Counseling Children and Adolescents

THE NATIONAL SOCIETY
FOR THE STUDY OF EDUCATION

Series on Contemporary Educational Issues
Kenneth J. Rehage, Series Editor

The 1976 Titles

Prospects for Research and Development in Education, Ralph W.
Tyler, Editor
Counseling Children and Adolescents, William M. Walsh, Editor
Public Testimony on Public Schools, National Committee for
Citizens in Education, Commission on Educational Governance

The National Society for the Study of Education also publishes Year-
books which are distributed by the University of Chicago Press. Inquiries regarding all publications of the Society, as well as inquiries
about membership in the Society, may be addressed to the Secretary-
Treasurer, 5835 Kimbark Avenue, Chicago, IL 60637. Membership
in the Society is open to any who are interested in promoting the
investigation and discussion of educational questions.

Counseling Children and Adolescents

AN ANTHOLOGY OF CONTEMPORARY TECHNIQUES

Edited By

WILLIAM M. WALSH

Northeastern Illinois University

McCutchan Publishing Corporation
2526 Grove Street
Berkeley, California 94704

Library of Congress Catalog Card Number 75-5097
ISBN 0-8211-2253-3

Printed in the United States of America

Contents

Contributors

Eugene D. Alexander is professor of psychology and education at Shippensburg State College in Pennsylvania.

Marilyn Bates is an assistant professor in the college of education at California State University in Fullerton.

Ernst G. Beier is professor of psychology and associate director of clinical training at the University of Utah in Salt Lake City.

Leif J. Braaten is professor of clinical psychology at Cornell University in Ithaca, New York.

Charles A. Bugg is an elementary school counselor in the American School in Dormstadt, Germany.

John J. Cody is a professor in the Guidance and Educational Psychology Department at Southern Illinois University in Carbondale.

Don Dinkmeyer is associated with the Alfred Adler Institute in Chicago.

Rudolf Dreikurs (deceased) was professor of psychiatry at the Chicago Medical School and director of the Alfred Adler Institute in Chicago.

Albert Ellis is executive director of the Institute for Advanced Study in Rational Psychotherapy and executive director of the Institute for Rational Living in New York.

Wayne E. Foley is a psychologist-consultant in the Seattle Public Schools, Washington.

William Glasser is a psychiatrist in Los Angeles, California.

Morley D. Glicken is a member of the Department of Social Work at Arizona State University in Tempe.

Richard R. Gronert is an elementary school counselor in Janesville, Wisconsin.

Richard M. Hawes is vice-president of the Institute for Reality Therapy in Los Angeles.

Ray E. Hosford is a professor in the Counseling Psychology Department at the University of California at Santa Barbara.

Ernest L. Johnson is professor of psychology at Mississippi State College for Women in Columbus.

Clarence D. Johnson is an assistant professor in the college of education at California State University in Fullerton.

C. Gratton Kemp is professor of psychology at Ohio State University in Columbus.

John D. Krumboltz is professor of education and psychology at Stanford University in California.

Arnold A. Lazarus is professor of psychology at Rutgers University in Princeton, New Jersey.

James L. Lister is professor of education at the University of Florida in Gainesville.

G. Roy Mayer is an assistant professor in the Guidance Department at California State University in Los Angeles.

George W. Murphy is a counselor in a junior high school in Baltimore County, Maryland.

C. H. Patterson is a professor in the Educational Psychology Department at the University of Illinois at Urbana.

Gerald J. Pine is professor of education at the University of New Hampshire in Durham.

Carl R. Rogers is a founder and staff member of the Center for Studies of the Person in La Jolla, California.

Carl E. Thoresen is associate professor of education at Stanford University in California.

Edwin E. Wagner is a professor at the University of Akron in Ohio.

Jean C. Waterland is assistant professor of educational psychology at the University of Wisconsin at Milwaukee.

James L. Widerman is a counselor at Martin Luther King High School in Philadelphia.

Eileen L. Widerman, at the time this article was written, was a psychiatric social worker in the Office of Mental Health-Mental Retardation of Philadelphia.

John W. Willson is a counselor-consultant in the Seattle Public Schools, Washington.

Introduction

> There is only one child
> And his name is all children.
>
> *—Carl Sandburg*

The counseling of children and adolescents is a relatively recent area of interest for professionals. The major growth in the field has taken place in the past twenty years. The early work of Sigmund Freud, at the beginning of this century, generated initial interest in the early childhood and adolescent years. However, this interest tended to settle in only two areas: the influence of early childhood experiences on later adolescent and adult behavior, and the development of effective therapeutic procedures for treating the severely disturbed client. The developmental needs of the majority of clients in this age group were largely overlooked.

In the past several years, professionals in psychology, counseling, social work, and the allied behavioral sciences have become increasingly aware of the void that exists in the treatment of adolescents and young children. These professionals have begun to respond to the demand for effective delivery systems and treatment processes by designing training and treatment programs to deal with this specialized population. Academicians and practitioners have found a real paucity of published material in this area. There is considerable research in the fields of psychiatry and clinical psychology that concerns itself primarily with aberrant or deviant behavior patterns, but these behavior patterns constitute only a small percentage of the presenting problems of preadolescent and adolescent children. Most of the children in this age group who seek counseling or therapy have less severe developmental and adjustment problems. In short, the counseling needs of children, particularly of preadolescents, have been largely overlooked or ignored.

A brief synopsis of the development of counseling and psychotherapy of children and adolescents may help to clarify the present position of the profession. Counseling, as a helping process, is not new or modern. It can be traced to the very roots of civilization. Many of the famous people of ancient and modern history performed the helping function of counseling. Other helpers, indeed the vast majority, were unknown, simple people: teachers, friends, relatives, and associates.

Only recently has the concept of interpersonal helping relationships been formalized into an academic discipline or science. The philosophers of the seventeenth and eighteenth centuries may be considered forerunners of today's psychological theorists. Men like Descartes, Locke, Hobbes, Hume, and Rousseau paved the way for modern concepts of behavior. Wilhelm Wundt is generally considered the father of modern psychology. He opened the first psychological measurement laboratory in 1879 in Leipzig, Germany. In succeeding years, the work of William James, Sigmund Freud, Alfred Binet, John Dewey, Carl Jung, Ivan Pavlov, John Watson, and Alfred Adler furthered the development of child counseling and therapy. In the United States, individuals like G. Stanley Hall emphasized the importance of working with children. Jesse Davis and Frank Parsons worked with youngsters at the inception of the vocational guidance movement. Clifford Beers generated interest in the mental health movement. The early twentieth century also witnessed the emergence of the child guidance movement.

Following the early years, despite the intrusion of world wars and a great depression, interest in child counseling continued to grow. More professionals began specializing in work with children and adolescents, primarily with classically oriented models. Interest in counseling adolescents accelerated before World War II with the work of E. G. Williamson and Carl Rogers. Little formal emphasis was given to the field of child counseling and psychotherapy until midcentury, however. In 1958, the National Defense Education Act provided considerable impetus for school counseling, and new nonclassical models began to gain wider acceptance. Training programs for child specialists expanded; counselors appeared in larger numbers in the elementary and secondary schools; and community mental health clinics expanded their personnel and services to include adolescents and younger children with less severe adjustment problems.

Today, the growth and expansion of the 1950s and 1960s is continuing. Professional associations have separate divisions for secondary school counselors, adolescent therapists, and child specialists; professional journals aimed specifically at the treatment of adolescents and preadolescents have appeared; and the focus on new treatment models and therapeutic approaches has intensified. The present book of readings is a response to this continued interest on the part of professionals and the lay population. It attempts to survey the newer, nonclassical models of counseling and therapy with children and adolescents, and to provide a wider variety of techniques to meet the needs of this population.

The readings are organized into sections, each treating a relatively distinct counseling model. The sections are arranged alphabetically, using the most commonly accepted title for that counseling approach. Each section contains an article that presents the major theoretical propositions of the model. This is followed by several readings that deal specifically with the practical application of that model in school and/or nonschool settings. All the counseling models are nonclassical in nature; that is, they are not analytically oriented. Each is a viable, professionally acceptable, effective process of therapy. The final section contains supplementary readings on each therapeutic model.

Classical therapeutic approaches are not covered in this text. These approaches consist of the analytic models, Freudian and neo-Freudian, that predominate in the fields of psychiatry and clinical psychology. They are used effectively with patients displaying abnormal or severely deviant behavior patterns in outpatient and inpatient settings. They are generally of longer duration than the approaches discussed here, and they focus on major personality reconstruction. However, as previously noted, clients displaying severely aberrant behavior are a minority of the child client population. The majority of preadolescent and adolescent clients are experiencing adjustment problems that may be treated more efficiently using short-term, nonanalytic counseling techniques. This assumption is a major premise of the present volume. Therefore, the book attempts to survey the new, nonclassical models of counseling and therapy with children and to provide counselors with a wider variety of techniques to meet the adjustment needs of the population. The reader who wishes to explore the analytic models of therapy may consult section IX, the supplementary readings at the end of the text.

The terms *counseling* and *therapy* are used interchangeably in this text. The word *counseling* may be substituted for *therapy* or *therapist* for *counselor* at any point in the readings. No attempt has been made to distinguish the two terms by way of specific problem orientation, duration of client involvement, or techniques. The processes involved in each are considered to be similar, if not identical, and are treated in this manner for the entire text.

A broad spectrum of therapeutic behaviors and techniques is represented in the various sections. Each approach is applicable to a variety of therapeutic settings in the school, the home, and the community. Several of the counseling processes emphasize directive behavior on the part of the counselor. Behavioral counseling, individual/developmental counseling, rational-emotive therapy, and reality therapy are examples of more active, cognitive counseling. Other sections emphasize less directive, more affective client-counselor involvement. Existential counseling, play therapy, and client-centered counseling are representative of this orientation. The reader should be able to identify with one or several approaches and incorporate these behaviors into his or her counseling practice. There is something for almost everyone—counselor educators, child therapists, counselors-in-training, classroom teachers, administrators, school psychologists, school counselors, special education therapists, family counselors, and professionals in allied fields who are concerned with the emotional development of children.

SECTION I

Behavioral Counseling

Without doubt, people have feelings, and many have learned
an extensive vocabulary for describing such feelings. I am
not against people feeling they understand and accept
themselves. I favor such feelings just as I favor people loving
justice, truth and beauty. My point is that, stated as goals of
counseling, such subjective feelings will not prove as useful
as more objective statements of behavior. Being sensitive to
the feelings of a client is certainly a necessary attribute for
any counselor. That it is sufficient is questionable.

—John Krumboltz

Behavioral counseling is an approach to therapy developed by John Krumboltz in the mid 1960s. In this model, counseling is viewed as a learning process. Behavioristic explanations of behavior and behavioristic change techniques form the core of Krumboltz's theoretical model. Among these are the importance of environmental factors in learning; the belief that all behavior is learned and can thus be unlearned or modified; the belief that modification or manipulation of the environment can produce change in the client; the focus on reinforcement and extinction techniques for changing behavior; and the importance of measurement in the counseling process.

Unlike the proponents of behaviorism, Krumboltz believes in the importance of the counseling relationship, and its power to affect a client's behavior. In this relationship, the mutual establishment of goals by counselor and client is an essential initial step. Once specific behavioral goals have been identified, the counselor can use one or more general techniques in the counseling process. Each technique incorporates the principles of reinforcement and extinction, and each is used only after a specific behavior has been identified. The techniques can be summarized as follows:

1. Operant learning: reinforcement of selected behaviors, giving special attention to the timing of reinforcement.

2. Imitative learning: use of behavioral models in the counseling process.

3. Cognitive learning: use of role-playing, client contracts, and verbal instructions.

4. Emotional learning: use of approaches patterned after the techniques of reciprocal inhibition.

Thus, behavioral counseling can be viewed as a process emphasizing specifics: specific identification of behavior, specific goal establishment, and specific changes in client behavior.

The first article in this section, by Ray Hosford, serves as a comprehensive introduction to behavioral counseling. He discusses the theory's major assumptions and presents an in-depth analysis of the techniques a counselor would use in this approach. Carl Thoresen, in the second article, uses the case example of a high school student to illustrate his interpretation of behavioral counseling and to present his rationale for its use in school situations. Case studies are also used by John Krumboltz and Ray Hosford in the third article to demonstrate how an elementary school counselor would use behavioral counseling techniques to remedy behavior problems. They discuss the importance of goals in the counseling process and provide a step-by-step program for counselor intervention. Counselor-teacher and counselor-parent consultations are emphasized in the remedial procedures.

The remaining readings in this section refer directly to the concepts of behavioral counseling presented in the first articles. Classroom behavior problems are treated by Wayne Foley and John Willson using a contract system. Their step-by-step analysis of the implementation of a contract procedure in consultation with the teacher is particularly helpful. Charles Bugg, in the final reading, describes the process of systematic desensitization. He explains how it can be readily applied to counseling situations, and presents several case studies to demonstrate its application in the school.

In summary, behavioral counseling is viewed as a learning process, using behavioristic principles and emphasizing the importance of the counseling relationship. An essential step in the process is mutual goal identification, followed by the modification or elimination of specific behavioral incidents using behavioristic reinforcement and extinction techniques.

RAY E. HOSFORD

Behavioral Counseling–
A Contemporary Overview

A "revolution" is taking place within the counseling profession, a revolution caused by counselors wanting to find more effective means for helping various kinds of clients with various kinds of problems. Both the questionable effectiveness of traditional counseling and the accumulation of research results emanating from learning theory have been great motivators in the "revolution" and the establishment of a rather new approach to helping clients: Behavioral Counseling. Because this new approach challenges much of what has been done in traditional counseling, the techniques and procedures developing from the scientific research findings of behavioral counselors have met with considerable resistance from some and with "open arms" by others.

Assumptions of Behavioral Counseling

Basically, behavioral theory holds that most behavior is learned, i.e., a function of one's environment. Man begins not as innately "good" or bad," but like a Lochian *tabula rasa,* upon which, Thorn-

Ray E. Hosford, "Behavioral Counseling—A Contemporary Overview," *Counseling Psychologist,* 1969, *1* (1), pp. 1-33. Reprinted by permission.

dike would say, nothing has been "stamped." Man is, however, a reactive being—reacting to stimuli he encounters in his environment. As he learns to react to his environment, his behavior and subsequent personality are formed. In addition to his environment, however, heredity and the interaction of heredity and environment also account for some of man's behavior; but, because we cannot control heredity (at least humanistically at present, though great strides are being made in this area), environmental manipulation is the "key" to altering behavior. The behavioral counselor is interested not only in the variables that control behavior, but, more appropriately, in determining how these variables might be utilized to promote the client's desired behavior change.

The use of environmental influences to solve human psychological problems has a long history with roots that can be traced back to Messmer in 1779 (Wolpe and Lazarus, 1966). However, it is Pavlov's (1927) early work in conditioning dogs that is usually associated with the beginnings of the theoretical rationale underlying the approach. His work helped to establish the principles of classical conditioning and subsequently the conceptualization of learning as a conditioning process. In addition to demonstrating that dogs could learn to respond with salivation to a neutral stimulus (a bell) if the presentation of that neutral stimulus were paired several times with an unconditioned stimulus (food), Pavlov also demonstrated that new learnings could be extinguished if the behaviors occurred and were not followed periodically by some sort of reinforcement.

In much the same way as Pavlov demonstrated conditioning in dogs, Watson showed that human neuroses could result from the same process. In the case of Albert (Watson and Rayner, 1920), the fear of white rats was conditioned in a child of eleven months by presenting the rodent to the boy and making a loud sound everytime he reached for the rat. Albert gradually reacted with fear to the rat even when the loud noise no longer accompanied its presence. This fear subsequently generalized to other animals and furry objects. The study showed that maladaptive behavior (in this case, anxiety to white rats) is a process of learning gained in much the same way as any behavior is learned.

Just as Watson and Rayner demonstrated that human neurosis (conditioned fear) was a process of learning, Jones (1924) was successful in eliminating such maladaptive behavior by using conditioning procedures different from those used in conditioning Albert. In this case, Jones worked with a boy, Peter, who had a severe fear of animals. To extinguish this fear, Jones exposed Peter to a rabbit caged some distance from him and at the same time gave him some of his favorite food to eat. Because eating is pleasurable and the relaxation which follows is physically antagonistic to the physical reactions accompanying anxiety or fear, the boy did not experience his previous anxiety. On succeeding days the rabbit was gradually moved closer to the boy until his fear was extinguished. Peter not only lost his fear of rabbits, but of other furry objects as well, i.e., the response-inhibiting fear generalized.

Jones was able to reverse the maladaptive conditioning (fear of animals) by pairing the noxious stimulus (the rabbit) with a non-noxious and pleasurable one (food). By making the pleasurable response stronger than the anxiety felt from the presence of the provoking stimulus, Jones weakened, and gradually extinguished, the bond between anxiety and the presence of animals.[1]

These experiments by Jones and Watson demonstrate that the relationship between reward and response which Pavlov found in animals also exists in humans. Unlike animals, however, as man develops he becomes capable of cognitive or mediating responses which allow him to react to his environment in new ways. He is not bound, as are animals, to prior conditioning but is able to plan and evaluate his responses to stimuli. Man's personality is "... the totality of ... [his] ... habits—of thought and action, musculoskeletal and autonomic (Lazarus, 1968)." Many find this concept hard to accept (cf: Ullmann and Krasner, 1965), and argue that, since it does not change the "real man," the changing of man's behavior is superficial. This assumes, of course, that there is a "real" personality underlying an individual's behavior, something "more real" than that which man demonstrates in his observable behavior. To this argument the behavioral counselor would respond that all that can be known about a man can be gained only from data obtained from his behavior, and that this behavior is useful only as long as it can be quantified and operationally defined.

Deviant Behavior

Man's personality consists of both his positive and his negative habits. Those habits which are inappropriate (i.e., deviant) are learned in much the same way as appropriate behaviors. Pavlov believed that abnormal behavior was the result of conditioning. He was able to demonstrate that dogs would acquire neurotic behaviors by conditioning them to expect food upon the presentation of a circle and no food when exposed to an oval. As he changed the oval more and more like a circle, the dogs became unable to distinguish between the stimuli and went berserk. Similarly, Wolpe (1958) developed "neurotic" behavior in cats by giving them electric shocks during the time he was feeding them. He then extinguished the neurotic behaviors by the process he later termed "desensitization."

On the whole, an individual's behavior is determined by the frequency and types of reinforcements he has received relative to the like situations he has encountered; and the interactions between various reinforcement social models and situations he has experienced. It is the culture or the situation within which the behavior occurs that determines whether that behavior is inappropriate.

Atypical behavior then differs from "normal" behavior not in the way it was acquired, i.e., learned, but only to the extent that the behavior is atypical or abnormal to the observers. A behavior seen as abnormal in one culture may be completely normal in another culture. (See Ullmann and Krasner (1969) for a more complete discussion and definition of abnormal behavior.)

Disease or "Bad Habits"

Traditionally, psychiatry and counseling have dealt with emotional problems and neurotic behavior as symptoms of some internal struggle, a disease within the organism which must be removed and resolved by self-awareness and insight before any "cure" can take place. Counseling or psychotherapy emanating from such a conceptualization is often referred to as "evocative therapy," in which the relationship or therapeutic situation is significant in itself in bringing about behavioral change. Both Freudians and Rogerians utilize this medical model approach as the principal means for helping clients solve psychological problems (Ullmann and Krasner, 1965). However, implying that the "cause" must be treated rather than the symptom (or behavior as the Behaviorists would say) intensifies the disease model and the process of treatment proceeds accordingly. The behaviorists have found this medical approach to treating psychological problems not only wanting but downright misleading (Bandura, 1967).

Treating psychological problems under the guise of mental illness was a major humanistic step in therapy from that of conceptualizing certain types of behavior as due to evil spirits, in which the "therapy" was to beat out the demons physically from the individual. This conceptualization of behavior problems as symptoms of mental illness, however, has probably done more to retard positive growth by the individual than to promote it. Therapists continue to find support for inner psychological constructs consistent with their own theoretical background but not for others. As the Freudians report evidence for "Oedipal Complexes," Adlerians for "inferiority feelings and power strivings," Rogerians for "inappropriate self-concepts," the existentialists look for and find support for "existential crises" and anxieties (Bandura, 1967). While it appears that we now have a "complex" rather than a "demon," we are still not too far removed from the old demon model. All things considered, we have not only developed a "sick" model in traditional therapy but in society as well. We have formed a culture built on being unhappy. If we report to a counselor that we are feeling good, we are apt to hear that we are resisting and be asked who we are kidding. One has to be "sick" if he is to receive the attention of the traditional therapist and often the attention of members of society as well. Is it any wonder that many of those who seek medical assistance are hypochondriacs and actually have nothing physically wrong with them?

Behavioral therapists restrict the conception of deviant behavior to objective phenomena and assume it unnecessary to posit the existence of any unobservable internal states to account for the behavior (Skinner, 1967). As stated above, symptomatic behavior is not viewed as emanating from any mental illness but simply as inappropriately learned behavior or "bad habits." These bad habits have been formed through a learning process and can be unlearned by the use of appropriate social models and the alteration of the response—reinforcement contingencies. Once the inappropriate behavior is modified, it is unnecessary to remove the hypothetical underlying pathology. Indeed, according to Szasz (1965, p. 26), the whole concept of mental illness has ". . . outlived whatever usefulness it may have had and it now functions merely as a convenient myth." "Sustained adherence to the myth of mental illness," he goes on to say, "allows people to avoid facing this problem, believing that mental health, conceived as the absence of mental illness, automatically insures the making of right and safe choices in one's conduct of life. But the facts are all the other way. It is the making of good choices in life that others regard, retrospectively, as good mental health."

Because they deal directly with overt behavior rather than some underlying "cause," behavioral counselors and psychotherapists have been criticized for focusing only on the symptoms and not the "real" problem. Bookbinder (1962), among others, suggests that symptom substitution, which in his opinion can cause severe negative effects, does indeed occur. Yet others (e.g., Yates, 1958; Grossberg, 1964; Bandura, 1969; Ullmann and Krasner, 1965) suggest that there is no such phenomenon as symptom substitution.

It is rather ironic that therapists have not really defined a symptom and cannot specify when symptoms should occur. The question of whether or not behavioral therapists are treating symptoms and not the "real cause" is often raised by those who find it difficult to accept deviant behavior as having been learned in much the same way as appropriate behavior. Although the evidence is far from complete, Beech (1969) says that the facts support the behavioral hypothesis:

There is no doubt that the psychoanalytic and related viewpoints have a clear cut prediction to make about the results of symptomatic treatment; it is that the removal of one symptom will give place to another. The prediction is bound up with the notion that an overt psychological disturbance is only the outward evidence of some internal complex, the tip of the iceberg, so to speak. It should follow from this, of course, that any attempt at symptomatic treatment will fail, for it does not remove the true source of disturbance. Only by dealing with the "inner roots" of the disorder could we hope to effect a "cure." The evidence here is quite compelling; the appearance of new symptoms to replace those removed is rare indeed, and it is not certain that these rare cases are examples of replacement at all. Furthermore, symptomatic treatment by behavior therapy often seems to produce evidence for better all-around adjustment, as if the more general aspects of maladjustment have stemmed from a failing attempt to deal with one isolated area of difficulty.

In summing up the issue, Bandura (1969, p. 49) says that ". . . if the concepts of symptom and mental disease were pertinent to behavioral dysfunctions, which they are not, the symptom substitution hypothesis could never be satisfactorily tested because it fails to specify specifically what constitutes a 'symptom,' when the substitution should occur, the social conditions under which it is most likely to arise and the form that the substitute symptom will take."

Whether symptom substitution exists is hypothetical, and, as Bandura suggests, cannot be verified scientifically. All forms of counseling and psychotherapy attempt to effect behavioral change, whether through evocative techniques or the use of behavior modification procedures. To dwell on the issue only retards rather than promotes discovering techniques which produce beneficial changes in psychological functioning. Neither behavior modification nor any other form of counseling will free an individual for life of the stresses and strains of life's experiences.

Diagnosis

Just as behaviorists reject in general the concept of mental illness so do they repudiate traditional nosological classifications of behavior adopted by the psychiatric and psychological professions. *Behavior is behavior* whether it be maladaptive or adaptive. Categorizing maladaptive behavior leads to categorizing persons in terms of presumed underlying illnesses. Ullmann and Krasner (1965) suggest that the motivation for therapists to classify behavior in terms of illnesses has to do more than anything else with social and historical pressures and presumed but not validated theoretical viewpoints. As Wolpe (1958) brings out in his discussion of the etiology of neuroses, the classification system used in psychiatric diagnoses is more a product of Kraepelin's imagination than scientific fact. The evidence that these classifications rarely hold up under research analysis, and the poor consistency found between therapists' diagnoses of the same individual's behavior (e.g., see Ash, 1949; Rotter, 1954; Katz et al., 1964; Ullmann and Krasner, 1969) have led behavior therapists to reject not only the classification system of pathological behaviors but other diagnoses in which operational definitions cannot be given in behavioral terms. Categories such as "aggression," "anxiety," and "fear" unless operationally defined are useless labels.

Many of the diagnostic and classificatory terms currently used in counseling should be questioned closely with respect to their empirical bases. Certainly many, if not most, serve only as self-fulfilling hypotheses for the evaluator. Moreover, free use of nosological classifications of behavior by counselors can promote the manifestation of the very same behavior in their clients. Those individuals sophisticated in the use of psychological classifications and terminology in describing behavior often display all the symptoms listed in whatever book they have read, or those described by their counselors (Kelly, 1955). During World War II, for example, more psychosomatic "illnesses" were found among the usually more sophisticated officers than the enlisted men.

One wonders how often clients give counselors what is expected and what the counselors want to hear. The reinforcement that counselors provide for client "sick talk" by their attention and comments only serves to promote such talk in the future. In mental hospitals, how many thousands of patients have learned from other patients and through the reinforcements of hospital staffs to demonstrate the role of the "good patient": that of passive and/or other "mentally ill" behavior? It may well be that most, if not all, "symptoms of the mentally ill" may be attributed to hospitalization rather than to illness, to immediate environment rather than childhood traumas. Kesey's *One Flew Over the Cuckoo's Nest* may be more truth than fiction!

Problem Identification

The behavioral counselor sees problem identification as being more effective and efficient than the traditional diagnosis generally in use. A diagnosis based on a functional analysis of what the individual can or cannot do provides continuity between the diagnostic procedures and the treatment techniques employed by the counselor. Because he utilizes a functional analysis, the behavioral counselor's assessment is directly related to his treatment. His first goal, with the help of the client, is to determine which behavior needs to be modified. The three steps utilized in such an analysis are similar to the three utilized by Kanfer and Saslow (1967, p. 376), in which the task of the counselor is to determine:

(1) Which specific behavior patterns require change in their frequency of occurrence, their intensity, their duration or in the conditions under which they occur.

(2) What are the best practical means which can produce the desired changes in this individual (manipulation of the environment of the behavior, or the self-attitudes of the patient).

(3) What factors are currently maintaining it and what are the conditions under which this behavior was acquired.

Rather than requiring that the counselor attempt to change the personality structure of the client, behavior analysis, such as that proposed by Kanfer and Saslow above, permits the counselor to utilize environmental events to explain the behavior in terms that can be objectively evaluated. The counselor can also use these environmental events to help promote the type of behavior which the client needs to learn in order to solve his problem (Ferster, 1965).

Analysis and clarification of the problem situation, the individual's motivation for change, his biological condition, self-control, social relationships and social-cultural environment, are all included in a functional assessment of behavior (Kanfer and Saslow, 1967). In the analysis of the problem situation, the counselor utilizes such variables as frequency, intensity, and duration in categorizing the client's behavior in terms of excesses and deficits.

By identifying situations (i.e., specific circumstances in which the behavior occurs) the counselor is better able to decide which techniques and procedures to use. That the client has a poor self-concept or lacks self-esteem indicates his need for counseling but it provides little help in revealing what behaviors he lacks or has in excess. This is not to suggest that the behavioral counselor is interested only in the client's overt behavior and not in his feelings. Feelings of self may and often are adjunct to any counseling problem. An increase in self-esteem is nearly always a secondary effect of any gain the client makes toward a desired behavior change. As was indicated earlier, feelings of self are derived from the feedback one does or does not get from his behavior. The postulation that discussion of client feelings leads to insight and changes in thought, subsequently manifested in changes in behavior has little scientific support. Further, insight, lifting of repressions, and making the unconscious conscious, are unnecessary for behavior change. Obviously, discussing client feelings in order to help him gain insight is not a *sine qua non* of counseling to the behavioral counselor. In fact, some therapists (e.g., Bandura, 1969) suggest that the counselor's preoccupation with helping the client gain insight into his behavior results in a complete disregard of the environmental influences that may be controlling that behavior. The client's verbal reports of feelings are important, however, as they provide strong clues to the motives and circumstances behind his behavior. By learning the conditions under which positive and negative feelings emerge, the counselor can better determine the way the client must act in order to solve his problem. The counselor's role, therefore, is to help the client translate his feelings into actions.

Goals of Counseling

One of the main problems in counseling has been the lack of specifying precisely what the counseling is to accomplish. Too often counseling goals are so vague and hypothetical that the client (if, in fact, not the counselor) has little idea as to what the client is to accomplish as a result of the counseling experience. The procedures a counselor employs should be those shown by experimental research to be effective in promoting a specific desired outcome. When the objectives of counseling are vague and indefinable in behavioral terms, the procedures a counselor uses are too often determined by his own preferences rather than the actual objective desired by the client. For any goal or objective to be meaningful in a counseling relationship, two factors must be present. First, the goal should describe in behavioral terms the desired outcome; i.e., it should specify what the client should be able to do differently as a result of the counseling. Second, the objectives should be formulated in such a way that the counselor has some idea as to which procedures and techniques he might employ to promote this desired behavior.

If the counselor's goals ignore the problem for which the client sought help, he is undermining the legitimacy of the client-practitioner relationship. By definition, the role of the client should be assumed by both the counselor and the client to be that of an individual seeking help, who has the right to direct jointly with the counselor the goals and procedures of his treatment. In addition, both should assume that the individual has the right to terminate the treatment.

In terms of goals, then, behavioral counseling differs principally from traditional counseling in terms of specificity (cf: Bijou, 1966). Whereas the goals of relationship counseling are usually formulated in terms of greater insight, self-understanding and self-reorganization (cf: Rogers, 1951), the behavioral counselor prefers to specify goals as overt changes in behavior rather than hypothetical constructs. Self-understanding is viewed, for example, as a vague goal and one seldom requested by the client (Krumboltz, 1966c). Observable behavior, on the other hand, according to Michael and Meyerson (1962, p. 395) ". . . is the only variable of importance in the counseling and guidance process, and the only criterion against which the outcome of the process can be evaluated." The assumption that behavior is a function of some underlying, if not unconscious, complex, is impossible to test experimentally. The traditional conceptualization that self-understanding is needed to gain effective behavior is the reverse of what probably is the relationship. Insight is not the cause but the result of behavior change (Hobbs, 1962). What is ultimately curative, however, is the behavior of the client, not the degree of self-insight gained.

The goals of a behavioral counselor can be organized into three

main categories (Krumboltz, 1966*a*; Krumboltz and Hosford, 1967):
(1) altering maladaptive behavior; (2) learning the decision-making
process; and (3) preventing problems. Such goals are not unlike those
of the educator. A teacher may be interested in helping a child learn
how to solve a quadratic equation; a counselor, on the other hand,
may need to help the child learn how to make wise decisions, be
more assertive with his peers, or speak up more in the class discussions.

The criteria for any set of goals in counseling have been defined by
Krumboltz (1966*a*, p. 155; 1966*c*, p. 4):

(1) The goals of counseling should be capable of being stated differently for
each individual client.

(2) The goals of counseling for each client should be compatible with, though
not necessarily identical to, the values of his counselor.

(3) The degree to which the goals of counseling are attained by each client
should be observable.

Many types of goals meet these criteria. Increasing the frequency
with which a student speaks up in class might be an appropriate goal
for a shy individual who wants to participate in classroom discussion,
but is unable to do so because he has not learned the behaviors necessary for speaking up in class or perhaps has learned to associate
anxiety with that particular behavior. Some other goals which a
counselor and client might develop are: increasing or decreasing
assertive responses; gaining alternative courses of action; relating to
the opposite sex with less anxièty; decreasing fear of situations or
objects; increasing the frequency with which the individual demonstrates sensitivity to others; or decreasing the amount of thumb
sucking.

It is important, however, that the goals of the counselor be relevant to those of the client. Unless counselors work with their clients
in developing goals which communicate specifically what the client
will be able to *do* when the counseling is terminated, there may be
times in which the outcome of counseling will have little relationship
to the problem for which the individual sought help (Vance, 1967).

In establishing goals it is often necessary to formulate intermediate
or day-to-day objectives to facilitate the gradual shaping of the desired behavior. Human behavior is very complex and often the desired behavior the client wishes to achieve consists of many lower
level behaviors which he has not yet learned. As was stated above,
the counselor's role in diagnosis is to determine which behaviors

related to his desired behavior change the client has learned and which he needs to learn or re-learn. Day-to-day goals are important in that they offer opportunities for the client to receive the immediate reinforcement necessary to promote the motivation needed for him to continue working toward his goal. Not only does the hierarchy of goals promote continual progress thereby keeping the level of positive reinforcement high, but it also makes it possible to minimize the client's chances of failure (Bandura, 1969). Just as a young boy needs to learn many sub-behaviors (e.g., batting, catching, running) before he becomes a baseball player, a male awkward in interpersonal relationships may need to learn how to say hello to girls, initiate conversations, ask a girl for a date, and many other intermediate behaviors before he can accomplish his overall goal of marriage. If such an individual were to attempt a behavior far too complex in relation to his prior learning, his probability of success would be almost nil and that of failure extremely high. The anxiety and discouraging results associated with such failure can often be avoided if the counselor and client establish a graded hierarchy of goals designed to promote successful experiences in the gradual learning of the desired complex behavior.

After the problem has been identified and the desired behavior change agreed upon by the counselor and client, the behavioral counselor is apt to employ a variety of counseling procedures to help the client acquire the behaviors necessary for the solution of his problem.

Choosing the Technique

Contrary to what one might read, techniques utilized in behavioral counseling do not supplant those used in traditional counseling. Rather, they are an addition to those generally utilized in a counseling relationship. There is nothing in behavioral counseling which restrains the counselor from offering the kinds of understanding and support stressed in traditional counseling. Krumboltz (1967, p. 224), for example, provides two reasons why empathetic understanding, the *sine qua non* of Rogerian counseling, is necessary for behavioral counselors. First of all, "The client is likely not to describe the totality of his problems unless he thinks his listener will understand things from his point of view"; and second, "the counselor's ability to communicate his understanding of the client's problem to him establishes the counselor as an important person in the client's life and therefore one able to be an influential model and effective reinforcing agent." The behavioral counselor, then, views traditional supportive elements, such as empathy, as necessary in the counseling relationship, but insufficient for promoting the desired behavioral change.

As is evident, the behavioral counselor does not rely only on face-to-face interviews or on any one set of procedures. Since most behavior is a function of environmental consequences, effective counseling techniques for promoting behavior change must depend upon the modification of the environmental contingencies which maintain the client's behavior. Because the interaction between the environment and man is unique to each individual, the counseling procedures used vary for different clients and are specifically designed for the particular problem of each individual (Krumboltz and Hosford, 1967). These techniques emanate from the findings of experimental research based, for the most part, on theories of learning. It is research in learning, however, rather than theories of learning, which provides the techniques a behavioral counselor employs. Traditional counseling procedures, on the other hand, stem primarily from clinical experiences in which, all too often, the counselor's personality (i.e., patterns of behavior) and experience cannot be separated from the results of the treatment (cf: Truax and Carkhuff, 1967). For the behavioral therapist, experimental conceptions and research needed for empirical justification precede rather than follow after the employment of the treatment procedures (Ullmann and Krasner, 1969).

Which technique the counselor might use depends on many variables. Among them might be the client's behavioral assets and deficits, the type of problem for which the client sought counseling, the type and value of the various reinforcers available in his environment, and the significant others (e.g., peers, teachers, and parents) important in his life who might assist the counselor in promoting the client's desired behavior change. If it appears that another person (e.g., teacher, friend or parent) may have established a close and positive contact with the client, he, rather than the counselor, might be utilized as the principal change agent. Not only do individuals react differently to various kinds of reinforcers, the value of the reinforcer is often directly related to the person who offers it. Just as edible or monetary reinforcers may be more effective than verbal praise in promoting behavior change among those of low socio-economic backgrounds, verbal praise administered by a teacher with whom the client has a valued relationship may be more effective than if it were given by the counselor. In addition, parents and teachers are with children for much greater amounts of time than are counselors and consequently have many more opportunities to use the reinforcement procedures (Krumboltz and Thoresen, 1969). Including others in the behavior modification program often has other positive side effects. By teaching teachers to reinforce shy students for participating in class discussions, Hosford (1969) found that not only did the students change their behaviors, but teachers began changing their teaching procedures. Bandura (1969) and Krumboltz and Thoresen (1969) provide evidence of many other cases in which parents, teachers and others have been utilized effectively by counselors as the principal therapeutic sources.

Operant Conditioning

The techniques most frequently employed by behavioral counselors involve operant conditioning, social modeling, and counterconditioning procedures. These and other techniques may be used independently or in various combinations to help clients achieve desired behavioral changes. The use of reinforcement (i.e., operant conditioning) is probably the one technique that behavioral counselors most often employ. This procedure involves modifying behavior by the alteration of its rewarding outcomes. There is nothing new in the use of positive reinforcement to shape behavior. Its use today, as in the time of the ancient Greeks, is just good common sense. What is new is the contingency between the behavior and the reinforcer. It is not enough to provide rewards if those rewards are not administered upon the demonstration of the desired behavior. Counselors often must arrange situations in such a way that it is almost impossible for the client to respond with any but the desired behavior which leads to the reinforcement.

In operant conditioning, the objective lies in strengthening an operant, that is, a behavior, by increasing the frequency of that response (Skinner, 1953). Although Pavlov called any event which strengthened behavior reinforcement, and the resulting changes conditioning, his procedure was in pairing a reinforcer with a stimulus rather than making the reinforcement contingent upon the response (Skinner, 1954). Principles of operant conditioning have been discussed in great detail in a number of books (e.g., Reynolds, 1968;

Bandura, 1969; Ullmann and Krasner, 1965, 1969; Krumboltz and Thoresen, 1969). However, for the present discussion, a few basic principles should suffice in providing a rationale for its use in counseling.

Operant behavior was first differentiated from respondent behavior by Skinner (1938). Basically, the premise of operant conditioning assumes that many, if not most, of our behaviors are random, emitted rather than elicited by particular stimuli. Acquiring a new behavior by operant conditioning follows one of the laws of learning discovered by Dr. Skinner (1938, 1953) which states, in effect, that if a particular response is followed by an environmental event which is reinforcing to the individual, then the probability of that behavior occurring again is increased. Thus, operant behavior is that behavior which is governed by its consequences. Learning a new behavior by operant conditioning is the reverse of classical (respondent) conditioning. In operant conditioning the individual must *first* emit a response which is shaped by the reinforcement which follows it. In classical conditioning, on the other hand, acquiring a new behavior is determined by the stimulus which elicited it. Recall the case of Albert (Watson and Rayner, 1920) discussed earlier. Albert's fear of white rats, which he had not demonstrated previously, was acquired through the frequent pairing of the white rat (heretofore a neutral stimulus) with a loud noise (unconditioned stimulus).

The objective in operant conditioning lies in strengthening a behavior by increasing the frequency with which it is emitted. The emphasis lies on increasing the frequency rather than on the strength or content of the response per se. Such conditioning, or learning, occurs daily in all our lives. A child learning to ride a bike is rewarded by the bike staying in motion if he performs certain behaviors. If he doesn't, the bike falls. Gradually, he learns more and more behaviors (e.g., to steer, pedal, and balance), and is rewarded for each new behavior by staying upright more easily. Many academic and social behaviors as well as other physical behaviors are learned in much the same way.

Skinner's premise that reinforcement must be contingent upon the response is not too different from Guthrie's Contiguity Theory (Hilgard, 1956). The factor in promoting learning according to Guthrie is the contiguity between the response and the reinforcement. When teachers shout at their students when they are noisy, they serve only to teach the students to be disorderly when teachers shout.[2] The principle of the contiguity between behavior and reinforcement can be seen in an actual consultation this writer once had with a seventh grade teacher. Her problem, she related, was that she constantly had to yell at her students to get them to begin working. It was suggested that she quit shouting and remain quiet, and then reward the students if and when they came in in a relatively quiet manner. Only three days later, when the students did come into the room and begin to work in an orderly manner, she told them how much she appreciated the mature way in which they came in and that as a result she would let them out a minute early for brunch. Thus, her students were first in line to buy ice cream bars sold by the student government during the 12-minute brunch period. In the past, her class was always too late to purchase the bars, or in many cases did not receive a brunch break at all. She had been punishing them for not quieting down by keeping the class in during brunch. In subsequent discussions, the teacher revealed that the suggestion to reward rather than punish her students had changed her whole method of teaching. She no longer had to shout at the class, and both she and the students ended the period on a "happy note" rather than on one of anger.

Four Crucial Elements

Four crucial elements are necessary in any counseling program implementing operant conditioning (positive reinforcement) procedures. First, it is necessary that the reinforcements which the counselor employs be potent enough to motivate the individual sufficiently to continue performing the behavior being reinforced. Children, for example, whose parents lavish money and material things on them could hardly be expected to be motivated by pennies. Social reinforcers, such as praise and demonstrations of "warmth," would probably be more reinforcing to these youngsters. Principles of satiation and deprivation need to be kept in mind in combination with the kinds of reinforcers a counselor might employ.

The second element necessary, and the one too often neglected, is the principle that the reinforcement must be applied systematically. To apply reinforcement procedures one day on a child to help him acquire the habit of paying attention to the teacher, and then to neglect to reinforce him for the next five days does little. It is especially necessary in the early stages of employing reinforcement procedures that the individual be reinforced every time he emits the

behavior. Closely associated with the systematic application of operant conditioning is the third element: the contingency involved between demonstration of the behavior and the application of the reinforcement. Many people, both professional and lay, state that they
use reinforcement all the time. Reinforcement per se is not new, but
knowing when and how to reinforce is. As Ayllon (1966, p. 2) suggests:

The new thing . . . [about reinforcement therapy] . . . is the contingency. Giving
rewards is not enough. You must know when to give them. You make certain
rewards contingent upon the exhibition of certain behavior, and you arrange the
situation in such a way that it is practically impossible for the . . . [client] . . . to
respond in any way but that which will lead to the specific reward.

The fourth component necessary in using reinforcement procedures is that the counselor must be able to elicit the behavior which
he plans to reinforce. Specific cueing (Ryan, 1967; Krumboltz and
Thoresen, 1967), social modeling procedures (Bandura, 1969), verbal
prompts (Baer and Wolf, 1967), and the use of successive approximations are some of the procedures shown effective for this purpose.

Factors Affecting Reinforcement

In addition to the four components discussed above, research has
shown several factors which may affect the degree to which reinforcement procedures promote behavior change. Principal among
these is the fact that in initiating a behavior, the reinforcement of
that behavior must be immediate upon its demonstration or the differential effect is lost (Skinner, 1953). An illustration of this principle in counseling can be seen in a study by Loree and Koch (1960).
In an effort to help students gain group discussion competencies,
tape recorded playbacks of their discussions were used with systematic verbal reinforcement. For one group, the authors stopped the
tape at various intervals and verbally reinforced the students for their
contributions. The other students received reinforcement only after
the complete play through of the tape. When immediate reinforcement procedures were employed, the students improved considerably
more than when reinforcement was applied only at the end of the
discussions.

The individual's susceptibility for conditioning also has been found
to affect his rate and degree of learning (Skinner, 1957). Strong
(1964), in reviewing verbal conditioning and counseling research,

reports that the individual's degree of change is influenced greatly by the relationship which exists between the counselor and himself, the effect of the reinforcement being related to who does the reinforcing. Peer reinforcement, for example, especially as it relates to verbal response in the classroom, can counter or supersede that of the teacher (Hively, 1959).

Several writers have proposed that personality variables such as anxiety (Patterson et al., 1960; Rogers, 1960; Zigler and Kanzer, 1962; Spielberger et al., 1963) and dependency (Cairns and Lewis, 1962) are related to the degree of success in operant conditioning. While some studies found high positive relationships, others found insignificant or negative relationships between combinations of the two variables. It appears that little consistent evidence is available to support a relationship between one's personality variables and one's rate of conditioning. The problem is probably due to the imprecise methods used in assessing personality differences (see Mischel, 1969).

The reinforcement history of the individual appears to be related strongly to the effectiveness of operant conditioning procedures. How motivated an individual is to perform a behavior is determined to a large extent by his past experience with reinforcements. Like most behaviors, motivation is learned and depends on both the expectation of reward and the value of the reinforcer. For example, candy, a primary reinforcer, is more effective than praise, reproof, or tokens with four and five year old children (Terrell and Kennedy, 1957). Verbal reinforcers such as "right" and "correct" were found by Zigler and Kanzer (1962) to promote greater learning among middle class students than among those of lower class. In contrast, "fine" and "good" were more effective with lower class than middle class students. And just as various reinforcers affect individuals in varying ways, the roles of reinforcement and punishment used by social agencies for controlling behavior produce differential effects among individuals of varying learning backgrounds (Ferster, 1958).

To determine an effective reinforcer for clients is not easy; what is reinforcing to one individual may not be reinforcing to another. The counselor may need to try several things before finding an adequate reinforcer for those having deficits in their cultural and learning backgrounds. Because people learn to respond to their environments in different ways, the value of objects within their environments varies. Just as those of low economic background may value money and/or food differently from those having backgrounds of affluence, so might delinquent boys be expected to react differently to reinforcements which the school or counselor has to offer, based upon their past experiences with rewards and punishments in their respective environments. According to Jeffrey (1961), deprivation of the reinforcers society has to offer leads to high incidence of criminal behavior among young males. "A middle class person secures food, clothing, automobiles, money, and sex gratification by non-criminal responses; he does not develop criminal responses to obtain these reinforcers (p. 17)." That deprivation conditions lead to deviant behavior is easily seen in penal institutions. "In prison camps prisoners eat rats and commit homosexual acts; they do not behave in this manner when beefsteak and females are available (Jeffrey, 1961, p. 17)." Similarly, when adolescents have histories of little verbal reinforcement in their school lives, they do not learn to value such reinforcement later. School counselors who represent adult middle class values to adolescent boys may find verbal reinforcement to have little effect with such clients (Cohen, 1955). In addition, the relationship between verbal expression and delinquency proneness was found to be highly negative by Jaffee and Polansky (1962), which would also suggest that reinforcers other than verbal ones would need to be used with such individuals.

Principally two kinds of reinforcers affect our behavior. Primary reinforcers, such as food, water, removal from pain, sex, etc., affect our behavior from the beginning. They are unconditioned stimuli, so to speak, because they affect our behavior the first time they are applied. Secondary reinforcers, such as praise, money, and grades, are perhaps the more important in shaping human behavior. After early childhood, primary reinforcers become increasingly less and less important in molding the behavior of human beings (Staats and Staats, 1964). A secondary reinforcer can be learned by pairing its presentation with a primary or other already learned secondary reinforcer. The principle may be easily demonstrated by the way in which school grades take on positive reinforcing value. "A" grades on papers of a first grader have little value initially unless paired with a primary reinforcer or another secondary reinforcer which already has taken on positive value. One child bringing home an "A" paper might be met with kisses and hugs and perhaps a special treat in addition to special attention when daddy gets home. He soon learns the value of "A" grades and will strive for the behaviors needed to acquire more "A" grades. Another first grader receiving an "A" grade, but not receiving such attention from his parents or others, is not as likely to learn the value of such secondary reinforcers until much later. He may learn vicariously that good things happen to those who receive "A" grades, but by this time his achievement level may be at a point so far removed from "A" work that, for him, such a goal seems impossible. He may then resort to other behaviors, some of which may be deviant, in order to receive attention and other reinforcement from his teachers and peers. Gradually, he acquires a deficit in the various types of positive reinforcers society has to offer. Indeed, one of the biggest problems in working with psychotics has been the absence of effective reinforcers. Ayllon and Azrin (1965) were able to solve this problem for some psychotics by observing closely what they did or tried to do in their free time, then using these behaviors with the patients as reinforcers for doing those behaviors connected with the therapy program.

Daley (1969) describes an interesting technique, the "Reinforcement Menu," for finding effective reinforcers for 8 to 11 year old retarded children. Principally, the idea is the same as that used by Ayllon and Azrin (1965) with psychotics. Daley prepared a picture book of 22 activities, such as coloring, dancing, swinging on a door, which he had observed the children doing most often. The children were then told, "You are going to be able to have time to do whatever you want to do that is in this book. Every time you finish your work, you will get to look at our book and pick what you want to do for four minutes (p. 43)." The reinforcers were found very effective in promoting verbal language skills. After only 15 thirty-minute sessions, the children demonstrated an increased ability, ranging from two years to two years six months in the level of improvement.

Keirsey (1969) offers another interesting technique that counselors might employ when the usual reinforcers available in the school setting appear not to have positive value for the student. With the use of a technique he calls behavior contracts, the privilege of remaining in school becomes the reinforcer for the child. Although some would question the alleged positive valence of remaining in school, Keirsey has shown in hundreds of cases that students have changed many of their behaviors in order to receive the privilege of attending school without parent or teacher nagging (Krumboltz and Thoresen, 1969).

A technique for determining which cultural experiences in the lives of Mexican-American children can act as reinforcers for them is presently being studied at the University of California—Santa Barbara by this writer and Dr. Stewart Shapiro. The procedure involves the "What if" technique (Shapiro, 1964), in which the children describe the activities in their various cultural traditions, such as Cinco de Mayo, which they particularly enjoy. The "What if" technique attempts to expand the children's imaginings of positive experiences in their lives by asking them to explore those experiences they would like to have if they had no negative feelings. For example, if a child relates something he would like to do but feels that he cannot or should not do, the counselor responds with, "What if you could," or "What if they didn't say no," etc. Whenever possible, the activities that appear to be most positive in the lives of these children are then used as reinforcers to shape desired behaviors.

Studies supporting the effectiveness of operant conditioning procedures per se are numerous and the technique hardly needs further demonstration in the counseling setting. Several examples in which counselors have used operant techniques along or in combination with other techniques can be found in the following section on social modeling. More complete discussions, however, of numerous as well as a variety of cases in which these procedures have been used effectively by counselors and other therapists can be found in the recent texts by Krumboltz and Thoresen (1969), Bandura (1969) and Ullmann and Krasner (1969).

Social Modeling Procedures

Social modeling procedures involve the provision of real or symbolic models who demonstrate the desired behavior that the client wishes to acquire. Almost any learning that results from direct experience can result also from an observational or vicarious learning situation. By viewing another person's behavior and its consequences for him, an observer can learn the behavior in much the same way as he would if he were to acquire it from direct experience. Bandura (1967, p. 79) suggests that ". . . providing an appropriate 'model' may accelerate the learning process, . . . [and that this process] . . . is particularly suitable in the treatment of gross deficits in behavior as in the case of a child who does not speak, interact with other people or even respond to their presence." Indeed, ". . . virtually all learning phenomena resulting from direct experiences can occur on a vicarious basis through observation of other persons' behavior and its consequences for them (Bandura, 1969, p. 118)."

The process of modifying behavior through imitation certainly isn't new. Discussions of similar techniques (e.g., Jersild and Holmes, 1935; Guthrie, 1938; Chittenden, 1942; Jack, 1934; Page, 1935) have long been in the literature. Recently, however, interest in the use of modeling procedures in counseling and psychotherapy has been greatly revived by research emanating from Social Learning Theory by Bandura and others (Bandura and Walters, 1963) and field studies by Krumboltz and his associates at Stanford University.

Bandura (1965a) suggests that modeling procedures can be used to help clients acquire responses that did not exist before in their behavior repertoires, to strengthen or weaken inhibitory responses and to elicit previously learned behaviors. It is rather ironic that while one of the most used procedures in counselor training is that of modeling, few counselors use this procedure to help clients learn new behaviors. Most of us observed professors and clinicians counseling clients as part of our training program. We also listened to audio tapes and observed films and video presentations of counseling in process. We then proceeded to "model" or imitate the behaviors demonstrated by the model counselor. Medical interns gain much of their learning by observing systematically other doctors performing the many behaviors necessary in the field of medicine. In much the same way as counselors learn to counsel and medical doctors learn to practice medicine, counselors can help clients learn new behaviors deficient in their lives.

Learning by observation then is a potent means of acquiring ways of behavior, and the counselor's systematic use of models can expedite the learning process. Often one or more presentations of the same social model may be all that is necessary for many client problems. For other problems, the process is not unlike that of Wolpe's desensitization (1958) or Skinner's (1953) successive approximations. After the counselor and the client have determined the client's problem and have specified the desired behavior to be learned, the counselor may need to develop a series of models of gradual degrees of difficulty toward the desired behavior. After observing one model presentation, the client practices and learns that behavior, then the next model on the hierarchy is presented, etc.

To understand fully when and how a counselor might employ modeling techniques, it is perhaps helpful to review some of the background and research relative to the development of modeling and vicarious learning procedures.

Social model learning involves the matching of the behavior of a social model by an observer. This process has been referred to as imitative learning, observational learning, identification, vicarious learning, matched dependent behavior, and indirect learning (Thoresen, 1964). Mowrer (1950) defines imitation as matching behavior which occurs in the presence of the model; however, he refers to identification as matching behavior occurring in the model's absence. Bandura (1962), on the other hand, employs a single concept, "imitation," to designate both kinds of matching behavior.

The importance of social model learning in changing the behavior of observer-learners has long been recognized by sociologists and anthropologists. Whiting (1941), nearly three decades ago, provided a social model learning description to describe how youth learns by observing the behavior of socially powerful and aggressive models. The anthropological field studies of Bateson (1936) and Nash (1958) have also recognized the primary impact of social model learning on the behavior of observers. Williams (1952) similarly describes the process of enculturation as gained primarily from observing the behavior of others.

Miller and Dollard (1941), however, were among the first to conceptualize imitative behavior as something other than an instinctive process. Their experiments treated the process of social learning which they referred to as "matched dependent behavior" as instrumental conditioning in which the subjects were reinforced for matching the responses of the model. Although Miller and Dollard demonstrated that individuals can learn by observing others, their studies included reinforcement of the subjects for matching the behavior of the social models and therefore were unable to account for the effect of the social model alone.

Mowrer (1960) takes a different view of social model learning. Although he recognizes that imitative learning occurs when the observer is reinforced for matching the model's responses, his proprioceptive feedback theory (1960) reduces imitative learning to the process of classical conditioning. According to this theory, reinforcement for matching the behavior of the social model is not necessary in order for the observer to acquire the responses. Mowrer suggests that rewarding the behavior of the model is sufficient to promote imitative behavior. As a result of the reinforcement provided the social model, the model's behavior acquires secondary reinforcing properties through the process of classical conditioning. By reproducing the model's positively valenced behavior, the observer, in effect, administers conditioned reinforcements to himself. Once the behavior is acquired by the observer, it may be effective in eliciting external reinforcement and therefore is maintained and enhanced by the process of instrumental conditioning.

Some evidence is available to support Mowrer's vicarious conditioning theory (Bandura and Huston, 1961; Bandura, Ross and Ross, 1963*b*; Bandura and McDonald, 1963). Bandura and Huston exposed nursery children to a model-rewarded or model-nonrewarded situation. The experimenter and an assistant engaged the subject in a game, the object of which was to guess which of two boxes contained two picture stickers. The subject observed while the model engaged in various verbal, motor, and aggressive behaviors totally irrelevant to the performance of the task to which the subject's attention was directed. In the model-rewarded condition, the model culminated the unrelated behaviors by choosing the box which contained the picture stickers. The model demonstrated the same irrelevant behaviors in the model-nonrewarded treatment, but chose the empty box. The results of the study showed those subjects in the model-rewarded situation engaged in a significantly greater amount of imitative behavior than did those individuals who observed the non-rewarded model.

A subsequent study by Bandura, Ross and Ross (1963*a*) showed that children who observed an aggressive model whose behavior was rewarded, displayed more imitative aggressive behavior than did children who saw the model punished. Four groups of nursery school children were used in the study: (1) aggressive model-rewarded; (2) aggressive model-punished; (3) a control group which had no exposure to the model; and (4) a second control group which observed highly expressive but non-aggressive models. Those children exposed to the punished model did not differ significantly in the amount of imitative behavior from those in the control group.

Bandura and McDonald (1963) combined the principles of imitation and operant conditioning in a study to determine whether the combined use of models and social reinforcement would be more effective than models alone in altering children's moral judgments. One of the findings of this investigation was that the presence of the rewarded model was sufficient to instigate matching behavior. Not only was the use of models alone as effective as the combination of models and reinforcement, but the former was also significantly more effective than reinforcement procedures alone. The findings of these studies provide evidence that much human behavior can be learned without any externally administered rewards to the observer.

While recognizing the value of both Miller and Dollard's instrumental conditioning and Mowrer's classical conditioning theories for explaining imitative learning, Bandura (1962, 1965a) criticizes these theories because, he says, they assume that in order for imitative learning to occur, the subject must perform the behavior and experience some reward contingent to the response. He suggests that the acquisition of imitative responses may depend solely upon observing the performance of a social model and does not necessarily entail the opportunity to perform the model's behavior in the exposure setting, or any reinforcements applied immediately to either the model or the observer. Bandura accounts for imitative learning under these conditions by the contiguity theory of observational learning (Bandura, 1965c). According to this theory, contiguity of sensory stimulation is the sole requirement for the acquisition of most forms of matching responses. This process is independent of motivation, reinforcement, overt practice and other factors. These variables are regarded as facilitative rather than necessary for the occurrence of imitative learning.

There is evidence that the acquisition of matching responses takes place through contiguity, whereas reinforcing the model and/or the observer influences the performance of the learned responses (Bandura, 1969). The 1961 and 1963c studies of Bandura, Ross and Ross showed that, although a number of subjects in the model-punished condition did not demonstrate the aggressive behavior, they were able, in post-experimental interviews, to describe the models' responses with considerable accuracy. Bandura states: "Evidently, they had learned the cognitive equivalents of the models' responses but they were not translated into their motoric form (Bandura, 1965a, p. 329)." Support for Bandura's view also comes from the area of communication. Sheffield and Maccoby's (1958) account of jet mechanics who learned faster by watching films than by actually engaging in and being reinforced in the learning process, indicates contiguous association of sensory events may be the only requirements needed in imitative learning.

It is important to point out, however, that Bandura's contiguity or no-trial learning theory (1965c) refers to the acquisition of imitative responses. According to Bandura, reinforcement is still important in imitative learning, but is viewed as influencing the performance of imitatively learned responses rather than their acquisition.

Symbolic Models

Several studies indicate that symbolic models in the form of recordings, films, video tapes, etc., and physically present models may be equally effective in influencing behavior (Walters et al., 1962; Bandura, Ross and Ross, 1963*b*; Schroeder, 1964; Thoresen, 1964; Lovaas et al., 1961). Bandura, Ross and Ross's replication of their 1961 study (1963*b*) used the same models but presented them on film. Analysis of the two sequential studies by the authors not only showed that children exposed to live or film models of aggressive behavior exhibited more aggressive behavior than did children exposed to non-aggressive models, but also that children who viewed real-life models did not differ in total aggressiveness from those exposed to film models. A later experiment by Bandura and Mischel (Bandura, 1965*a*) found that both live and verbally presented symbolic models were successful in modifying children's delay-of-reward patterns. The changes produced by the symbolic model, however, were less stable over time. Lovaas (1961), working with nursery school age children, similarly found film models effective in promoting aggressive behavior. He demonstrated that, after viewing aggressive behavior on film, subjects chose to operate aggressive-type toys to a greater extent than subjects viewing non-aggressive films. Contrary to the hydraulic energy model of psychoanalytic theory, which predicts that children will discharge pent-up aggressions by vicarious participation in aggressive behavior of others, Lovaas' results provide evidence that aggressive models presented on film make children more aggressive rather than less aggressive.

The possibility that symbolic models are effective in promoting subjects' imitative behavior has direct applicability to the counseling situation. If behavior can be acquired by exposure to symbolic social models, counseling procedures utilizing models presented by means of video and audio media may be effective in shaping and modifying a large number of behaviors among clients.

Social Models and Counseling

New procedures for counseling have been and are being developed with principles of social model learning. The effect of symbolic social models as a source of patterns of behavior has been investigated as a variable for promoting information-seeking behavior among high school students (Krumboltz and Schroeder, 1965; Krumboltz and Thoresen, 1964; Krumboltz, Varenhorst and Thoresen, 1967; Thoresen, Hosford and Krumboltz, 1969; Thoresen and Krumboltz, 1968; Thoresen and Hamilton, 1969).

Krumboltz and Schroeder investigated both model-reinforcement and reinforcement counseling techniques on the information-seeking behavior of fifty-four high school juniors. The model-reinforcement procedure consisted of presenting an audio tape of a counselor-student interview in which the counselee modeled the desired behavior and was verbally reinforced by the model counselor. After listening to the audio tape, the subject was reinforced by the experimental counselor for verbal responses that indicated imitation of the model's behavior.

When reinforcement counseling procedures alone were used, the counselor verbally and nonverbally rewarded the subject for any information-seeking response made during the interview. The criterion adopted for the study was the number and variety of information-seeking activities engaged in by the subject within a three-week period following the experimental treatment. Follow-up interviews with the subjects were conducted at the end of the time period by individuals not otherwise connected with the study. These findings indicate that: (1) experimental subjects engaged in more information-seeking behavior outside the interview than control subjects; (2) reinforcement counseling produced significantly more external information-seeking behavior among females than among controls, but this did not hold true for males; (3) for males, but not for females, model-reinforcement counseling produced significantly more external information-seeking behavior than control procedures; and (4) the ratio of information-seeking responses to other responses in the interview was positively correlated with external information-seeking behaviors.

The authors suggest that model-reinforcement counseling may have been more effective for males than for females because the model was a male who discussed only male interests and concerns. In addition, eight of the nine experimental counselors were female, which the authors postulate may have been a factor in the effectiveness of the reinforcement-only counseling.

Significant results for the use of social models in counseling were also found by Krumboltz and Thoresen (1964). Their study represented a replication and extension of the investigation by Krumboltz and Schroeder discussed above. The problem of this study was to determine which of the two counseling techniques investigated in the earlier study would be more effective for promoting the criterion behavior when applied in dyadic or small group settings. The major findings of this investigation were: (1) model-reinforcement and reinforcement counseling were both significantly more effective in promoting information-seeking behavior in both individual and group settings than were the two control group procedures; (2) model-reinforcement counseling was more effective than reinforcement counseling for males; and (3) group model-reinforcement counseling was more effective for males than individual model-reinforcement counseling. For girls no significant differences were found between reinforcement or model-reinforcement procedures or between the types of group settings.

Among the procedures investigated by Thoresen and Hamilton (1969) for promoting the utilization and collection of relevant career information among eleventh grade male students were two social modeling treatments: video-presented peer social models and video-presented peer social models combined with structured stimulus materials. Scores on a knowledge test and on a simulated vocational decision test as well as frequency and variety of career exploratory behaviors carried out by the subjects were the criteria used to assess the efficacy of the various treatments. Although the treatment effects were mixed and inconsistent (i.e., no one treatment was consistently effective across schools), the study does raise an important question for counselors to consider when using social modeling procedures. The models in this study merely talked about ways of setting up career expectations, asking important questions, etc. Perhaps having the models merely talk about rather than actually demonstrate the behavior to be learned decreased the potency of the modeling effect.

One very significant finding to both the Krumboltz and Schroeder and Krumboltz and Thoresen studies was that model-reinforcement counseling was more effective for males than females. These findings suggest that certain model or subject characteristics, or both in combination, may be important variables to consider in using social model procedures for counseling.

Social Model Characteristics

The need to explore the specific characteristics and behaviors of social models as well as special characteristics of observers to determine how they can be effectively utilized by counselors has been pointed out several times in the literature (Magoon, 1964; Robinson, 1963; Williamson, 1962). There is some evidence to indicate that certain model and subject characteristics significantly affect the degree to which observers emulate the behavior of models. A difference between the sex of the model and the sex of the subject may influence the extent to which modeling behavior will be observed and imitated (Bandura, 1962; Bandura, Ross and Ross, 1961, 1963c; Rosenblith, 1959; Thoresen, Krumboltz and Varenhorst, 1965; Krumboltz and Schroeder, 1965; Krumboltz and Thoresen, 1964). Rosenblith (1959) found male experimenters to be more effective than females in influencing kindergarten children's behavior. Bandura, Ross and Ross (1961) obtained similar results in an investigation carried out to determine the influence of the sex of the model on the observer's imitative behavior. These experimenters exposed one half of the subjects to a model of the same sex and the rest to a model of the opposite sex. In general, an aggressive male model provided a more powerful stimulus for imitative aggressive behavior for both sexes than did an aggressive female model.

Thoresen, Krumboltz, and Varenhorst (1965) report results indicating the sex factor influences the degree of imitative behavior in model-reinforcement counseling. These authors found that various combinations of models, subjects and counselors arranged according to sex, influenced the degree to which the subject emulated behavior. Four types of social model audio tapes were used in this study: (1) male counselor and male student; (2) male counselor and female student; (3) female counselor and male student; and (4) female counselor and female student. For male subjects, a male counselor-male student model was most effective when presented by a male counselor. However, for females, it made little difference whether a male or female model was used; instead, the significant variable was the sex of the counselor. Both models were more effective when presented by a male counselor.

Other studies have also demonstrated the influence of sex differences in imitative learning. Bandura (1965b) found that boys produced more imitative responses than girls, especially under conditions in which the model's behavior was punished rather than rewarded. Similarly, Brown (1956, 1952) showed boys more susceptible to influence by masculine models than girls. Brown's findings indicate female subjects displayed ambivalence to the masculine role preference exhibited by the male models.

While the results of these studies indicate the sex of the model may be a salient factor in influencing the degree of imitative behavior, the issue may also be discussed in terms of sex-appropriate behaviors. In the Krumboltz and Schroeder (1965) and Krumboltz and Thoresen (1964) studies, for example, the models discussed typically male-oriented concerns and decisions. Thus the behavior of the model was more suitable for male imitation. A study by Heilbrun (1964) indicates that the sex-appropriate imitative behavior of an individual may be a function of the models to which he has been exposed. Heilbrun investigated the relationship between the sex role behavior in adolescents and the nurturance of their parents. He found that males raised in homes of more masculine and more nurturant fathers displayed more sex-appropriate behaviors than did males raised in less masculine and less nurturant homes.

Bandura, Ross and Ross (1963*a*) also found the sex factor a significant variable in imitative learning. Their study showed that male subjects exposed to a female controller of rewards in the presence of a powerless and ignored male imitated the male more strongly than the female controller. In every other treatment situation (male dominant-female consumer; male dominant-female ignored; female dominant-male consumer), the controller of resources was the more strongly imitated. It may well be, as the study of Fauls and Smith (1956) suggests, that individuals learn to imitate models of the same sex because parents have reinforced sex-appropriate behavior and have punished sex-inappropriate behavior.

Social Power

Bandura and Walters (1963) suggest that models who are ". . . rewarding, prestigeful, competent, . . . high status, and who have control over rewarding resources are more readily imitated than are models who lack these qualities (p. 107)." Merely telling the subjects that the model was competent was found by Rosenbaum and Tucker (1962) to produce significantly greater imitative behavior among subjects than describing the model as incompetent. Subjects exposed to a warm, nurturant model (Bandura and Huston, 1961) also exhibited significantly greater imitative behavior than did individuals exposed to a cold, distant model. A study by Lefkowitz, Blake, and Mouton (1955) used models attired in different clothing to simulate high or low status. The subjects (random groups of individuals on various street corners in Austin, Texas) observed the models violating traffic regulations, i.e., walking across the street against the red light. The authors observed the consequent behavior on the part of the subjects and found that the behavior of the high status models was imitated to a greater degree than that of models of low status.

Numerous other attributes of social models have been studied to determine what model factors promote learning through imitative behavior. Models who are prestigeful (Asch, 1948; Maccoby, 1959; Mussen and Distler, 1959; Mausner, 1953; Krumboltz, Varenhorst and Thoresen, 1967), competent (Mausner and Bloch, 1957; Rosenbaum and Tucker, 1962), and powerful (Bandura, Ross and Ross, 1963a) have all been shown effective for promoting certain behaviors. Similarly, several studies indicate that certain subject characteristics may also serve to facilitate imitative behavior. Individuals who are incompetent (Kanareff and Lanzetta, 1960), lacking in self-esteem (de Charms and Rosenbaum, 1960; Gelfand, 1961), dependent (Kagan and Mussen, 1956), and who have been frequently rewarded for imitative behavior (Lanzetta and Kanareff, 1959; Miller and Dollard, 1941) are especially predisposed to imitate the behavior of models. On the other hand, differences in the extent to which male eleventh grade subjects were influenced by exposure to social modeling treatments were not found related to differences in subject perceptual field orientations (independence-dependence) or to differences in subject personality types (extroversion-introversion) (Thoresen, Hamilton and Bergland, 1969).

The above investigations, however, strongly suggest that certain model characteristics and subject characteristics affect the degree to which observers emulate the behavior of models. A study by Krumboltz, Varenhorst, and Thoresen (1967) suggests that the degree of model counselor attentiveness and prestige may also be significant variables for increasing the frequency and variety of information-seeking behaviors. In this study, two video tapes were shown to female high school students. One tape presented a "low attentive" counselor, who seldom smiled or looked at the student, doodled, or sorted cards; the other tape presented a "high attentive" counselor, who smiled frequently, nodded and attended fully to the student. Counselor prestige was varied by introductory statements preceding the showing of the video tapes. The behavior of the student model and the verbal content were identical on both tapes. The results indicated that model-reinforcement counseling procedures were significantly more effective than the two control procedures in promoting criterion behavior. A significant result of this study, however, was the failure of differences in the model counselor's attentiveness or prestige to affect significantly the information-seeking behavior of the student observers. During subsequent evaluation interviews, the authors found that the student observers attended primarily to the student model instead of the counselor in watching the video tape. This finding strongly suggests the need to explore experimentally specific characteristics of student models and their effect on the behavior of student observers.

Peer Social Models

According to the power theory of social influence (Maccoby, 1959; Mussen and Distler, 1959), adolescent models having considerable social power (prestige) should present a more potent stimulus for imitative behavior than models with low prestige. Social power, as defined by Bandura and Walters (1963), is the ability of a person to influence the behavior of others. Although the studies already reviewed indicate numerous attributes of a model are effective in promoting imitative behavior, no experimental evidence is currently available relating the social power hypothesis to the imitative behavior of adolescents.

Havighurst and Neugarten (1962) point out that the peer group is a powerful force in molding the behavior of individuals. Because the adolescent is always in a subordinate position in the adult world, he turns to the peer group in which he has equal status for learning many behaviors. These authors also maintain that certain areas of teaching and information-giving have become the special province of the peer group, and that it is this group which decides what knowledge is important and what is not. "Parents," Grinder (1965) alleges, "tend to relax their control with the advent of adolescence, while concurrently, peer and school models burgeon in their salience as administrators of cultural rewards and punishments."

There is some evidence (Coleman, 1961; Gordon, 1957; Havighurst and Neugarten, 1962; Tannenbaum, 1960) that high school students are very sensitive to and aware of the athletic, academic, and social success of peers. According to Coleman, "Just as the adult society has models of success, so does the adolescent culture, perhaps to an even greater extent, since the adolescent culture is in greater flux. Its models of immediate success are other boys within the culture and may include boys who have achieved success in various fields (pp. 144-145)."

Gordon (1957) studied the social organization of the high school and found that four major groups—athletic, music and club, dating, and academic—were the main sources of prestige in the school. Similar findings were obtained by Coleman (1961) in a study of ten high school subcultures. In general, the student subcultures centered around non-academic values. For boys, athletic success, dating and extra-curricular activities were found to be the main sources of status. Coleman summarizes his data in the following terms: "In short, despite wide differences in parental background, type of community, and type of school, there was little difference in the standards of prestige, the activities which confer status, and the values which focus attention and interest. In particular, good grades and academic status had relatively low status in all schools (p. 338)."

A study by Tannenbaum (1960) supports the findings of Gordon (1957) and Coleman (1961). He had high school students rank their peers into eight categories. In this study the most popular student was perceived as bright (but not studious) and athletic.

Although the above results must be interpreted cautiously since they were almost entirely sociometric studies rather than investigations having a behavioral reference as a criterion, they do indicate that students are aware of and sensitive to the athletic, academic and social success of their peers. In addition they suggest that students want to be like and tend to emulate those individuals having high social status in the peer culture. Similar support for this postulation can be found in research studies of reference groups, attitude formation, and attitude change (Krech, Crutchfield and Ballachey, 1962). Thus the peer prestige hierarchy appears to be constructed in terms of athletic, social, and academic ability. Consequently, these kinds of ability could be potent factors in making social models more effective in influencing the behavior of observing students.

Recent studies by Thoresen and Krumboltz (1968) and Thoresen, Hosford and Krumboltz (in press) indicate that the kind of model as well as the model's degree of success on that dimension does affect the degree of observer emulation. Indeed, Thoresen and Krumboltz found that different athletic-model success levels caused significant differences in the frequency of information-seeking behaviors by students. During a three-week period following the counseling, those subjects who had been exposed to a high success athletic model demonstrated significantly more of the criterion behavior than did those exposed to athletic models of moderate or low success. Variations in academic success levels did not produce significant differences in the extent to which the students sought educational and career information. Thoresen, Hosford and Krumboltz (in press) found that while the kind of success (academic, social or athletic) ascribed to the model did not significantly affect the extent to which subjects increased their information-seeking activities, the degree of athletic success did. Again, as in the Thoresen and Krumboltz study, subjects exposed to peer models of high or medium success carried out more and greater variety of information-seeking behaviors than subjects exposed to models of low athletic success.

A second important finding of this study was that low self-concept subjects (those who perceived themselves low athletically, socially or academically) aspiring to high success sought more information after exposure to low or medium models than to high models. This finding suggests that further research is needed to determine more fully the ways in which the aspiration level of an individual affects the extent of his emulating behavior.

The fact that "low-but-aspiring" individuals engaged in greater imitative behavior after exposure to low or medium models than after exposure to high models has strong implications for further research. Some possible reasons for this phenomenon were given by the authors (Thoresen, Hosford and Krumboltz, 1969):

It may be that the social distance between the aspiring subjects and the high models was sufficiently great that the model in effect became an aversive stimulus. Although such individuals may have a strong desire to be academically, socially, or athletically successful, they may react negatively to peer models who exhibit high success because they are already painfully aware of their own level of success. Subsequent research needs to explore a greater range of success levels to determine what constitutes an "extreme" difference between the subject and model. At what point does the model start to become an aversive stimulus for low-but-aspiring individuals? It may be that the success of the model becomes an aversive stimulus not at a point of "extreme" difference, but at a point of "crucial" difference. For example, a successful peer athlete may represent a highly negative model to a low-but-aspiring athlete while a professional sports figure may represent a high positive model.

Similarity of Models and Subjects

Another factor in peer social models that may be an important variable in influencing imitative behavior is the similarity between the model and the observer. One of the major motives that mediates behavior change, according to Kagan (1958), is the desire of the individual to maximize similarity to a model. Subjects wish to maximize similarity to a desirable model in order to share vicariously in his resources. This process leads to identification with the model, which Kagan holds is of major importance in the establishment of unusually strong motivations for careers. Although there is little research at present which explores specifically the differential effect of providing peer social models highly similar to subjects, a few recent studies suggest self-perceived similarity of the subject to the model may be an important variable for promoting imitative behavior.

Burstein, Stotland, and Zander (1961) report a study in which children were found to accept the preferences of the model more readily when he was introduced to them as having a very similar background to themselves. Similarly, Sapolsky (1960) showed that the effectiveness of reinforcement in verbal conditioning may depend in part on the relationship between the experimenter and the subject. The author matched subjects with experimenters for similarity on the basis of a personality test, and found that subjects compatible with the experimenters, as determined by the similarity of test scores, conditioned better than those who were incompatible.

The effectiveness of model and subject similarity as a factor promoting reflective behavior among impulsive first grade children was investigated by Kagan et al. (1965). The authors compared the effectiveness of training in reflection under two conditions: (1) a normally nurturant condition between the child and tutor; and (2) one in which the child was persuaded to believe that he shared the same attributes with the tutor and by becoming more reflective could increase the number of shared characteristics. The authors assumed that the subject's desire to maximize similarity to a model would motivate the child to add to the number of shared similarities. Thus if the subject believed the tutor valued reflection he would be highly motivated to imitate this behavior. Significant results were not obtained, but the findings indicate the perceived similarity to the tutor facilitated reflective training for girls, but not for boys. Kagan and his associates point out, however, that the results suggest that future work with this variable might prove extremely valuable.

The two studies discussed above (Thoresen and Krumboltz, 1968; Thoresen, Hosford and Krumboltz, 1969) also tested the similarity hypothesis as a factor for promoting client imitative behavior. Both studies found that the subjects were more prone to imitate the behavior of high status models than models similar to themselves. As a matter of fact, the means of the Thoresen, Hosford and Krumboltz

(1969) study were in the opposite direction to that suggested by the similarity hypothesis; that is, subjects exposed to models representing higher or lower success performed more of the criterion behavior than those subjects exposed to models of similar success to themselves. Because little research has been done in this area, further studies need to be carried out before any conclusions regarding the efficacy of the similarity hypothesis can be made. The studies by Thoresen and Krumboltz and Thoresen, Hosford and Krumboltz suggest that the similarity between the model and observer in terms of age, socio-economic status, ethnic group, grade level and occupational preference might be explored to test further the applicability of this hypothesis to the use of social models in counseling.

Summary

It is evident that modeling procedures are effective means of changing behavior, and it appears that the limits have yet to be established as to the types of client problems for which such techniques are applicable. For some problems modeling techniques themselves may be sufficient to promote the client's desired behavior change. For others, the systematic use of models combined with other techniques may enhance counselor effectiveness. Although operant conditioning procedures are exceedingly reliable and effective when clients need only to strengthen or maintain behaviors which they have already learned, they are sometimes laborious and time consuming, especially when clients need to learn completely new or highly complex behaviors. In such cases, social modeling or combinations of social modeling and operant techniques might be used to promote the desired behavior change.

One main advantage of using modeling techniques in counseling, as shown by the Krumboltz and Thoresen (1964) study, is that they apparently work as well with groups of clients as they do in one-to-one situations. Also, the effective use of audio, video, and film recorded models in helping clients learn various behaviors offers great potential in preventing problems. If counselors were to construct counseling films designed to demonstrate ways clients can learn to make decisions, cope with and reduce anxiety, and acquire numerous other appropriate behaviors, many of the problems clients have could be greatly lessened if not extinguished before the inappropriate behaviors have a chance to become strongly learned habits.

Counselors should be aware of the sources of imitative learning within the home and school settings; i.e., they should recognize the types of behavior to which the individual is exposed. Certainly school counselors should be well aware of the negative effect various grouping policies can have on students' personality development. Too often we separate the "emotionally disturbed," mentally retarded, and others from students in the regular school program. When individuals who act atypically are exposed only to others who also act atypically, is it any wonder that these students soon acquire larger repertoires of deviant behavior? If we expect deviant-acting students to learn more positive ways of behaving, we should not expose them exclusively to models who demonstrate consistent examples of deviant behavior.

This writer recalls one of his first exposures to "group counseling." I was invited to sit in with a group of students identified by teachers and a psychologist as having "emotional problems." The group was formed in October and lasted until March. I recall that at first members of the group came in, sat down and talked. During the course of events, I noticed a continual increase in the frequency and variety of deviant behaviors. The foul language increased; loud boisterous remarks and demonstrations of aggression and hostility became more apparent. If a frequency count of deviant behaviors emitted by the group had been done during the beginning weeks of the counseling and again near the end, the increase in the number of "deviant behaviors" certainly would have reached respectable levels of statistical significance. It was soon evident that the members of this group were increasing their repertoires of deviant behavior from their exposure to the inappropriate behavior of other members of the group. I observed many times, for example, individuals turning off the lights, walking on the table, pulling shades which put the room in total darkness, and yelling profanity that might shock the most sophisticated sailor. Few of these behaviors were performed by the same individuals during the first sessions of the "counseling."

Desensitization

Many problems for which clients seek counselor help involve anxiety; anxiety about taking tests, speaking before groups, traveling in airplanes—the list is endless. A variety of inappropriate behaviors have been related to anxiety. Indeed, Wolpe (1958) suggests that anxiety is the major causal determinant of unadaptive avoidance behavior. To be overly shy or aggressive, to hear strange sounds or be functionally deaf, or to suffer from constipation or diarrhea are but a few of many behaviors that have been attributed to anxiety (Kamin et al., 1955). Wolpe (1958) suggests that for many individuals, muscle tension that seriously impairs coordination, tremors, headaches, stomach distress, and interference with sexual performance, are the result of the person's inability to deal effectively with stressful situations. For such problems, counselors can often design counterconditioning procedures by which the client gradually learns a new behavior for a given situation (e.g., relaxation, assertive responses, etc.) which counteracts the previously learned anxiety.

Before discussing the technique behavioral counselors most often employ with clients having problems of anxiety, it might be well to conceptualize anxiety from a behavioral point of view. If one adheres to a psychoanalytic frame of reference, for example, anxiety is likely to be regarded as the resulting conflict of repression of the id, super ego, or sex aggression (Cattell, 1958; Metzner, 1961). Fenichel (1945), in his discussion of the psychoanalytic view of neurosis, says that the neurosis-producing situation is a result of contradictory impulses between an instinct striving for discharge and impulses in the usual manner. As a result, tension accumulates and the organism is subjected to an amount of excitation greater than it can master. The neurotic symptoms are regarded as distorted discharges as a consequence of the state of damming up.

From a behavioral point of view, on the other hand, anxiety reactions, be they behavioral inhibitions, phobic or other avoidant responses, result from formerly inappropriate stimuli which have acquired the capacity to elicit high-intensity emotional reactions (Bandura, 1969). This model, of course, follows the classical conditioning paradigm which has shown that anxieties and other unadaptive behaviors are learned in much the same way other behaviors are learned. Wolpe's early work with experimental neurosis (cf: Wolpe, 1952*a*, 1952*b*, 1958) led him to believe not only that anxiety was learned, but also that there is no physiological difference between the fear response one emits to an objective threat (e.g., a rattlesnake) and an anxiety (or unadaptive) response elicited by a kitten. Neurotic behavior, of which anxiety is the central constituent, is to Wolpe a persistent unadaptive behavior acquired by learning in a physiologically normal organism. He emphasizes the physiologically normal organism because he readily admits that hyperthyroidism, epilepsy, and other abnormal states can be accompanied by prominent anxiety.

Although all individuals respond to the same laws of learning, the resulting behavior which each of us demonstrates in a given situation may differ greatly from that of another individual. Many factors may be responsible for these differences. The amount and variety of reinforcements the individual has had in the past and his experiences with people (i.e., the amount and kinds of prior learnings) determine not only to a large degree whether a given situation will be anxiety-provoking to the individual, but also the subsequent behavior he might use to reduce the anxiety. Whether an individual chooses withdrawal or aggressive behavior to reduce anxiety in a given situation, for example, is due in part to the kinds of reinforcement he has received in the past for such behavior. This withdrawal or assertion, or any other such response, becomes a "normal" behavior for the individual whenever he encounters the anxiety-provoking situation which first prompted that behavior. The more often he employs that behavior and the more the behavior serves to aid him in escaping or lowering his anxiety, the stronger the behavior becomes; i.e., it becomes a habit.

Desensitization Procedures

The behavioral counseling procedure used with the most success with clients having problems of anxiety has been desensitization. This technique was first employed experimentally by Mary Cover Jones (1924) some 45 years ago. The Jones experiment (discussed earlier) demonstrated how a young boy was successfully deconditioned for the fear of small animals by gradually exposing him to the aversive stimuli (rabbit) while providing him with his favorite food. It was not until 1952, when Wolpe published his paper (Wolpe, 1952b) on an objective psychotherapy of neuroses, however, that any systematic rationale for desensitization as a therapeutic technique was available. Wolpe's subsequent work provided the rationale for his theory Psychotherapy by Reciprocal Inhibition (1958). The principle of reciprocal inhibition, upon which the treatment of desensitization is based, involves associating an incompatible response (e.g., relaxation) with the unadaptive learned behavior (anxiety) in the presence of the situation which elicits the unadaptive behavior. Both responses cannot occur simultaneously because they are incompatible; i.e., one cannot be relaxed and anxious at the same time. Wolpe's theory was developed in part from his experimental observations of animal behavior. He noticed that neurotic behavior among animals often disappeared when feeding occurred in the presence of the anxiety-provoking stimuli. He subsequently inferred and demonstrated that individuals can overcome habits of experiencing anxiety by forming new and reciprocal habits in the same stimulus situations. Wolpe reasoned that helping individuals learn and demonstrate, in the presence of an anxiety-provoking stimulus, responses opposite to those of anxiety (e.g., assertive behaviors, relaxation, sexual and certain avoidance responses) would weaken the bond between the anxiety and the eliciting stimuli. Through the repeated inhibition of the unadaptive anxiety, not only can the potency of the new behavior (relaxation) be increased, but a gradual extinction of the previously learned anxiety will occur. In effect, the desensitization "... seeks to undo a phobia by having the patient unlearn the emotional behavior that is the neurosis (Wolpe, 1969a, p. 35)."

Because the continuum of anxiety reactions (e.g., sexual problems and unique social concerns) presents the problem of having the client actually perform or be exposed to the anxiety-provoking situation, Wolpe developed the procedure of having the aversive stimuli presented to the client gradually in visualized scenes. In essence, this technique involves three separate sets of operations: (1) training in deep muscle relaxation; (2) construction of anxiety hierarchies to be used later in the scenes the client is asked to visualize; and (3) counterposing relaxation and anxiety-evoking stimuli from the hierarchies. After receiving training in relaxation, the client, with the help of the counselor, works out a graduated list of stimuli to which he has been responding with unadaptive anxiety. During the subsequent counseling sessions, the client is made to relax and is then asked to imagine as vividly as possible the weakest item on the hierarchy. As the client learns to relax to scenes higher on the hierarchy, he gradually reaches the point where he can be exposed to the original phobic situation without experiencing the accompanying anxiety.

Crucial Factors

Despite the vast number of studies published supporting desensitization as an effective technique for helping clients with a variety of problems, negative outcomes can occur if the procedure is incorrectly administered (Lazarus, 1964, 1968). It is in the presentation of the anxiety-evoking stimuli to the imagination of the relaxed client that Lazarus suggests most problems occur. For example, if a client repeatedly signals anxiety even to the weakest item on the hierarchy, it is important that the counselor terminate the "scene," reinstating deep relaxation, possibly by presenting several neutral scenes, so that the client will not terminate the counseling session in a state of anxiety. To leave the client anxious could cause him to associate anxiety with the desensitization process itself.

Other factors which Lazarus (1964) points out as critical to the success of the desensitization process include knowing how long the client should visualize the scene, the optimal length of the relaxation interval between scenes, the recommended number of scenes per session, the number of sessions needed and whether an optimal interval should elapse between sessions. These factors are discussed by Lazarus (1964). The counselor planning on using desensitization procedures should familiarize himself with these specific methodological issues before employing the technique. In addition, step by step procedures for constructing hierarchies as well as for utilizing the whole technique are available in sufficient detail so that counselors not specifically trained in behavioral counseling can learn to use these procedures with clients having anxiety-related problems (see, for example, Wolpe and Lazarus, 1966; Emery, 1969; Weinstein, 1969; Bandura, 1969; Wolpe, 1969b).

Types of Problems and Treatment Success

Desensitization procedures appear to be applicable to a great variety of specific and non-specific behaviors. Problems of "free floating" anxiety (Wolpe, 1958), as well as inappropriate behaviors of aggression, dependency, sex and other interpersonal problems (Bandura, 1969) appear to be significantly altered by this counterconditioning process. Indeed, Bandura (1969, p. 464) asserts that ". . . desensitization procedures are not restricted, either on theoretical or practical grounds, to any particular set of emotion-arousing stimuli." He suggests further that such procedures could even ". . . be employed to neutralize the negative valence of Oedipal fantasies in clients for whom this might constitute a problem."

That desensitization is an effective counseling technique for a variety of client problems has considerable support in the literature. Wolpe (1961), in the first published statistical study relating to the efficacy of desensitization, used a sample of 39 cases randomly selected from his files. Of the 39 clients, 19 had multiple anxieties necessitating evaluations of 68 anxiety-response hierarchies used in the treatments. The systematic desensitization procedures were found effective for helping 35 of the 39 clients. Success was operationally defined as "complete or almost complete freedom from phobic reactions to all situations in the area of the phobia encountered in actuality," or "improvement of response such that the phobia is judged by the patient to have lost at least 80 percent of its original strength (Wolpe and Lazarus, 1966, p. 96)." Complete freedom of the phobic reactions was found for 45 of the anxiety response habits for which desensitization hierarchies were constructed, while 17 were "markedly ameliorated." The combined success rate was 90 percent. Control groups, however, were not used, nor was any direct comparison made to matched cases receiving other types of treatment. Such a comparison, however, was made by Lazarus (1961), in which he matched and randomly assigned 15 claustrophobics, 11 acrophobics and five impotent men to either group desensitization or group interpretation (a form of insight therapy) treatments. Lazarus reports that the group desensitization procedures were significantly more effective in helping the clients overcome their phobic reactions than were the interpretation methods. Whereas two-thirds of the subjects experiencing desensitization overcame their phobias in an average of 20.4 sessions, only 2 of 17 in the interpretation group were found symptom-free.

After reviewing over 50 case articles and 20 experimental studies in which controls were used, Paul (1968a, 1968b) concluded that "The findings were overwhelmingly positive, and for the first time in the history of psychological treatments, a specific therapeutic package was found to reliably produce therapeutic benefits for clients across a broad range of distressing problems where anxiety is a fundamental importance."

Some of the specific problems for which desensitization procedures have been employed successfully include test anxiety (Emery, 1969; Weinstein, 1969), school phobia (Garvey and Hengrenes, 1966), sexual deviations (Lazarus, 1963; Lazarus and Rachman, 1957; Wolpe, 1958; Stevenson and Wolpe, 1960), traffic and automobile anxieties (Wolpe and Lazarus, 1966; Kraft and All-Issa, 1965), public speaking (Paul and Shannon, 1966), concern over possible disasters (Ashen, 1963), insomnia (Geer and Katkin, 1966), exhibitionism (Bond and Hutchinson, 1960), fear of animals (Friedman, 1966) and nervous diarrhea (Cohen and Reed, 1968). Extensive discussions of many other cases in which desensitization procedures have been used effectively can be found in reviews by Paul (1968*a*, 1968*b*, 1968*c*) and recent publications by Bandura (1969) and Krumboltz and Thoresen (1969).

Several innovations in the use of desensitization procedures have been carried out and are worthy of consideration. Donner (1967), for example, used a programmed desensitization procedure successfully with and without the therapist being present. Similarly, Migler and Wolpe (1967) report a case in which a client, unable to attend staff meetings due to severe anxiety created by having to speak before groups, successfully desensitized himself at home through the use of tape recordings which presented the relaxation instructions and graduated scenes of public speaking situations. Role playing situations rather than visualized scenes were used by Hosford (1969) to desensitize a child to the anxiety she experienced in reading, giving a report, or performing in any manner before a group. Rather than imagine the stimulus situation on the hierarchy, as is the usual procedure, the client role-played those behaviors which were associated with her anxiety. When she was able to perform a particular behavior in the practice situation with little or no anxiety, the next stimulus situation on the hierarchy was role played. Systematic desensitization procedures have also been employed successfully with groups of clients having similar problems (e.g., Paul, 1968*c*; Paul and Shannon, 1966) as well as groups of clients with dissimilar problems (Lazarus, 1961, 1968).

Innovations in the types and construction of the stimulus hierarchies have also been tested experimentally. For example, Wolpe (1958) utilized actual stimulus situations rather than imagined scenes in the successful desensitization of college students concerned with test anxiety. While both groups demonstrated a significant reduction in test anxiety, no difference was found between those students using standard hierarchies and those using the individual hierarchies.

An interesting study in which several extensions of the classic desensitization process were tested experimentally was carried out by Thoresen and Bergland (1969). In an attempt to promote greater transfer to real life of the extinction effects from the desensitization process, three treatment combinations were tested experimentally: (1) desensitization followed by performance tasks carried out in the counselor's office; (2) desensitization followed by performance tasks carried out in real-life settings; and (3) *in-vivo* desensitization, in which the subjects, after being given help in constructing the anxiety hierarchies and training in relaxation by the counselor, carried out the desensitization procedures *in-vivo* without the counselor present. Briefly, the results indicate that systematic desensitization *with performance tasks* was more effective in reducing anxiety about participating in class, measured by a questionnaire, than systematic desensitization or *in-vivo* desensitization. However, the frequency of participation responses as measured by classroom observers and instructor ratings was not appreciably increased and anxiety was *not* consistently reduced in the classroom setting when heart rate and muscle tension were used as criteria. The results suggest the need for sequential or concomitant treatments, where at least some subjects receive desensitization to reduce anxiety coupled with an observation-operant treatment, such as live modeling and positively reinforced behavioral rehearsal. The study established the feasibility of using telemetered physiological assessment in actual life situations such as the classroom. In addition, the multiple criteria data from this study strongly supports the concept of intraindividual response patterning, i.e., very different and low intercorrelations between subjects and within individual subjects on different criterion measures.

Summary

There appears to be sufficient evidence to support the fact that many phobias and inhibitions can be effectively eliminated by the use of counterconditioning procedures such as desensitization. The effectiveness of this technique is not limited to helping clients overcome a few specific phobias. On the contrary, it appears that these procedures can be used to neutralize the negative valence of many types of emotion-arousing stimuli for many types of clients in a wide variety of settings and situations. Further, the innovations in the use of classical desensitization procedures presently being tested may make the technique even more efficacious. When counselors can tailor individually the technique to the type of client, the type of problem, and the type of situation in which the problem occurs, greater success no doubt will occur.

An important side effect resulting from desensitization should be generalized improvements in other areas of behavioral performance. In addition to the great relief the client experiences by the reduction or elimination of the anxiety per se, it should follow that the reduction in anxiety would be accompanied by a chain reaction in which positive approach behaviors would begin to appear. An example of this can be seen in the theoretical case of an anxious client who acquires a large repertoire of avoidance behaviors in order to escape a particular anxiety-provoking situation such as the giving of an oral presentation before a group of classmates. The behaviors he has learned are, in effect, maintained by the reinforcement he receives by not having to undergo the tremendous anxiety he has learned to associate with speaking before a group; i.e., the anxiety acts as a negative reinforcer. For this client, as for many others, avoidance of a negative stimulus such as anxiety is often a stronger reinforcer for promoting inappropriate behavior than social approval and the other reinforcers available in the individual's environment are for promoting appropriate behavior. Eliminating the anxiety by desensitization therefore eliminates the reinforcer which has been maintaining the inappropriate avoidance behavior. Because these behaviors no longer "pay off," the individual is free to try new and more appropriate behaviors. And, it would follow that if these new behaviors were to meet with favorable feedback from self and others, other positive behaviors as well as the strengthening of the newly learned behavior would occur.

If, as this model suggests, behavioral functioning in other areas often follows specific induced changes in anxiety or other behavior,[3] rather than looking for possible areas of "symptom substitution" when clients have significantly altered their anxieties or other behavior, the counselor should be observing closely for any emergence of new and appropriate behaviors. He would then be prepared to make sure that any attempt on the part of the client to perform approach or other positive behaviors would be met with reinforcement. Indeed, the counselor could employ social modeling procedures during or near the end of the desensitization process to elicit such new approach behaviors. Those behaviors to be elicited would, of course, need to have a neutral or low anxiety valence for the client so as not to interfere with the desensitization process.

The counselor is not, of course, limited to any one technique or to only those discussed in this paper. Although operant, modeling and desensitization procedures are perhaps used by behavioral counselors more than any other techniques, others (e.g., assertive training, behavior rehearsal, and behavior contracts) are often employed. Nor is the counselor limited only to those procedures developed within the behavioral counseling framework. Any morally and legally sound treatment that offers a solution to the problem for which a client seeks counseling may be employed. Whether or not a procedure is used depends more upon its demonstrated ability to survive subjection to empirical tests than upon whether it is a "counseling" technique, or a behavioral counseling practice for that matter. Indeed, the fields of instruction, technology, and industry, along with other sources, have available a large array of techniques that counselors can test out and use.

Comments and Conclusions

New approaches to counseling and psychotherapy come and go. Some are met with great zeal by the profession only to peter out when they are subjected to the test of empirical research. The techniques that have endured this test have not been those derived from philosophy. Nor have they been those developed from the counselor's own needs, or from reflections of what he thought took place during the counseling process. The fact that the principles and techniques of behavioral counseling have emanated from controlled scientific studies would suggest that the approach is here to stay. The probability is infinitesimal, however, that behavioral counseling or any other approach will ever prove to be 100 percent effective with all clients or with all types of problems.

Many of the issues raised in the counseling literature by behaviorists and those adhering to other approaches are word games: semantic arguments for which answers cannot be gained. As behavioral scientists, we should be dealing with things that can be verified. To do otherwise only retards our efforts to discover effective techniques which can be used to solve the problems for which individuals seek counseling. Whether it is a symptom or a behavior with which the counselor must deal is irrelevant. To give credence to the argument of symptom substitution probably only legitimizes the question because proof one way or the other is impossible.

A second issue often raised is whether or not the counselor should manipulate and control the behavior of the client. This, too, is another semantic argument, perhaps best left to philosophers rather than scientists. Rogers's phenomenology is just as manipulative as Krumboltz's or Skinner's behaviorism. None of us is beyond the reach of controlling techniques; people constantly control and manipulate each other by words and gestures. The techniques used by governmental, religious and educational institutions to control human behavior are powerful indeed. The by-products of such control, much of which is accomplished by aversive means, can be very detrimental, causing such negative responses as fear, anxiety, depression and anger to name a few.

Freedom is always restrictive. In fact it is the restrictions in freedom which bring clients to counselors. Individuals who have few friends because they do not know how to relate with people; those who are preparing themselves for careers they do not want because they have not learned to survey other alternatives, to collect and utilize information on each option, and to consider the consequences of each before making a decision; and the multitudes of others who have deficits in many types of learning, are all restricted in the degrees of freedom open to them. The freedom of each of these individuals to choose alternatives and courses of action, which will lead to a fuller and more productive life, is directly related to the variety of behaviors he has learned and the extent to which he has learned them.

The techniques that a counselor uses are neither moral nor immoral. It is the end product, not the counselor's techniques, which must be looked at to determine whether the manipulation and control is ethically and morally sound. If by manipulating factors within an individual's environment he learns to relate to others, or to make more effective decisions, or to speak before groups without anxiety, we are increasing his degrees of freedom. He has many new responses available to him which he can now use to increase the array and frequency of reinforcements which otherwise were closed to him.

Manipulation and control of course can be bad. On one hand, they can make our clients dependent, conforming, or any one of a variety of other negative behavioral patterns. On the other, they can be used to promote just as many positive outcomes. The danger lies in not being aware that as counselors we are controlling human behavior. Not only should we be aware of this constant control, but we must make special effort to use its potentialities in helping clients achieve their desired changes in behavior. To leave this control of behavior to others or to chance is to forfeit our opportunity and responsibility to help individuals attain the goals they wish to achieve in life.

Some counselors have referred to behavioral counseling as just good common sense. But perhaps we should describe the approach as good sense—common sense in this field just is not common.

Footnotes

1. Although these experiments demonstrated that human anxieties could be learned and unlearned, clinicians have only recently begun utilizing these principles in counseling and psychotherapy. Some recent works from which many of the principles and techniques of behavioral counseling have been developed are: Wolpe's *Psychotherapy by Reciprocal Inhibition* (1958); Eysenck's *Behavior Therapy and the Neuroses* (1960); Bandura and Walters' *Social Learning and Personality Development* (1963); and Skinner's *Science and Human Behavior* (1953). These all provide major bases from which counselors and psychotherapists can develop techniques for behavioral change based on learning principles. However, to suggest that behavioral counseling has its roots entirely in psychology would be in error. Much of the theoretical rationale from which techniques of behavioral counseling have been developed stems from the contributions of philosophy, biology, and physiology. Other major works to present counseling and psychotherapy as a learning process include those of Rotter (1954), Salter (1961), Franks (1961), Krasner and Ullmann (1965), Ullmann and Krasner (1965), Bandura (1969), Wolpe (1969b) and Ullmann and Krasner (1969). Specifically concerned with counseling from a learning point of view are *Revolution in Counseling* edited by John D. Krumboltz (1966b) and *Behavioral Counseling: Cases and Techniques* edited by Krumboltz and Thoresen (1969).

2. Actually, Guthrian theory differs considerably from that of Skinner. Guthrie did not see the need for rewards in strengthening a behavior. The full associative strength is gained on the first stimulus and response pairing. Rewards, according to Guthrie, only protect the unlearning of the newly acquired behavior (Hilgard, 1956). Whether reinforcement affects the strengthening of a response is still debatable. But Bandura (1969, p. 225) says that the "overall evidence would seem to indicate that reinforcers can have both associative strengthening and performance-enhancing effects."

3. There is some evidence to suggest that change in specific areas of behavioral functioning does indeed result in generalized improvement in other areas. See, for example, Bandura (1969) and Krumboltz and Thoresen (1969). More research, however, is badly needed in this area.

References

Allyon, T. In: *Reinforcement therapy* (a supplement to the film: *Reinforcement therapy*). Philadelphia: Smith, Kline and French, 1966.

Allyon, T. & Azrin, N. H. The measurement and reinforcement of behavior of psychotics. *Journal of Experimental Analysis of Behavior*, 1965, *8*, 357-383.

Asch, S. E. The doctrine of suggestion, prestige, and imitation in social psychology. *Psychological Review*, 1948, *55*, 250-277.

Ash, R. Reliability of psychiatric diagnosis. *Journal of Abnormal and Social Psychology*, 1949, *44*, 272-277.

Ashem, B. The treatment of a disaster phobia by systematic desensitization. *Behavior Research and Therapy*, 1963, *1*, 81-84.

Baer, D. M. & Wolf, M. M. The entry into natural communities of reinforcement. Paper read at the American Psychological Association meeting, Washington, September, 1967.

Bandura, A. Psychotherapy as a learning process. *Psychological Bulletin*, 1961, *58*, 143-159.

Bandura, A. Social learning through imitation. In Marshal Jones (Ed.), *Nebraska symposium on motivation*, 1962. Lincoln: University of Nebraska Press, 1962.

Bandura, A. Behavioral modifications through modeling procedures. In Krasner, L. & Ullmann, L. (Eds.), *Research in behavior modification*. New York: Holt, Rinehart and Winston, 1965. (*a*)

Bandura, A. Influence of models' reinforcement contingencies on the acquisition of imitative responses. *Journal of Social Psychology*, 1965, *1*, 589-595. (*b*)

Bandura, A. Vicarious processes: A case of no-trial learning. In Berkowitz, L. (Ed.), *Advances in experimental social psychology. Vol. II*. New York: Academic Press, 1965. (*c*)

Bandura, A. Behavioral psychotherapy. *Scientific American*, 1967, *216*, No. 3, 78-86.

Bandura, A. *Principles of behavior modification*. New York: Holt, Rinehart and Winston, 1969.

Bandura, A. & Huston, A. C. Identification as a process of incidental learning. *Journal of Abnormal and Social Psychology*, 1961, *63*, 311-318.

Bandura, A. & McDonald, F. J. The influence of social reinforcement and the behavior of models in shaping children's moral judgments. *Journal of Abnormal and Social Psychology*, 1963, *67*, 274-281.

Bandura, A., Ross, D. & Ross, S. A. Transmission of aggression through imitation of aggressive models. *Journal of Abnormal and Social Psychology*, 1961, *63*, 575-582.

Bandura, A., Ross, D. & Ross, S. A. A comparative test of the status envy, social power, and secondary reinforcement theories of identificatory learning. *Journal of Abnormal and Social Psychology*, 1963, *67*, 527-534. (*a*)

Bandura, A., Ross, D. & Ross, S. A. Imitation of film-mediated aggressive models. *Journal of Abnormal and Social Psychology*, 1963, *66*, 3-11. (*b*)

Bandura, A., Ross, D. & Ross, S. A. Vicarious reinforcement and imitative learning. *Journal of Abnormal and Social Psychology*, 1963, *67*, 601-607. (*c*)

Bandura, A. & Walters, R. *Social imitation and personality development*. New York: Holt, Rinehart and Winston, 1963.

Bateson, G. *The naven*. Stanford: Stanford University Press, 1936.

Beech, H. R. *Changing man's behavior*. Baltimore: Penguin Books, 1969.

Bijou, S. W. Implications of behavioral science for counseling and guidance. In Krumboltz, J. D. (Ed.), *Revolution in counseling: Implication of behavioral science*. Boston: Houghton Mifflin, 1966.

Bond, I. K. & Hutchinson, H. C. Application of reciprocal inhibition therapy to exhibitionism. *Canadian Medical Association Journal*, 1960, *83*, 23-25.

Bookbinder, J. L. Simple conditioning vs. the dynamic approach to symptoms and symptom substitution: A reply to Yates. *Psychological Reports*, 1962, *10*, 71-77.

Brown, D. E. Sex-role development in a changing culture. *Psychological Bulletin,* 1958, *55,* 232-242.

Brown, D. E. Sex-role preference in young children. *Psychological Monograph,* 1956, *70,* 17.

Burnstein, E., Stotland, E. & Zander, A. Similarity to a model and self-evaluation. *Journal of Abnormal and Social Psychology,* 1961, *62,* 257-264.

Cairns, R. B. & Lewis, M. Dependency and the reinforcement value of a verbal stimulus. *Journal of Consulting Psychology,* 1962, *26,* 1-8.

Cattell, R. B. & Scheier, I. H. The nature of anxiety: A review of thirteen multivariate analyses comprising 814 variables. *Psychological Reports,* 1958, *4,* 351-388.

Chittenden, G. E. An experimental study in measuring and modifying assertive behavior in young children. *Monographs of the Society for Research in Child Development,* 1942.

Cohen, A. K. *Delinquent boys: The culture of the gang.* Glencoe: The Free Press, 1955.

Cohen, S. I. & Reed, J. L. The treatment of "nervous diarrhea" and other conditioned autonomic disorders by desensitization. *British Journal of Psychiatry,* 1968, *117,* 1275-1280.

Coleman, J. S. *The adolescent society.* New York: The Free Press of Glencoe, 1961.

Daley, M. F. The "reinforcement menu": finding effective reinforcers. In Krumboltz, J. D. & Thoresen, C. E. (Eds.), *Behavioral counseling: Cases and techniques.* New York: Holt, Rinehart and Winston, 1969.

de Charms, R. & Rosenbaum, M. E. Status variables and matching behavior. *Journal of Personality,* 1960, *28,* 492-502.

Donner, L. Effectiveness of a pre-programmed group desensitization treatment for test anxiety with and without a therapist present. Unpublished Ph.D. dissertation, Rutgers University, 1967.

Emery, J. R. Systematic desensitization: reducing test anxiety. In Krumboltz, J. D. & Thoresen, C. E. (Eds.), *Behavioral counseling: Cases and techniques.* New York: Holt, Rinehart and Winston, 1969.

Emery, J. R. & Krumboltz, J. D. Standard versus individualized hierarchies in desensitization to reduce test anxiety. *Journal of Counseling Psychology,* 1967, *14,* 204-209.

Eysenck, H. J. *Behavior therapy and the neuroses.* Oxford: Pergamon Press, 1960.

Fauls, L. B. & Smith, W. D. Sex-role learning of five year olds. *Journal of Genetic Psychology,* 1956, *89,* 105-117.

Fenichel, O. *The psychoanalytic theory of neurosis.* New York: Norton and Co., 1945.

Ferster, C. B. Reinforcement and punishment in the control of human behavior by social agencies. *Psychiatric Research Reports,* 1958, *10,* 101-118.

Ferster, C. B. Classification of behavioral pathology. In Krasner, L. & Ullmann, L. (Eds.), *Research in behavior modification.* New York: Holt, Rinehart and Winston, 1965.

Franks, C. M. *Conditioning techniques in clinical practice and research.* New York: Springer, 1961.

Friedman, D. Treatment of a case of dog phobia in a deaf mute by behavior therapy. *Behavior Research and Therapy,* 1966, *4,* 141.

Garvey, W. P. & Hegrenes, J. R. Desensitization techniques in the treatment of school phobia. *American Journal of Orthopsychiatry,* 1966, 147-152.

Geer, J. H. & Katkin, E. S. Treatment of insomnia using a variant of systematic desensitization. *Journal of Abnormal and Social Psychology,* 1966, *7,* 161-164.

Gelfand, D. M. The influence of self-esteem on rate of conditioning and social matching behavior. Unpublished Ph.D. dissertation, Stanford University, 1961.

Gordon, C. W. *The social system of the high school.* Glencoe: The Free Press, 1957.

Grinder, R. E. Peer status, academic performance, and motivation for social dating. A paper presented at the American Educational Research Association symposium, *Youth Culture and the High School: Co-Agents of Socialization,* Chicago, February, 1965.

Grossberg, J. M. Behavior therapy. A review. *Psychological Bulletin,* 1964, *62,* 73-88.

Guthrie, E. R. *The psychology of human conflict.* New York: Harper and Row, 1938.

Havighurst, R. J. & Neugarten, B. L. *Society and education.* Boston: Allyn and Bacon, Inc., 1962.

Heilbrun, A. B., Jr. Parental model attributes, nurturant reinforcement and consistency of behavior in adolescents. *Child Development,* 1964, *35,* 151-167.

Hilgard, E. R. *Theories of learning.* (Second Ed.) New York: Appleton-Century-Crofts, 1956.

Hively, W. Implications for the classroom of B. F. Skinner's analyses of behavior. *Harvard Educational Review,* Winter, 1959.

Hobbs, N. Sources of gain in psychotherapy. *American Psychologist,* 1962, *17,* 741-747.

Hosford, R. E. Teaching teachers to reinforce student participation. In Krumboltz, J. D. & Thoresen, C. E. (Eds.), *Behavioral counseling: Cases and techniques.* New York: Holt, Rinehart and Winston, 1969.

Jack, L. M. An experimental study of ascendant behavior in preschool children. *University of Iowa Studies in Child Welfare,* 1934, *9,* 3-65.

Jaffee, L. D. & Polansky, N. Verbal inaccessibility in young adolescents in showing delinquent trends. *Journal of Health and Human Behavior,* 1962, *3,* 105-111.

Jeffrey, C. R. Behavior theory and criminology. Paper presented at the annual meeting of the American Association for the Advancement of Science, Denver, 1961.

Jersild, A. T. & Holmes, F. B. Methods of overcoming children's fears. *Journal of Psychology,* 1935, *1,* 75-104.

Jones, M. C. A laboratory study of fear: The case of Peter. *The Pedagogical*

Seminary and Journal of Genetic Psychology, Child Behavior, Animal Behavior and Comparative Psychology, 1924, *31*, 308-315.

Kagan, J. & Mussen, P. H. Dependency themes on the TAT and group conformity. *Journal of Consulting Psychology*, 1956, *20*, 29-32.

Kagan, J., Pearson, L. & Welsh, L. The modifiability of an impulsive tempo. (mimeo), Harvard University, 1965.

Kamin, L. J., Bindra, D., Clark, J. & Wakesburg, H. The interrelations among some behavioral measures of anxiety. *Canadian Journal of Psychology*, 1955, *9*, 79-83.

Kanareff, V. T. & Lanzetta, J. Effects of success-failure experiences and probability of reinforcement upon the acquisition and extinction of an imitative response. *Psychological Review*, 1960, *67*, 373-379.

Kanfer, F. H. & Saslow, G. Behavioral analysis: an alternative to diagnostic classification. In Millon, T. (Ed.), *Theories of psychopathology*. Philadelphia: W. B. Saunders, 1967.

Katz, M. M., Cole, J. O. & Lowery, H. A. Nonspecificity of diagnosis of paranoid schizophrenia. *Archives of General Psychiatry*, 1964, *11*, 197-202.

Kelly, G. A. *Psychology of personal constructs, Vol. II. Clinical diagnosis and psychotherapy*. New York: Norton, 1955.

Keirsey, D. W. Systematic exclusion: Eliminating chronic classroom disruptions. In Krumboltz, J. D. & Thoresen, C. E. (Eds.), *Behavioral counseling: Cases and techniques*. New York: Holt, Rinehart and Winston, 1969.

Kesey, K. *One flew over the cuckoo's nest*. New York: Signet, 1962.

Kraft, T. & All-Issa, I. The application of learning theory to the treatment of traffic phobia. *British Journal of Psychiatry*, 1965, *111*, 277-279.

Krasner, L. & Ullmann, L. F. (Eds.) *Research in behavioral modification*. New York: Holt, Rinehart and Winston, 1965.

Krech, D., Crutchfield, R. S. & Ballachey, E. L. *Individual in society*. New York: McGraw-Hill, 1962.

Krumboltz, J. D. Behavioral goals for counseling. *Journal of Counseling Psychology*, 1966, No. 2, 13. (*a*)

Krumboltz, J. D. (Ed.) *Revolution in counseling: Implications of behavioral science*. Boston: Houghton Mifflin, 1966. (*b*)

Krumboltz, J. D. Stating the goals of counseling. *California Counseling and Guidance Association Monograph*, 1966, No. 1. (*c*)

Krumboltz, J. D. Changing the behavior of behavior changers. *Counselor Education and Supervision*, Special publication, Spring, 1967.

Krumboltz, J. D. & Hosford, R. E. Behavioral counseling in the elementary school. *Elementary School Guidance and Counseling*, 1967, *1*, 27-40.

Krumboltz, J. D. & Schroeder, W. W. Promoting career exploration through reinforcement. *Personnel and Guidance Journal*, 1965, *44*, 19-26.

Krumboltz, J. D. & Thoresen, C. E. The effect of behavioral counseling in group and individual settings on information-seeking behavior. *Journal of Counseling Psychology*, 1964, *11*, 324-333.

Krumboltz, J. D. & Thoresen, C. E. *Behavioral Counseling: Cases and Techniques*. New York: Holt, Rinehart and Winston, 1969.

Krumboltz, J. D., Varenhorst, B. & Thoresen, C. E. Non-verbal factors in effectiveness of models in counseling. *Journal of Counseling Psychology*, 1967, *14*, 412-418.

Lanzetta, J. T. & Kanareff, V. T. The effects of a monetary reward on the acquisition of an imitative response. *Journal of Abnormal and Social Psychology*, 1959, *59*, 120-127.

Lazarus, A. A. Group therapy of phobic disorders by systematic desensitization. *Journal of Abnormal and Social Psychology*, 1961, *63*, 504.

Lazarus, A. A. The treatment of chronic frigidity by systematic desensitization. *Journal of Nervous and Mental Disease*, 1963, *136*, 272-278.

Lazarus, A. A. Crucial procedural factors in desensitization therapy. *Behavior Research and Therapy*, 1964, *22*, 65-70.

Lazarus, A. A. Behavior therapy in group. In Gazda, G. M. (Ed.), *Basic approaches to group psychotherapy and group counseling*. Springfield: Charles C Thomas, 1968.

Lazarus, A. A. & Rachman, S. The use of systematic desensitization in psychotherapy. *South African Medical Journal*, 1957, *311*, 934-937.

Lefkowitz, M., Blake, R. R. & Mouton, J. S. Status factors in pedestrian violation of traffic signals. *Journal of Abnormal and Social Psychology*, 1955, *51*, 704-705.

Loree, M. R. & Koch, M. Use of verbal reinforcement in developing group discussion skills. *Journal of Educational Psychology*, June, 1960.

Lovass, O. I. Effect of exposure to symbolic aggression on aggressive behavior. *Child Development*, 1961, *32*, 37-44.

Maccoby, E. E. Role-taking in childhood and its consequences for social learning. *Child Development*, 1959, *30*, 239-252.

Magoon, T. Innovations in counseling. *Journal of Counseling Psychology*, 1964, *11*, 342-347.

Mausner, B. Studies in social interaction: III. Effect of variation in one partner's prestige on the interaction of observer pairs. *Journal of Applied Psychology*, 1953, *37*, 391-393.

Mausner, B. & Bloch, B. L. A study of the additivity of variables affecting social interaction. *Journal of Abnormal and Social Psychology*, 1957, *54*, 250-256.

Metzner, R. Learning theory and the therapy of neurosis. *The British Journal of Psychology*. Monograph Supplement. Cambridge: Oxford University Press, 1961.

Michael, J. & Meyerson, L. A behavioral approach to counseling and guidance. *Harvard Educational Review*, 1962, *32*, 382-492.

Mischel, W. *Personality assessment*. New York: Wiley, 1969.

Migler, B. & Wolpe, J. Automated self-desensitization: A case report. *Behavior Research and Therapy*, 1967, *5*, 133-135.

Miller, N. E. & Dollard, J. *Social learning and imitation*. New Haven: Yale University Press, 1941.

Mowrer, O. H. *Learning theory and personality dynamics*. New York: Ronald, 1950.

Mowrer, O. H. *Learning theory and the symbolic processes*. New York: John Wiley and Sons, 1960.

Mussen, B. H. & Distler, L. Masculinity identification and father-son relationships. *Journal of Abnormal and Social Psychology*, 1959, *59*, 350-356.

Nash, M. Machine age Maya: The industrialization of a Guatemalan community. *American Anthropologist*, 1958, *60*, no. 2, Part 2 (memoir no. 87).

Page, M. L. The modification of ascendant behavior in preschool children. *University of Iowa Studies in Child Welfare*, 1936, *12*, 7-69.

Patterson, G. R., Helper, M. E. & Wilcott, R. C. Anxiety and verbal conditioning in children. *Child Development*, 1960, *31*, 101-108.

Paul, G. L. Outcome of systematic desensitization. I: Background, procedures and uncontrolled reports of individual treatment. In Franks, C. M. (Ed.), *Assessment and status of the behavior therapies*. New York: McGraw-Hill, 1968. (*a*)

Paul, G. L. Outcome of systematic desensitization. II. Controlled investigations of individual treatment, technique variations, and current status. In Franks, C. M. (Ed.), *Assessment and status of the behavior therapies*. New York: McGraw-Hill, 1968. (*b*)

Paul, G. L. Two-year followup of systematic desensitization in therapy groups. *Journal of Abnormal Psychology*, 1968, *73*, 119-130. (*c*)

Paul, G. L. & Shannon, D. T. Treatment of anxiety through systematic desensitization in therapy groups. *Journal of Abnormal Psychology*, 1966, *71*, 124-135.

Pavlov, I. P. *Conditioned reflexes*. Trans. by G. V. Anrep. New York: Liveright, 1927.

Reynolds, G. S. *A primer of operant conditioning*. Glenview, Illinois: Scott, Foresman, 1968.

Robinson, F. P. A cubist approach to the art of counseling. *Personnel and Guidance Journal*, 1963, *41*, 670-676.

Rogers, C. R. *Client-centered therapy*. Boston: Houghton Mifflin, 1951.

Rogers, J. M. Operant conditioning in a quasi-therapeutic setting. *Journal of Abnormal and Social Psychology*, *60*, 247-252.

Rosenbaum, M. E. & Tucker, I. F. The competence of the model and the learning of imitation and non-imitation. *Journal of Experimental Psychology*, 1962.

Rosenblith, J. F. Learning by imitation in kindergarten children. *Child Development*, 1959, *30*, 69-80.

Rotter. J. B. *Social learning and clinical psychology*. Englewood Cliffs, N.J.: Prentice Hall, 1954.

Ryan, T. A. *Effectiveness of counseling in college residence halls on students' study behavior*. U.S. Dept. of Health, Education, and Welfare, Office of Education, Research Project No. 3269. Corvallis: Oregon State University, 1967.

Salter, A. *Conditioned reflex therapy*. New York: Capricorn Books, Putnam's Sons, 1961.

Sapolsky, A. Interpersonal relationships and verbal conditioning. *Journal of Abnormal Psychology*, 1960, *60*, 241-246.

Schroeder, W. W. The effect of reinforcement counseling and model-reinforcement counseling upon the information-seeking behavior of high school students. Unpublished Ph.D. dissertation, Stanford University, 1964.

Shapiro, S. Explorations in positive experience. *Los Angeles Society of Clinical Psychologists News*, 1964, *6*, No. 3, 11-21.

Sheffield, F. D. & Maccoby, N. Summary and interpretation of research on organizational principles in constructing filmed demonstration. In Lumsdaine, A. A. (Ed.), *Student response in programmed instruction.* Washington: National Academy of Sciences-National Research Council, 1961, 117-131.

Skinner, B. F. *The behavior of organisms.* New York: Appleton, 1938.

Skinner, B. F. *Science and human behavior.* New York: Macmillan Co., 1953.

Skinner, B. F. *Verbal behavior.* New York: Appleton-Century-Crofts, 1957.

Skinner, B. F. What is psychotic behavior? In Milton, T. (Ed.), *Theories of psychopathology.* Philadelphia: Saunders, 1967.

Spielberger, C. D., Berger, A. & Howard, K. Conditioning of verbal behavior as a function of awareness, need for social approval and motivation to receive reinforcement. *Journal of Abnormal and Social Psychology*, 1963, *67*, 241-246.

Staats, A. W. & Staats, C. K. *Complex human behavior.* New York: Holt, Rinehart and Winston, 1964.

Stevenson, I. & Wolpe, J. Recovery from sexual deviations through overcoming of non-sexual neurotic responses. *American Journal of Psychiatry*, 1960, *116*, 737-742.

Strong, S. R. Verbal conditioning and counseling research. *Personnel and Guidance Journal*, 1964, *42*, 654-659.

Szasz, T. The myth of mental illness. In Milton, O. & Wahler, R. (Eds.), *Behavior disorders, perspectives and trends.* New York: Lippincott, 1965.

Tannenbaum, A. J. Adolescent attitude toward academic brilliance. Unpublished Ph.D. dissertation, New York University, 1960.

Terrell, G. & Kennedy, W. A. Discrimination learning and transposition in children as a function of the nature of the reward. *Journal of Experimental Psychology*, 1957, *53*, 257-260.

Thoresen, C. E. An experimental comparison of counseling techniques for producing information-seeking behavior. Unpublished Ph.D. dissertation, Stanford University, 1964.

Thoresen, C. E. The counselor as an applied behavioral scientist. *Personnel and Guidance Journal*, 1969, *47*, 841-848. (*b*)

Thoresen, C. E. (Personal communication) 1969. (*c*)

Thoresen, C. E. & Bergland, B. W. Behavioral and physiological outcomes of counterconditioning in increasing classroom participation: An exploratory study. Unpublished manuscript, Stanford University, 1969.

Thoresen, C. E. & Hamilton, J. A. Encouraging adolescent career behavior with peer modeling and stimulus materials in counseling groups. Unpublished manuscript, Stanford University, 1969.

Thoresen, C. E., Hamilton, J. A. & Bergland, B. W. Using perceptual and personality differences to predict treatment effects on adolescent career behaviors. Unpublished manuscript, Stanford University, 1969.

Thoresen, C. E., Hosford, R. E. & Krumboltz, J. D. Determining effective models for counseling clients of varying competencies. *Journal of Counseling Psychology.* (in press)

Thoresen, C. E. & Krumboltz, J. D. Similarity of social models and clients in behavioral counseling: Two experimental studies. *Journal of Counseling Psychology*, 1968, *15*, 393-401.

Thoresen, C. E., Krumboltz, J. D. & Varenhorst, B. The sex factor in model reinforcement counseling. *American Psychologist*, July, 1965.

Truax, C. B. & Carkhuff, R. R. New directions in clinical research. In Berenson, B. G. & Carkhuff, R. R. (Eds.), *Sources of gain in counseling and psychotherapy*. New York: Holt, Rinehart and Winston, 1967.

Ullmann, L. P. & Krasner, L. *A psychological approach to abnormal behavior*. Englewood Cliffs, N.J.: Prentice-Hall, 1969.

Ullmann, L. P. & Krasner, L. *Case studies in behavior modification*. New York: Holt, Rinehart and Winston, 1965.

Vance, B. The counselor—an agent of what change? *Personnel and Guidance Journal*, 1967, *45*, 1012-1016.

Walters, R. H., Llewellyn, T. E. & Acker, C. W. Enhancement of punitive behavior by audio-visual displays. *Science*, 1962, *136*, 872-873.

Watson, J. B. & Rayner, P. Conditioned emotional reactions. *Journal of Experimental Psychology*, 1920, *3*, 1.

Weinstein, F. Reducing test anxiety. In Krumboltz, J. D. & Thoresen, C. E. (Eds.), *Behavioral counseling: Cases and techniques*. New York: Holt, Rinehart and Winston, 1969.

Whiting, J. M. W. *Becoming a woman*. New Haven: Yale University Press, 1941.

Williams, R. M., Jr. *American society: A sociological interpretation*. New York: Alfred Knopf, 1952.

Williamson, E. G. The counselor as technique. *Personnel and Guidance Journal*, 1962, *41*, 108-111.

Wolpe, J. Experimental neuroses as learned behavior. *British Journal of Psychology*, 1952, *53*, 243-268. (*a*)

Wolpe, J. Objective psychotherapy of the neuroses. *South African Medical Journal*, 1952, *26*, 824-829. (*b*)

Wolpe, J. *Psychotherapy by reciprocal inhibition*. Stanford: Stanford University Press, 1958.

Wolpe, J. The systematic desensitization treatment of neuroses. *Journal of Nervous and Mental Disease*, 1961, *132*, 189-203.

Wolpe, J. For phobia: A hair of the hound. *Psychology Today*, 1969, *3*, 34-37. (*a*)

Wolpe, J. *The practice of behavior therapy*. New York: Pergamon Press, 1969. (*b*)

Wolpe, J. & Lazarus, A. *Behavior therapy techniques: A guide to the treatment of neuroses*. New York: Pergamon Press, 1966.

Yates, A. J. Symptoms and symptom substitution. *Psychological Review*, 1958, *65*, 371-374.

Zigler, E. & Kanzer, P. The effectiveness of two classes of verbal reinforcers on the performance of middle- and lower-class children. *Journal of Personality*, 1962, *30*, 157-163.

CARL E. THORESEN

Behavioral Counseling: An Introduction

Just what is behavioral counseling? Why should a counselor really give serious consideration to this approach? Let's take an example presented by a student to convey some basic features of behavioral counseling.

The Case of Bob

Bob, a bright high school junior, came into my office to talk about his poor grades. He complained of difficulty in concentrating on his studies, particularly math. "I just seem to go through the motions—I mean I can't remember what I read. . . ." Bob also said that he got very nervous and tense before taking tests, especially in United States history. "Sometimes I get so tied up my mind goes blank!" He brought up his reluctance to participate in class discussions: "I know that Miss Stein really expects us to speak up, but—well, you know, I feel so kinda stupid—and then sometimes other kids say just what I was thinking." Bob pointed out that his parents were very concerned about his grades but felt in general that it was really up to him to try

Thoresen, C. E. Behavioral counseling: an introduction. *The School Counselor,* 1966, *14*(1), 13-21. Copyright 1966 American Personnel and Guidance Association. Reprinted with permission.

harder. He expressed great dissatisfaction with his school work, especially his performance on tests, his short concentration span, and his inability to participate. I asked Bob how he felt about involving his parents and teachers in helping solve his problems. He said, "It's O.K. with me. I know they're worried. . . . Well, uh, can you help me?"

Behavior Is Learned

Behavioral counseling uses the adjective "behavioral" to emphasize that counseling seeks to bring about changes in student behavior. In the problem cited, Bob asked for assistance in changing his behavior; that is, he wanted help in improving his ability to concentrate, in reducing tension just before tests, and in increasing his oral participation in class. A basic assumption in behavioral counseling is that most behavior is learned and is therefore potentially changeable. The individual's environment is recognized as being very influential in what is learned and how it is learned. Significant changes in behavior may take place if the individual's environment is systematically modified.

Reinforcing Behavior

How can Bob be assisted in changing his behavior? Let's look first at his problem of concentration. In talking with Bob, I found that he usually studied after dinner. He complained of loss of concentration after about 10 minutes of studying, especially with math. After that, the more he tried to concentrate, the less he was able to do so. I suggested that Bob start the next evening with his math and that he study it for only a 10-minute period. If he felt that he had really concentrated during that time, he was free to take a five-minute break and do something that he really enjoyed. Bob said he could look through a car magazine, something he enjoyed immensely, or he could practice his uke or he might get something to eat. He asked if he should try studying his math again after the break. I suggested he try one more 10-minute session and then do something he thoroughly enjoyed.

I asked Bob to stop by my office each morning during the first week to tell me how long he had studied his math. I deliberately made an encouraging comment (e.g., "Bob, that's very good!") when he told me how long he had spent on his math. During the second week I asked him to come by three times and twice during the third week. Over a period of time he was gradually able to build up his "good study time" (as he called it) in math to 40 minutes.

In assisting Bob to improve his concentration, I drew upon a demonstrated principle of learning: behavior which is rewarded or reinforced, especially immediately after it occurs, is strengthened and is more likely to occur again. Bob was rewarding himself for concentrating by doing something he enjoyed, immediately after he had successfully studied his mathematics. The counselor was also reinforcing Bob with attention and approval for his changed behavior. By chance, Bob's father also became involved. (It should be noted that the counselor could have deliberately asked the parents to participate.) His father asked him to check with him after studying math each evening. He would praise Bob for his progress in increasing his "good" studying time and also talk with him about other things. In effect, he was specifically rewarding Bob for his progress.

A Variety of Tailored Procedures

Behavioral counseling does not rely on any one set of procedures. In particular, this approach does not expect the counselor himself to function personally as the most important or influential source of change. The following definition of counseling makes an important point: "Counseling consists of whatever ethical activities a counselor undertakes in an effort to help the client engage in those types of behavior which will lead to a resolution of the client's problems" [12, p. 4]. The point is that counselors can develop and use a wide variety of procedures, often specifically involving significant persons in the student's life, to assist him in solving problems. Procedures can be tailored to the individual situation. Counselors need not (and should not) place exclusive reliance on the face-to-face, one-to-one interview. It may be that parents, classroom teachers, and peers can be far more influential in helping to bring about desired changes in behavior. Many writers in counseling have recently urged the creation and use of new counseling procedures, procedures which would move the activities of counselors beyond use of the interview per se and which would take the counselor away from his desk and out of his office [13, 18, 23, 27, 29, 32].[1]

Specific Change as Success

How about Bob's tenseness just before tests? Bob said that this problem seemed to have developed recently, especially in his English and history classes. He said that both teachers used essay tests which have always bothered him. "I really get excited and nervous because I never know how to get started right—I mean, I, uh, always never have enough time . . . can't figure out how to say it." I asked Bob if he knew someone in class who did well on essay tests. My suggestion was that he read over some of his past test papers to get an idea of what the finished product looked like. I also suggested he talk with the student as to how he went about organizing his ideas during the test. My hunch was that Bob's tenseness was in part a function of his poor essay test skills. If he could acquire greater proficiency he might begin to feel more relaxed and therefore less tense about essay tests. Looking over good examples of well-written essay answers could provide Bob with a kind of model to emulate.

I also talked briefly with his English and history teachers, explaining Bob's problem of tenseness and eliciting their assistance. I suggested that these teachers take particular note of Bob in class just prior to taking a test. Specifically, I asked that they make some reassuring comment, coming by his desk before he started the test, or use a non-verbal expression, such as a smile or nod. Such behavior might assist Bob to relax a little more prior to the test. His English teacher suggested that making encouraging remarks could also be done immediately following the test, especially if Bob had appeared more relaxed. I suggested that Bob might actually practice writing essay answers before school in the same classroom, with the teacher present. Experience in writing an essay response in a near-reality setting (i.e., the classroom) with the support and approval of the teacher, would be less anxiety-arousing for Bob. His increased ability to be more relaxed as well as skillful while writing an essay answer would, in effect, counteract his anxiety and tenseness. His increased calmness would then generalize into the actual class situation. (This procedure may be thought of as a way of "desensitizing" Bob to an anxiety situation.) I also agreed to stop by the classroom several times before school to encourage Bob in his efforts.

After three weeks, Bob reported feeling much more relaxed about taking essay tests. In addition, his grade in history had improved by one letter grade. His English grade, due to some problems on grammar quizzes, remained the same, although he was getting higher essay test grades.

The counselor here was effective in assisting Bob to reduce his tension about tests. Counseling effectiveness, as viewed in behavioral counseling, must depend on having specifically defined outcomes. Did the behavior in question—in this case tension about taking essay tests—show any change? Often counseling effectiveness is judged solely from what happens during the counseling interview; i.e., how does the counselor conduct the interview and what does the student say? While interview behavior is crucial, especially in establishing a relationship that will permit the counselor to tailor procedures to the individual problem, relevant changes in student behaviors *outside* the interview remain the most significant yardstick of counseling effectiveness.

Modeling Behavior

Bob's third problem, you may recall, concerned his oral participation in history. Since several junior students had recently talked with the counselor about this problem, I asked Bob if he would like to work with a small group of students on this. He and eight other students met with the counselor for three sessions. During each, the counselor played a short, rehearsed audio tape-recording of a student group, which had also been concerned with problems of participation—principles of good discussion, specific steps for improving participation, and expectations for trying them out in class. During the sessions the group reacted to the tapes, talking about how they felt their situation resembled or differed from those presented on the tapes. Their "participation" in the group was encouraged by the counselor with approving comments, smiles, and nods. During the third session an attempt was made to simulate the reality of the classroom by role playing a history discussion.

Most students, including Bob, reported feeling much more comfortable in voluntarily making a comment in class. Bob's history teacher also noted an increase in the number of his voluntary comments in class. In talking with her, it became clear that the teacher was thinking about responding to Bob more positively.

This illustrates an important point: assisting a student in modifying a specific behavior, such as increasing his oral participation, may have several positive consequences; i.e., the change in a particular behavior may contribute to changes in other behaviors in the person and in others. Besides the increased feelings of self-mastery and esteem experienced by the student himself, the behavior of others toward him in other situations (including their perceptions and expectations) may undergo change.

The use of tape-recorded peers as "social models" in a group situation, in which students can make comments and immediately experience an encouraging response from the counselor and other members of the group, is based on research and theory in social learning. Behavioral counseling freely and deliberately draws upon social learning principles and experimentation to develop counseling procedures. In this situation, for example, the peer group was employed specifically to provide social reward for participation behavior.

The problem of Bob as presented is admittedly fragmentary and incomplete. With him the procedures described above proved effective. Other procedures might have been equally or more effective. In addition, Bob may still have problems. But he has experienced some success with the counselor in changing certain specific problem behaviors. As a result, he may be more receptive to approaching the counselor in the future with more "dynamic, deep-seated" difficulties or he may have started to learn how to handle and resolve his own problems. Then, too, these procedures may not have a positive effect with a student who is less desirous of changing or with a student from a different subculture. (The dramatic Streetcorner Research Project by Schwitzgebel and Kalb, involving work with "unreachable" delinquents, demonstrates how behavioral counseling procedure can be successfully tailored to the individual problem [25].

Some Basic Points

Bob's problem as presented does, however, serve to introduce some basic points which characterize behavioral counseling:

1. Most human behavior is learned and is therefore subject to change.

2. Specific changes of the individual's environment can assist in altering relevant behaviors; counseling procedures seek to bring about relevant changes in student behavior by altering the environment.

3. Social learning principles, such as those of reinforcement and social modeling, can be used to develop counseling procedures.

4. Counseling effectiveness and the outcome of counseling are assessed by changes in specific student behaviors outside the counseling interview. Interview behavior per se is not a satisfactory measure of effective counseling.

5. Counseling procedures are not static, fixed, or predetermined, but can be specifically designed to assist the student in solving a particular problem.

What Behavioral Counseling Is Not

Behavioral counseling is not, as Patterson, McCully, and Jourard have recently suggested, cold, impersonal, or manipulative counseling [22, 17, 10]. It does not consider the counseling relationship as totally irrelevant, nor does it seek to "dehumanize man" or to manipulate the client subtly against his will. It has not created, nor does it seek to create, mechanical, technique-ridden counselors or slavish clients. "A behavioral approach to counseling and guidance does not consist of a bag of tricks to be applied mechanically for the purpose of coercing unwilling people" [20, p. 382].

I think the alarm of some may stem from these sources: (1) misinformation about behavioral counseling; (2) the connotation and semantic confusion about certain psychological terms; and (3) perceived philosophical implications of the scientific method in counseling, i.e., counseling as a behavioral science.

Pigeons and Patients

Aware of the successful work of B. F. Skinner at Harvard with pigeons and other animals, some categorically condemn behavioral counseling as "Skinnerian . . . pigeon-oriented." While Skinner does offer established principles and provocative ideas about the learning of human behavior [25, pp. 503-515], behavioral counseling can and does draw upon the experimentation and principles of *several* learning theories as well as other behavioral sciences.

Others, aware of the research in behavior modification with severely disturbed persons, in which abnormal behavior has been dramatically changed with the use of social learning procedures [6, 7, 11, 28, 30], may err in generalizing to the school setting these special situations in which the client does not necessarily request help in changing certain behaviors. In these studies, psychotic patients have, for example, been "taught" to pick up utensils before entering the dining room and to eat properly in a few weeks, after years of being "unreachable." Procedures developed to do this were based on reinforcement learning principles, where patients were consistently verbally and non-verbally reinforced for their successive approximation of relevant behaviors. Their cooperation was not necessarily elicited in advance. In the school setting, on the other hand, the behavioral counselor does *not* arbitrarily and secretly influence the student against his will. Instead, he uses what is known about how learning occurs and how it can be changed to help the student modify his behavior in directions desired by the student himself.

Manipulation

The emotional and very negative connotation for some of the commonly used scientific and psychological terms creates problems. Consider the term "manipulation." As used in psychological research, for example, it means management of certain factors to control a particular situation. To many, however, the term suggests some devious activity, perhaps with a questionable ulterior motive. Therefore, when the phrase "manipulate the environment" is encountered, many react negatively. The same may be said for such terms as "conditioning" and "programming." Actually, as Patterson, a proponent of client-centered counseling, recently pointed out: "We must recognize that anything we do in or out of counseling, has some influence on others, that it is not possible, in this sense, to avoid some control or manipulation of the behavior of others . . . everyone, including the client-centered counselor, manipulates" [22, p. 683].

The Individual in Control

I think counseling can move toward becoming a behavioral science, using methods scientifically developed, without dehumanizing the client (or the counselor). Some seem to believe that the increased use in counseling research and practice of social learning principles and experimentation ignores basic human values and philosophical questions in counseling. This does not follow. The counselor will always be confronted with value judgments and ethical issues. He cannot function, as several studies have demonstrated, without involving in some way his perceptions of what is desirable. Making the counselor more effective in solving problems by, for example, having clients view a video tape, does not mechanize him or make him impersonal. Using the methods of science, testing hunches derived from principles of social learning, studying the client's environment and how he interacts with it—these do not ignore man as a complex entity or leave him ". . . sitting off in a corner, quite alone" [1].

Actually, clients will come to exercise more self-control and self-direction by learning specifically how factors in their environment influence their behavior and how to modify their own behavior in desired directions. The shy girl, for example, who after working with a behavioral counselor feels more comfortable in a group situation such as the classroom and is able to take part in discussions, has acquired greater freedom. She can now choose to participate or not. "Really, man becomes free only when he has attained self-mastery" [5]. One might say that the client's potential for exercising freedom and responsibility is greatly enhanced. He sees his own behavior as learned, as a product of his environment, and as subject to change by himself.

Behavioral counseling in many ways is very demanding on the counselor. He must constantly study the environment and social learning history of students and try out hunches. He does not know the complacent security of one set of fixed procedures. He experiences the inevitable frustrations and failures. Yet he has the satisfaction at times of observing the consequences of his procedures: changes in the behavior of students. The extent of his ingenuity, openmindedness, and creativity may be the only limitation in his developing more effective procedures. Perhaps the real limitation is what John Gardner recently termed the tyranny of tradition and "proper procedures," which often become encased in a hard, almost impregnable change-defying shell [8, p. 56].

Recommended Readings

The following introductory list of readings is suggested for counselors and others who wish to learn more about behavioral counseling.

John D. Krumboltz. Behavioral counseling: rationale and research. *Personnel Guid. J.*, 1965, *44*, 383-387. Discusses how goals of counseling can be determined for each client, how behavioral counseling can achieve them, and what are the limitations on counselor activities. Several counseling research studies are presented.

John D. Krumboltz. Parable of the good counselor. *Personnel Guid. J.*, 1964, *43*, 118-123. Presents a counseling problem and how two counselors—"behavioral" and "client-centered"—might handle it. Discusses similarities and differences in assumptions and procedures between behavioral and client-centered counseling.

John D. Krumboltz & Carl E. Thoresen. The effect of behavioral counseling in group and individual settings on information-seeking behavior. *J. Counsel. Psychol.*, 1964, *11*, 324-333. Reports an experimental counseling study (11th grade students) in which a 15-minute audio tape and encouraging comments by counselors were found effective in helping students seek information relevant to their future plans.

Jack Michael. Guidance and counseling as the control of behavior. In E. Landy and P. Perry (Eds.) *Guidance in American education: backgrounds and prospects.* Cambridge, Mass.: Harvard University Press, 1964, 71-83. A more readable treatment than the Michael and Meyerson article of a behavioral approach. Defines reinforcement learning terms with many good examples. Good discussion of implications of behavioral approach to educational practice.

Jack Michael & Lee Meyerson. A behavioral approach to counseling and guidance. In Ralph L. Mosher, Richard F. Carle, & Chris D. Kehas (Eds.) *Guidance on examination.* New York: Harcourt, Brace & World, 1965, pp. 24-48. Also in *Harv. Educ. Rev.*, 1962, *32*, 382-402. Presents the behavioral approach to many problems faced in counseling, using the sometimes confusing terminology of the experimental learning psychologist. Defines several learning terms such as operant conditioning, positive reinforcers, and aversive stimuli. Stresses use of environmental changes to modify behavior.

Thomas Magoon. Innovations in counseling. *J. Counsel. Psychol.*, 1964, *11*, 343-347. Offers several novel ideas about how counselors can develop more effective procedures in such areas as occupational information and career planning.

Albert Bandura. Psychotherapy as a learning process. *Psychol. Bull.*, 1961, *58*, 143-159. Appears in O. Milton (Ed.), *Behavior disorders.* New York: Lippincott, 1965, 185-207. Thorough discussion and review of attempts to use principles of learning in psychotherapy. Discusses some objections to a social learning approach.

Israel Goldiamond. Justified and unjustified alarm over behavioral control. In O. Milton (Ed.), *Behavior disorders.* New York: Lippincott, 1965, 237 ff. Provocative, stimulating and well-written discussion of misunderstandings and confusions about a behavior approach to human problems.

Leonard Ullman & Leonard Krasner (Eds.) *Case studies in behavior modification.* New York: Holt, Rinehart & Winston, 1965. Examples of how counseling and psychotherapeutic procedures based on social learning can be designated to change specifically a wide variety of problem behaviors.

Ralph Schwitzgebel & D. Kolb. Inducing behavioral change in adolescent delinquents. *Behav. Res. Ther.*, 1964, *1*, 297-304. Forty "unreachable" delinquent boys are given part-time jobs which involved talking into tape recorders, learning how to read, etc. Counselors successfully used a variety of rewards (positive reinforcers) to encourage non-delinquent behavior.

John D. Krumboltz, Barbara B. Varenhorst, & Carl E. Thoresen. Non-verbal factors in the effectiveness of models in counseling. Paper read at American Educational Research Association Convention, Chicago, February, 1965. Experimental counseling study used two video-taped counseling interviews (woman counselor and junior year girl) to help girls with their future planning. Differences in counselor attentiveness and prestige were involved. Available from authors, c/o School of Education, Stanford University, Stanford, California.

Arthur Bachrach (Ed.) *Experimental foundations of clinical psychology.* New York: Basic Books, 1962. Several chapters cover such topics as verbal conditioning, operant behavior, and small groups. Excellent source of references to research literature.

Footnote

1. I am reminded here of recent articles by Schwebel, Wrenn, and Lifton [24, 32, 16] on "counselor encapsulation"; i.e., how counselors have become, among other things, trapped in the exclusive use of traditional techniques.

References

1. Arbuckle, Dugald S. Foreword to Carlton Beck, *Philosophical foundations of guidance.* Englewood Cliffs, N.J.: Prentice-Hall, 1963.
2. Ayllon, Teodoro, & Michael, Jack L. The psychiatric nurse as a behavioral engineer. *J. Exp. Anal. Behav.,* 1959, *2,* 323-334.
3. Bachrach, Arthur (Ed.) *Experimental foundations of clinical psychology.* New York: Basic Books, 1962.
4. Bandura, Albert. Psychotherapy as a learning process. *Psychol. Bull.,* 1961, *58,* 143-159.
5. De Rougemont, Denis. *Love in the western world.* New York: Pantheon, 1956.
6. Eysenck, Hans J. (Ed.) *Experiments in behavior therapy.* New York: Macmillan, 1964.
7. Frank, Cyril M. *Conditioning techniques in clinical practice and research.* New York: Springer, 1965.
8. Gardner, John W. *Self-renewal.* New York: Harper & Row, 1964.
9. Goldiamond, Israel. Justified and unjustified alarm over behavioral control. In O. Milton (Ed.), *Behavior disorders.* New York: Lippincott, 1965, 237-261.
10. Jourard, Sidney. On the problem of reinforcement by the psychotherapist of healthy behavior. In Franklin Shaw (Ed.), *Behavioral approaches to counseling and psychotherapy.* Montgomery: University of Alabama Press, 1961.
11. Krasner, Leonard, & Ullmann, Leonard P. (Eds.) *Research in behavior modification.* New York: Holt, Rinehart & Winston, 1965.
12. Krumboltz, John D. Parable of the good counselor. *Personnel Guid. J.,* 1964, *43,* 118-123.
13. Krumboltz, John D. Behavioral counseling: rationale and research. *Personnel Guid. J.,* 1965, *44,* 383-387.

14. Krumboltz, John D., & Thoresen, Carl E. The effect of behavioral counseling in group and individual settings on information-seeking behavior. *J. Counsel. Psychol.,* 1964, *11,* 324-333.

15. Krumboltz, John D., Varenhorst, Barbara B., & Thoresen, Carl E. Non-verbal factors in the effectiveness of models in counseling. Paper read at American Educ. Res. Assn. Convention, Chicago, February, 1965.

16. Lifton, Walter. The culturally encapsulated counselor faces reality. Paper read at Annual Meeting of American Psychol. Assn., Philadelphia, August, 1963.

17. McCully, C. Harold. The two secrets of the gods. Paper read at Iota Alpha Banquet, Pennsylvania State University, May, 1964.

18. Magoon, Thomas. Innovations in counseling. *J. Counsel. Psychol.,* 1964, *11,* 342-347.

19. Michael, Jack. Guidance and counseling as the control of behavior. In E. Landy & P. Perry (Eds.), *Guidance in American education: backgrounds and prospects.* Cambridge, Mass.: Harvard University Press, 1964, 71-83.

20. Michael, Jack, & Meyerson, Lee. A behavioral approach to counseling and guidance. *Harv. Educ. Rev.,* 1962, *32,* 382-402.

21. Patterson, Cecil H. Comment on John D. Krumboltz, Parable of the good counselor. *Personnel Guid. J.,* 1964, *43,* 124.

22. Patterson, Cecil H. Control, conditioning and counseling. *Personnel Guid. J.,* 1963, *41,* 680-686.

23. Robinson, Francis P. A cubist approach to the art of counseling. *Personnel Guid. J.,* 1963, *41,* 670-676.

24. Schwebel, Milton. Ideology and counselor encapsulation. *J. Counsel. Psychol.,* 1964, *11,* 366-369.

25. Schwitzgebel, Ralph, & Kolb, D. Inducing behavioral change in adolescent delinquents. *Behav. Res. Ther.,* 1964, *1,* 297-304.

26. Skinner, B. F. Operant behavior. *Amer. Psychologist,* 1963, *18,* 503-515.

27. Truax, Charles B., and Carkhuff, Robert R. The old and the new: theory and research in counseling and psychotherapy. *Personnel Guid. J.,* 1964, *41,* 108-111.

28. Ullman, Leonard P., & Krasner, Leonard (Eds.) *Case studies in behavior modification.* New York: Holt, Rinehart & Winston, 1965.

29. Williamson, E. G. The counselor as technique. *Personnel Guid. J.,* 1962, *41,* 108-111.

30. Wolpe, Joseph, Salter, Andrew, & Leyna, L. J. *The conditioning therapies.* New York: Holt, Rinehart & Winston, 1964.

31. Wrenn, C. Gilbert. *The counselor in a changing world.* Washington: American Personnel and Guidance Association, 1962.

32. Wrenn, C. Gilbert. The culturally encapsulated counselor. *Harv. Educ. Rev.,* 1962, *32,* 444-449.

JOHN D. KRUMBOLTZ
RAYMOND E. HOSFORD

Behavioral Counseling in the Elementary School

"Same ol' run-around again," said Miss Ford as she returned from her conference with the school counselor.

"What's the problem?" asked Joe Peterson, a fellow teacher.

"You remember that I referred Don to the counselor because he would go into a terrible rage and kick and scream whenever he didn't get his own way. Everyone was afraid of him. I didn't know what to do. I had tried everything from sending him to the principal to standing him in a corner. Nothing seemed to work."

"Well, what did the counselor suggest?"

"Nothing, really. That's the trouble. The counselor said that Don's responses on the various tests indicate he is a very anxious and aggressive child who has a low self-concept. So what? I already know all that."

"Didn't the counselor have any ideas of what to do?" insisted Mr. Peterson.

"The only real suggestion I got was that Don needs to learn how to get along with others. But that is precisely why I referred him—I want to help him learn to get along with the other boys and girls, but

Krumboltz, J. D., & Hosford, R. E. Behavioral counseling in the elementary school. *Elementary School Guidance and Counseling*, 1967, *1*(1), 27-40. Copyright 1967 American Personnel and Guidance Association. Reprinted with permission.

I don't know how. I guess I was hoping for something more from the counselor," said Miss Ford with more sadness than anger.

"I know what you mean," Joe said. "Early in the year I referred Mickey, you know, the shy little girl who clams up whenever she is asked to give a report in front of the class. The counselor told me that she has an inferiority complex as the result of a fixation at a premature level of development. If knowing those words does any good, it sure doesn't show. Mickey, poor scared kid, is just as mousy as ever. I wish I knew how to help her."

"Maybe the counselor would like to be more helpful but doesn't know how either," suggested Miss Ford thoughtfully.

"Maybe so. But just once I'd like to see the counselor produce some results."

The complaints of these two teachers certainly do not apply to all counselors. But they do have one important implication: A counselor's success is judged by the degree to which he can help pupils engage in more appropriate types of behavior. When a teacher refers Don to a counselor because of his frequent temper tantrums, she hopes in some way that Don will decrease the frequency of these tantrums. She is not asking the counselor to improve Don's self-concept or to reconstruct his personality. If a teacher wants to help shy, withdrawn Mickey to learn how to participate in class, he eventually expects Mickey to talk more in class. He is not asking for the counselor's opinion about the origin of the problem or for a hypothesis about the inner state of the child's mind. The success of the counselor's work, regardless of the intervening processes used, will necessarily be judged by the observed improvement in the child's behavior. In this article we propose that a behavioral approach to elementary school guidance offers counselors an effective way to specify and accomplish the purposes of counseling. We will first show how a behavioral counselor would handle the problems of Don and Mickey by applying some principles of learning. We will then consider some broader implications and problems of behavioral approaches to counseling.

The two problems described here are based on actual cases referred to an elementary school counselor who applied learning principles to resolve them. Though names and identifying data have been changed, these cases will be used to illustrate how actual behavior problems can be solved through systematic attention to the reinforcing consequences associated with different kinds of behavior.

Mickey, a bright sixth-grade girl, was referred to the counselor because she became extremely anxious when asked to give an oral book report before the class. Because Mickey had sometimes participated in class discussions, the teacher was surprised to see her become too nervous to continue. He quickly suggested that she give her presentation another time.

In talking with the counselor, Mickey explained that she wanted very much to talk in front of the class but had never been able to do so. Her cumulative record showed that her former teachers seldom asked her to give oral reports because of anxiety she developed when speaking before a group. The counselor thought the best approach would be to help her learn gradually the behaviors necessary in giving a report. Thus a program of counseling activities was formulated to accomplish this goal.

A combination of procedures was used by the counselor in helping Mickey learn the behaviors necessary to solve her problem. In the counseling setting, Mickey met with the counselor once a week for six weeks and practiced getting out of her seat, coming to the front of the room, and saying a few words. The counselor suggested she begin with brief reports and gradually build up to longer presentations. Mickey was always free to stop and sit down whenever she felt anxious about talking. During each session the counselor smiled, said "very good, Mickey," and gave other types of reinforcement as Mickey successfully role-played the part of giving a report.

The counselor also worked closely with Mickey's teacher in setting up a program for gradually increasing Mickey's ability to speak before a group. The teacher agreed to progressively include Mickey in a social studies committee which was giving oral presentations on various countries. At first Mickey was asked to help only by pointing on a large map to the city, river, or area that was being discussed by other members of the committee. Members of the group, at the suggestion of the teacher, gradually involved Mickey more in the discussions. Each week Mickey was asked to tell a little more about the location and terrain of a country while the other members of the committee covered the political, social, and economic aspects. At the end of the two and one-half months, Mickey's presentation was about the same length as that of other members of the committee.

Mickey was often thanked for helping out and was given praise and approval by the teacher and members of the committee each time she participated in the panel. The two co-chairmen of the committee were also encouraged to tell Mickey she did very well as she increased her participation, thus providing for peer reinforcement. Mickey gradually became more comfortable while in front of the class and eventually was able to give reports on her own. She was also among the students who volunteered to give an oral presentation at the end of the year when a few parents attended the culmination of the social studies unit.

The role-playing allowed Mickey to practice the behavior under low-stress conditions. When an individual role-plays a behavior enough times, the role becomes part of his repertoire of behavior. He is then better able to perform the behavior in other situations. In this case, the role-playing also gave the counselor an excellent opportunity to reinforce and encourage Mickey as she made increasingly better approximations to the desired behavior.

The counselor helped to arrange a program of systematic positive reinforcement in the classroom as well as in his office to help Mickey learn how to talk before a group. Behavior that is reinforced or rewarded is more likely to occur again (Skinner, 1953). Thus, to increase the occurrence of a particular behavior (in this case, Mickey's oral reports) it is often only necessary to insure that reinforcement be given soon after the behavior occurs.

A grades, approving gestures, and verbal remarks such as "very good" and "well done" are a few of the reinforcing stimuli effective for encouraging most school children in our society. The important aspect in Mickey's case was that reinforcement was given for any improvement in speaking before a group. She did not need to make a polished speech before receiving the approval and attention of her teacher, counselor, and peers. Each gradual step toward improvement was reinforced.

Several studies in counseling (Johnson, 1964; Krumboltz & Schroeder, 1965; Krumboltz & Thoresen, 1964) have shown that reinforcement procedures can be used very effectively in school counseling to promote or change a particular behavior. The annotated bibliography contains references that may suggest other principles and examples as well as theoretical formulations derived from research in learning.

An effective technique for eliminating undesired behavior is "extinction"—arranging for no reinforcements to follow the inappropriate behavior. The use of this procedure can be seen in the case of Don. Don was a third-grade boy who often gave rather violent displays of temper on the playground whenever he did not get his way. Since he was relatively new to the school, his teacher, Miss Ford, thought the tantrums would decrease as Don adjusted to the school situation. Rather than decrease, Don's tantrums became more frequent.

After talking with Miss Ford and the boy's mother, the counselor arranged to be on the playground to observe Don. He noticed that when Don began to scream and pick fights with others, the teacher would quickly respond and attempt to quiet him down. Don usually calmed down when Miss Ford sat on the playground bench with her arm around him. Miss Ford said that she felt Don needed a feeling of security since he responded very quickly to words of reassurance from her.

The next day when Miss Ford came to see the counselor, she asked what was causing the tantrums and what she should do about them. The counselor felt that in this case the increase in the tantrums resulted from the reinforcement Don received from Miss Ford whenever he kicked, screamed, or picked a fight. In effect, Don had more tantrums because he had learned that such behavior usually gave him the undivided attention of the teacher. The tantrum behavior apparently had been learned at home and generalized to the school situation.

The counselor explained to the teacher that behavior previously learned through reinforcement can often be eliminated by permitting it to recur without any reinforcement. Thus, a program for the extinction of the behavior was formulated with the specific goal of decreasing the number of Don's tantrums. In this case the principal of the school and the child's mother were included in the process. It was agreed that when Don began a display of bad temper on the playground, Miss Ford would busy herself with the others and in general ignore his behavior. The same procedure was used in the classroom. In those instances when the class was disturbed too much, Miss Ford would quietly escort Don to the hallway, and the principal would take him to the nurse's room where he would remain until he calmed down.

The conference with Don's mother revealed that the same type of behavior was manifested at home. After considerable effort on the part of the counselor, Don's mother also agreed not to provide him with reinforcement for the tantrum behavior. It was agreed that Don would be left in his room to "cry it out" each time he resorted to displays of temper. In a very short time Don stopped having tantrums both at home and in school—the tantrum behavior was extinguished.

By providing for no reinforcement after the tantrums, Don's counselor, teacher, and parents were able to eliminate the undesirable behavior. Extinction procedures as used here as well as other procedures (e.g., Wolpe, 1958) have been shown to be effective counseling techniques for weakening or eliminating deviant behaviors. It is possible that other methods could have helped Don learn to control his temper. However, a warm understanding approach would not only be ineffective in this case but, as used here, was actually partly responsible for maintaining and promoting the undesirable behavior.

The behavioral counselor does not rely on any one set of counseling procedures but instead tailors specific techniques for specific problems. The techniques the counselor uses are employed to aid the student in learning those behaviors necessary to the solution of his problem. If the underachiever, for example, is referred for counseling, the behavioral counselor would not devote his time and energy to trying to determine what is "abnormal" about the individual's personality by administering various personality tests. Rather, he would attempt to devise techniques and procedures that would be effective in helping the individual to improve his achievement. He would seek ways of providing more encouragement for constructive efforts at improving his school work.

Specific techniques for specific problems are not readily available but must be devised by the counselor to fit each individual problem. Procedures described in various research studies may be suggestive, however. The use of systematic positive reinforcement (Krumboltz & Schroeder, 1965; Johnson, 1964), tape recordings of students modeling a desired behavior (Krumboltz & Thoresen, 1964; Bandura, 1965), programmed instruction (Bruner, 1965), video-taped presentations and films (Krumboltz, Varenhorst, & Thoresen, in press), "behavior contracts" and role-playing (Keirsey, 1965), and systematic desensitization of anxieties (Wolpe, 1958; Lazarus, 1961) are some examples of procedures counselors might try to help students learn the behaviors necessary for the solution of their particular problems.

The central purpose of counseling and the main reason for its existence is to assist each student, teacher, or parent with the specific problem for which he is seeking help. The main task then for counselors is to assist the individual in learning those behaviors which will result in a solution to his problem.

From a behavioral approach, all relevant goals and objectives of counseling must be focused on behavior. Thus, the counselor would state his counseling goals in terms of observable behavior rather than of some abstract inner personality process (Krumboltz, 1966). Since students' problems are different from each other, the goals of counseling would be stated differently for each individual. Broad general goals for all individuals, e.g., self-understanding or increased ego strength, are deemed by the behavioral counselor as too abstract to be useful in specifying the purposes to be accomplished.

The goals of the behavioral counselor may be organized into three categories: (1) altering maladaptive behavior, (2) learning the decision-making process, and (3) preventing problems. In each category the objectives of the counselor are specified changes in behavior sought by or for the student and agreed to by the counselor.

The situations of Mickey and Don provide good examples of goals that the behavioral counselor would use in instances of maladaptive behavior. For Mickey the goal of counseling was an increase in the skills necessary for giving oral reports before the class. For Don, the counselor's goal was to decrease the number of tantrums he was displaying at school. For both problems, observable changes in behavior were the explicit objectives of the counseling process.

The advantages of this approach can be easily seen. By avoiding ambiguous abstract terms, e.g., to increase Mickey's ego strength, the counselor was able to communicate with the teacher and Mickey as to what they were trying to accomplish. Thus, the counselor, teacher, and Mickey had a clear understanding of the goals of the counseling; all were able to take active roles in the process; and all could see progress being made toward the goal.

A second major category of objectives in behavioral counseling is aiding students in learning how to make good decisions. Many personal and educational problems can often be solved when individuals know how to go about making a decision. Counselors can be effective in helping elementary school children to learn how to (1) construct alternative behaviors, (2) seek relevant information about each alternative, (3) weigh the possible outcomes and values of each alternative, and (4) formulate tentative plans of action.

Consider Frankie and Brian. Frankie blurts out incorrect answers without taking sufficient time to think through a problem. Brian, on the other hand, vacillates from one side of the question to the other and can never make up his mind. Both boys could benefit from some systematic help in learning how to make decisions wisely.

Research studies have shown that presenting information on probable outcomes (Gelatt, 1964) and reinforcing either deliberation or decision-type responses (Ryan & Krumboltz, 1964) influences the decision-making process. By aiding students to learn how to use the steps involved in the decision-making process, counselors and teachers are in effect providing students with problem-solving skills and attitudes which will aid them in meeting new problems in the future.

The third type of goal for counseling is that of preventing problems. By setting up educational programs that help students learn the behaviors necessary in the decision-making process, counselors can be effective in assisting students to solve some of their future personal, educational, and vocational decisions. But counselors must also be concerned about other educational practices.

Students who are discouraged because of harsh punishment for low grades or feel inadequate because of a constantly dissatisfied teacher or parent are all too often seen by a counselor after the damage is done. By asking for and taking an active role in the curricular and extracurricular programs of the school, counselors can help prevent educational practices which stifle the desire for learning and create serious emotional maladjustment.

The way we conceptualize a student's problem will determine our goals and procedures in counseling. It is important then that school counselors conceptualize student problems in ways that suggest steps for solving them. As we have seen in the cases of Mickey and Don, the behavioral counselor does not view deviant student behaviors as symptoms of pathology but as inappropriate behaviors that have been learned in the same way that any other behavior is learned. The counseling process is a learning situation in which the counselor aids the counselee in learning those behaviors necessary to the solution of his problem. How behavior is learned and how it may be unlearned or altered become central issues for the behavioral counselor.

Since most learning is a function of environmental consequences, effective procedures for producing behavior change depend on the arrangement of the student's environment. In reality, environmental modification is the only channel open to counselors for influencing human behavior. The behavioral counselor thus looks at the student's environment to see what is maintaining the behavior and what changes in the environment would significantly aid the individual to learn those behaviors necessary for solving his problem.

Conceptualizing the problem as one of learning guides the counselor in the goals that must be accomplished and allows him to monitor progress objectively. Since counseling is seen as a learning process, the counselor becomes an integral part of the educational system and joins with teachers, administrators, and parents in helping children learn how to lead fuller, richer lives.

A behavioral approach to counseling offers elementary school counselors an effective means for helping students with specific problems. This approach has several unique characteristics:

1. Since most human behavior is learned, it treats the counseling process as a learning process.

2. It assumes that effective procedures for producing desired behavioral change lie in arranging the student's environment to promote the desired learning rather than in manipulating hypothetical processes or entities within the individual.

3. The outcomes and goals of counseling are stated and assessed as specific changes in behavior shown by the student.

4. The counseling interview itself is only a small part of the total process of helping the student learn to solve his problems. Teachers, parents, and peers are all seen as important persons in providing an environment conducive to new learning.

5. Counseling procedures vary for different individuals and are specifically designed for the particular problem of each individual.

6. Counseling procedures and techniques are derived from scientifically based knowledge of the learning process.

Some counselors have said that the behavioral approach is just good common sense. Parents, counselors, and teachers frequently use effective learning principles without realizing the application they are making. However, it is important for the counselor to know why certain procedures are used, when to apply them and for what types of students and which specific problems, and to accomplish which goals. The counselor can thus become an integral part of the educational process.

Annotated Bibliography

Bandura, Albert. Psychotherapy as a learning process. *Psychological Bulletin*, 1961, *58*, 143-159. Surveys many experimental and clinical studies using behavioristic psychotherapy. Relates that many types of deviant behavior have been treated successfully by direct focusing on the behavior itself.

Krumboltz, John D. Behavioral counseling: rationale and research. *Personnel and Guidance Journal,* 1965, *44,* 383-387. Asserts that the goals of counseling must be in terms of some end condition and not the means to achieve that end. Rationale for the behavioral approach, counselor limitations, and useful counselor activities are discussed.

Krumboltz, John D. Parable of a good counselor. *Personnel and Guidance Journal,* 1964, *43,* 118-123. This article provides a comparison of behavioral and client-centered approaches to a counseling problem. The similarities and differences in the assumptions and procedures of the two approaches are discussed.

Krumboltz, John D. (Ed.) *Revolution in counseling: implications of behavioral science.* Boston: Houghton Mifflin, 1966. Chapters by Krumboltz, Bijou, Shoben, McDaniel, and Wrenn explore the possibilities and problems arising from application of learning principles to counseling.

Krasner, Leonard, & Ullmann, Leonard P. (Eds.) *Research in behavior modification.* New York: Holt, Rinehart & Winston, 1965. Fifteen articles of research in personality, child, clinical, social, general, and experimental psychology are presented. Such areas as learning principles, the interview, vicarious reinforcement, verbal conditioning, modeling, small groups, and hypnosis are covered.

Magoon, Thomas. Innovations in counseling. *Journal of Counseling Psychology,* 1964, *11,* 343-347. Magoon presents possibilities in using audio-visual materials in career counseling.

Michael, Jack, & Meyerson, Lee. A behavioral approach to counseling and guidance. *Harvard Educational Review,* 1962, *32,* 382-402. A behavioristic model for counseling is presented as an approach for the development of a scientific approach to guidance. The phenomena of conditioning are discussed in terms of the experimental learning psychologist.

Ullmann, Leonard P., & Krasner, Leonard (Eds.) *Case studies in behavior modification.* New York: Holt, Rinehart & Winston, 1965. The writers present a variety of behavioral problems in which psychotherapeutic procedures derived from social learning theory are applied. Cases are drawn from a wide variety of clinical and non-clinical settings.

References

Bandura, A. Behavioral modifications through modeling procedures. In L. Krasner & L. P. Ullmann (Eds.), *Research in behavior modification.* New York: Holt, Rinehart & Winston, 1965.

Bruner, Fern. The effect of programmed instruction on information-seeking behavior in tenth-grade students. Unpublished doctoral dissertation, Stanford Univ., 1965.

Gelatt, H. B. The influence of outcome probability data on college choice. Unpublished doctoral dissertation, Stanford Univ., 1964.

Johnson, C. J. The transfer effect of treatment group composition on pupils' classroom participation. Unpublished doctoral dissertation, Stanford Univ., 1964.

Keirsey, D. W. Transactional casework; a technology for inducing behavior change. Paper read at California Assn. of School Psychologists and Psychometrists, San Francisco, 1965.

Krumboltz, J. D. *Stating the goals of counseling*, Monograph No. 1, California Counseling and Guidance Assn., 1966.

Krumboltz, J. D., & Schroeder, W. W. Promoting career exploration through reinforcement. *Personnel and Guidance Journal*, 1965, *44*, 19-26.

Krumboltz, J. D., & Thoresen, C. E. The effect of behavioral counseling in group and individual settings on information-seeking behavior. *Journal of Counseling Psychology*, 1964, *11*, 324-333.

Krumboltz, J. D., Varenhorst, Barbara B., & Thoresen, C. E. Nonverbal factors in the effectiveness of models in counseling. *Journal of Counseling Psychology*, in press.

Lazarus, A. A. Group therapy of phobic disorders by systematic desensitization. *Journal of Abnormal and Social Psychology*, 1961, *63*, 504-510.

Ryan, T. Antoinette, & Krumboltz, J. D. Effect of planned reinforcement counseling on client decision-making behavior. *Journal of Counseling Psychology*, 1964, *11*, 315-323.

Skinner, B. F. *Science and human behavior.* New York: Macmillan, 1953.

Wolpe, J. *Psychotherapy by reciprocal inhibition.* Stanford, Calif.: Stanford University Press, 1958.

WAYNE E. FOLEY
JOHN W. WILLSON

Contracted Behavioral
Counseling: A Model for
Classroom Intervention

Students who exhibit various forms of maladaptive academic or social behavior are frequently referred by teachers to counselors. In response to such referrals, counselors usually assume independent responsibility for diagnosis and treatment. They prepare case studies that may include individual and group test scores, family histories, and anecdotal teacher impressions and classroom observations. Rarely included, however, are specific workable suggestions as to how to plan and implement a program of behavioral remediation for such students.

Although the referring teacher may gain a greater understanding of a student's problem from a comprehensive case study, she is nevertheless primarily concerned with seeing improved classroom performance in the problem student.

A relatively new methodology, contracted behavioral counseling, adapted from the works of Lloyd Homme (1969) and John D. Krumboltz (1966), provides counselors with a specific and expedient program for intervention. Contracted behavioral counseling is a systematic application of the "laws of learning," providing incentive for

Foley, W. E. & Willson, J. W. Contracted behavioral counseling: a model for classroom intervention. *The School Counselor,* 1971, *19*(2), 126-130. Copyright 1971 American Personnel and Guidance Association. Reprinted with permission.

students to learn new kinds of adaptive behaviors. This procedure requires that the teacher share joint responsibility with the counselor as an active participant in behavioral change rather than a recipient of counseling outcomes. This model of intervention assumes that the referred problem is being controlled or maintained by consequences operative in the classroom environment; therefore, the remediation takes place in the classroom or environment from which the problem generates. Each contract is individually designed to meet the specific needs of a particular problem student.

Implementation of such counseling follows these steps:

Step 1. Referral of maldaptive behavior. The counselor and teacher jointly define the referred problem in behavioral terms. The referral is stated so as to identify the actual behavior or actions that constitute the problem (Vance, 1967).

Step 2. Selection of terminal behaviors. The desired adaptive or terminal behaviors are identified by the teacher and counselor as mutually expected counseling outcomes or goals. Also identified are those intermediate behaviors or successive approximations that lead to the terminal behavior.

Step 3. Construction of a reinforcement menu. A list of positively reinforcing consequences or events is compiled from the counselor's and teacher's observations and conversations with the student. The student is allowed to select his own reinforcer from the reinforcement menu.

Step 4. A token economy is developed. The counselor assists the teacher in developing a point system or token economy and demonstrates how to dispense positive reinforcers (i.e., points and teacher praise) in formulating and shaping adaptive student behaviors (Ayllon & Arzin, 1968).

Step 5. Initiation of a contractual agreement. The counselor and the teacher discuss the maladaptive classroom behavior with the problem student. The student is asked if he would like to participate in a program designed to improve his performance. If the student chooses to participate, the program's contingencies and consequences are discussed leading toward contractual agreement.

Step 6. Specification of contractual terms. The terms of the contract are completed when the student agrees to perform certain social or academic behaviors, while the teacher agrees to award a specified number of points. The student and the teacher mutually agree on the number of points needed before free time may be spent for any item on the reinforcement menu.

Step 7. The contract is formalized. The exact behaviors and contingencies to be carried out by the teacher and the student are explicitly stated in a written document. The contract (cosigned by the student and the teacher) serves to remind the signees of their cooperative efforts to solve the problem. The teacher initials the contract only after the student's behavior has met the contractual requirements (see Figure 1).

Step 8. Contractual pay-off. As the student performs successive approximations to the terminal behaviors, points are accumulated that are cashed in at specified times. Points are converted for minutes of free time activities listed on the reinforcement menu (Premack, 1959).

Step 9. Renegotiation of the contract. Since the objective of contracted behavioral counseling is to produce behavioral change in small steps or successive approximations, the contract must be renegotiated and increased as the teacher and the student accomplish the intermediate behaviors. The same procedures are followed in the renegotiation process.

Summary

Usually by the time a teacher requests the counselor's assistance with a problem student, he has already attempted a variety of approaches to improve the student's academic or social performance. At this point he has experienced failure and, probably, so has the student.

Contracted behavioral counseling provides a method of intervention that removes the conflict from centering directly between student and teacher. The counselor as a neutral to both parties may offer his skills in behavioral contracting in securing their cooperative effort to resolve the impasse or conflict situation that they have reached.

Communication problems existing between student and teacher expectations are minimized by the use of behavioral statements written into the formalized contract. Also, the terms of the contract are mutually negotiable and acceptable; therefore, the contractual arrangements are viewed as fair and honest.

Figure 1. An Example of a Contract Used in Increasing
Academic Behaviors

Student: John B. Goode

Terminal Behavior: John will complete each written Math assignment in the
   allotted time with a minimum of 90% accuracy.[a]

Behavior Contract

Terms of the Contract: (Contract One—beginning requirements)

1. John is to complete each written Math assignment in the allotted time with
   a minimum of 50% accuracy.[b]
2. John must only complete written Math assignment in the allotted time
   with 50% accuracy to gain the teacher's signature.
3. By completing each assignment as stated above, John gains 10 points. The
   contract is issued daily and signed by both the teacher and the student.
4. Total points necessary for cash-in is set at 30.

Period	Subject	Teacher's Initials	Room
1			
2			
3	Math		23
4			
5			
6			

_____
Teacher

_____
Student

   a. That point which the student and the teacher have mutually defined as
the eventual behavioral goal.

   b. As John is able to consistently meet the requirements of this contract,
the percentage of accuracy will be systematically increased. As one academic
subject comes under control, others may be added.

An important aspect of contracted behavioral counseling is that as a result of the teacher's participation in the planning and execution of the intervention program, he gains useful skills in dealing with this and future classroom behavior problems. Teacher training in problem identification and intervention procedures is a necessary and intrinsic element of this model. Further, since the referral identifies the precise observable behaviors that constitute the problem it is compatible with measurement requirements. That is, empirical data may be collected on the frequency of occurrence of the referred problem and used to evaluate the success or failure of the intervention program. The actual written contract may be constructed to provide a daily written summary of performance data, as well as serve as a constant reminder of the student's and teacher's cooperative efforts to remediate the problem. Even without the collection of empirical data, the specific identification of the terminal behaviors and those intermediate behaviors (successive approximations) provide observable and objective criteria for evaluating behavioral change.

The utilization of contracted behavioral counseling gets the counselor out of his office and in direct contact with teachers and students in arranging effective classroom environments to meet individualized student problems.

References

Ayllon, T. & Azrin, N. H. *Token economy.* New York: Appleton-Century-Crofts, 1968.

Homme, L., Csaryi, A. P., Gonzales, M. & Rech, J. R. *How to use contingency contracting in the classroom.* Champaign, Ill.: Research Press, 1969.

Krumboltz, J. D. (Ed.) *Revolution in counseling.* Boston: Houghton Mifflin, 1966.

Premack, D. Toward empirical behavior laws: I. Positive reinforcement. *Psychological Review,* 1969, *66,* 219-233.

Vance, B. The counselor—an agent of what change? *Personnel and Guidance Journal,* 1967, *45,* 1012-1016.

CHARLES A. BUGG

Systematic Desensitization:
A Technique Worth Trying

During the past four years, I have noted that a substantial proportion of children's self-referrals for counseling concern problems in
which anxiety related to specific events or situations is the major
causal element. One particularly common reason they seek counseling is test anxiety. Another is stage fright associated with public-
speaking situations (e.g., making reports, reading in class, speaking in
student election campaigns, performing in plays and talent shows). I
assume that other working counselors encounter similar client problems and therefore in this article I will briefly describe the technique
of systematic desensitization and then relate my own experiences in
using a modified form of this technique in a public school setting.

Although the experiences reported here occurred in a school setting, systematic desensitization is a general technique and may be
useful to many persons, regardless of age or setting, whenever minor
specific anxieties are causing some debilitating effect. Counselors in
settings other than the schools should be able to extend and generalize the experience reported here to their own clients in their own
settings.

Bugg, C. A. Systematic desensitization: a technique worth trying. *The Personnel and Guidance Journal*, 1972, *50*(10), 823-828. Copyright 1972 American Personnel and Guidance
Association. Reprinted with permission.

Systematic Desensitization

Systematic desensitization is one limited purpose form of behavior therapy based upon the principle of reciprocal inhibition. Wolpe (1961) describes reciprocal inhibition,

If a response inhibitory to anxiety can be made to occur in the presence of anxiety-evoking stimuli so that it is accompanied by a complete or partial suppression of the anxiety response, the bond between these stimuli and the anxiety response will be weakened (p. 189).

The essential principle of reciprocal inhibition is that an organism cannot make two contradictory responses at the same time. Behavior therapy assumes that anxiety responses are learned (conditioned) behaviors and may be extinguished by reconditioning. If the response that is contradictory to anxiety results in a more pleasant state or more productive behavior for the subject, the new response to the anxiety-evoking stimuli will gradually replace the anxiety response.

Wolpe (1961, 1966) restricted his use of systematic desensitization to cases involving minor neurotic anxieties, simple phobias related to specific situations and objects (fear of high places, fear of dogs, etc.) and those not resulting from interpersonal relations. He claims 90 percent effectiveness in treating patients when he uses systematic desensitization.

Systematic desensitization consists of three steps: (a) training in deep muscle relaxation, the primary anxiety-inhibiting response; (b) construction of anxiety hierarchies for the patient (ordered from stimuli that produce slight anxiety to those that produce great anxiety); and (c) counterposing relaxation and anxiety-evoking stimuli from the hierarchies. Usually the patient is hypnotized. (Other researchers have demonstrated that hypnosis is unnecessary in the settings and for the clients with which most counselors deal.) Wolpe (1961) describes the process in these words:

In brief, the desensitization method consists of presenting to the imagination of the deeply relaxed patient the feeblest item in a list of anxiety-evoking stimuli—repeatedly, until no more anxiety is evoked. The next item of the list is presented, and so on, until eventually, even the strongest of the anxiety-evoking stimuli fails to evoke any stir of anxiety in the patient. It has consistently been found that at every stage a stimulus that evokes no anxiety when imagined in a state of relaxation will also evoke no anxiety when encountered in reality (p. 191).

Wolpe's Method

To illustrate the technique developed and used by Wolpe, I will use as an example a patient with an irrational fear of cats. First, a hierarchy is constructed. The greatest anxiety is evoked by a scarred, ugly alley cat hissing and snarling in the walkway as the patient goes down the street. A pet cat in a friend's house causes great anxiety, but not so much as the alley cat. Little kittens cause anxiety, but not as much as grown cats. Pictures of cats evoke fear, but not so much as real cats. A picture of little kittens playing with a ball of yarn causes just noticeable tenseness.

Second, the patient is taught the method of deep muscle relaxation.

Third, the therapist relaxes the patient and begins to describe the picture of little kittens—the item producing the most feeble anxiety reaction. When the patient signals that he feels tense or anxious, he is ordered to relax. After a few seconds' relaxation, the stimulus is described again until the patient again signals anxiety and is relaxed. These steps are repeated until the stimulus finally evokes no anxiety in the patient. Then the process is repeated with the second weakest stimulus, and so on up the line. The process works very rapidly, and it is not unusual for a patient to have two or more sessions with the therapist per day.

Nonmedical Research

A number of recent studies have involved modifications of Wolpe's method of systematic desensitization. Two of these are of particular significance to those who work in nonmedical settings.

Emory (1967) found desensitization effective in reducing test anxiety in college students, and, very importantly, his results indicated no significant differences in reduction of test anxiety between students treated with individually developed hierarchies and students treated by the use of a standardized hierarchy for relief of test anxiety.

Paul and Shannon (1966) worked with college students whose anxiety about public speaking restricted their academic success. Their study compared group desensitization, insight-oriented therapy (with psychoanalytically oriented therapists), attention-placebo treatment, and individual desensitization. They found that both group and individual desensitization techniques proved to be effective and both were superior to insight-oriented therapy and attention-placebo treatment in reducing anxiety. Group desensitization was not significantly different in its effect from individual desensitization. Furthermore, Paul and Shannon used a modified form of deep muscle relaxation requiring less training than Wolpe's method, and none of the subjects was hypnotized. The results of a study by Dixon (1966), however, reported no difference between a group method of desensitization and conventional group therapy in reducing test anxiety.

In the School Setting

Almost every day the working school counselor encounters students whose educational, social, and personal development and success are hampered by some specific anxiety, usually in a testing or public speaking situation. In my work during the past four years, I have observed that a modified form of systematic desensitization can help counselees with such problems, provided that the following two conditions exist:

1. The counselor must spend enough time listening to the student, reflecting his feelings and concerns, and helping him describe and clarify his problem situation to determine that anxiety is in fact the culprit and to gain some reasonable idea of the counselee's hierarchy. (A student may flunk tests because he plays around and is not prepared rather than because anxiety causes him to tense up and forget everything he has learned.)

2. The counselee must conscientiously apply the techniques of systematic desensitization at every opportunity in both imagination and reality.

As I use it, systematic desensitization is a technique taught to and applied by the counselee. Ordinarily, one or two half-hour sessions are sufficient for the counselee to learn the basic principles of the technique and how to apply it. I discuss the principle of reciprocal inhibition and the technique of systematic desensitization in non-technical language until I feel that the counselee understands them. Then we discuss the counselee's specific problem until he understands not only the major situation that causes him anxiety and problems but also a number of related situations (his hierarchy) in which the technique should and can be applied to alleviate the problem. The basic test of the counselee's understanding is to have him describe in his own words the technique and how it can and will be applied to his personal situation.

The student learns to relax himself by using three basic steps in words to this effect. "First, whenever you are in the situation or imagine yourself in it, take a deep breath and let it go suddenly. This forces relaxation for a split second. Second, tell yourself to be calm and relax. Third, think of something very pleasant for a few seconds before bringing yourself back to the problem situation and repeating the whole process."

The student is instructed to imagine himself in situations related to his strongest anxiety-evoking situation and to relax. He is told to do this over and over again, hundreds of times if necessary. Gradually, he works himself through his hierarchy in imagination. He also practices the techniques of relaxation and desensitization whenever he finds himself in such a situation in reality. I stress that if the technique is to work, the counselee must apply it repeatedly at every possible opportunity in reality and imagination, both in the problem situation and in related situations.

Examples

The following case studies from my own experience illustrate the use that has been made of systematic desensitization.

William, a seventh-grader, came into my office just before semester exams and declared that he had a serious problem in math. He anticipated failing the quarter test two days hence and getting a D for his quarter grade. He expected to follow that up by flunking the semester exam a few days later and getting a D for the final semester grade. The result would be that his parents would place him on restriction for the next nine weeks or until the grade went to C or above. William was known to be a strong, conscientious student. He diagnosed his own case, stating that he studied math regularly, sometimes with his father who knew math well, and that he was certain he understood the material. He added,

I always get good grades for homework. I can answer any question or work any problem in class that the teacher wants me to do, but I just can't pass a test. I get all excited and nervous and then make stupid mistakes or just completely forget how to work the problems. When he gives the test back, I can work any of the problems that I have missed without any help at all.

I explained systematic desensitization to William and told him that the method might not work as quickly as he needed in order to pass the tests, but that at least it could help him get off restriction by the end of nine weeks. Two days later he said, "Man, what you told me to try sure works. I made a B on the test and got a C for my quarter grade." A few days later he repeated this high performance getting a B on the semester final.

Because he wasn't much concerned about his other subjects and felt confident that he basically knew the math, William had devoted almost full time during those two days to desensitizing himself for the math test. He imagined himself in the math room and relaxed. He imagined himself speaking with the math teacher and relaxed. As he studied math, he relaxed himself. He imagined himself taking tests in other subjects and relaxed. He imagined taking the math test and relaxed. When he finally took the test, he relaxed himself as much as possible beforehand and then took the test one problem at a time, relaxing in between. He kept telling himself, "Just be calm and relax. You know this stuff, and if you don't get shook, you'll make a good grade." After resolving his test anxiety, William continued in counseling to discuss concerns that he had about dating and sexual behavior and values.

Rita, in second grade, presented a problem that combines test anxiety and fear of public speaking. She said that whenever the teacher called on her to work something on the board she got upset, started crying, and couldn't do the work. Like William, she knew how to do the work. There was just something about being asked to do it on the board that upset her so much that she couldn't do it. She practiced the same techniques prescribed for William in both imagination and reality and added a wrinkle of her own.

When she came back for her second meeting a week later, Rita reported that on that very morning the teacher had asked her to go to the board to work a math problem and that she had felt nervous about it but had done it without crying. She said that she had been working very hard that week on trying to relax herself. Then she added,

Last weekend, I had three of my best friends over. I told them about my problem and what you had told me to try to solve it. We played school almost all day. They played the teacher, and they called on me a lot to go to the board and work. I was nervous, but I just kept taking deep breaths and relaxing. That helped me a lot.

John, in ninth grade, was an outstanding student and a natural leader. Although he hadn't sought either office, he had been elected as a student council representative and as the top officer of another major school activity. Just before the deadline for filing as a candidate for one of the four major student council offices, he was asked why he hadn't signed up to run for one of them. His reply was:

I would love to serve in one of the offices, but I couldn't possibly run, because I would have to make a speech to the student body. I can't even read out of a book in class when the teacher calls on me. I know the material perfectly, but I get so nervous that I either start stuttering or else just can't get anything to come out at all.

Assured that his problem could be overcome, John agreed to run for one of the offices. Two weeks later, he made an excellent speech to the student body and was elected. Afterward, his office required him to speak to a number of groups to explain student council plans and policies. He spoke successfully on every occasion.

To achieve this result, John imagined himself engaged in spontaneous debate with his peers in student council (this caused only slight anxiety) and relaxed himself. He imagined himself reading in class and relaxed. He relaxed himself as he wrote his speech. He practiced in front of the mirror and relaxed. He practiced in front of his parents and relaxed. He practiced in front of his friends and campaign managers and relaxed. Called upon to read or speak in class, he relaxed himself and did the best he could. In both imagination and reality, he found and practiced opportunities to employ the techniques of systematic desensitization during the two weeks prior to his election speech.

Systematic desensitization is a technique that has worked for a substantial proportion of the pupils who have come to me for help. It is a technique with which all counselors should be familiar. One of its distinct advantages is the time it saves for the counselor to devote to other cases that require other approaches. With most counselees whom the technique can help, only one or two short sessions are needed. It can also be used in group counseling, and students who have been taught the technique can teach it to others without the intervention of the counselor. On many occasions, a student has approached me and said:

I had planned to make an appointment with you, but I was talking with my friend. He told me why he saw you and what you suggested. My problem was the same, so I tried the same thing and it worked. I don't need to see you now.

In Other Settings

No great stretch of the imagination should be required for counselors in settings other than the schools to apply the principles of systematic desensitization to their own clients. Sooner or later most counselors are likely to encounter clients who are afflicted by specific anxiety to some degree and for whom desensitization may contribute to more effective functioning. The client who is well qualified for a position but who becomes so nervous during a job interview that he is judged unfavorably is a prime candidate for desensitization. Another example of someone who would benefit from the technique is the person who becomes so anxious while being taught the responsibilities and techniques of a new job that he fails to learn properly or makes mistakes that may cause him to lose the job or not advance in it in accord with his true abilities. A toning down of the stage fright associated with public speaking in both large and small groups would enable people to communicate their ideas more effectively, would free them to utilize more of their basic talents as human beings, and would enable them to live more effective, more productive, and more rewarding personal, civic, business, and social lives. Whatever the counselor's setting, whenever he encounters a client whose functioning is hampered by some specific minor anxiety, he might use systematic desensitization to help his client overcome the negative effects of the anxiety and achieve his goals and potential.

Relax and Try It

Do you get a little worked up about using something from the behavioral school? Imagine yourself hearing a counselee describe his problem and thinking that you know what is wrong. Just before that puts you into a catatonic seizure, take a deep breath and let it go. Relax. Think about something less threatening for a moment. Now, repeat that until you stop feeling tense and nervous about having such a thought. Next, imagine yourself saying, "I think I know what your problem is, and I know what you can do to solve it." When that makes you feel uneasy, relax. Keep trying this in your imagination until you feel comfortable with it, then try it out on a real live counselee. Chances are good that it will help him and save you time for others whose concerns are of a different nature and require a more extended application of your reflective skills.

References

Dixon, F. S. Systematic desensitization of test anxiety. *Dissertation Abstracts,* 1966, *27* (4-b), 1301-1302.

Emory, J. R. An evaluation of standard versus individualized hierarchies in desensitization to reduce test anxiety. *Dissertation Abstracts,* 1967, *27* (7-b), 2510-2511.

Paul, G. L. & Shannon, D. T. Treatment of anxiety through systematic desensitization in therapy groups. *Journal of Abnormal Psychology,* 1966, *71,* 124-135.

Wolpe, J. The systematic desensitization treatment of neuroses. *Journal of Nervous and Mental Disease,* 1961, *132,* 189-203.

Wolpe, J. The conditioning and deconditioning of neurotic anxiety. In C. D. Spielberger (Ed.), *Anxiety and behavior.* New York: Academic Press, 1966, 179-190.

Suggested Reading

(These two chapters provide an excellent brief overview of Wolpe's work and of the principles and techniques of systematic desensitization.)

Ford, D. H. & Urban, H. B. *Systems of psychotherapy.* New York: Wiley & Sons, 1963, 273-303.

Patterson, C. H. *Theories of counseling and psychotherapy.* New York: Harper & Row, 1966, 154-178.

SECTION II

Client-centered Counseling

For constructive personality change to occur, it is necessary that these conditions exist and continue over a period of time:

1. Two persons are in psychological contact.

2. The first, whom we shall term the client, is in a state of incongruence, being vulnerable or anxious.

3. The second person, whom we shall term the therapist, is congruent or integrated in the relationship.

4. The therapist experiences unconditional positive regard for the client.

5. The therapist experiences an empathic understanding of the client's internal frame of reference and endeavors to communicate this experience to the client.

6. The communication to the client of the therapist's empathic understanding and unconditional positive regard is to a minimal degree achieved.

No other conditions are necessary. If these six conditions exist, and continue over a period of time, this is sufficient. The process of constructive personality change will follow.

—Carl Rogers

Client-centered counseling has had a profound effect on the development of counseling and therapy for the past three decades. Many training institutions emphasize this approach in theory and practicum courses, and consequently a large proportion of practicing counselors adhere to its basic premises and techniques. It has been widely used as a treatment modality with adolescent and adult populations. The child population has been less extensively, and only recently, treated with this model. Thus, specific adaptation of its techniques for the preadolescent population has not been emphasized. Research in this area is conspicuously absent. Despite this handicap, the basic conceptual model is readily adaptable to the child clientele.

Client-centered counseling is built on the foundation of phenomenological psychology. Phenomenological assumptions focus on several major concepts: the phenomenological field, the self system, and individual perception. The field is the environment in which an individual exists, and particular attention is directed to the individual's perception of environmental events. His or her unique perceptions govern the development and growth of the self system. Faulty perceptions lead to incongruence in the self system, which is the basis for inconsistent behavior and maladjustment.

Carl Rogers has been the major spokesman for the client-centered approach to counseling. Accepting the tenets of phenomenological theory, he has constructed a theory of counseling that is noticeably free of specific techniques. He prefers to focus his attention on the counselor-client relationship. For Rogers, the relationship is the major change agent in therapy. This relationship has certain definable characteristics that are essential to effective counseling. Among them are: empathy, genuineness, warmth, and unconditional positive regard. The primary behaviors of the counselor in this relationship are listening and reflection of feeling. In general, the focus of client-centered counseling is on the affective growth of the client in the context of the helping relationship.

The article by C. H. Patterson that opens this section provides a comprehensive overview of the phenomenological school of thought. Patterson begins by defining phenomenology comprehensively and comparing it to the more classical systems of psychotherapy. Eight major tenets of the theory are discussed, and special emphasis is given to the development and maintenance of the individual's self-concept.

In the second reading, Carl Rogers addresses the importance of the counselor-client relationship. He feels that this relationship is the major factor in constructive personality or behavior change. Surveys of pertinent studies on this relationship compare client-centered techniques with other major schools of thought in psychotherapy. Rogers creatively seeks to present his view of the helping relationship by asking the reader to consider ten questions that are central to client-centered relationships. He concludes by stating that affirmative responses to these questions will lead to helping relationships that foster personality growth and change.

Roy Mayer and John Cody, in the third article, approach the client-centered model from an unusual perspective. They relate Festinger's concept of cognitive dissonance to Rogers's concept of incongruence in the self system, by proposing that the concepts are similar and that both produce psychological discomfort in an individual. In an atmosphere of discomfort, positive growth is inhibited. This type of threatening environment will lead to defensive reactions on the part of the client. Mayer and Cody relate the concepts of cognitive dissonance and incongruence specifically to school counseling via the counseling relationship and suggest more effective counseling behaviors. Excerpts from a case transcript with a twelve-year-old client, and a brief summary of the case of an eleven-year-old boy illustrate their topic. The counselor's use of reflection techniques is particularly apparent in the transcript illustration.

The concluding article, by Ernst Beier, focuses specifically on the involuntary client in the school setting. Beier uses case examples creatively to demonstrate a client-centered approach with clients of different age levels and presenting problems. The school counselor frequently encounters involuntariness and resistance, and Beier's presentation offers ways of dealing with these phenomena.

C. H. PATTERSON

Phenomenological Psychology

It is a basic tenet of so-called depth or dynamic psychology that behavior is determined by deep unconscious motives, and that in order to understand, predict, or control behavior one must understand these motives. This is not a simple matter, since one cannot easily recognize motives. The apparent or obvious motives, or the motives reported by the subject, are not the real motives. Indeed, the so-called real motives are commonly the reverse of those reported by the subject. Thus nothing can be accepted at face value. Nothing is what it appears to be. Reports of subjects are not to be trusted. The widespread acceptance of this point of view, by lay as well as professional people, attests to the influence of Freud and psychoanalysis.

There is another point of view, which has not been widely accepted, but which is increasing its influence in psychology. This approach suggests that for the purpose of understanding and predicting behavior it is profitable to make the assumption that things *are* what they appear to be, that the significant determinants of behavior are not some mysterious unconscious motives, nor some so-called reality, but the individual's perceptions of himself and his environ-

Patterson, C. H. Phenomenological psychology. *The Personnel and Guidance Journal,* 1965, *43*(10), 997-1005. Copyright 1965 American Personnel and Guidance Association. Reprinted with permission.

ment. "There is more to seeing than meets the eyeball" (Hanson, 1958). "We see things," to quote Gibson (1951, p. 98) "not as *they* are but as *we* are." Or to say it another way, it is not "seeing is believing," but "believing is seeing." In more technical terms, the response defines the stimulus, rather than the stimulus defining the response. Gombrich, in a discussion of art and illusion (1960, p. 394) notes that ". . . we can never neatly separate what we see from what we know." "The individual sees what he wants to see, not in the sense that he manufactures out of whole cloth, but in the sense that he appropriates to himself, from what is given, the pattern that he needs" (Murphy, Murphy, & Newcomb, 1937, p. 218).

This second point of view is phenomenology. It is not widely accepted. Snygg (1961), in reviewing a recent book, states: "Phenomenology is not in this country an honored, going concern with a historical past. American phenomenologies therefore emerge rather suddenly, as workers in applied fields run into problems they cannot solve by the traditional objective approach, are forced to develop conceptual models better suited to their needs and then go on to apply them in wide fields." It is interesting to list some of the names of those who have come to entertain a phenomenological approach. They include William James, John Dewey, George H. Mead, the Allports, Wertheimer, Koffka, Koehler, Kurt Lewin, Adelbert Ames, and Carl Rogers.

Phenomenology and Introspection

A number of years ago a colleague declared that Rogers had set psychology back by 50 years. His basis for the statement was the identification of phenomenology with introspection. It is not necessarily undesirable that we go back 50 years, since it might be contended that psychology has been on the wrong track or in a blind alley during this time, and that it is necessary to go back and pick up a new fork in the road. Psychology has been dominated in the past 50 years by behaviorism and psychoanalysis. While these two approaches or systems are antithetical in many respects, they are similar in that they view the individual from an external position, as an object. Phenomenology, on the other hand, takes the internal form of reference, and in this respect is related to introspection. However, there is a difference. Introspection was concerned only with the subject's report or description of his conscious sensations and feelings.

Phenomenology is concerned with the individual's report, not only of his own sensations and feelings, but of his perceptions of the external world as well as of himself. While phenomenology is thus related to introspection, and to some extent grew out of it, phenomenology as represented by Gestalt psychology, as Boring (1953) points out, was a protest against classic introspection.

Phenomenology, using introspection in the form of verbal reports, produced extensive and significant experimental research in perception. In using verbal reports, phenomenological experiments are no different from psychophysical experiments, in which the subject reports psychical sensations or judgments. In fact, much of current experimental psychology, including behavioristic psychology, depends upon verbal reports, so that phenomenology cannot be condemned as unscientific because it also utilizes verbal report. It is true that there are problems involved in the use of self-reports, but as Bakan (1953) points out, in this respect the method is no different from any other method of science. And there is no other way in many instances to study certain significant problems, such as the self-concept, or to determine the perceptual field of the subject. Nevertheless, it must be recognized that the description of the perceptual field by a subject is not identical with the field itself.

It is interesting that stimulus-response psychology supports the phenomenological point of view. It has been noted that for phenomenology, the response defines the stimulus. Experimental psychologists have come to realize this in the recognition that the same objective or physical stimulus means different things to different subjects, and that if the stimulus situation is to be standardized, it must be in terms of the subjects' perceptions of the stimulus, not the stimulus as objectively defined, or as perceived by the experimenter. In this respect all stimuli are response-inferred (Jessor, 1956; Wylie, 1961, 13-21).

Phenomenology Defined

What is phenomenology? It is the purpose of this paper to attempt to describe briefly the phenomenological approach to behavior. English and English (1958, p. 387) define phenomenology as follows: "A theoretical point of view which advocates the study of phenomena or direct experience taken naively at face value; the view that behavior is determined by the phenomena of experience rather than by external, objective, physically described reality." Phenomenalism is defined as "a philosophical doctrine teaching that human knowledge is limited to appearances, never reaching the true nature of reality" (English & English, 1958, p. 386). Phenomenology as a distinct philosophical point of view is a development mainly of the present century, usually being associated with the philosopher Husserl whose phenomenological writings date from the early years of the century (Spiegelberg, 1960). A brief description of philosophical phenomenology is impossible, in part because of differences among its exponents; there are phenomenologies rather than a school. But they agree in that they are all concerned with experience as the basic data of knowledge. Knowledge can come only from experience, whether sensory or nonsensory, or extrasensory. Whether there is some reality that gives rise to experiences, and if so what is the nature of this reality, is unimportant, since it can only be known through experience. Taking this experience, phenomenology attempts to study it, through observing, describing, and analyzing it, attempting to generalize from the particular experiences, determining relationships, studying the various appearances of phenomena and the development of perceptions and conceptions in the phenomenological field.

The position that we can never know the true nature of reality is resisted, both by those who feel that common sense indicates that there is a reality, as when we stub a toe on a brick, by those whose needs or desires require the certainty of some reality and by scientists who accept their objective measurements and operational definitions as reality. But it should be obvious, both to common sense and to objective observation and measurement, that "reality" varies with different attitudes, motives, desires, or points of view, and with different operations. Whether or not these individual realities add up to a general, absolute, natural reality is a question that has little if any practical significance, for reasons that will become apparent. Philosophically, a phenomenologist may or may not be a realist. Phenomenology represents a "neutralism with regard to reality rather than an outright commitment to realism" (Spiegelberg, 1960, p. 636).

Spiegelberg (1960) in his history of philosophical phenomenology, notes that "Phenomenology is hardly one of the leading philosophical movements in the United States." He later states that "actually in the United States phenomenology has had a much bigger impact on extraphilosophical studies such as psychology and theology, though to be sure in forms which differ considerably from those stressed by the philosophical phenomenologists" (p. 637). In psychology, he continues, "the reaction against behaviorism takes more and more the form of developing a wider phenomenological approach, which tries to give introspection as objective and critical refinement as possible" (pp. 643-644).

While, as has been indicated, the Gestaltists were essentially phenomenological, as well as a number of social psychologists identified with sociology, notably G. H. Mead, the first specific treatment of phenomenological psychology was the 1941 article by Snygg (1941). At the present time perhaps the most definitive statement of phenomenological psychology is that of Snygg and Combs, first published in 1949, and recently revised (Combs & Snygg, 1959).

A Synthesis of Phenomenological Psychology

What is phenomenological psychology? What are its distinguishing features? Phenomenology in psychology did not develop from philosophical phenomenology, but arose almost independently, although psychologists such as James, Koehler, and Lewin had some contact with the latter. There is, as yet, no formal school of phenomenological psychology. It is thus not possible to present a statement of a formal or complete system. The outline of the characteristics of a phenomenological approach to human behavior that follows is an attempt to synthesize or integrate the ideas of those who have been identified as phenomenological in their psychological approach to behavior. The attempt rests most heavily, perhaps, on Combs and Snygg (1959).

1. *The individual is a living, and therefore active, organism engaged in the attempt to organize its world.* Two characteristics of this fact are important.

a. The individual is not an empty organism, waiting to be prodded into action by external or even internal stimuli. The response seeks the stimulus, rather than waiting for the stimulus to evoke it.

b. The interaction of the organism with its environment is the basis for experience. This experience constitutes the basic data of psychology. It consists of, or underlies and gives meaning to, overt behavior. Phenomenological psychology is concerned with the study of the experiencing individual.

2. *The organization which the individual gives to the world is known as his perceptual or phenomenal field.* This is more than the area of sensory perception, including cognition, conceptions, and knowledge. The importance of phenomenology was first recognized by perceptual psychology, since the study of perception was the focus of early psychology and the lack of a constant relation of perception to the objective stimulus became apparent.

The phenomenal field is the universe, including the individual himself, as it is perceived and experienced by him. It consists not of the so-called "reality," but of the world as it appears to him, as he perceives it. He can only know the world through his perceptions, and there is no reality for the individual other than what constitutes his perceptual or phenomenal field. "To each individual, his phenomenal field *is* reality; it is the only reality he can know" (Combs & Snygg, 1959, p. 21). The perceptual field of the individual is influenced by his needs and beliefs. "What is perceived is not what exists, but what one believes exists, . . . what we have learned to perceive as a result of our past opportunities or experiences" (Combs & Snygg, 1959, pp. 84, 85).

Perceptions are often referred to as accurate, true, veridical, or inaccurate, wrong, or distorted. It is probably better not to think of perceptions in these terms, since they involve an evaluation from an external frame of reference. All perceptions, from the point of view of the perceiver, are accurate and true, since there is no other experience, at the time of perceiving, with which they may be compared and evaluated. A perception may not agree with the perceptions of others under the same conditions, or with the perception of the same individual at another time or from another vantage point. All perceptions are thus true or accurate, as perceptions. In the case of so-called illusion, such as the Ames demonstrations, the illusion is a true perception. What is in error, what is wrong, is the inference from a perception regarding the nature of the stimulus. What is perceived, from one angle, as a chair, is found not to have the qualities of a chair from another angle and is not perceived as a chair from the changed position. Thus, inferences regarding the stimuli may be changed, or corrected, on further experience with a stimulus. The same point of view may be taken with regard to what have been called distorted perceptions resulting from the needs of the perceiver (Combs & Snygg, 1959, pp. 154-155). It is not the perceptions that are distorted—they are experienced as clear and unambiguous. It is the stimuli which are distorted.

3. *The individual can act only on the basis of his perceptions, his phenomenal field.* As Combs and Snygg state it, "All behavior, without exception, is completely determined by, and pertinent to, the perceptual field of the behaving organism" (1959, p. 20). Appearances may be deceiving, but we act on them, nevertheless. We can act on nothing else, of course. "People can behave only in terms of what seems to them to be so" (Combs & Snygg, 1959, p. 5).

Some confusion has arisen because of a lack of understanding of the nature of the phenomenal field. Two problems in particular may be mentioned.

a. Combs and Snygg state that the perceptual field is "each individual's personal and unique field of awareness" (1959, p. 20). This word awareness has been equated with consciousness by some, and the phenomenological approach criticized for neglecting unconscious motivation (Smith, 1950). The concept of unconscious motivation cannot be dealt with here, other than to say that both the concept of the unconscious and of motivation are so fuzzy that when combined it is doubtful that the resulting construct has any real meaning or value. But the point to be made is that awareness is a matter of degree. As Combs & Snygg point out, "Although the perceptual field includes all the universe of which we are aware, we are not aware of all parts with the same degree of clarity at any moment" (1959, p. 27). Much of the field is ground, rather than figure, in Gestalt terminology. But what is in the ground is not unconscious. The individual may not be able to label or to report all the elements of his perceptual field, but unreportability is not to be equated with the unconscious. (See Phillips, 1956, Chapter 3, for a consideration of this problem.)

b. A second problem has arisen because of the apparent ahistorical nature of phenomenology. If all behavior is determined by the perceptual field at the moment of action, then are not we leaving out of consideration the important historical determinants of behavior? The answer to this is relatively simple. Snygg and Combs (1950) reply that "certainly the events of an individual's life affect his behavior. But it is important for us to recognize that it is the perceptions of these events and not the events themselves which are the *immediate* causes of behavior." Earlier events are part of the phenomenal field; as Lewin (1943) puts it: "The behaver's field at any given instant contains also the views of the individual about his past and future. ... The psychological past and the psychological future are simultaneous parts of the psychological field existing at a given time." It must also be recognized that it is not the event as it occurred objectively, nor even the individual's perception of it as it occurred at the time, but his present perception of it which is a determinant of behavior. This fact perhaps explains the lack of a strong relationship between early significant or presumably traumatic events and later behavior, and suggests a phenomenological approach to the study of the relation of childhood events to later behavior.

4. *The phenomenal field is an inference, and thus a hypothetical construct.* It is an inference of the subject as well as of the observer. It is not open to direct observation. Inferences concerning the phenomenological fields of individuals may be developed in several ways.

a. The phenomenal field may be inferred from the observation of behavior. While this is an objective method, it is limited, and inferences can be dangerous. Sufficient observation may not be possible, the observer may project himself into the situation, and his inferences may be interpretations which force behavior to fit a preconceived theory or system of behavior analysis.

b. The individual may be asked to report on his phenomenal field. The ability of the human subject to verbalize his perceptions offers us an approach to his phenomenal field. However, there are limitations. First, the subject may not wish to communicate certain aspects of his experience or perceptions. Second, he may not be able to report accurately, because of the lack of clarity and low awareness level of much of the field. Third, the conscious concentration upon the field changes the field. While attention to the field may crystallize something for the first time, and bring into clearer focus or awareness parts of the field that were at a lower level of awareness, the field then changes and further report is influenced by the changed field. Fourth, some aspects of the field may not be capable of being expressed in words, or may not be represented adequately by verbalizations.

c. The phenomenal field may be studied by means of tests and inventories. The usefulness of this approach is limited, however, by the lack of data upon which to make inferences regarding the perceptual field. Tests and inventories have been studied almost entirely in terms of empirical relationships to external behavior, or, in the case of some projective techniques, external evidence of internal experience or hypothesized dynamic characteristics. A technique such as the Rorschach might be useful in understanding the phenomenal fields of individuals if we knew how to assess the meanings of the stimuli to the individual or convert the responses into information relevant to the subjects' perceptual fields. It is my hypothesis that insofar as the Rorschach is useful it is a result of its use in this way, and the generally negative results of its use are related to the fact that it is not usually employed in this manner.

d. Perhaps the most useful approach to inferring the phenomenal field of another is the use of the free, unstructured interview. The free interview method is less likely to impose the investigator's structure on the subject's field. It also minimizes some of the disadvantage of the self-report, in that the subject's attention or concentration is less consciously directed at analysis of the field. In other words the report may be more clearly descriptive rather than interpretive. This approach leads us to a basic distinction between the so-called objective and the phenomenological approach to the study of behavior.

5. *Phenomenology, as should be apparent by now, takes the internal frame of reference rather than the external frame of reference in its study of behavior.* As Snygg (1941) points out, this is similar to the common-sense approach, when an observer, in attempting to understand "Why did he do that?" asks "Under what circumstances would I have done that?" This approach has been resisted, both because it is seen as subjective, and perhaps too close to common sense. The approach, however, is useful with animals as well as humans. Koehler (1931) pointed out long ago the common error of animal psychologists of structuring the test situation in terms of their own perceptual and conceptual field rather than in terms of the rat's. Tolman once said (1938), in response to a question or charge of anthropomorphism, that he would "go ahead imagining how, if I were a rat, I would behave" because it gave him insight and understanding of his results. Snygg (see references in Snygg, 1941) has demonstrated the fruitfulness of this approach in developing hypotheses, which were confirmed, regarding the perceptual behavior of rats.

In using the internal frame of reference the investigator attempts to place himself, insofar as possible, in the subject's place in order to view the world and the subject as the subject does. This is the approach to the unstructured interview suggested above for the investigation of another person's phenomenal field. The investigator avoids as much as possible the influence of his own phenomenal field on the subject's report by refraining from structuring, probing or direct questioning, or interpreting or evaluating the productions of the subject.

6. *Since the phenomenal field of the individual determines his behavior, prediction for the individual becomes possible when one knows the behaver's phenomenal field, which is then projected into the future field.* Understanding of the inferred future field makes possible the prediction of future behavior. Such predictions for an individual should be more accurate than predictions based upon group characteristics and memberships. The process is complicated, not only by the difficulty of inferring the present field, but because some aspects of the future field, which will be affected by external conditions, cannot be known. Nevertheless, such an approach to prediction is promising. It is similar to the proposals of the Pepinskys (1954), Koester (1954), Parker (1958), McArthur (1954), and Soskin (1959) that suggest the development of a hypothetical model of an individual. The application of this method, as in the studies by McArthur and Parker, have not been successful, however. These investigators suggest that the counselors were too hasty and premature in building their models of the clients. Another more important reason for the lack of success might be the failure to build the model on the basis of the phenomenal field of the subject.

7. We finally come to the matter of the self and the self-concept. *The self is part of the individual's phenomenal field.* It includes all the perceptions and conceptions he has about himself, his attitudes and beliefs about himself. Whether there is a real self apart from the perceptual or phenomenal self is a hypothetical or philosophical question. The phenomenal self is the real self in terms of the individual's behavior. The perceptions which others have of an individual's self may influence the phenomenal self. But the perceptions of others, even though in agreement, are still phenomenal, and do not necessarily constitute any "real" self.

The phenomenal self is a most significant part of the phenomenal field since it is the central or pivotal part of the field, about which perceptions are organized: it is the frame of reference for the individual. "All perceptions . . . derive their meaning from their relation to the phenomenal self" (Combs & Snygg, 1959, p. 131). "What a person thinks and how he behaves are largely determined by the concepts he holds about himself and his abilities" (Combs & Snygg,

1959, p. 122). Combs and Snygg (1959, pp. 126-127) distinguish between the phenomenal self and the self-concept, the latter being
defined as "those perceptions about self which seem most vital or
important to the individual himself." However, the difficulty of
defining and applying criteria to make this differentiation would
seem to give it little usefulness. It is no doubt true that some perceptions about the self are more central and vital than others, but it is
doubtful that there is any dividing line that can be drawn between
these and other less vital self-perceptions. We shall therefore make no
distinction between the phenomenal self and the self-concept.

Since the self-concept is the crucial point about which the phenomenal field is organized, its importance in understanding the field
and making inferences about it for predictive purposes is apparent.
The centrality of the self in phenomenological psychology is indicated in the postulate that the single motive for behavior is the
preservation and enhancement of the phenomenal self.

8. We have indicated that since perceptions, particularly the perceptions of the self, determine behavior, in order to change behavior
we must first change perceptions. What are the conditions under
which perceptions change? *Essentially, perceptions change under
those conditions that have relevance to the basic need for the preservation and enhancement of the self.* Conditions that are not relevant
to this need are not perceived. It appears then, that the first condition for perceptual change is an experience which is relevant to the
self or self-concept. But if the experience, even though relevant, is
consistent with or reinforces the self-concept, it seems clear that
change is not likely to occur. To lead to change, the experience must
be inconsistent with the existing self-perception, raise a question, or
pose a problem. Since the existing self-concept is the object of the
need for preservation, it is apparent that it is resistant to change, and
that experiences that are inconsistent with the self-concept may not
enter into or become the figure in the perceptual field. The so-called
mechanisms of defense, the misinterpretation of stimuli or experiences, the failure to perceive which is represented by tunnel vision,
and the denial of the experience are ways in which the self resists
perceiving experiences that are inconsistent with the self-concept. It
would thus appear that the less important or more peripheral aspects
of the self will change more readily than the central core.

This reaction of the organism to preserve its perceptual field, particularly the phenomenal self, is the characteristic reaction to threat.

It would seem to be apparent, then, that an individual under threat does not easily change his perceptions, but instead becomes resistant to change. Stimuli or experiences that are perceived as threatening, tend to be relegated to the ground rather than being focused upon a figure. Now this does not mean that threat does not change behavior —it is obvious that threat results in withdrawal, resistance, aggression, or other kinds of obstructing behavior. It may also result in acquiescence, submission, etc. These are all the result of changes in perception of the individual, and the recognition of the threat, leading to attempts to cope with it by capitulation if this is felt to be necessary or desirable for the preservation or enhancement of the self. Thus, behavior, and perceptions, can be influenced and changed by threat, or by other forms of manipulation. The question is raised as to whether this is desirable, from an ethical and moral standpoint, and whether, even though the goal of the manipulator is claimed to be for the good of the person manipulated or influenced, whether the ends justify the means, or even whether the ends are acceptable under any circumstances, since they are imposed from the outside and thus deny the individual freedom of choice and independence of action. Thus, if voluntary changes of behavior are desired, behavior which is responsible and independent, it would appear that threat should be avoided. Combs and Snygg (1959, pp. 163-196) suggest that ". . . other things being equal, change in the self is most likely to occur in situations which do not force the individual to self defense."

It appears, then, that for the phenomenal field to change, there must be a clear experience that is relevant to but inconsistent with the existing field, yet not highly threatening to the self.

In Summary

This paper has attempted to present the nature of phenomenological psychology. While this approach to human behavior begins with a common sense level, it goes beyond this to an analysis of the nature and conditions of behavior and its changes. The central nature of perception in behavior leads to the study of perception in all its aspects, including the perception of the self as the point about which the phenomenal field is organized.

There is evidence that psychology is turning to the study of experience, and to the phenomenological method. Koch, the editor of the monumental *Psychology: A Study of Science,* indicates the trend as follows: "Behavioral epistemology is under stress; behaviorism is on the defensive, while neobehaviorism enfolds itself in a womb of its own manufacture. There is a strongly increased interest in perception and central process even on the part of the S-R theorists; in fact a tendency for the central area of psychological interest to shift from learning to perception. There is a marked, if as yet unfocused, disposition on the part of *even* fundamental psychologists to readdress human phenomena and to readmit questions having experiential reference" (Koch, 1961). In other words, psychology is becoming psychological, and is returning to a study of experience in its psychological aspects, after a half century of wandering in search of the objectivity of physics on the one hand, and the subjectivity of depth psychology on the other. From the extremes of the empty organism of the behaviorists and the organism seething with unconscious desires and motives of the depth psychologists, we are striking the happy medium of the experiencing organism interacting with and being shaped by and shaping its environment. This approach promises to lead to a fruitful era in the understanding of human behavior.

References

Bakan, D. A reconsideration of the problem of introspection. *Psychol. Bull.*, 1954, *51*, 105-118.

Boring, E. G. A history of introspection. *Psychol. Bull.*, 1953, *50*, 169-189.

Combs, A. W. A phenomenological approach to adjustment theory. *J. Abnorm. Soc. Psychol.*, 1949, *44*, 29-35.

Combs, A. W., & Snygg, D. *Individual behavior.* Rev. ed. New York: Harper, 1959.

English, H. B., & English, Ava C. *A comprehensive dictionary of psychological and psychoanalytical terms.* New York: Longmans, Green, 1958.

Gibson, J. J. Theories of perception. (In Dennis, W. (Ed.), *Current trends in psychological theory.* Pittsburgh: Univ. of Pittsburgh Press, 1951.)

Gombrich, E. H. *Art and illusion. A study in the psychology of pictorial representation.* New York: Pantheon Books, 1960.

Hanson, N. R. *Patterns of discovery: an inquiry into the conceptual foundations of science.* New York: Cambridge Univ. Press, 1958.

Ittelson, W. H. *The Ames demonstrations in perception.* Princeton, N.J.: Princeton Univ. Press, 1952.

Jessor, R. Phenomenological personality theories and the data language of psychology. *Psychol. Rev.*, 1956, *63*, 173-180. (In Kuenzli, A. E. (Ed.), *The phenomenological problem.* New York: Harper, 1959, pp. 280-294.)

Jessor, R. Issues in the phenomenological approach to personality. *J. Indiv. Psychol.*, 1961, *17*, 28-38.

Koch, S. Psychological science versus the science-humanism antinomy: intimations of a significant science of man. *Amer. Psychologist*, 1961, *16*, 629-639.

Koehler, W. *The mentality of apes.* London: Kegan Paul, Trench, Trubner & Co., 1931.

Koester, G. A. A study of the diagnostic process. *Educ. Psychol. Measmt.*, 1954, 473-486.

Kuenzli, A. E. (Ed.) *The phenomenological problem.* New York: Harper, 1959.

Landsman, T. Four phenomenologies. *J. Indiv. Psychol.*, 1958, *14*, 29-37.

Lewin, K. Defining the "field at a given time." *Psychol. Rev.*, 1943, *50*, 292-310.

MacLeod, R. B. The phenomenological approach to social psychology. *Psychol. Rev.*, 1947, *54*, 193-210. (In Kuenzli, A. E. (Ed.), *The phenomenological problem.* New York: Harper, 1959, pp. 149-181.)

McArthur, C. Analyzing the clinical process. *J. Counsel. Psychol.*, 1954, *1*, 203-208.

Murphy, G., Murphy, Lois B., & Newcomb, T. M. *Experimental social psychology.* Rev. ed. New York: Harper, 1957.

Parker, C. A. As a clinician thinks . . . *J. Counsel. Psychol.*, 1958, *5*, 253-261.

Patterson, C. H. *Counseling and psychotherapy: theory and practice.* New York: Harper, 1959.

Patterson, C. H. The self in recent Rogerian theory. *J. Indiv. Psychol.*, 1961, *17*, 5-11.

Pepinsky, H. B., & Pepinsky, Pauline. *Counseling: theory and practice.* New York: Ronald, 1954.

Phillips, E. L. *Psychotherapy: a modern theory and practice.* Englewood Cliffs, N.J.: Prentice-Hall, 1956.

Smith, M. B. The phenomenological approach in personality theory: some critical remarks. *J. Abnorm. Soc. Psychol.*, 1950, *45*, 510-522. (In Kuenzli, A. E. (Ed.), *The phenomenological problem.* New York: Harper, 1959, pp. 253-267.)

Snygg, D. The need for a phenomenological system of psychology. *Psychol. Rev.*, 1941, *48*, 404-424. (In Kuenzli, A. E. (Ed.), *The phenomenological problem.* New York: Harper, 1959, pp. 3-30.)

Snygg, D. Review of Kilpatrick, F. P. (Ed.) Explorations in transactional psychology. *J. Indiv. Psychol.*, 1961, *17*, 230.

Snygg, D., & Combs, A. W. The phenomenological approach and the problem of "unconscious" behavior: a reply to Dr. Smith. *J. Abnorm. Soc. Psychol.*, 1950, *45*, 523-528. (In Kuenzli, A. E. (Ed.), *The phenomenological problem.* New York: Harper, 1959, pp. 268-279.)

Soskin, W. F. Influence of four types of data on diagnostic conceptualizations in psychological testing. *J. Abnorm. Soc. Psychol.*, 1959, *38*, 69-78.

Spiegelberg, H. *The phenomenological movement: a historical introduction.* 2 vols. The Hague: Martimus Nijhoff, 1960.

Tolman, E. C. Determiners of behavior at a choice point. *Psychol. Rev.*, 1938, *57*, 243-259.

Wylie, Ruth C. *The self concept: a critical survey of pertinent research literature.* Lincoln: Univ. Nebraska Press, 1961.

CARL R. ROGERS

The Characteristics of
a Helping Relationship

My interest in psychotherapy has brought about in me an interest in every kind of helping relationship. By this term I mean a relationship in which at least one of the parties has the intent of promoting the growth, development, maturity, improved functioning, improved coping with life of the other. The other, in this sense, may be one individual or a group. To put it in another way, a helping relationship might be defined as one in which one of the participants intends that there should come about, in one or both parties, more appreciation of, more expression of, more functional use of the latent inner resources of the individual.

Now it is obvious that such a definition covers a wide range of relationships which usually are intended to facilitate growth. It would certainly include the relationship between mother and child, father and child. It would include the relationship between the physician and his patient. The relationship between teacher and pupil would often come under this definition, though some teachers would not have the promotion of growth as their intent. It includes almost all counselor-client relationships, whether we are speaking of educa-

Rogers, C. R. The characteristics of a helping relationship. *The Personnel and Guidance Journal,* 1958, 37(1), 6-16. Copyright 1958 American Personnel and Guidance Association. Reprinted with permission.

tional counseling, vocational counseling, or personal counseling. In this last-mentioned area it would include the wide range of relationships between the psychotherapist and the hospitalized psychotic, the therapist and the troubled or neurotic individual, and the relationship between the therapist and the increasing number of so-called "normal" individuals who enter therapy to improve their own functioning or accelerate their personal growth.

These are largely one-to-one relationships. But we should also think of the large number of individual-group interactions which are intended as helping relationships. Some administrators intend that their relationship to their staff groups shall be of the sort which promotes growth, though other administrators would not have this purpose. The interaction between the group therapy leader and his group belongs here. So does the relationship of the community consultant to a community group. Increasingly the interaction between the industrial consultant and a management group is intended as a helping relationship. Perhaps this listing will point up the fact that a great many of the relationships in which we and others are involved fall within this category of interactions in which there is the purpose of promoting development and more mature and adequate functioning.

The Question

But what are the characteristics of those relationships which *do* help, which do facilitate growth? And at the other end of the scale is it possible to discern those characteristics which make a relationship unhelpful, even though it was the sincere intent to promote growth and development? It is to these questions, particularly the first, that I would like to take you with me over some of the paths I have explored, and to tell you where I am, as of now, in my thinking on these issues.

The Answers Given by Research

It is natural to ask first of all whether there is any empirical research which would give us an objective answer to these questions. There has not been a large amount of research in this area as yet, but what there is is stimulating and suggestive. I cannot report all of it but I would like to make a somewhat extensive sampling of the studies which have been done and state very briefly some of the findings. In so doing, over-simplification is necessary, and I am quite aware that I am not doing full justice to the researches I am mentioning, but it may give you the feeling that factual advances are being made and pique your curiosity enough to examine the studies themselves, if you have not already done so.

Studies of Attitudes

Most of the studies throw light on the attitudes on the part of the helping person which make a relationship growth-promoting or growth-inhibiting. Let us look at some of these.

A careful study of parent-child relationships made some years ago by Baldwin and others [1] at the Fels Institute contains interesting evidence. Of the various clusters of parental attitudes toward children, the "acceptant-democratic" seemed most growth-facilitating. Children of these parents with their warm and equalitarian attitudes showed an accelerated intellectual development (an increasing IQ), more originality, more emotional security and control, less excitability than children from other types of homes. Though somewhat slow initially in social development, they were, by the time they reached school age, popular, friendly, non-aggressive leaders.

Where parents' attitudes are classed as "actively rejectant" the children show a slightly decelerated intellectual development, relatively poor use of the abilities they do possess, and some lack of originality. They are emotionally unstable, rebellious, aggressive, and quarrelsome. The children of parents with other attitude syndromes tend in various respects to fall in between these extremes.

I am sure that these findings do not surprise us as related to child development. I would like to suggest that they probably apply to other relationships as well, and that the counselor or physician or administrator who is warmly emotional and expressive, respectful of the individuality of himself and of the other, and who exhibits a nonpossessive caring, probably facilitates self-realization much as does a parent with these attitudes.

Let me turn to another careful study in a very different area. Whitehorn and Betz [2, 18] investigated the degree of success achieved by young resident physicians in working with schizophrenic patients on a psychiatric ward. They chose for special study the seven who had been outstandingly helpful, and seven whose patients had shown the least degree of improvement. Each group had treated about 50 patients. The investigators examined all the available evidence to discover in what ways the A group (the successful group) differed from the B group. Several significant differences were found. The physicians in the A group tended to see the schizophrenic in terms of the personal meaning which various behaviors had to the patient, rather than seeing him as a case history or a descriptive diagnosis. They also tended to work toward goals which were oriented to the personality of the patient, rather than such goals as reducing the symptoms or curing the disease. It was found that the helpful physicians, in their day by day interaction, primarily made use of active personal participation—a person-to-person relationship. They made less use of procedures which could be classed as "passive permissive." They were even less likely to use such procedures as interpretation, instruction or advice, or emphasis upon the practical care of the patient. Finally, they were much more likely than the B group to develop a relationship in which the patient felt trust and confidence in the physician.

Although the authors cautiously emphasize that these findings relate only to the treatment of schizophrenics, I am inclined to disagree. I suspect that similar facts would be found in a research study of almost any class of helping relationship.

Another interesting study focuses upon the way in which the person being helped perceives the relationship. Heine [11] studied individuals who had gone for psychotherapeutic help to psychoanalytic, client-centered, and Adlerian therapists. Regardless of the type of therapy, these clients report similar changes in themselves. But it is their perception of the relationship which is of particular interest to us here. When asked what accounted for the changes which had occurred, they expressed some differing explanations, depending on the orientation of the therapist. But their agreement on the major elements they had found helpful was even more significant. They indicated that these attitudinal elements in the relationship accounted for the changes which had taken place in themselves: the trust they had felt in the therapist; being understood by the therapist; the feeling of independence they had had in making choices and decisions. The therapist procedure which they had found most helpful was that the therapist clarified and openly stated feelings which the client had been approaching hazily and hesitantly.

There was also a high degree of agreement among these clients, regardless of the orientation of their therapists, as to what elements had been unhelpful in the relationship. Such therapist attitudes as lack of interest, remoteness or distance, and an over-degree of sympathy, were perceived as unhelpful. As to procèdures, they had found it unhelpful when therapists had given direct specific advice regarding decisions or had emphasized past history rather than present problems. Guiding suggestions mildly given were perceived in an intermediate range—neither clearly helpful nor unhelpful.

Fiedler, in a much quoted study [7], found that expert therapists of differing orientations formed similar relationships with their clients. Less well known are the elements which characterized these relationships, differentiating them from the relationships formed by less expert therapists. These elements are: an ability to understand the client's meanings and feelings; a sensitivity to the client's attitudes; a warm interest without any emotional over-involvement.

A study by Quinn [15] throws light on what is involved in understanding the client's meanings and feelings. His study is surprising in that it shows that "understanding" of the client's meanings is essentially an attitude of *desiring* to understand. Quinn presented his judges only with recorded therapist statements taken from interviews. The raters had no knowledge of what the therapist was responding to or how the client reacted to his response. Yet it was found that the degree of understanding could be judged about as well from this material as from listening to the response in context. This seems rather conclusive evidence that it is an attitude of wanting to understand which is communicated.

As to the emotional quality of the relationship, Seeman [16] found that success in psychotherapy is closely associated with a strong and growing mutual liking and respect between client and therapist.

An interesting study by Dittes [4] indicates how delicate this relationship is. Using a physiological measure, the psychogalvanic reflex, to measure the anxious or threatened or alerted reactions of the client, Dittes correlated the deviations on this measure with judge's ratings of the degree of warm acceptance and permissiveness on the part of the therapist. It was found that whenever the therapist's attitudes changed even slightly in the direction of a lesser degree of acceptance, the number of abrupt GSR deviations significantly increased. Evidently when the relationship is experienced as less acceptant the organism organizes against threat, even at the physiological level.

Without trying fully to integrate the findings from these various studies, it can at least be noted that a few things stand out. One is the fact that it is the attitudes and feelings of the therapist, rather than his theoretical orientation, which is important. His procedures and techniques are less important than his attitudes. It is also worth noting that it is the way in which his attitudes and procedures are *perceived* which makes a difference to the client, and that it is this perception which is crucial.

"Manufactured" Relationships

Let me turn to research of a very different sort, some of which you may find rather abhorrent, but which nevertheless has a bearing upon the nature of a facilitating relationship. These studies have to do with what we might think of as manufactured relationships.

Verplanck [17], Greenspoon [8] and others have shown that operant conditioning of verbal behavior is possible in a relationship. Very briefly, if the experimenter says "Mhm," or "Good," or nods his head after certain types of words or statements, those classes of words tend to increase because of being reinforced. It has been shown that using such procedures one can bring about increases in such diverse verbal categories as plural nouns, hostile words, statements of opinion. The person is completely unaware that he is being influenced in any way by these reinforcers. The implication is that by such selective reinforcement we could bring it about that the other person in the relationship would be using whatever kinds of words and making whatever kinds of statements we had decided to reinforce.

Following still further the principles of operant conditioning as developed by Skinner and his group, Lindsley [12] has shown that a chronic schizophrenic can be placed in a "helping relationship" with a machine. The machine, somewhat like a vending machine, can be set to reward a variety of types of behaviors. Initially it simply rewards—with candy, a cigarette, or the display of a picture—the lever-pressing behavior of the patient. But it is possible to set it so that many pulls on the lever may supply a hungry kitten—visible in a separate enclosure—with a drop of milk. In this case the satisfaction is an altruistic one. Plans are being developed to reward similar social or altruistic behavior directed toward another patient, placed in the next room. The only limit to the kinds of behavior which might be rewarded lies in the degree of mechanical ingenuity of the experimenter.

Lindsley reports that in some patients there has been marked clinical improvement. Personally I cannot help but be impressed by the description of one patient who had gone from a deteriorated chronic state to being given free grounds privileges, this change being quite clearly associated with his interaction with the machine. Then the experimenter decided to study experimental extinction, which, put in more personal terms, means that no matter how many thousands of times the lever was pressed, no reward of any kind was forthcoming. The patient gradually regressed, grew untidy, uncommunicative, and his grounds privilege had to be revoked. This (to me) pathetic incident would seem to indicate that even in a relationship to a machine, trustworthiness is important if the relationship is to be helpful.

Still another interesting study of a manufactured relationship is being carried on by Harlow and his associates [10], this time with monkeys. Infant monkeys, removed from their mothers almost immediately after birth, are, in one phase of the experiment, presented with two objects. One might be termed the "hard mother," a sloping cylinder of wire netting with a nipple from which the baby may feed. The other is a "soft mother," a similar cylinder made of foam rubber and terry cloth. Even when an infant gets all his food from the "hard mother" he clearly and increasingly prefers the "soft mother." Motion pictures show that he definitely "relates" to this object, playing with it, enjoying it, finding security in clinging to it when strange objects are near, and using that security as a home base for venturing into the frightening world. Of the many interesting and challenging implications of this study, one seems reasonably clear. It is that no amount of direct food reward can take the place of certain perceived qualities which the infant appears to need and desire.

Two Recent Studies

Let me close this wide-ranging—and perhaps perplexing—sampling of research studies with an account of two very recent investigations. The first is an experiment conducted by Ends and Page [5]. Working with hardened chronic hospitalized alcoholics who had been committed to a state hospital for 60 days, they tried three different methods of group psychotherapy. The method which they believed would be most effective was therapy based on a two-factor theory of learning; a client-centered approach was expected to be second; a psychoanalytically oriented approach was expected to be least efficient. Their results showed that the therapy based upon a learning theory approach was not only not helpful, but was somewhat deleterious. The outcomes were worse than those in the control group which had no therapy. The analytically oriented therapy produced some positive gain, and the client-centered group therapy was associated with the greatest amount of positive change. Follow-up data, extending over one and one-half years, confirmed the in-hospital findings, with the lasting improvement being greatest in the client-centered approach, next in the analytic, next the control group, and least in those handled by a learning theory approach.

As I have puzzled over this study, unusual in that the approach to which the authors were committed proved *least* effective, I find a clue, I believe, in the description of the therapy based on learning theory [13]. Essentially it consisted (1) of pointing out and labelling the behaviors which had proved unsatisfying, (2) of exploring objectively with the client the reasons behind these behaviors, and (3) of establishing through re-education more effective problem-solving habits. But in all of this interaction the aim, as they formulated it, was to be impersonal. The therapist "permits as little of his own personality to intrude as is humanly possible." The "therapist stresses personal anonymity in his activities, i.e., he must studiously avoid impressing the patient with his own (therapist's) individual personality characteristics." To me this seems the most likely clue to the failure of this approach, as I try to interpret the facts in the light of the other research studies. To withhold one's self as a person and to deal with the other person as an object does not have a high probability of being helpful.

The final study I wish to report is one just being completed by Halkides [9]. She started from a theoretical formulation of mine regarding the necessary and sufficient conditions for therapeutic change [14]. She hypothesized that there would be a significant relationship between the extent of constructive personality change in the client and four counselor variables: (1) the degree of empathic understanding of the client manifested by the counselor; (2) the degree of positive affective attitude (unconditional positive regard) manifested by the counselor toward the client; (3) the extent to which the counselor is genuine, his words matching his own internal feeling; and (4) the extent to which the counselor's response matches the client's expression in the intensity of affective expression.

To investigate these hypotheses she first selected, by multiple objective criteria, a group of 10 cases which could be classed as "most successful" and a group of 10 "least successful" cases. She then took an early and late recorded interview from each of these cases. On a random basis she picked nine client-counselor interaction units—a client statement and a counselor response—from each of these interviews. She thus had nine early interactions and nine late interactions from each case. This gave her several hundred units which were now placed in random order. The units from an early interview of an unsuccessful case might be followed by the units from a late interview of a successful case, etc.

Three judges, who did not know the cases or their degree of success, or the source of any given unit, now listened to this material four different times. They rated each unit on a seven point scale, first as to the degree of empathy, second as to the counselor's positive attitude toward the client, third as to the counselor's congruence or genuineness, and fourth as to the degree to which the counselor's response matched the emotional intensity of the client's expression.

I think all of us who knew of the study regarded it as a very bold venture. Could judges listening to single units of interaction possibly make any reliable rating of such subtle qualities as I have mentioned? And even if suitable reliability could be obtained, could 18 counselor-client interchanges from each case—a minute sampling of the hundreds or thousands of such interchanges which occurred in each case—possibly bear any relationship to the therapeutic outcome? The chance seemed slim.

The findings are surprising. It proved possible to achieve high reliability between the judges, most of the inter-judge correlations being in the 0.80's or 0.90's, except on the last variable. It was found that a high degree of empathic understanding was significantly associated, at a 0.001 level, with the more successful cases. A high degree of unconditional positive regard was likewise associated with the more successful cases, at the 0.001 level. Even the rating of the counselor's genuineness or congruence—the extent to which his words matched his feelings—was associated with the successful outcome of the case, and again at the 0.001 level of significance. Only in the investigation of the matching intensity of affective expression were the results equivocal.

It is of interest too that high ratings of these variables were not associated more significantly with units from later interviews than with units from early interviews. This means that the counselor's attitudes were quite constant throughout the interviews. If he was highly empathic, he tended to be so from first to last. If he was lacking in genuineness, this tended to be true of both early and late interviews.

As with any study, this investigation has its limitations. It is concerned with a certain type of helping relationship, psychotherapy. It investigated only four variables thought to be significant. Perhaps there are many others. Nevertheless it represents a significant advance in the study of helping relationships. Let me try to state the findings in the simplest possible fashion. It seems to indicate that the quality of the counselor's interaction with a client can be satisfactorily judged on the basis of a very small sampling of his behavior. It also means that if the counselor is congruent or transparent, so that his words are in line with his feelings rather than the two being discrepant—if the counselor likes the client, unconditionally, and if the counselor understands the essential feelings of the client as they seem to the client—then there is a strong probability that this will be an effective helping relationship.

Some Comments

These then are some of the studies which throw at least a measure of light on the nature of the helping relationship. They have investigated different facets of the problem. They have approached it from very different theoretical contexts. They have used different methods. They are not directly comparable. Yet they seem to me to point to several statements which may be made with some assurance. It seems clear that relationships which are helpful have different characteristics from relationships which are unhelpful. These differential characteristics have to do primarily with the attitudes of the helping person on the one hand and with the perception of the relationship by the "helpee" on the other. It is equally clear that the studies thus far made do not give us any final answers as to what is a helping relationship, nor how it is to be formed.

How Can I Create a Helping Relationship?

I believe each of us working in the field of human relationships has a similar problem in knowing how to use such research knowledge. We cannot slavishly follow such findings in a mechanical way or we destroy the personal qualities which these very studies show to be valuable. It seems to me that we have to use these studies, testing them against our own experience and forming new and further personal hypotheses to use and test in our own further personal relationships.

So rather than try to tell you how you should use the findings I have presented I should like to tell you the kind of questions which these studies and my own clinical experience raise for me, and some of the tentative and changing hypotheses which guide my behavior as I enter into what I hope may be helping relationships, whether with students, staff, family, or clients. Let me list a number of these questions and considerations.

1. Can I *be* in some way which will be perceived by the other person as trustworthy, as dependable or consistent in some deep sense? Both research and experience indicate that this is very important, and over the years I have found what I believe are deeper and better ways of answering this question. I used to feel that if I fulfilled all the outer conditions of trustworthiness—keeping appointments, respecting the confidential nature of the interviews, etc.—and if I acted consistently the same during the interviews, then this condition would be fulfilled. But experience drove home the fact that to act consistently acceptant, for example, if in fact I was feeling annoyed or skeptical or some other non-acceptant feeling, was certain in the long run to be perceived as inconsistent or untrustworthy. I have come to recognize that being trustworthy does not demand that I be rigidly consistent but that I be dependably real. The term congruent is one I have used to describe the way I would like to be. By this I mean that whatever feeling or attitude I am experiencing would be matched by my awareness of that attitude. When this is true, then I am a unified or integrated person in that moment, and hence I can *be* whatever I deeply *am*. This is a reality which I find others experience as dependable.

2. A very closely related question is this: Can I be expressive enough as a person that what I am will be communicated unambiguously? I believe that most of my failures to achieve a helping relationship can be traced to unsatisfactory answers to these two questions. When I am experiencing an attitude of annoyance toward another person but am unaware of it, then my communication contains contradictory messages. My words are giving one message, but I am also in subtle ways communicating the annoyance I feel and this

confuses the other person and makes him distrustful, though he too may be unaware of what is causing the difficulty. When as a parent or a therapist or a teacher or an administrator I fail to listen to what is going on in me, fail because of my own defensiveness to sense my own feelings, then this kind of failure seems to result. It has made it seem to me that the most basic learning for anyone who hopes to establish any kind of helping relationship is that it is safe to be transparently real. If in a given relationship I am reasonably congruent, if no feelings relevant to the relationship are hidden either to me or the other person, then I can be almost sure that the relationship will be a helpful one.

One way of putting this which may seem strange to you is that if I can form a helping relationship to myself—if I can be sensitively aware of and acceptant toward my own feelings—then the likelihood is great that I can form a helping relationship toward another.

Now, acceptantly to be what I am, in this sense, and to permit this to show through to the other person, is the most difficult task I know and one I never fully achieve. But to realize that this *is* my task has been most rewarding because it has helped me to find what has gone wrong with interpersonal relationships which have become snarled and to put them on a constructive track again. It has meant that if I am to facilitate the personal growth of others in relation to me, then I must grow, and while this is often painful it is also enriching.

3. A third question is: Can I let myself experience positive attitudes toward this other person—attitudes of warmth, caring, liking, interest, respect? It is not easy. I find in myself, and feel that I often see in others, a certain amount of fear of these feelings. We are afraid that if we let ourselves freely experience these positive feelings toward another we may be trapped by them. They may lead to demands on us or we may be disappointed in our trust, and these outcomes we fear. So as a reaction we tend to build up distance between ourselves and others—aloofness, a "professional" attitude, an impersonal relationship.

I feel quite strongly that one of the important reasons for the professionalization of every field is that it helps to keep this distance. In the clinical areas we develop elaborate diagnostic formulations, seeing the person as an object. In teaching and in administration we develop all kinds of evaluative procedures, so that again the person is perceived as an object. In these ways, I believe, we can keep ourselves from experiencing the caring which would exist if we recognized the relationship as one between two persons. It is a real achievement when we can learn, even in certain relationships or at certain times in those relationships, that it is safe to care, that it is safe to relate to the other as a person for whom we have positive feelings.

4. Another question the importance of which I have learned in my own experience is: Can I be strong enough as a person to be separate from the other? Can I be a sturdy respecter of my own feelings, my own needs, as well as his? Can I own and, if need be, express my own feelings as something belonging to me and separate from his feelings? Am I strong enough in my own separateness that I will not be downcast by his depression, frightened by his fear, nor engulfed by his dependency? Is my inner self hardy enough to realize that I am not destroyed by his anger, taken over by his need for dependence, nor enslaved by his love, but that I exist separate from him with feelings and rights of my own? When I can freely feel this strength of being a separate person, then I find that I can let myself go much more deeply in understanding and accepting him because I am not fearful of losing myself.

5. The next question is closely related. Am I secure enough within myself to permit him his separateness? Can I permit him to be what he is—honest or deceitful, infantile or adult, despairing or over-confident? Can I give him the freedom to be? Or do I feel that he should follow my advice, or remain somewhat dependent on me, or mold himself after me? In this connection I think of the interesting small study by Farson [6] which found that the less well adjusted and less competent counselor tends to induce conformity to himself, to have clients who model themselves after him. On the other hand, the better adjusted and more competent counselor can interact with a client through many interviews without interfering with the freedom of the client to develop a personality quite separate from that of his therapist. I should prefer to be in this latter class, whether as parent or supervisor or counselor.

6. Another question I ask myself is: Can I let myself enter fully into the world of his feelings and personal meanings and see these as he does? Can I step into his private world so completely that I lose all desire to evaluate or judge it? Can I enter it so sensitively that I can move about in it freely, without tramping on meanings which are precious to him? Can I sense it so accurately that I can catch not only the meanings of his experience which are obvious to him, but

those meanings which are only implicit, which he sees only dimly or as confusion? Can I extend this understanding without limit? I think of the client who said, "Whenever I find someone who understands a *part* of me at the time, then it never fails that a point is reached where I know they're *not* understanding me again. . . . What I've looked for so hard is for someone to understand."

For myself I find it easier to feel this kind of understanding, and to communicate it, to individual clients than to students in a class or staff members in a group in which I am involved. There is a strong temptation to set students "straight," or to point out to a staff member the errors in his thinking. Yet when I can permit myself to understand in these situations, it is mutually rewarding. And with clients in therapy, I am often impressed with the fact that even a minimal amount of empathic understanding—a bumbling and faulty attempt to catch the confused complexity of the client's meaning—is helpful, though there is no doubt that it is most helpful when I can see and formulate clearly the meanings in his experiencing which for him have been unclear and tangled.

7. Still another issue is whether I can be acceptant of each facet of this other person which he presents to me. Can I receive him as he is? Can I communicate this attitude? Or can I only receive him conditionally, acceptant of some aspects of his feelings and silently or openly disapproving of other aspects? It has been my experience that when my attitude is conditional, then he cannot change or grow in those respects in which I cannot fully receive him. And when—afterward and sometimes too late—I try to discover why I have been unable to accept him in every respect, I usually discover that it is because I have been frightened or threatened in myself by some aspect of his feelings. If I am to be more helpful, then I must myself grow and accept myself in these respects.

8. A very practical issue is raised by the question: Can I act with sufficient sensitivity in the relationship that my behavior will not be perceived as a threat? The work we are beginning to do in studying the physiological concomitants of psychotherapy confirms the research by Dittes in indicating how easily individuals are threatened at a physiological level. The psychogalvanic reflex—the measure of skin conductance—takes a sharp dip when the therapist responds with some word which is just a little stronger than the client's feelings. And to a phrase such as, "My, you *do* look upset," the needle swings almost off the paper. My desire to avoid even such minor threats is

not due to a hypersensitivity about my client. It is simply due to the conviction based on experience that if I can free him as completely as possible from external threat, then he can begin to experience and to deal with the internal feelings and conflicts which he finds threatening within himself.

9. A specific aspect of the preceding question but an important one is: Can I free him from the threat of external evaluation? In almost every phase of our lives—at home, at school, at work—we find ourselves under the rewards and punishments of external judgments. "That's good"; "that's naughty." "That's worth an A"; "that's a failure." "That's good counseling"; "that's poor counseling." Such judgments are a part of our lives from infancy to old age. I believe they have a certain social usefulness to institutions and organizations such as schools and professions. Like everyone else I find myself all too often making such evaluations. But, in my experience, they do not make for personal growth and hence I do not believe that they are a part of a helping relationship. Curiously enough a positive evaluation is as threatening in the long run as a negative one, since to inform someone that he is good implies that you also have the right to tell him he is bad. So I have come to feel that the more I can keep a relationship free of judgment and evaluation, the more this will permit the other person to reach the point where he recognizes that the locus of evaluation, the center of responsibility, lies within himself. The meaning and value of his experience is in the last analysis something which is up to him, and no amount of external judgment can alter this. So I should like to work toward a relationship in which I am not, even in my own feelings, evaluating him. This I believe can set him free to be a self-responsible person.

10. One last question: Can I meet this other individual as a person who is in process of *becoming,* or will I be bound by his past and by my past? If, in my encounter with him, I am dealing with him as an immature child, an ignorant student, a neurotic personality, or a psychopath, each of these concepts of mine limits what he can be in the relationship. Martin Buber, the existentialist philosopher of the University of Jerusalem, has a phrase, "confirming the other," which has had meaning for me. He says "Confirming means . . . accepting the whole potentiality of the other . . . . I can recognize in him, know in him, the person he has been . . . *created* to become . . . . I confirm him in myself, and then in him, in relation to this potentiality that . . . can now be developed, can evolve" [3]. If I accept the

other person as something fixed, already diagnosed and classified, already shaped by his past, then I am doing my part to confirm this limited hypothesis. If I accept him as a process of becoming, then I am doing what I can to confirm or make real his potentialities.

It is at this point that I see Verplanck, Lindsley, and Skinner, working in operant conditioning, coming together with Buber, the philosopher or mystic. At least they come together in principle, in an odd way. If I see a relationship as only an opportunity to reinforce certain types of words or opinions in the other, then I tend to confirm him as an object—a basically mechanical, manipulable object. And if I see this as his potentiality, he tends to act in ways which support this hypothesis. If, on the other hand, I see a relationship as an opportunity to "reinforce" *all* that he is, the person that he is with all his existent potentialities, then he tends to act in ways which support *this* hypothesis. I have then—to use Buber's term—confirmed him as a living person, capable of creative inner development. Personally I prefer this second type of hypothesis.

Conclusion

In the early portion of this paper I reviewed some of the contributions which research is making to our knowledge *about* relationships. Endeavoring to keep that knowledge in mind I then took up the kind of questions which arise from an inner and subjective point of view as I enter, as a person, into relationships. If I could, in myself, answer all the questions I have raised in the affirmative, then I believe that any relationships in which I was involved would be helping relationships, would involve growth. But I cannot give a positive answer to most of these questions. I can only work in the direction of a positive answer.

This has raised in my mind the strong suspicion that the optimal helping relationship is the kind of relationship created by a person who is psychologically mature. Or to put it in another way, the degree to which I can create relationships which facilitate the growth of others as separate persons is a measure of the growth I have achieved in myself. In some respects this is a disturbing thought, but it is also a promising or challenging one. It would indicate that if I am interested in creating helping relationships I have a fascinating life-time job ahead of me, stretching and developing my potentialities in the direction of growth.

I am left with the uncomfortable thought that what I have been working out for myself in this paper may have little relationship to your interests and your work. If so, I regret it. But I am at least partially comforted by the fact that all of us who are working in the field of human relationships and trying to understand the basic orderliness of that field are engaged in the most crucial enterprise in today's world. If we are thoughtfully trying to understand our tasks as administrators, teachers, educational counselors, vocational counselors, therapists, then we are working on the problem which will determine the future of this planet. For it is not upon the physical sciences that the future will depend. It is upon us who are trying to understand and deal with the interactions between human beings— who are trying to create helping relationships. So I hope that the questions I ask of myself will be of some use to you in gaining understanding and perspective as you endeavor, in your way, to facilitate growth in your relationships.

References

1. Baldwin, A. L., Kalhorn, J., & Breese, F. H. Patterns of parent behavior. *Psychol. Monogr.*, 1945, *58*, No. 268, 1-75.
2. Betz, B. J., & Whitehorn, J. C. The relationship of the therapist to the outcome of therapy in schizophrenia. *Psychiat. Research Reports #5. Research techniques in schizophrenia.* Washington, D.C.: American Psychiatric Association, 1956, 89-117.
3. Buber, M., & Rogers, C. Transcription of dialogue held April 18, 1957, Ann Arbor, Mich. Unpublished manuscript.
4. Dittes, J. E. Galvanic skin response as a measure of patient's reaction to therapist's permissiveness. *J. Abnorm. Soc. Psychol.*, 1957, *55*, 295-303.
5. Ends, E. J., & Page, C. W. A study of three types of group psychotherapy with hospitalized male inebriates. *Quar. J. Stud. Alcohol,* 1957, *18*, 263-277.
6. Farson, R. E. Introjection in the psychotherapeutic relationship. Unpublished doctoral dissertation, University of Chicago, 1955.
7. Fiedler, F. E. Quantitative studies on the role of therapists' feelings toward their patients. In Mowrer, O. H. (Ed.), *Psychotherapy: theory and research.* New York: Ronald Press, 1953, Chap. 12.
8. Greenspoon, J. The reinforcing effect of two spoken sounds on the frequency of two responses. *Amer. J. Psychol.*, 1955, *68*, 409-416.
9. Halkides, G. An experimental study of four conditions necessary for therapeutic change. Unpublished doctoral dissertation, University of Chicago, 1958.
10. Harlow, H., & Associates. Experiment in progress, as reported by Robert Zimmerman.

11. Heine, R. W. A comparison of patients' reports on psychotherapeutic experience with psychoanalytic, nondirective, and Adlerian therapists. Unpublished doctoral dissertation, University of Chicago, 1950.

12. Lindsley, O. R. Operant conditioning methods applied to research in chronic schizophrenia. *Psychiat. Research Reports #5. Research techniques in schizophrenia.* Washington, D.C.: American Psychiatric Association, 1956, 118-153.

13. Page, C. W., & Ends, E. J. A review and synthesis of the literature suggesting a psychotherapeutic technique based on two-factor learning theory. Unpublished manuscript, loaned to the writer.

14. Rogers, C. R. The necessary and sufficient conditions of psychotherapeutic personality change. *J. Consult. Psychol.,* 1957, *21,* 95-103.

15. Quinn, R. D. Psychotherapists' expressions as an index to the quality of early therapeutic relationships. Unpublished doctoral dissertation, University of Chicago, 1950.

16. Seeman, J. Counselor judgments of therapeutic process and outcome. In Rogers, C. R., and Dymond, R. F. (Eds.), *Psychotherapy and personality change.* Chicago: University of Chicago Press, 1954, Chap. 7.

17. Verplanck, W. S. The control of the content of conversation: reinforcement of statements of opinion. *J. Abnorm. Soc. Psychol.,* 1955, *51,* 668-676.

18. Whitehorn, J. C., & Betz, B. J. A study of psychotherapeutic relationships between physicians and schizophrenic patients. *Amer. J. Psychiat.,* 1954, *111,* 321-331.

G. ROY MAYER
JOHN J. CODY

Festinger's Theory of
Cognitive Dissonance
Applied to School Counseling

Descriptions of human behavior in the sociological and psychological literature are abounding. Festinger's (1957) theory of cognitive dissonance has received more widespread attention from personality and social psychologists in the past 10 years than any other contemporary statement about human behavior (Bem, 1967). It is a theory concerned with process. Since counseling theories are process-oriented also, it seems reasonable to consider possible relationships between these two areas of study. Aspects of Festinger's (1957) theory and Rogers' (1951) theoretical approach to counseling are similar and are supported by research. However, only limited attempts have been made to generalize aspects of Festinger's (1957) theory to counseling. The purpose of this presentation is (a) to describe aspects of Festinger's theory of cognitive dissonance which appear similar to Rogers' description of incongruence, and (b) to apply the apparently complementary notions of Rogers and Festinger to the *practice* of counseling for behavioral modification through "public commitment" in the school setting.

Mayer, G. R., & Cody, J. J. Festinger's theory of cognitive dissonance applied to school counseling. *The Personnel and Guidance Journal,* 1968, 47(3), 233-239. Copyright 1968 American Personnel and Guidance Association. Reprinted with permission.

Dissonance and Incongruence Defined

Dissonance, according to Festinger (1957), is an uncomfortable state which an individual attempts to alleviate or change by bringing his cognitions closer together. The term "cognitive" or "cognition" simply emphasizes that the theory deals with relations among items of information. The items might relate to behavior, feelings, opinions, or things in the environment. Any two items of information which psychologically do not fit together are said to be in a dissonant relation to each other. Thus, if "a person knows various things which are not psychologically consistent with one another, he will, in a variety of ways, try to make them more consistent" (Festinger, 1957).

Rogers (1951), in a similar vein, referred to a discrepancy between the self as perceived and the actual experience of the individual as a state of incongruence. He emphasized that the source of conflict is between the self-concept and organismic experiences, and that this disturbance tends to be reflected in an unrealistic self-ideal or an incongruence between self and ideal self.

Incongruence and dissonance then seem to refer essentially to an intrapersonal mediating state during which an individual experiences contradictory perceptions either about himself or his environment. Both of the terms, incongruence and dissonance, represent an uncomfortable state of affairs for the individual, or feelings of tension and conflict, which an individual attempts to reduce or alleviate. And both suggest that the individual is, as a consequence, motivated to lessen the incompatibility of the perceptions or cognitions.

Means of Reducing Psychological Discomfort

Individuals must change if they are to mature mentally, psychosocially, and physically, and dissonance or incongruence increases the likelihood of change. A variety of ways of reducing psychological discomfort (dissonance or incongruence) apparently exist. An individual may resort to denial or distortion. To deny or distort sensory or visceral experiences with a resultant nonsymbolization into the self is likely to result in psychological maladjustment, according to Rogers (1951).

Changing the physical situation is another means which an individual might use to reduce psychological discomfort. A student might request that a teacher allow him to sit among a group of boys rather than between two girls in a specific class. By changing the situation he may find greater security. However, it seems clear that in many situations manipulation of the environment is unlikely. Due to tradition and the rigid structure of some classroom situations, the likelihood of a student changing the situation seems remote. Behavioral standards, regulated social interactions, adult controls, and mass educational practices are apparently formidable obstacles to a student who seeks to modify his immediate environment.

A third means is personal change. An individual may attempt to adapt his behavior to the requirements of a particular set of circumstances. That is, rather than denying or distorting his experiences, an individual might examine his contradictory perceptions in order to symbolize and organize his experiences into some acceptable relationship with his perceptions of self. In this sense, change is not necessarily an extrinsic force molding an individual's behavior to some predetermined value structure. Rather, change may be regarded as a modification of personal perception or behavior as a result of some intrinsic motivation to alleviate personal tension. In this structure, school counselors, behavioral modifiers, and teachers might employ relatively distinct methods to enhance the possibility of a self-directed and initiated change, which at the same time permits these practitioners to preserve their unique values relative to the rights and nature of the human organism.

Present school practice suggests that the third means, personal change, is indeed important and perhaps essential to the enhancement of a student's maturational process. Educators, including school counselors, are generally most concerned with providing conditions which will facilitate "positive" personal changes in student attitudes, knowledge, and behavior. Rogers (1951, 1954, 1957, 1959, 1961, 1962, 1964) and his colleagues (Barrett-Lennard, 1962; Gendlin, 1961, 1962; Truax, 1963, 1965a, 1965b) have massed considerable evidence to support their contention that under certain conditions, primarily involving absence of threat to the self-structure, experiences which are inconsistent with the self may be perceived and examined, and the structure of the self revised to assimilate and include such experiences.

Festinger's work has led to a number of similarly related postulates. For example, research has suggested that a person who is induced under minimal pressure, threat, or reward to listen to, to say, or to do something that is contrary to his private opinion, the greater is the probability that he will change his opinion and bring it in line with what he has heard, said, or done (Janis & King, 1954; Hovland, Campbell, & Brock, 1957; Cohen, Terry, & Jones, 1959; Festinger & Carlsmith, 1959; Brehm & Cohen, 1962; Brock, 1962; Bem, 1965, 1967; Elms & Janis, 1965). Furthermore, the probability that he will change his opinion and bring it in line with what he has said or done seems increased if he is informed that his parents or other significant human figures are aware, or will be made aware, of the newly expressed attitude or behavior (Hovland, Campbell, & Brock, 1957; Brehm, 1959; Brehm & Cohen, 1962; Bem, 1965, 1967). Brehm's (1959) study provides an example of this latter relationship. He obtained like-dislike ratings from eighth graders for 34 vegetables. Each student was given a small reward if he would eat a vegetable he heartily disliked. Some of the subjects were then casually informed that as part of the experiment a letter was to be sent home to the parents indicating which vegetable that person had eaten. The subjects were then asked to rate the 34 vegetables again. Both groups gave higher ratings to the test vegetables after having eaten them. However, the subjects whose behavior was allegedly reported to their parents changed significantly more in their ranking of the previously disliked vegetable than those whose behavior was not allegedly reported to their parents.

It should be noted that student performance in the post-evaluation situation described in Brehm's (1959) study was not the actual behavior of eating foods which was initially avoided. Obtaining a reported attitude change is not a direct means of evaluating behavior in a life situation. However, it seems reasonable to assume that change in behavior is likely when an individual is capable of verbalizing or reporting a change in perception, attitude, or opinion.

Implications for School Counseling

Several implications for school counseling can be drawn from the concepts and findings discussed above. Rogers' and Festinger's positions persuasively suggest that it is important for the school counselor to realize that students should feel relatively threat-free during counseling, and should not be forced or pressured into receiving counseling. Caution should be exercised, however, in interpreting the term "threat-free" as synonymous with a special set of interview techniques or a specific counseling persuasion. The present discussion is confined to a consideration of only limited aspects of the counseling process applicable to several counseling persuasions. Furthermore, this discussion does not deny that observable behavioral change can occur under conditions of threat, pressure, or punishment. It does contend, however, that an individual is less likely to change his self-perception under threatening conditions. For example, Rogers (1951) contended that the characteristic reaction to threat, punishment, or pressure is for the individual to behave in a manner which will permit him to maintain his perceptions of his environment and self. Patterson (1965), in agreement with Rogers (1951), contended that the phenomenal self, when threatened, is typically preserved through denial or distortion, or by the person becoming acquiescent, submissive, withdrawn, resistant, aggressive, or obstructing. These latter behavioral changes or capitulations are, however, not usually considered to be very positive or permanent. Moreover, Combs and Snygg (1959) corroborated this point when they stated, "Other things being equal, change in the self is most likely to occur in situations which do not force the individual to self-defense."

Another implication for counseling is that the student or counselee is likely to experience dissonance, a prerequisite to attitudinal and behavioral change, if he has seen, heard, expressed, or initiated an attitude, opinion, or behavior contrary to his deeply held opinion or previous behavior. Counselors, then, are confronted with the major responsibility of recognizing that some individuals probably need and perhaps seek assistance in developing sufficient dissonance, or an awareness of their dissonance, in order to enhance or stimulate alternative thoughts and courses of action. Some might consider this latter point as undue intervention on the part of the counselor, especially if the dissonance is initiated or increased by the counselor. However, if man is viewed in the process of "becoming" (Rogers, 1951, 1961, 1964), dissonance or incongruence seems an essential element in an individual's maturational process, perhaps sufficiently to justify its instigation by the counselor. As a scholar is seldom satisfied with his current level of knowledge, a maturing individual seems unsatisfied with his present status of psychological development.

A dissonance-creating situation, yet one that minimizes threat, can be fostered in several ways. For example, a counselor might express verbally what the counselee is "experiencing" (Gendlin, 1961), though not necessarily verbalizing, and accept this experiencing. The counselee will have heard a statement which will create dissonance providing that which was verbalized for him by the counselor was contradictory to or inconsistent with his previously held beliefs and attitudes. By *verbalizing* and *accepting* the counselee's experiencing, the counselor also has made it easier for the counselee to express verbally and clarify his *own* experiencing (Gendlin, 1961).

The counselor should also be able to provide a dissonance-creating situation in a relatively threat-free counseling relationship by permitting the client the freedom to confront himself under the safety and security of the postulated "necessary and sufficient conditions" (Rogers, 1957). When the counselor is perceived by the student as being genuinely himself—one who expressed liking with no "strings attached," and who is empathic in his total behavior—the student can voice dissonance in the form of doubts and other forms of self-exploration.

To help the student perceive the counselor as being genuinely himself, the counselor might express his own experiencing as advocated by Rogers (1961, 1962, 1964) and Gendlin (1961, 1962). An expression of the counselor's experiencing could introduce an attitude, behavior, or some other item of information inconsistent with the counselee's opinion or attitude, thus creating dissonance. For example, a student may express doubt concerning the counselor's respect for him (the counselee). The counselor would attempt to communicate his understanding of this expression of concern and also express (verbally and non-verbally) his personal experiencing of high respect for the student. Thus, a dissonance-creating situation would be enhanced. Perhaps the recognition by the student that there is incongruence between his perception and that of the counselor could be the first step toward the resolution of this difference (Rogers, 1964).

Since the counseling process is usually characterized by conditions of minimal threat, the dissonance or incongruence created within the student is likely to result in a personal change congruent with the newly stated attitude (Janis & King, 1954; Hovland, Campbell, & Brock, 1957; Festinger & Carlsmith, 1959; Brock, 1962; Elms & Janis, 1965). But what if the newly expressed or performed attitude, opinion, or behavior is socially undesirable? Will the counselee change in a "negative" direction in order to reduce his dissonance? Rogers (1951) contended that in counseling, where an atmosphere of safety and acceptance prevails, the firm and defensive boundaries of the self are relaxed, and an individual is better able to evaluate *objectively* his contradictory perceptions and experiences. If Rogers is correct, the described counseling environment appears to encourage independence of thought and expression. In such an environment the individual would seem able to evaluate the consequences of his behavior more rationally. Thus, he would probably select or retain behavior which would avoid negative social consequences such as punishment. It would seem then that a new, negative expression or behavior would *less* likely be retained than a positive one, since the student in counseling is better able to evaluate objectively and rationally his contradictory perceptions in the light of environmental reality and social consequences. If some form of negative behavior occurs, as determined by the school, the counselor is left with an ethical decision of whether to accept this as a natural outcome and ignore it, or refer the counselee for some other form of treatment, or select some other possible alternative.

An additional finding from certain of the previously mentioned studies (Hovland, Campbell, & Brock, 1957; Brehm, 1959; Bem, 1965, 1967) seems to have important implications related to counseling. The results of the studies suggest that intra-personal change would be facilitated if the counselee were to inform his important significant others (teachers, parents, and possibly peers) as to the outcomes or decisions he arrived at during the counseling process. This change would likely result, provided he was not forced to do so (Brehm & Cohen, 1962) and he usually tells them the truth (Bem, 1965). If he did not usually tell his significant others the truth, his statements to them concerning his decisions arrived at in the counseling relationship would not likely result in an attitudinal or behavioral change (Bem, 1965). Such statements would not be meaningful or dissonance-creating (Bem, 1965, 1967). Furthermore, as indicated earlier, the counselee should not be forced or pressured into behaving in a manner against his will. Thus, he should not be pressured into informing others of his decisions. Providing, then, that the assumptions of truthfulness and minimal pressure are met, the activity of informing significant others (teachers, parents, or peers) would seem to facilitate the counselee's self-directed change through publicly committing him to change (Hovland, Campbell, & Brock, 1957; Brehm, 1959; Bem, 1965, 1967).

Excerpts from two counseling sessions should help clarify the practical application of public commitment in counseling. The first excerpt was taken from the context of the second interview with a 12-year-old, sixth grade boy who achieved an IQ equivalent to 107 on the Wechsler Intelligence Scale for Children.

Student: I guess good grades are more important than I figured—before.

Counselor: You just discovered that good grades are important to you.

Student: No, I knew it all the time. I just never wanted to admit it. Because once you admit something then you have to do it. You know if I really believe—like religion—then you have to—like study and that stuff.

Counselor: Then doing something about getting good grades is really important to you now.

Student: I hope so, but I guess there's no way of knowing, is there? How can you tell if I really mean it?

Counselor: Perhaps we can tell if you really mean it. Are you willing to give yourself a test?

Student: That depends what kind of test.

Counselor: Are you willing to go either alone or with me to your teacher and your mother and tell them that you are really going to work hard and bring your grades up?

Student: What if I don't?

Counselor: I don't know, what do you think?

Student: OK, I'll go with you.

Counselor: You want me to go with you?

Student: You really think it will help?

Counselor: Do you really respect these people, your mom and teacher? Do you really want to improve?

Student: I hope it does because I am kind of sick of having everyone think I'm lazy.

Sometimes the student needs assistance in publicly committing himself. In the above situation, the student and the counselor went together to respected adults. In the example that follows, the student (an 11-year-old) went by himself to inform significant others of intended action.

Student: Yeah, I gotta be a winner. I shouldn't. I gotta lose sometime. It ain't that bad. Maybe I can live it a little. A little at first maybe and then a lot more. Yeah, that's the way to do it. Just a little then some more.

Counselor: You don't sound sold on it.

Student: Yes I am. (Pause) I need a helper. Somebody should say stop—don't get mad, laugh. (Pause) Uh huh, a helper, a dwarf.

Counselor: Maybe your best friend could be that dwarf.

Student: Oh Zippie ain't much, he's the same. He might help. You talk to him, too? I can help him. He can help me. That's the way. You go get Zip.

Counselor: Zip is my friend?

Student: I don't know, he's mine.

Counselor: Maybe we . . .

Student: Yeah, I'll get him to do it. I'll tell him my idea.
Counselor: You're sure it'll help you?
Student: Huh. (Nods yes.)
Counselor: Maybe you could tell the whole group you reformed. Then you would have a lot of helpers.
Student: No, they're not—yeah—no way to do it.
Counselor: Why not kid them, you know, say in a kind of teasing way.
Student: Like—I reformed—my counselor says I got to—OK you can help that way.
Counselor: It might be worth a trial.
Student: Maybe—OK, I'll try.

This 11-year-old managed to tell his classmates using the counselor as the "goat." He managed it, however. It seems that under some circumstances public commitment flows naturally out of the situation.

As a result of being publicly committed to change, significant others now *expect,* and are likely to reinforce the new attitude or behavior, particularly if they perceive the new attitude or behavior as positive. Furthermore, since the client knows that important others have been told of his change, he is likely to perceive others as seeing him in this new light. If we tend to perceive ourselves and behave as we believe others perceive us, as Cooley (1902) indicated, notifying significant others of a change would seem to increase the chances of the change lasting through changing the "looking glass self" (Cooley, 1902). Bem (1967) has presented considerable evidence indicating that self-perception explains the cognitive dissonance phenomena. Perhaps, then, this explains why several of the previously mentioned studies have indicated that intra-personal change is more likely to persist if a child's important others (teachers, peers, or parents) are told that a change in attitudes or behavior, which is contrary to the child's previous attitudes or behavior, has taken place.

Conclusion

Counseling students within the school seems to offer an excellent environment in which the complementary notions of "dissonance" and "incongruence" and the concept of "public commitment" might be employed with little difficulty. The reader should be cautioned, however, that the counselor activity of publicly committing students must be viewed as suggestive. Its particular value or the particular circumstances under which it may be of value (i.e., when and when not to employ it) has not, as yet, been experimentally demonstrated in the school setting. For this reason, some of the conclusions reached must be viewed (a) as tentative and suggestive of the kinds of school counselor activities which may increase the counselor's effectiveness in facilitating change, but (b) in need of systematic and detailed research.

References

Barrett-Lennard, G. T. Dimensions of therapist response as causal factors in therapeutic change. *Psychological Monographs*, 1962, *76*, Whole No. 562.

Bem, D. J. An experimental analysis of self-persuasion. *Journal of Experimental Social Psychology*. 1965, *1*, 199-218.

Bem, D. J. Self-perception: an alternative interpretation of cognitive dissonance phenomena. *Psychological Review*, 1967, *74*, 183-200.

Brehm, J. W. Increasing cognitive dissonance by a *fait accompli. Journal of Abnormal Social Psychology*, 1959, *58*, 379-382.

Brehm, J. W., & Cohen, A. R. *Explorations in cognitive dissonance.* New York: Wiley, 1962.

Brock, T. C., & Blackwood, J. E. Dissonance reduction, social comparison and modification of others' opinions. *Journal of Abnormal Social Psychology*, 1962, *65*, 319-324.

Cohen, A. R., Terry, H. I., & Jones, C. B. Attitudinal effects of choice in exposure to counterpropaganda. *Journal of Abnormal Social Psychology*, 1959, *58*, 388-391.

Combs, A. W., & Snygg, D. *Individual behavior: a perceptual approach to behavior.* (Rev. ed.) New York: Harper, 1959.

Cooley, C. H. *Human nature and the social order.* New York: Scribner, 1902.

Elms, A. C., & Janis, I. L. Counternorm attitudes induced by consonant versus dissonant role playing. *Journal of Experimental Research on Personality*, 1965, *1*, 50-60.

Festinger, L. A. *A theory of cognitive dissonance.* Evanston, Ill.: Row, Peterson, 1957.

Festinger, L., & Carlsmith, J. M. Cognitive consequences of forced compliance. *Journal of Abnormal Social Psychology*, 1959, *58*, 203-210.

Gendlin, E. T. Experiencing: a variable in the process of therapeutic change. *American Journal of Psychotherapy*, 1961, *15*, 233-245.

Gendlin, E. T. Client-centered developments in psychotherapy with schizophrenics. *Journal of Counseling Psychology*, 1962, *9*, 205-211.

Hovland, C. I., Campbell, E. H., & Brock, T. The effects of "commitment" on opinion change following communications. In C. I. Hovland, et al., *The order of presentation in persuasion.* New Haven, Conn.: Yale University Press, 1957.

Janis, I. L., & King, B. T. The influence of role-playing on opinion-change. *Journal of Abnormal Social Psychology*, 1954, *49*, 211-218.

Patterson, C. H. Phenomenological psychology. *Personnel and Guidance Journal*, 1965, *43*, 997-1005.

Rogers, C. R. *Client-centered therapy.* Boston: Houghton Mifflin, 1951.

Rogers, C. R., & Dymond, R. F. (Eds.) *Psychotherapy and personality change.* Chicago: University of Chicago Press, 1954.

Rogers, C. R. The necessary and sufficient conditions of therapeutic personality change. *Journal of Consulting Psychology,* 1957, *21,* 95-103.

Rogers, C. R. A theory of therapy, personality and interpersonal relationships as developed in the client-centered framework. In S. Koch (Ed.), *Psychology: a study of a science,* Vol. 3. New York: McGraw-Hill, 1959. Pp. 184-256.

Rogers, C. R. *On becoming a person.* Boston: Houghton Mifflin, 1961.

Rogers, C. R. The interpersonal relationships: the core of guidance. *Harvard Educational Review,* 1962, *32,* 416-429.

Rogers, C. R. Client-centered therapy. In S. Arieti (Ed.), *American handbook of psychiatry.* 1964, in press.

Truax, C. B. Effective ingredients in psychotherapy: an approach to unraveling the patient-therapist interaction. *Journal of Counseling Psychology,* 1963, *10,* 256-263.

Truax, C. B., & Carkhuff, R. R. Client and therapist transparency in the psychotherapeutic encounter. *Journal of Counseling Psychology,* 1965a, *12,* 3-9.

Truax, C. B., & Carkhuff, R. R. Experimental manipulation of therapeutic conditions. *Journal of Consulting Psychology,* 1965b, *29,* 119-124.

ERNST G. BEIER

Client-centered Therapy and the Involuntary Client

It is generally recognized that the most favorable condition for successful psychotherapy exists when the client himself feels ready to seek help for his problems. Rogers [8] lists the client's wish for help as one of "the most significant steps in therapy." Fenichel [3] states "the method of psychoanalysis is based on the cooperation of a reasonable ego." Freud's "basic rule" certainly can only be followed by an analysand who desires to be helped by analysis.

However, there is increasing evidence that therapists of all orientations have been called upon to make their services available to clients who do not seek their assistance. We need only to think of the efforts of some workers to give psychotherapeutic treatment to juvenile delinquents [4], to prisoners [7], to court referrals [6], to employees [2], to students referred by deans' offices, and, last but not least, to children who, after all, rarely come to the clinic of their own free will.

It is the intent of this paper to discuss methods available to the therapist to assist the "involuntary" client—the client who does not make the decision for therapeutic help himself—to make appropriate

Ernst G. Beier, "Client-centered Therapy and the Involuntary Client," *Journal of Consulting Psychology*, 1952, *16*, pp. 332-337. Copyright 1952 by the American Psychological Association. Reprinted by permission.

use of the therapeutic hour. It should be understood from the outset that assisting an involuntary client toward "therapy-readiness" can never mean that the therapist is attempting to make a client out of a nonclient. Rather, the therapist can hope to work with an "unready client" only if he deals with a *client* in the first place, i.e., an individual who engages in maladaptive behavior and who has some wish to free himself of such behavior. An involuntary client, then, would be an individual in whom resistance toward giving up symptoms and substitute gratifications is greater than his desire for help. With an involuntary client, the therapist must still attempt to support the client's own motivation for treatment.

The phase of the psychological contact which deals with supporting the client's own readiness for therapeutic help shall be called here the "pretherapeutic phase." In clinical experience, various types of pretherapeutic phases seem to be recognized. As yet, no information is available to indicate that one approach is more successful than another. It is likely that none of the approaches practiced can be "successful" per se, but that each approach can achieve its maximum gain in dealing with specific syndrome-constellations. Accordingly, in the following presentation, we are not aiming at finding a panacea. All we wish is to present a few incidents with involuntary clients, follow them through to success or failure (does the client become ready to seek help on his own?), and discuss their implications, perhaps with a hint here and there concerning how this problem can be investigated more properly [5]. We will, however, present the incidents in some order, being guided in this respect by our recognition of some types of "pretherapeutic" approaches which can easily be distinguished.

In our experience, counselors who are confronted with the involuntary client generally deal with him in one of the following ways:

A. They do not accept him, but "wait him out," until he is ready to seek help on his own.[1]

B. They accept him and actively engage in resistance reflections.

C. They accept him and discuss with him in an "above-board" fashion the fact that he is considered a client and the ways he can go about helping himself (anxiety-arousal).

Below we will present incidents and discussions relative to each of these major approaches for dealing with the involuntary client.

A. *The counselor does not accept the involuntary client but decides to "wait him out" until he is ready to seek help on his own*

Incidents:

1. Billy, aged 7, was referred to the clinic because of aggressive behavior. His parents brought Billy to the clinic against his will and he refused to follow the play therapist to the playroom. The worker accepted Billy's refusal and permitted him to stay downstairs in the waiting room. The parents, themselves engaged in a counseling hour, were given to understand that it was felt desirable for Billy to make his own decision and they accepted this. For the second session, Billy stayed for only 10 minutes and left again. In the third session, Billy stated that he really liked to come, and stayed for the whole hour. At this time the parents reported that even after so few contacts Billy's behavior had changed markedly. To what extent this change was due to parent counseling was not clear but the worker felt that Billy's early freedom of choice had much to do with it.

2. Johnny, a withdrawn child, aged 7, did not want to enter the playroom. He was given free choice to leave. The mother, in a counseling session, was informed as to the purpose of the free choice for Johnny. After three meetings, during which Johnny never entered the playroom, the mother decided to leave. She stated that Johnny was too immature to make such a decision. The workers felt that the mother would have given the clinic more time if Johnny had been *taken* to the playroom. She felt that by offering Johnny a free choice, he was presented with an unnecessary, and at this time insurmountable, problem.

3. Brown, a student, referred by the dean's office because he "literally fell asleep in class," protested during the first hour that he had no problems and did not wish to come to the clinic. The therapist structured to him that he did not have to come, even though the dean's office had sent him. Brown, first making certain that he had understood correctly, almost instantaneously began to make use of the hour.

4. Smith, a young woman, was referred to the clinic by the dean's office for "emotional rehabilitation." Smith felt that she did not want to come to a psychological clinic. She was given free choice in the matter of entering into a counseling relationship and decided to leave. After two months the report came to the clinic that Smith had had a nervous breakdown and had left school.

5. An athletic team was requested by the administration to report to the psychologist for the purpose of helping with the team's *esprit de corps*. The members of the team, deeply resentful of their coaches, transferred this resentment toward the psychologist and made an agreement that none of them would talk. The psychologist structured to them at their first session that they *did* have to be present but *did not* have to talk. As was hoped, a long discussion ensued which was directed toward their relationship with their coaches. The very permission "not to talk" had effected in the team a feeling that the psychologist was on their side.

6. A student had to enter a counseling relationship by court order. He sat through twelve silent hours with the therapist. The therapist had structured to

him that he did not have to talk and the client accepted this at face value. Reflections of silence were recognized by the client but not utilized. From the diagnostic record, severe emotional disturbances were indicated, and the worker felt by the end of the time that no gains had been made, that the silence had been a sign of defiance. Follow-up information supported this diagnosis and the worker's opinion.

Discussion. In all these incidents, the therapist's intent was to assist the involuntary client in his motivation toward therapy and growth. Following the thinking of client-centered theory, the therapist communicates to the client from the start that he respects the integrity of his client, that he does not identify with the referral agency, and that he has faith and confidence in the client's ability to be a person and to make his own decisions. The quickly achieved "therapy-readiness" in Cases 1, 3, and 5 supports the therapist's decision to offer free choice to the involuntary client from the start. The clients clearly benefited from this acceptance and seemed to utilize it well.

An analysis of Cases 2, 4, and 6, however, indicates that the same approach—with different clients—may fail. Here, too, the therapist tried to communicate his acceptance, but the clients, particularly 2 and 4, were not ready to sense permissiveness or acceptance. Throughout their life experience they had possibly never been asked to make a major decision by themselves, and now they were suddenly presented with this opportunity. They were not ready, not free enough emotionally, to make this decision objectively. Perhaps these two clients may even have been burdened by this choice. They were confronted with an additional difficult problem. The therapist's communication, "you alone can decide whether or not you need me," might have been easily misunderstood by them as another rejection. They had never had the opportunity to get to know the therapist and might have misinterpreted his statement as one of indifference. Case 6, the "forced" involuntary client, illustrates very neatly how the client persisted in thinking of the therapist in defiance. The therapist had accepted the court referral because of pressure ("you take him, or off he goes"), but he had given the boy free choice to use the hour as he wished. Apparently, the boy was so preoccupied with the idea that he was forced into this situation that he never could sense the therapist's acceptance. There were indications that he perceived permissiveness as hypocrisy.

Misunderstanding, misinterpretation, and the possible lack of readiness to admit and sense permissiveness are hindrances in making this pretherapeutic phase effective with some involuntary clients. It seems to be effective with clients of a certain maturity, but fails to work where emotional factors are in the way. The obvious questions that one would have to investigate more closely would be: What are these emotional factors that prevent some clients from being effectively reached? What are the behavioral correlates? Which cues can the therapist take into account to determine whether or not he should give free choice to a client without taking the risk of losing him altogether (Case 4)? Are other, more adequate methods available?

It should be carefully noted that we are speaking of approaches to therapy and not of the basic attitudes of the counselor. The respect for the integrity of the client and the acceptance of the client are not intended to be placed in doubt as basic requirements. When we speak of various approaches to helping motivate the involuntary client, we mean ways of responding to very real needs of the client.

B. *The counselor accepts the involuntary client and engages in resistance reflections*

Incidents:

1. The mother of a young child, who, at an earlier contact, had refused to enter into a counseling relationship, was asked to "give it a chance." The staff had decided, in this case, not to take the child (aged 3) unless the mother would also accept counseling for herself. The mother reluctantly agreed. She stated in her first session that she really had no problem and that she did not know what she could discuss. The therapist reflected her anger about being pushed into the counseling situation. He also commented during the hour on other manifestations of resistance, her embarrassment (perpetual laughing), her ambivalence (twice leaving the room), her difficulty in starting (silences, laughing, stating that she was talking in circles), and finally her very real wish to obtain help herself (although not based on *expressed* communication). What seems here to have been a merciless onslaught on the part of the therapist was understood by the client as very deep concern for her, as supported by the client's own "testimonial" after the pretherapeutic phase had long since passed into a therapeutic one: "For the first time in my life (during the first hour), I felt that somebody was concerned with *my* troubles." The therapist felt that without his very real effort to communicate understanding to the client, the client would have maintained her feeling that nobody could be interested in her feelings and would have stayed out of the relationship. It should be noted that considerable dependency had been established between the therapist and the client which had to be worked through in later contacts.

2. Another involuntary client, a young woman, came to the clinic and told the therapist that her husband had sent her because she was "upset too easily." She

expressed some resentment toward her husband's behavior, particularly that he had not come with her. She stated that she did not know what to talk about and thought that her husband certainly would not want her "to give away secrets." She was seen for six one-hour sessions, in which she either kept silent or discussed her bus trip to the clinic. In staff discussion, she was seen as an involuntary client who was badly in need of help and who was unable to break through her feelings of resistance. In the seventh hour, the therapist, in order to help her to feel more deeply understood and to establish a more therapeutic relationship, reflected to her a feeling that was implicit in many of her previous statements. She had never directly expressed the feeling, of which she was either unaware or could not yet bring herself to communicate, namely, hostility toward her husband. She felt her husband seemed to hold her responsible for all difficulties in the family. A statement to that effect, however, although cautiously worded, did not at all assist her towards a deeper relationship, but increased her resistance to the point where she had good reason to break the contact.

3. Another involuntary client, a delinquent boy of 15, had been accepted for therapy by court order. He had decided that he did not need us as he was not "nuts" and for two hours the boy maintained silence, a remarkable feat for a 15-year-old. We were convinced that the boy had severe emotional problems (he had been caught prowling in a number of buildings, stealing women's dresses), and decided in staff conference to consider reflection of resistance. The therapist reflected the boy's unexpressed feeling of bewilderment in this situation, his unexpressed fear that this might not be confidential, his fear of being called "nuts," his resentment and helplessness (biting of fingernails), and the stress under which the silence placed him. Rapport was established when the therapist used four-letter words to reflect the boy's feeling of anguish. He began to feel more at ease and work proceeded on more therapeutic lines. The therapist had established himself as a person who did not identify himself with authority, and in effect the boy could feel that he was being understood.

4. A girl was sent over by the dean's office because she was unable to do her schoolwork efficiently. She claimed that she was blind in one eye, although medical examination revealed no defect. The student stated that she had no problems and accepted her blindness without any signs of anxiety. She stayed with the therapist for a number of hours which seemed most unproductive. She would say that she knew that she had to come to the clinic but that there was nothing wrong with her. After twelve contacts, a more active pretherapeutic phase was recommended by the staff. During the next few hours, the therapist reflected her unexpressed ambivalence about coming to the clinic (there was no pressure from the dean's office), her unexpressed worry about the effects of her symptom (fear of getting behind in her classes), her feeling about the therapist (fear of dependency), and her anger about the university (the dean had discussed with her suspicions of sexual promiscuity). The therapist felt that the effect of his closer participation and his communication of concern helped the girl to become more thoroughly motivated toward the counseling relationship. The student brought more intimate material for discussion and the contact lasted for some 35 hours. The girl left school and recent reports state that she is free from her symptoms.

5. Another involuntary client, a student who had been referred to the clinic by the student court, had four contacts during which he was clearly evasive. He would pointedly talk about the weather and related subjects. From the record, it was evident that the student was under great tension; he was also known to engage in homosexual behavior. After the fourth hour, the therapist began to participate more readily, reflecting on the meaning of the evasive comments, reflecting unexpressed feelings such as resentment over being sent in and the fear that he might reveal unpleasant material during the hour. No change in behavior on the part of the client was noted, and he came for the remaining eight hours with the very same attitude we had witnessed in the beginning. (The student court was requested not to use the clinic in this manner in the future.)

Discussion. We assume that the therapist can only help an "involuntary" client to become a motivated client if the "involuntary" client is an individual with crippling problems, and who is either unaware of them, or does not wish to communicate a need for assistance. The approach utilized in the above incidents is one in which the therapist tries to assist the client toward accepting therapeutic help by reflecting unexpressed and unrecognized needs (resistance reflections) in order to communicate to the client his deep concern for him [1]. The therapist's attempt to understand the client better than he understands himself is meant to be supportive in nature, a support needed to work through feelings of resistance.

While advantages and disadvantages of approach A are closely related to the maturity of the client (will he sense the acceptant atmosphere?), the present approach is more directly involving the activity of the counselor. The maturity of his judgment would be an important variable. The bias of the free-choice approach (A) is: "I behave toward the involuntary client as if he can help himself (and I take the risk that he can*not*)." This stands in contrast to the bias of the second approach (B): "I behave toward the involuntary client as if he needs my support (Cases 1, 3, and 4); and I take the risk that my specific support is unacceptable to him (Cases 2 and 5)." The therapist not only has decided to give support, but has to decide throughout the contact where to give support. Such an attitude on the part of the therapist seems to contradict orthodox client-centered counseling, and yet the contradiction is only superficial. In the cases cited, the therapist's basic attitude has been to base the counseling on the second tenet of client-centered counseling: to present a non-threatening situation. Support was given not to establish the authority of the counselor, but to help the client to perceive the deep concern of the counselor for him and his unexpressed needs.

It seems clear to us that with support, some clients will be reached who otherwise would leave the situation. The obvious questions which arise with such an approach would be the following: Who are the clients who would profit by such support? What sort of behavior will we have to differentiate to make a decision with confidence? At which state of his own development as a therapist is the worker ready to make "adequate" judgments with respect to the client? Answers to such questions will help us to evaluate the effectiveness of various types of pretherapeutic approaches.

C. *The counselor discusses in an "above-board" fashion the fact that the involuntary client is really a client (anxiety-arousal)*

Incidents:

1. A group of parents had been asked to participate in counseling sessions along with play therapy for their children. For seven hours these parents discussed their children's problems almost exclusively. The therapist felt that the parents were operating according to a preconceived set and that there was some need for reorientation. At the eighth hour, he started the session by considering with the parents the need for discussing one's own problems in order to understand other people's problems a little better. He put it squarely up to them to see themselves as clients.

The parents reacted in an expected way with some confusion and some silence. This phase of the contact was understood by the therapist as a time of reorientation in which the older defenses (talking about children only) no longer worked. The therapist reflected the silence and the aroused anxieties of the parents. Our records indicate that during this hour, as well as the following hours, the parents discussed their own relationships and problems to a much larger extent and the counselor felt that he had a closer relationship with the parents.

2. An involuntary client, a school teacher who had been sent to the clinic by her supervisor, discussed some personal problems of her supervisor and the effects of these problems on the faculty. Afterwards she inquired of the worker what she was to do in this hour, and the worker structured the hour to her as an opportunity during which she would be able to talk about anything she wished. He also stated something to the effect that sometimes people can be helped to become happier when they have an opportunity to talk about themselves and their problems. This statement was apparently very threatening to the teacher. She said to the counselor: "I only talk to God about my problems," and left the contact.

3. A student was referred to the clinic (and to the infirmary) by the dean's office. The student suffered from paranoid delusions and insisted that other students stuck pins into his legs. He rationalized his being sent to see a psychologist with a very neat delusionary system. He demanded that the psychologist attend to his mother who, in his own words, was "the queerest woman you have ever seen." He described certain behaviors of his mother which were clearly delusionary (sleeping with his uncle the very day that he, the student, had poisoned his

father). The student stated that he did not wish to come back until the psychologist had evaluated his mother's state of mind. The therapist, in order to motivate the student toward working through his own problems, discussed with him for some four continuous hours various aspects of the situation as the student saw them. During this phase, the therapist accepted the student's delusions but also participated with such observations as the fact that the student would be in a much more favorable position if he himself would be less tense. Although certain anxieties were aroused by the therapist, it appeared that these anxieties, when recognized, deepened the rapport. The student saw the therapist daily during the following week at the end of which he was referred to a therapist near his home (as he had to leave school), now more highly motivated toward seeking help on his own.

Discussion. The "above-board" method, telling the involuntary client that he is a client and should behave as one, is a crude method at best. It can be understood as an attempt by the therapist to support the involuntary client's own motivation toward help by arousing motivating anxiety. Such a method would seem clearly to contradict the basic tenets of client-centered therapy. And yet, in a search for appropriate ways of dealing with various clients, the therapist's active participation, his attempt to arouse motivating anxiety which will help the involuntary client to become more ready to accept therapy, may very easily have a place in special cases. Case 1, perhaps, is not a good case in question. It can be argued that the therapist had a preconceived notion as to what parents should talk about and his relationship developed more readily when the parents acquiesced. Case 3, on the other hand, seems to be more specifically suited to this approach and therapists who have worked with schizophrenic patients may have had occasion to wonder about this problem. It is here, with special clients, that client-centered therapy will have to expand its views. Again some obvious questions come to mind: Which are the best methods to arouse just enough anxiety so that it is motivating and yet does not serve to terminate the contact (Case 2)? When is anxiety arousal the most adequate pretherapeutic procedure? How, precisely, is the therapist's challenge perceived by the client? If we have even tentative answers to some of these questions, the therapist may be in a position to differentiate his clients' needs more clearly.

Concluding Statement

It is probably true that we will never have a science of psychotherapy which takes all variables into account. Each client, and each therapist, is an individual in his own right, and not too consistent an individual at that. What we can hope for, at best, is a more thorough understanding of the therapeutic process and this by way of gathering many observations. Such observations may indicate general trends which hold true for many clients and many therapists. With regard to an evaluation of a pretherapeutic procedure designed to assist the involuntary client in becoming a motivated client, we face the very same difficulties. We will never know if a given approach was just the right one with a given client, or if another approach would have worked as well or even more effectively. We can, however, make it our practice to observe closely, to report and evaluate our observations, and last but not least, become psychologists who ask the right questions.

Footnote

1. Category A actually deals with "involuntary clients" who *can* absent themselves and those who *cannot* absent themselves from the therapeutic hour. The latter, who cannot absent themselves from the hour (court referral), present an extra problem.

References

1. Beier, E. G. The problem of anxiety in client-centered therapy. *J. Consult. Psychol.,* 1951, *15,* 359-362.
2. Cantow, L. A., Brickman, H., Edgecomb, W., & Kallen, A. A psychiatric approach to the problem of human relations in industry. *Personnel,* 1951, *27,* 431-439.
3. Fenichel, O. *The psychoanalytic theory of neurosis.* New York: Norton, 1945.
4. Gerstenlauer, C. Group therapy with institutionalized male juvenile delinquents. *Amer. Psychologist,* 1950, *5,* 325. (Abstract)
5. Grant, J. D., & Grant, Marguerite Q. "Therapy readiness" as a research variable. *J. Consult. Psychol.,* 1950, *14,* 156-157.
6. Guttmacher, M. S. Adult court psychiatric clinic. *Amer. J. Psychiat.,* 1950, *106,* 881-888.
7. Powelson, H., & Bendix, R. Psychiatry in prison. *Psychiatry,* 1951, *14,* 73-86.
8. Rogers, C. R. *Counseling and psychotherapy.* Boston: Houghton Mifflin, 1942.

SECTION III

Eclectic Counseling

> *The most compelling indication for adopting the eclectic approach to behavioral study and psychotherapy is the complexity of the psychological states and life situations involved in even the simplest clinical problems. Behavior normally is in constant flux and change. Behavior occurs phenomenally in a sequence of psychological states of Being, each reactive to a constantly changing existential situation. Integrative dynamics not only are tremendously complex but also determined by almost infinite permutations and combinations of organizing factors. Only the eclectic approach is capable of dealing with such complexity and change.*
>
> *—Frederick C. Thorne*

To be eclectic means to develop a combination of theoretical approaches that effectively deal with human behavior. The eclectic counselor is not satisfied with one theorist's explanation of behavior and therapeutic change agents. He or she feels this is too restrictive, confining, and ineffective. To be effective, the counselor must use the experience of many divergent theorists in his or her own practice. In order to do this he or she must borrow from a spectrum of theoretical approaches those that are most relevant for his or her clientele.

Frederick Thorne is one of the leading proponents of the eclectic position in psychotherapy and counseling. He strongly advocates that all therapists examine a number of different theoretical models in order to find the best personal combination of theory and technique. However, consistency throughout the theoretical framework is essential. All the varying elements must form an interdependent, interrelated system. Every counselor must eventually settle on one philosophy and theory of personality that explains human behavior for him or her. The specific techniques of counseling are chosen from those that have proved effective in therapeutic settings. The best features of each approach are then selected for inclusion in the personal framework. When the counselor adds new techniques that he or she feels will increase his or her effectiveness, they must be consistent and congruent with the existing framework.

The readings in this section are intended as facilitators for encouraging the reader to consider the eclectic position. In the first article, Arnold Lazarus presents a thoughtful plea for therapists to continually seek additional techniques that will broaden their practical expertise. He emphasizes the need for a system or framework of therapy and for incorporating new techniques into the total system. James Lister, in the second reading, discusses eclecticism from the theoretical and technical perspectives. Synthesis of different theoretical models into a sound, consistent framework for counseling practice is the method he advocates for counselors.

The two remaining articles deal with several combinations of theoretical positions that exemplify eclectic frameworks. Richard Gronert presents a model of counseling that combines reality therapy, Adlerian psychology, and behavior modification. He concludes by applying the model to specific cases involving preadolescent clients. Ernest Johnson synthesizes existential counseling and client-centered counseling by comparing their major theoretical constructs.

In summary, eclecticism may be characterized by both diversity and consistency. Diverse theoretical positions are synthesized into a consistent framework that is personally satisfying and professionally effective.

ARNOLD A. LAZARUS

In Support of
Technical Eclecticism

The plethora of psychological theories is exceeded only by the dearth of testable deductions emanating therefrom. Harper (1959), for instance, described 36 separate systems of psychotherapy which he regarded as "the main types of psychological treatment." There are, in fact, many other clearly identifiable "systems" which can be added to Harper's list. These would include: Transactional Analysis, Psychosynthesis, Reality Therapy, Reparative Psychotherapy, Integrity Therapy, Implosive Psychotherapy, and Morita Therapy, to mention a few.

Faced with this complex, contradictory, and often confusing array of psychological theories and systems, most practitioners seek refuge in those notions which best satisfy their own subjective needs. Yet one may legitimately inquire whether the consequence of adhering to a particular school of thought is to exclude from one's armamentarium a significant range of effective procedures. Who, even in a lifetime of endeavor, can hope to encompass such a diverse and multifarious range of thought and theory? Indeed, an attempt to imbibe and digest this overwhelming mass of information (and misinformation) may be no more rewarding than gluttony at any other level. Is there a way out of this morass?

Reprinted with permission of author and publisher from: Lazarus, A. A. In support of technical eclecticism. *Psychological Reports*, 1967, *21*, 415-416.

To luxuriate in a metaphor, we might conceivably wield Occam's razor the way Alexander the Great used his sword, to cut *through* the Gordian knot instead of becoming involved in its intricacies. Occam taught that explanatory principles should not be needlessly multiplied. In keeping with this, the general principle of scientific thinking is that given two equally tenable hypotheses the simpler of the two is to be preferred. Add to this London's (1964) profound observation that: "However interesting, plausible, and appealing a theory may be, it is techniques, not theories, that are actually used on people. Study of the effects of psychotherapy, therefore, is always the study of the effectiveness of techniques."

Can a practicing psychotherapist afford to ignore any effective technique, regardless of its theoretical origins? Obviously, a technique derived from a source or system which is at variance with one's own theoretical beliefs may nevertheless possess healing properties— not necessarily for reasons which attach to the theories of its originator. Consider the case of a highly anxious patient who received relaxation therapy (Jacobson, 1964) to diminish his over-all tensions, while receiving systematic desensitization (Wolpe, 1961; Wolpe & Lazarus, 1966) to various subjectively threatening situations and also being trained to be "excitatory" (Salter, 1949) by assertively standing up for his rights and by giving vent to his feelings. This was extended to embrace self-disclosure (rather than a life of concealment and camouflage) as a means of achieving social harmony (Jourard, 1964). The patient's irrational ideas were handled along lines advocated by Ellis (1962).

Now, the theoretical notions espoused by Jacobson, Wolpe, Salter, Jourard, and Ellis are very much at odds with one another. The eclectic theorist who borrows bits and pieces from divergent theories in the hope of building a composite system must inevitably embrace contradictory notions and thus is likely to find himself in a state of confusion worse confounded. But it is not necessary to accept or reconcile divergent theoretical systems in order to utilize their techniques.

And so it is with Harper's (1959) three-dozen systems and the dozens of others we could add to his original list. To attempt a theoretical *rapprochement* is as futile as seriously trying to picture the edge of the universe. But to read through the vast mass of literature on psychotherapy, *in search of techniques,* can be clinically enriching and therapeutically rewarding.

However, this should not presuppose a random melange of techniques taken eclectically out of the air. While the basic point of this paper is a plea for psychotherapists to try several effective techniques (even those not necessarily prompted by the logic of their own theories), it is nevertheless assumed that any selected maneuver will at least have the benefit of empirical support. Complete unity between a systematic theory of personality and an effective method of treatment derived therefrom remains a cherished ideal. Meanwhile it is well for the practicing psychotherapist to be content in the role of a technician rather than that of a scientist and to observe that those who impugn technical proficiency are often able to explain everything but to accomplish almost nothing.

References

Ellis, A. *Reason and emotion in psychotherapy.* New York: Lyle Stuart, 1964.

Harper, R. A. *Psychoanalysis and psychotherapy: 36 systems.* Englewood Cliffs, N.J.: Prentice-Hall, 1959.

Jacobson, E. *Anxiety and tension control.* Philadelphia: Lippincott, 1964.

Jourard, S. M. *The transparent self.* New York: Van Nostrand, 1964.

London, P. *The modes and morals of psychotherapy.* New York: Holt, Rinehart & Winston, 1964.

Salter, A. *Conditioned reflex therapy.* New York: Creative Age Press, 1949.

Wolpe, J. The systematic desensitization treatment of neuroses. *J. Nerv. Ment. Dis.,* 132, 189-203.

Wolpe, J., & Lazarus, A. A. *Behavior therapy techniques.* Oxford: Pergamon Press, 1966.

JAMES L. LISTER

The Eclectic Counselor: An Explorer

"Eclectic counseling" can mean many different things. The label "eclectic" by itself does not tell what a counselor believes or how he behaves. One knows what to expect from counselors who call themselves client-centered or psychoanalytic; but further inquiry is necessary of the person who says he is eclectic. To some it means finding "something that works." Others consider themselves eclectic because they use only techniques that have been scientifically validated. Counselors who borrow from many theories and disciplines in developing a counseling theory usually consider themselves eclectic. And many believe they are eclectic because they alternate in the use of "directive" and "nondirective" techniques.

The examples cited indicate that eclectic counseling encompasses a wide range of counseling methods and techniques. It appears to this author that eclectic counseling can be considered in terms of two general types, *theoretical* and *technical*. These two types are in no sense "pure"; they only illustrate different emphases within eclectic counseling. Consideration of the values and limitations of these two emphases should help counselors develop more effective approaches.

Lister, J. L. The eclectic counselor: an explorer. *The School Counselor*, 1967, *14*(5), 287-293. Copyright 1967 American Personnel and Guidance Association. Reprinted with permission.

Eclecticism: Theoretical and Technical

Departures from orthodox counseling approaches can emphasize modifications in theory, techniques, or both. Some eclectic counselors adhere closely to one theory while modifying or varying their counseling techniques. Others modify their theoretical framework of counseling with little emphasis on techniques.

Theoretical

The eclectic counselor of this emphasis is more concerned with developing a comprehensive rationale for his counseling than with the particular techniques he uses. He seeks an internally consistent theoretical position that is satisfying in view of his students, his school setting, and his own life style. The Freudian emphasis on early experience may be needed to explain his students' difficulties with their parents. He may, however, find the pervasive emphasis on sex unacceptable and therefore look to one of the social theorists for elements more compatible with his view of human behavior.

Counselors may be eclectic in theory because the use of various theories helps them explain the behavior of different students. Tyler has illustrated this:

Every personality has many facets. Different theories of personality are like spotlights focused on the individual from different directions. The same facets do not show up when one turns on the light labeled Freud that appear clearly when one throws the Rogers switch. And while Freudian concepts may enable a counselor to understand and to help Bill Amory, they may hinder him from seeing what is really the dominant factor in the life of Sarah Peele [15, p. 3].

In the same paper, Tyler described the kind of synthesizing she has done in developing her theoretical framework. Her presentation highlights critical areas to consider in such an undertaking. Tyler emphasized that her synthesis was uniquely hers and cautioned:

I am not recommending this particular synthesis for anyone else because I am convinced that each person needs to produce his own. My purpose is to point the way to a sort of *theorizing* counselors can employ rather than to a sort of *theory* they should adopt [p. 3, italics in original].

The essential nature of theoretical eclecticism is that either the synthesis or variation occurs largely within the framework from which the counselor operates. While important, counseling techniques are considered means for achieving desired goals.

The primary advantage of theoretical eclecticism is that it enables the counselor to work out for himself an internally consistent, coherent rationale for his counseling behavior. It helps him reconcile those aspects of theory which do not seem to fit; he may develop a point of view more personally meaningful than any existing orthodox position; he may acquire a tool for explaining student behavior; guided by his "feel" for what makes sense, he may conceptualize the counseling process in a way that meshes comfortably with his own life style.

A serious limitation of this approach is that it is uneconomical. Most orthodox theories are developed to the point where they provide consistency and comprehensiveness which few counselors can equal. Theories should lend themselves to continual modification through research or day-to-day counseling practice. Because they are usually stated less explicitly, most "home-grown" theories would not be particularly fruitful in generating research hypotheses.

Another limitation is that the counselor risks incorporating incompatible theoretical elements. One reason for this is a terminology problem. Is the self-concept the same for all "self" theorists? How does it differ from the ego? And is the ego the same among different Freudian and psychoanalytic theorists? And what about student learning: does it occur through conditioning, trial-and-error, or insight and discovery? It is extremely difficult to disentangle the conceptual and semantic snarls that hinder smooth translation from one theory to another. A more basic difficulty is that some elements, without redefinition, may be inconsistent with elements already included within the counselor's theoretical framework. A counselor might find very appealing Rogers' hypothesis of the individual's inherent tendency toward positive growth, but it could hardly be incorporated within a framework already including the Freudian emphasis on man's destructive instinct.

In fitting a theory to his personality, a counselor may reshape the theory to fit a distorted view of human behavior. A counselor should question his inability to accept a theory that does not "fit" his personal style. Shoben [13] has suggested that the particular theory a counselor selects may reflect the counselor's personality. Similarly, those aspects of theory the counselor rejects can also reflect his personality. Counselors are too often encouraged to find an approach that "feels comfortable" without considering the scientific validity of the approach. Patterson's [6] questions about the use of "counselor comfort" as a basis for counseling behavior apply also to the selection of theoretical principles.

The counselor may become so involved in explaining student behavior and in developing a rationale for operating that his theoretical principles are not translated into action. The best theory cannot help the student unless it is acted upon. A counselor should not rest on his laurels once he has achieved a unified theory of counseling.

Technical

These eclectic counselors are more concerned with counseling techniques than with theoretical or philosophical foundations. They are generally unconcerned about whether Freud, Skinner, or Rogers has presented the most accurate view of human behavior. Of more immediate importance are questions such as when to be "directive" or "nondirective." The counselor who is technically eclectic spends little time developing a rationale for his counseling. He is mainly concerned with techniques that work.

These counselors often develop their technique repertoires from lists such as those of Robinson [9] and Porter [8]. Choice of technique depends on factors such as student need, time limitations, and administrative viewpoint toward counseling. Callis [1] compared the one-technique counselor with a mechanic whose only tool is a screwdriver. The assumption is that different techniques are required in different situations. Virtually every counseling technique is therefore useful for achieving some desirable outcome. It would be argued that advice, punishment, and moralizing are appropriate techniques under certain circumstances.

There are advantages in technical eclecticism. It enables the counselor to be practical, flexible, and task-oriented. He need not feel his hands are tied because he has only one or two techniques at his disposal. Much of the resistance to nondirective techniques stems from the feeling that their exclusive use prevents a counselor from taking the steps necessary to help students.

There is evidence that students prefer counselors who direct the counseling process [7] and that younger students prefer a more dependent relationship with their counselors [3]. Students might therefore feel more secure with counselors who, by exhibiting a vast technique repertoire, appear to be "doing something." The school staff may likewise feel that the counselor is effective because he displays numerous techniques for helping students.

Technical eclecticism enables the counselor to economize on time and effort. Some techniques are more rapid and direct than others. For example, a counselor might decide that a student needs to engage in some activity in which he can succeed. If reasonably certain the student can succeed, the counselor will not hesitate to use the technique of urging to induce the student to give the activity a try. According to this counselor's judgment, urging would be much preferred to reflection of feelings.

The counselor who is technically eclectic might be more able to choose techniques that fit his personality. Shoben [13] hypothesized that the counselor's personality may influence his choice of counseling theory; it is likewise possible that the counselor's personality might influence his preference for certain techniques. It would be difficult for an energetic, argumentative person to rely exclusively on reflection and clarification. Urging, persuasion, and interpretation would be equally out of character for an unassertive counselor.

The technical emphasis in eclecticism poses certain hazards for the counselor. Orthodox counseling approaches are often criticized as inapplicable in the school because they take so much time. To find something quicker, the counselor often switches techniques when change is not immediate. But in doing so he may prematurely abandon a valid technique for one yielding immediate but temporary results.

When counseling techniques are varied from student to student, it is difficult to account for success. Many students make plans, reach decisions, and solve personal problems without the aid of counseling. Because desirable changes do occur *without* counseling, it is hazardous to adopt a technique because it happened to "work" with a particular student. This is the pitfall about which Deutsch and Murphy warned beginning psychiatrists:

> Our experience as supervisors taught us how far the deterioration of a psycho-therapeutic approach can go when the inexperienced psychiatrist, *left to his own devices and enticed by accidental successes,* considers a systematic approach as dispensable . . . we also realize how much more difficult it is to teach and to restrain a student who has already tasted the narcissistic gratification of those successes which he prefers to the effort of a consciously controlled therapeutic procedure [2, p. 9, italics added].

The counselor's readiness to modify his approach to fit the immediate situation can prevent mastery of basic techniques. What appears to be an inappropriate technique is often the ineffective use of the technique. Reflection of feeling, an important technique in all counseling approaches, is often discarded as ineffective before it is really learned. Many counselors mistakenly believe they are using reflection of feeling when they repeat or closely paraphrase the student's remarks. This is not reflection of feeling but it is about all that can be achieved in the beginning. Through experience and careful supervision, counselors learn to infer and state the *implied* feelings and meanings in the student's statements. It is one thing to use judiciously a technique over which one has acquired control; it is quite another to use it so sporadically it is never really learned.

Counselors who vary their techniques may confuse their students. Switching from active to passive techniques with the same student can confuse him about the counselor's estimate of his capacity to work things out for himself. Using different techniques with different students can confuse students about what to expect from the counselor.

The technically eclectic counselor may be unable to present a well-defined professional image to the school administration, staff, and student body. By widely varying his techniques and practices, he may have difficulty showing a consistent underlying policy. The eclectic counselor who cannot convey that he has a unified counseling position may be regarded as a general trouble-shooter whose chief distinction is his bag of tricks.

The most serious hazard in technical eclecticism is that it allows the counselor to avoid dealing openly with vital issues in counseling. Preoccupation with "what works" can prevent clear thinking about desired outcomes of counseling. The counselor who adopts an orthodox counseling approach is provided with a clear notion of how students behave and how they can be helped. His counseling techniques are subordinate to the purposes derived from the theoretical position. The counselor who lacks a sound theoretical framework, however, often works toward goals he does not clearly perceive. Eclectic counselors usually assume they accept the same goals as orthodox counselors but that they do so in practical ways that fit the school situation. For example, a counselor may say he agrees with client-centered *theory* but modifies his techniques because it is too time-consuming to listen to students discuss their feelings and aspirations at great length. This apparent compromise on *method* is actually a disagreement on *purpose.* This counselor *says* that students should be helped to make their own plans and reach their own decisions. His *action* suggests more expedient concerns—number of students seen per day, number of students who plan four-year programs, how quickly the student can be led to see that he should not question his teacher's fairness, etc. Such objectives imply that neither the counselor's techniques *nor* his objectives are client-centered. His *techniques* suggest an unspoken belief that counseling should cause students to fit into school procedures with a minimum of friction, that students need to be told what is best for them, that short-run efficiency is valued over long-run personal development.

In Quest of a Synthesis

The counselor who wishes to develop an alternative to existing counseling approaches has the task of developing a synthesis that avoids the pitfalls and incorporates the best aspects of the theoretical and technical emphases. The following considerations may be helpful in working toward such a synthesis.

A counselor behaves in terms of what he believes is true. A theoretical point of view cannot influence his behavior until it becomes a part of his belief system. One way of approaching such a synthesis is to begin by examining one's personal beliefs about the nature of people and the nature and purpose of the helping task. It has been suggested [5] that each counselor has formed, long before exposure to formal counseling theories, hypotheses about the nature of people and how best to help them. These implicit assumptions, or personal theories, can provide a point of departure in developing one's counseling approach. As the counselor clarifies his basic assumptions, he may find that his life style and personal philosophy are entirely consistent with some systematic theoretical position; consequently, he does not require an eclectic approach. He may find that his personal theory does not coincide with any existing approach and that he does need a synthesis. He may, however, find that he has operated according to beliefs that on examination are irrational, inappropriate bases for counseling; if so, he faces the dual task of changing his beliefs and developing a viable counseling approach.

Changes in one's theoretical framework occur very slowly. One cannot alter his concept of the nature of human behavior from one student to another, but he can vary his counseling techniques according to the student. Theoretical principles and counseling objectives comprise the counselor's base of operations, the framework *within* which he selects and varies techniques. Sound technical eclecticism cannot exist outside a theoretical framework—however conceived—that provides a stable and consistent foundation.

One can never regard his theory as a finished product. As new concepts of behavior and counseling emerge, the counselor has new elements to consider in strengthening his theory. For example, during the last decade the concept of tension reduction as a primary goal of human behavior has been questioned. There is evidence that some behavior is directed toward actually increasing tension. This concept suggests that students might make choices and decisions which reduce comfort and security, that freedom from worry and anxiety may not be sought by all healthy persons.

While personal style and individual preference are important determinants of one's counseling approach, the findings of sound research must be carefully considered. Just because a counselor's theoretical position is logically consistent and fits his personal style, there is no guarantee that he will be effective in helping students. He may have to admit the possibility that the way of counseling he finds personally rewarding may actually be harmful to students. Findings of carefully controlled research can suggest the approaches that are effective under certain circumstances. To illustrate, two different lines of research have recently yielded findings with significant implications for counseling.

Rogers and others [10, 14] have studied the kinds of relationships that lead to personal growth in clients. These studies have suggested that clients experience personal growth in relationships with counselors who can accurately understand their personal, subjective feelings, counselors who are dependably real in the relationships, counselors who value them unconditionally as persons. This line of research suggests that when these conditions are offered at a high level, positive personal development occurs, irrespective of the counselor's "school" or techniques. A sobering aspect of this research is the finding, with more disturbed clients, at least, that the absence of these conditions leads to personal disintegration and withdrawal. It may be that counseling can hurt as well as help.

The second line of research, conducted by Krumboltz and others [4, 11, 12], has studied the effectiveness of verbal reinforcement during the counseling interview. The findings have shown that students' information-seeking behavior, study habits, and attitudes can be modified through selective reinforcement of statements made during the interview. These findings suggest that counselors may soon acquire the techniques for influencing a wide range of student behavior. The possibilities for deliberate and systematic shaping of student behavior are clearly evident.

The counselor needs to keep "in touch" with himself as an instrument in the helping process. Research findings and theory development are indispensable guidelines for developing one's approach, but they are only guidelines. They must be individually interpreted and modified by each counselor. Each must know how students perceive him. He must know how effective he is with certain techniques. He must know the situations in which he is most helpful to students and those in which he fails miserably. He needs to communicate with himself in order to know when things are going well in the relationship and when communication is being impaired.

Every counseling theory should provide a blueprint for action. It is not enough to develop a theoretical base of operations. Theoretical principles must be translated into counseling behavior within one's particular school setting. If one believes that students learn best by experience and that independence is acquired through being independent, what can one *do* to provide such opportunities?

A mature eclectic approach is far more demanding than acceptance of an established point of view. It is *not* the easy way out. Professional counseling requires a sound theoretical framework. There is no longer a question of whether to have a counseling theory. It is abundantly clear that each counselor already has a set of guiding principles, whether openly stated or not. But it is only when operational theories *are* explicitly stated that they can be examined, tested, and modified by rational means. The eclectic counselor is very much an explorer. And as such, he must be courageous enough to explore beyond the well-marked path and responsible enough to map clearly the new terrain.

References

1. Callis, Robert. Toward an integrated theory of counseling. *J. Coll. Stu. Personnel*, 1960, *1*, 2-9.
2. Deutsch, Felix, & Murphy, William F. *The clinical interview*. Vol. 2. New York: International Universities Press, Inc., 1955.
3. Gilbert, Norman S. When the counselor is a disciplinarian. *Personnel Guid. J.*, 1965, *43*, 485-491.

4. Krumboltz, John D., & Thoresen, Carl E. Effect of behavioral counseling in group and individual settings on information-seeking behavior. *J. Counsel. Psychol.*, 1964, *11*, 324-333.
5. Lister, James L. The counselor's personal theory. *Counselor Educ. Supervis.*, 1964, *3*, 207-213.
6. Patterson, C. H. A note on counselor personality and therapeutic techniques. *J. Counsel. Psychol.*, 1961, *8*, 89-90.
7. Patterson, C. H. Client expectations and social conditioning. *Personnel Guid. J.*, 1958, *37*, 136-138.
8. Porter, E. H. *An introduction to therapeutic counseling.* Boston: Houghton Mifflin, 1950.
9. Robinson, Francis P. *Principles and procedures in student counseling.* New York: Harper & Bros., 1950.
10. Rogers, Carl R. The interpersonal relationship: the core of guidance. *Harv. Educ. Rev.*, 1962, *32*, 416-429.
11. Ryan, T. Antoinette. Reinforcement counseling with small groups in modifying study behavior of college students. Paper read at American Personnel and Guidance Assn., Minneapolis, 1965.
12. Schroeder, W. W. Effect of selective reinforcement and model interviews on information seeking behavior. Paper read at American Personnel and Guidance Assn., San Francisco, 1964.
13. Shoben, Edward Joseph, Jr. The counselor's theory as personal trait. *Personnel Guid. J.*, 1962, *40*, 617-621.
14. Truax, Charles B., & Carkhuff, Robert R. The old and the new: theory and research in counseling and psychotherapy. *Personnel Guid. J.*, 1964, *42*, 860-866.
15. Tyler, Leona E. Theoretical principles underlying the counseling process. *J. Counsel. Psychol.*, 1958, *5*, 3-10.

RICHARD R. GRONERT

Combining a
Behavioral Approach
with Reality Therapy

This study is an attempt to demonstrate how behavioral counseling and a Reality Therapy approach in elementary education can work together in the child's total development. Data for these two cases come from my work as an elementary school counselor in Janesville, Wisconsin.

Inasmuch as this paper deals with combining counseling approaches, it is necessary to examine the relationships of Reality Therapy, Adlerian Psychology, and Behavioral Modification.

Glasser's Reality Therapy (Glasser, 1965) is an excellent tool for identifying situations and problems; it serves well in helping a troubled client to internalize the fact that he is acting irresponsibly. When the counselor involves himself with the client's situation, then alternative client behaviors can be explored effectively. The client also is made to realize that he alone is responsible for his successes and failures, and if he is going to extend an accusing finger toward someone, he should point it at himself. Reality Therapy employs both positive and negative reinforcements for the purpose of "administering" life's consequences, i.e., reality. Examples of this are scat-

Gronert, R. R. Combining a behavioral approach with reality therapy. *Elementary School Guidance and Counseling,* 1970, 5(2), 104-112. Copyright 1970 American Personnel and Guidance Association. Reprinted with permission.

tered generously through chapter three of Glasser's work cited above which discusses the Ventura School for girls. He defines reality as that which has long-range benefits for the client as opposed to more immediate reinforcement of short-term pleasures.

Reality Therapy sets the stage and arranges the counseling relationship for the introduction of the Adlerian Psychology of Dreikurs (Dreikurs & Stolz, 1964) because it has determined that the total responsibility of the client's actions are directly on his own shoulders. Therefore, logical and natural consequences of the client's behavior are consistent and appropriate (Dreikurs & Stolz, p. 76). One of the tenets of this paper is that Adlerian Psychology aids in situation identification because the counselor begins to focus on the determinants of a situation when he considers the natural and/or logical consequences of the client's behavior. Even though Dreikurs does not endorse punishment, his view of Adlerian Psychology nevertheless serves as a bridge to Behavioral Modification in that his discussion points out the necessity for the parent or teacher to determine to what behaviors they will attend. Behavioral Modification goes a bit farther than Dreikurs because it endorses positive and negative reinforcement (Glasser, 1965; Krumboltz & Thoresen, 1969; Patterson & Gullion, 1968).

In combining a method of using natural and/or logical consequences with behavioral positive and negative reinforcement, we may think of the teacher or parent as analogous to a hot stove. A hot stove cooks meals (positive reinforcement). The logical consequence of using a hot stove properly is to eat hot meals; but, if one misuses the stove by bumping into it, he will be burned (negative reinforcement/natural consequence). Touching a hot stove repetitively would be similar to frequent disruption of a teacher's class by inappropriate behavior. The decision regarding how to use the hot stove is up to the individual, and he experiences in his behavior the natural consequences (good and bad). From such coping-experiences with life's consequences the client should developmentally learn to side-step problems.

After a situation is identified with the resulting realities of natural and logical consequences, then Behavioral Modification can be very useful. Reality Therapy combined with Adlerian Psychology can be thought of as setting the stage for Behavioral Modification.

The relationship between Adlerian Psychology and Behavioral Modification is strong because both methods indicate that the administrators of the child (parent, teacher, counselor, psychologist) need to sort out their own behaviors in a specific situation and quietly determine which behaviors in the children they will attend. (The act of responding is reinforcement—social reinforcements are smiles, praise; material reinforcements are M&M's, playtime, etc.) They must also determine which inappropriate behavior they will attempt to ignore and hope for considerable reduction in behavior. Any positive reinforcement is an encouragement that acts as a cement in strengthening the desired behavior. As the appropriate behavior sets, it usually carried its own reward (i.e., accomplishment, social acceptance, etc.) for the individual, as the behavior becomes assimilated, the material reinforcement gradually diminishes.

Jane's Case

Jane, eleven and a half, had had two years of ineffective psychological counseling concerning her grossly inappropriate, hyperactive classroom behavior with little or no results. Her behavior was so gross that the school psychologist said that any method that would cure this problem would be a rare accomplishment in psychological case studies.

Jane's five teachers approached me at the point of complete exasperation and stated their feeling that she should be sent away—perhaps to Mendota State Hospital. With reservations, however, they agreed to work with me in a behavioral approach. So, the challenge for elementary counseling was on.

First, a staffing was held with Jane's teachers to identify one of her most disturbing behaviors, namely, her vociferous outbursts. Second, it was explained that only one major behavior change should be dealt with at a time; teachers should ignore the behaviors that did not disrupt too much, thus not reinforcing other inappropriate attention-getting mechanisms. They also agreed to reinforce Jane's appropriate behaviors that they wanted her to repeat, thus encouraging desirable behavior. One teacher was asked to chart the frequency of Jane's vociferous outbursts. Finally, we agreed on the most important part of the method—the administration of a psychologically sterile Time-Out. When her behavior became so gross that it could not be ignored, the teachers had to act. In Jane's case we used a Time-Out in order not to reinforce her inappropriate means of getting attention (Briskin & Gardner, 1968).

A Time-Out is a physical area relatively void of visual or auditory stimulation though not frightening for the youngster. It is rigid, but in Jane's case it probably serves as one of the most loving acts in her behalf because it caused her to taste the realities of a balance between her inappropriate/appropriate behavior. The choice of appropriate versus inappropriate behavior is hers alone. The teachers are to reinforce her selected behavior if it is appropriate, attempt to ignore her mild inappropriate behavior, and, when the behaviors are gross, arrange the logical consequence for handling an inappropriate attention-getting mechanism. Then Jane goes to a Time-Out.

With no visible emotion, the teachers were to send Jane to the Time-Out area for each vociferous outburst no matter how many times a day it occurred. The Time-Out area is a blind, semidark, narrow, hallway far removed from other people but close enough to my office for both visual and auditory observation. This device not only helped Jane but it also immediately took the pressure off the teachers and the classroom when it was most urgent. A Time-Out might possibly become a damaging experience for one's psychological makeup; therefore, it should be administered in school only with the advice of a psychologist or a counselor. If improperly administered, a Time-Out could perhaps teach a child to withdraw, so it would become a reality-avoidance mechanism. What is meant by proper administration of a Time-Out is the significance of such a procedure with each individual. A child is evaluated by the counselor and/or psychologist to determine whether he has withdrawal tendencies. If so, he is not placed in a Time-Out.

Jane's teachers watched for her next vociferous outburst which came soon, followed by her first Time-Out experience. Jane had already experienced a trusting counseling relationship; therefore, it was explained to her that her own behavior had put her in this situation and when she decided to behave appropriately again according to classroom standards she would be welcomed back in class. Her first Time-Out lasted 35 minutes; she did not enjoy it because she had nothing to do. Her purse, pencils, books, etc., were all removed, leaving her with nothing to do but sit in boredom.

Purpose of the Time-Out

The purpose of the Time-Out is to produce a larger conflict for Jane than her present conflict of appropriate classroom behavior. Because her major goal has been getting attention inappropriately, we were convinced that by removing Jane's audience we would thwart her attention-getting fulfillment. The removal to the Time-Out area then became a negative reinforcer stimulating less maladaptive behavior and raising in Jane a conflict that needed resolution. When she chose appropriate alternative behavior, it was positively reinforced, thus achieving a welcome balance in the consequences of her behavior. An inference from Piaget's conflict resolution through alternative exploration would be that we choose the lesser of two conflicts by resolving the greater conflict by means of choosing alternative action or by avoidance (Piaget & Inhelder, 1958).

The victory in behavioral changes came from the staff's consistent actions and emotions. There was no reason to attach a label to Jane in an attempt to "pigeon-hole" her psychological behavior. Her name was the only label used in describing her. Jane was handled behaviorally with positive and negative reinforcements combined with Reality Therapy in which she had to admit that her behavior had been inappropriate at times and that she alone must pay for her irresponsibility (Glasser, 1969).

Table 1 shows what I consider the cycle of a person's behavior.

Table 1. Cycle of a Person's Behavior

According to:	Leads to:	Leads to:	Leads to:
G: Responsibility	Irresponsibility	Consequence	Responsibility
P: Conflict	Avoidance	Larger conflict	Lesser conflict
D: Classroom be-havior	Misuse of class	Painful consequence	Appreciation of class
J: Jane's behavior	Vociferous out-burst	Time-Out	Responsible be-havior

Note—Glasser (G); Piaget (P); Dreikurs (D); Jane's case (J).

Within three days of this consistent, nonemotional teacher reaction, Jane was very much improved. It took two days of the teachers' appropriate behavior in ignoring Jane's mild misbehaviors, their reinforcements of her slightest attempt to behave appropriately, and their consistently sending her to a Time-Out room for gross behavior (two times in two days). The Time-Out served as a strong reminder for Jane to think twice before she misbehaved in class. By the end of the week the teachers were delighted with the modification of Jane's behavior and they began to realize that she had something to offer. More importantly Jane realized this herself, so her self-concept began to improve. Her peers began to accept her and teasing diminished. Jane began to effectively cope in life and her job became that of a student with little time for excuses or crutches.

One day a teacher even left Jane alone in charge of the class and she was pleasantly overwhelmed by such attention. She had found that appropriate behavior was much less a conflict than inappropriate behavior because she had tasted the reality of consequences. The quality of the psychologically sterile Time-Out is what delivered that reality to her and she experienced a necessary comparison between the consequences of her appropriate and inappropriate behavior. (Since this episode a new Time-Out area has been devised, which is a multi-sided opaque screen that can be used in an open-pod area.) The positive reinforcement/encouragement effort effected a significant balance in Jane's experience of the pleasure of appropriate behavior and the painful consequence of inappropriate behavior. After the first week with these behavioral methods, Jane went for one month without a Time-Out and her teachers praised her instead of registering complaints. One day Jane said to me, "How come the teachers are being so nice to me?" In reply I asked her if it might be because she was being nice to her teachers.

Jane is fully aware that she alone is responsible for her behavior and about every four weeks her behavior (described as hyperactive) sends her to a Time-Out. She is no longer dreaded by teachers, however. Frequently, while she is behaving appropriately she comes to me for general attention, counseling, window-washing therapy, and folk guitar sessions. Jane certainly has earned these privileges and they are timed to encourage only the behaviors we want repeated.

Jane was helped because of an effective combination of behavioral counseling, Reality Therapy, Adlerian Psychology, and teacher cooperation which is an important element—because without their support, elementary counseling effectiveness is severely diminished. Perhaps two words synthesize the combined approach—encouragement and involvement.

The major limitation in this approach is that the frequency charts of Jane's inappropriate behavior were not carefully maintained by the teacher. However, everyone felt the impact of Jane's swift behavior modification, and they were convinced the system was operating efficiently and saw little need for charts as proof. I kept my "druthers" to myself on this less significant point because teachers are very busy people with many things to chart.

The only danger now is that the teachers will rest on their oars in consistently dealing with Jane because she is no longer a threat; and they have been consulted on this point. If they let up in consistency of balancing positive and negative reinforcement, she may experience more reversals than necessary.

Mark's Case

Mark's case is more baffling and also more difficult than Jane's. However, the above methods were used to return Mark to appropriate behavior in the classroom and at home.

Since age two Mark had constantly wet his pants as many as five times or more a day. Mark was still wetting when he was referred to us. He was, and is, in second grade. He wet so often that his clothes were thoroughly saturated both at the end of the morning session and again at the end of the afternoon session, which had been preceded by a fresh change of clothing.

In despair, his teacher brought him to me. Mark was saturated and stank. His teacher was nauseated and desperate. Mark visited three teachers every day and the situation was urgent because he had been thoroughly wet every day of the first month of school. He remained soaked at school because he refused to cooperate with his teachers or mother in this elimination process. This was not a healthy condition mentally or physically and Mark was shunned by his peers. The next morning, after studying sphincter control, etc., and receiving no useful information, Mark and I went into the following Reality Therapy session. I explained to him that no longer would he sit in the pod (multiclass area) with wet pants because it was not sanitary or fair to the others around him or to himself. Besides, wet pants really smell bad (the realization of how he smelled was a direct thrust of Reality Therapy). His mother had mentioned that he had brain damage, but we determined that brain-damaged or not, Mark had to keep living in the world. Mark (and his mother) had had several years of psychological, neurological, psychiatric, and occupational therapy sessions with no progress.

Mark's mother had mentioned that he did not take enough time to go to the bathroom. Therefore, this morning he was told that he was going to have as much time as he needed for elimination. In fact, he was instructed to stay in the extremely small toilet area of the nurse's office until he did eliminate and I would stay outside the door to hear the water tinkle.

Before Mark went into the toilet area, we chose three pieces of candy that were placed on the desk outside the toilet area. He was told that if he eliminated he would get the three pieces of candy, if he did not eliminate then I was going to eat them.

Within 10 seconds after Mark entered the toilet area, I heard the water tinkle. Mark was pleased and I was jubilant. Not only did he get the candy but also he was made to feel as if he had won an election by the principal, his teachers and me. Mark came in to the nurse's toilet four times that day, and four times that day Mark was 100 percent successful. He went home with a pocket bulging with eight pieces of candy in a pair of dry trousers. He was so proud he did not even eat the candy; he wanted to save them to show his mother.

For one month, Mark had no reversals in school. We set him on an hour and a half schedule to visit the nurse's toilet and coordinated this as best we could with his home routine. The schedule was set up this way in case Mark could not feel bladder distentions; also, we needed a string of victories to reinforce our efforts. Later, the candy reinforcements became intermittent but we always used social reinforcements. We tried extending the schedule to an hour and 45 minutes, but the teachers had more difficulty keeping track of Mark's schedule so we returned to the original schedule. Mark did become somewhat dependent on seeing me for his eliminations and we tried to get him to take the initiative. He is now much more successful in initiating the elimination response independently.

Just before Thanksgiving Mark had three days of reversals after a month of successes. His mother said this was because of an upsetting weekend with her divorced husband disrupting the home atmosphere and Mark was reacting violently. The therapist and psychiatric social worker thought that Mark was purposely not cooperating because he felt hostile toward his mother because of the divorce situation. When asked to see the data supporting this idea they avoided responding four times and eventually admitted they had nothing to substantiate this claim. (What is this need for labels—brain damage, revenge, etc.? Do therapists really believe that a label aids treatment?)

When Mark was wet he did not go back to the class at any time. He spent two long sessions in a sanitary Time-Out situation, which he did not like. He wanted to be back in class and felt most uncomfortable. He knew his wetting behavior put him in the Time-Out, but he persisted. In fact, he missed the Thanksgiving party because the last day before vacation Mark spent considerable time in the Time-Out. It was Mark's fault that he was wet; and he could not sit in the pod area because of sanitation and damage to his increasing peer acceptance. Some may feel Mark was being punished, but, if so, he punished himself.

After Thanksgiving vacation, Mark was right back on a no-wetting schedule and is still functioning well. He had suffered the logical consequences of a lonesome Time-Out because he was wet. While consulting with his mother, we determined that she needed fresh legal advice concerning her divorce status for Mark's sake and for the whole family.

If Mark cannot feel bladder distention, then later when he can tell time, he can have a wrist alarm watch to remind him to visit the toilet. The diabetic needs to remind himself to take insulin, and there is no reason Mark cannot go through life as a normal person.

Instead of labeling irresponsible behavior and then using the label as a crutch to continue on irresponsibly, we could instead start without a label and realize that the troubled person, no matter what he is called, has to make it through life. Because of the urgency of some of our client's cases, we had better begin employing usable alternative behaviors that will adequately substitute for irresponsibility. This means, however, that we must get involved.

It seems that the younger the client, the more effective a behavioral reinforcement technique is. This presents a strong case for the great need for elementary school counselors who are capable of coordinating behavioral approaches with other approaches, such as Adlerian, developmental, Reality Therapy, self-concept, and therapy.

References

Briskin, A., & Gardner, W. Social reinforcement in reducing inappropriate behavior. *Young Children,* December 1968, *24* (2), 84-89.

Dreikurs, R., & Stolz, V. *Children: The challenge.* New York: Meredith Press, 1964. Pp. 76, 276-277.

Glasser, W. *Reality therapy.* New York: Harper & Row, 1965. Pp. 67-106.

Glasser, W. *Schools without failure.* New York: Harper & Row, 1969. Pp. 21, 131.

Krumboltz, J., & Thoresen, C. *Behavioral counseling.* New York: Holt, Rinehart & Winston, 1969. Pp. 89-114.

Patterson, G., & Gullion, M. E. *Living with children.* Champaign, Ill.: Research Press, 1968.

Piaget, J., & Inhelder, B. *The growth of logical thinking from childhood to adolescence.* New York: Basic Books, 1958. Pp. 339-340.

ERNEST L. JOHNSON

Existentialism, Self Theory, and the Existential Self

Several investigators have observed connections between Rogers' self theory and existentialist concept (Arbuckle, 1965; Landsman, 1961; Maslow, 1961; Pervin, 1960). In this study an attempt is made to identify some similarities and differences and suggest areas where a synthesis is indicated. Client-centered theory and the existential psychotherapies have evolved independently and simultaneously, are among the most recent developments in psychotherapy on two continents, and are characterized by their tentative and unfinished state of development. Their similarities should suggest confirmation, their differences may identify weaknesses, and a unification could result in the emergence of a better model of the individual.

Rogers' theory is itself a synthesis of several American personality theories that stress self-processes, phenomenology, holistic and organismic processes (see Rogers, 1951, p. 482). Rogers draws directly from Maslow, Angyal, Snygg and Combs, Raimy, Lecky, Goldstein, Allport, Stagner, and others. Rogers begins with the *individual*, or *organism*, in his private world of experience. The individual differentiates and selects experience, hence he helps to make his own

Johnson, E. L. Existentialism, self theory and the existential self. *The Personnel and Guidance Journal*, 1967, 46(1), 53-58. Copyright 1967 American Personnel and Guidance Association. Reprinted with permission.

world (phenomenal field). The individual, or organism, as used by Rogers, describes what is known in personality theory as the self-as-process, or the self-as-doer (Hall & Lindzey, 1957, p. 468).

The *self* in Rogers' theory is differentiated out of the other perceptual objects of the phenomenal field and refers to the "I" or "me." The *self-concept* refers to all the self-definitions and descriptions that the individual holds about himself. The *self structure* includes the self, self-concept, and the values that are attached to them. All these terms refer to "objects" and are governed by the same organizational principles that govern other perceptual objects. Although the self structure (self-as-object) is differentiated and defined by the individual, it finally appears to become rather organized, structured and autonomous in governing the experience of the individual.

Rogers believes that much of the self structure consists of values introjected or taken over from other people. The child may deny his real feelings because they contradict the picture that others appear to have of him, which is later assimilated by the child himself. Therefore, the "objective self," which may be the introjected values of other people or society at large, may determine the behavior or even the perceptions of the "subjective self."

Maladjustment, as viewed by Rogers, "exists when the organism denies to awareness significant sensory and visceral experiences, which consequently are not symbolized and organized into the gestalt of the self-structure" (1951, p. 510). In psychotherapy, Rogers seeks a congruence between the experience of the organism and the conceptual structure of self.

Some Existential Concepts

Existentialism also is often regarded as a synthesis. Heidegger combined Husserl's phenomenology, Nietzsche and Kierkegaard's expressions of individuality, and his own creative thinking to lay the cornerstone of the modern movement. The writings of Jaspers and Sartre helped propel it into the limelight.

Existentialism has been known as a philosophy that is concerned with the search for identity in times when selfhood is threatened by theoretical systems, mass reactions, mechanistic and technological production, exploitive mass media, and industrial and governmental hierarchical organizations. The philosophy is usually defined by several themes that permeate certain modern European philosophies, themes such as alienation and self-estrangement, transcendence, self-assertion, meaning in life, authentic living, existence in the face of death, and many others.

The philosophy places existence prior to essence. "Essence," which refers to the substance of things that is permanent and unchangeable, has been sought by the natural sciences. "Existence" on the other hand refers merely to the apparent fact of "being there." Existence, according to Sartre (1947), is just plain, absolute "to be." This existence is neither created by man, nor can he analyze it through his logical systems of thinking. Thus, his thinking does not create his existence, as Descartes would have it. According to existentialists, man exists first and then he speculates and contemplates it.

By stressing existence, existentialism undercuts the dichotomy between subject and object. Man is not a subject who perceives an object, but he exists with his objects. Subject and object become one in being-in-the-world. Man is with and a part of every object he encounters. Existentialism is said to be anti-scientific because science seeks essence and is concerned with the objects impersonally. But every object is a personal object, and according to the existentialists the individual must be fitted into every scientific observation and equation.

The individual's existence is the central factor in the analysis of things, because he creates his world and gives meaning to phenomena. He creates the objects of his experience through his *intentions* and goals. Man is viewed as being on his way toward his essence, as bridging the gap between the finite and infinite. There is nobody or no system outside of man that can affect his existence. Sartre states that "man is that which he makes himself," and therefore is responsible for what he is. If essence, what a man consists of, preceded existence, the fact that man is, then man would be determined. However, since man does not have a previously given essence, he is free, and he himself must take the responsibility for what he is.

Man's freedom and responsibility are the main sources of his anxiety. He may feel alone and isolated without some external authority to guide his behavior. This explains man's craze toward conventionality, and his tendency to "escape from freedom" (Riesman, 1950; Fromm, 1941). He also may feel abandoned when thrown into a meaningless world where he must invent purpose and projects that will confer meaning on both himself and the world of objects. Not to see possibility, not to find reason to existence, is to lose the authentic self and thus to exist in bad faith.

Anxiety and despair are the inevitable qualities of being. Man faces an uncertain future and an ultimate death. He alone must take the consequences for his choices and decisions. If he alienates himself by identifying with some corporation, organization, or system, or if he becomes "other-directed," his life is characterized by apathy, boredom, and a zombie-like existence. On the other hand, if he actualizes value, creates meaning, and takes on responsibility he suffers existential loneliness and dread. Yet this latter course of expressing his full potentiality and creativity has to be done if he is to achieve selfhood and authenticity.

Phenomenology and the Subject-Object Problem

It is evident from the preceding that both viewpoints stress the importance and significance of the individual, his capacity for growth and his freedom in realizing his own potential. Both approaches are phenomenological in that they begin with the subjective side of the subject-object relationship in examining the meaning that events have for the individual. They view the individual as active in "changing his own world" through the differentiation process of altering figure and ground. However, Rogers is concerned only with the individual's "reality," and feels that it is not necessary for the psychologist to become involved with the metaphysical question of "true" reality. "For psychological purposes, reality is basically the private world of individual perceptions" (Rogers, 1951, p. 484), and behavior is a function of this perceived reality. In contrast, the existentialists have founded their position on an attempt to resolve the epistemological dichotomy, which separates noumena from phenomena. *Being-in-the-world* implies a unity that cannot be broken down into (1) man and his sensory equipment or (2) the physical energy systems which are generally regarded as activation of this equipment. For the existentialists, existence or *Dasien* is the basic element in reality, and the polar terms *subject* and *object* are synthesized.

Rogers' approach here is phenomenological but not existential. His "reductionistic" ideas coincide with Husserl's method, which suspended judgment about real existence and stated that mental processes and ideal objects were the appropriate subject matter for science. There appears to be a subtle and indirect link between Rogers' and Husserl's brand of phenomenology. Self theory is grounded in Gestalt psychology which in turn was influenced by Husserl. This point may account for the observed similarities between self theory and existentialism, since Husserl is also regarded as one of the founding figures of existentialism (Johnson, 1966, p. 36). Thus, self theory and existentialism may have a common ancestor in Husserl.

The subject-object problem is one of long standing among the self theorists in regard to the relationship between "self-as-process" and "self-as-object" (Hall & Lindzey, 1957). Rogers makes no explanation as to how the "objective self" (the self, self-concept, self structure), is related to the "subjective self" (the organism or individual). The implications are that they are rather distinct and the self structure can become rather independent in directing experience and behavior. The existentialists, by using such concepts as *being-in-the-world*, would unify not only self and real object, but also self and perceived object. Thus, the subjective self would be in unity with the objective self, or, in Rogerian terms, the individual, or organism, would be synthesized with the self or self structure. In such a synthesis the self structure could never become an autonomous determinant of perception, but would be inseparably linked with an active, or becoming self.

Self-actualization and Determinism

Both self theory and existentialism emphasize man's movement toward self-actualization. Rogers' quote from Angyal could easily have been said by an existentialist: "Life processes do not merely tend to preserve life but transcend the momentary status quo of the organism, expanding itself continually and imposing its autonomous determination upon an ever-increasing realm of events" (Rogers, 1951, p. 488).

The term "existence" as defined by the existentialists means to *stand out,* to emerge; it is a process of becoming rather than a state of being: "Existence is projection; it 'becomes.' With every passing moment it becomes more (or less) than it is. Existence and temporality are thus practically synonymous" (Kneller, 1958, p. 25). For Tillich, man is "asked to make himself what he is supposed to become, to fulfill his destiny. In every act of moral self-affirmation man contributes to the fulfillment of his destiny, to the actualization of what he potentially is" (1952, p. 52).

A major difference between the two viewpoints is Rogers' more deterministic treatment of this directional tendency. It appears to be a natural law that applies to all living things: "The directional trend we are endeavoring to describe is evident in the life of the individual organism from conception to maturity, at whatever level of organic complexity" (Rogers, 1951, p. 488). The implication here is that striving is innate and based upon organic evaluation. The existentialists, on the other hand, view self-actualization as a goal toward which the person could *choose* to strive. However, it is the responsibility of the person to make of himself what he potentially is, and to shrug off this responsibility is to dwell in inauthentic existence. Plans, purposes and goals are strictly human creations, and when man makes them and acts on them his being becomes unique and quite distinct from that of the other objects and organisms in the world.

Experienced Values Versus Incorporated Values

Both Rogerian and existentialist positions agree that certain preferences and values become culturally defined and often assimilated through vicarious rather than actual experience. Some "values" are considered by society to be better than others, and, therefore, should be taught by parents and teachers. Cultural values may, however, eventually contradict real, experienced values, and thus the individual is thrown into conflict. Rogers believes that both non-experienced (incorporated) and experienced values are included in the self structure, and that the individual may be directed more by the incorporated or "false" values.

Both Kierkegaard and Heidegger fear that man is losing contact with his own concrete experience by accepting, or at least pretending to accept, non-chosen values. This leads to inauthentic existence; the person becomes an object among other objects in the world, or as Sartre puts it, a "being-in-itself" instead of a "being-for-itself." Kierkegaard viewed these unreal values as assimilated for the purpose of maintaining a false picture the individual has of himself as a result of expectations from other people. The individual is thus severed from his subjectivity and lives in pretense.

Values, according to the existentialists, are not detached and apart from the individual, but they are one and the same with his choices. A value always involves free choice without a "good" or "bad." Arbuckle (1965, p. 564), in relating existential treatment of values to counseling, states that every act that is labeled "bad" by someone is labeled "good" by someone else. Sartre implies that man has no hierarchy of values or universal ethics to guide his choices and therefore must act on his own responsibility. If universal values were valid then man would have no choice nor freedom, and, therefore, essence, a determined state, would be prior to existence.

One result of therapy, according to Rogers, is the replacement of a value *system* by a valuing *process*. Then the individual relies on his own physiological equipment for providing data for making value judgments and for continuously revising them. While this appears at first to coincide with existentialist ideas, a significant difference is involved. Rogers implies that there must be evidence upon which to make a value judgment, and that evidence comes from the individual's own sense-data. It appears that Rogers visualizes values emerging out of fact, which is the experiential evidence of the person.

According to the existentialists, notably Sartre, values are created by the free act of a human being, and they have nothing to do with facts. Existentialists believe that values are on a different realm from fact, and, unlike the pragmatists, hold that the former can never be generated out of an accumulation of the latter. Rogers, therefore, appears to be more pragmatic than existentialistic in this respect.

Phenomenological Self Versus Existential Self

Rogers' adherence to lawfulness follows the American trend toward predictability and exactitude. His "determinism" not only rests on the assumption that the directional tendency motivates all behavior, but also upon the proposition that if behavior is "determined by the phenomenal field, then of course, he has no choice, and he can hardly be held 'responsible' for his actions" (Arbuckle, 1965, p. 560). Rogers' theory, like that of Snygg and Combs, is deterministic to the extent that the field is more important than the individual in determining behavior.

The self structure (phenomenal self) is the most influential aspect of the field in determining perceptual selectivity and defense. But the goals of client-centered therapy appear to be toward freeing the individual from these influences so that he can choose experience that had previously been denied. Rogers sees the goals of therapy, then, as a movement of the individual toward a fuller grasp of reality so that he may become less determined by inaccurate perceptions of himself. Viewed another way, this is the movement of a phenomenal self toward an existential self, or the movement from an ideal of perceived reality to one that actually exists.

The existential self has been rather well defined by Rogers' concept of the fully functioning person. Rogers states that "... the self and personality would emerge *from* experience, rather than experience being truncated or twisted to fit the preconceived self-structure" (1951, p. 90) and "that there would be no barriers, or inhibitions which would prevent the full experiencing of whatever was organismically present" (p. 87). The fully functioning person would be a participant in and an observer of the ongoing process of organismic experience. With this concept, Rogers shifts his emphasis from a structural and consistent self-as-object, to a self that is active, subjective, and open to reality. He appears to be less phenomenological and more existential at this point.

Braaten, working within the Rogerian theory, found that the more successful a client was rated by a therapist and a TAT diagnostician the more likely it was that he showed a movement toward greater emphasis upon an immediate, emotional experiencing of the self. These "successful" clients became more truly open to their existence "right there and then" (Braaten, 1961, p. 10). Hence, Braaten poses the following as a major theme from the viewpoint of psychotherapy: "Your own experiencing is the highest authority—be fully present in the immediacy of the moment" (1961, p. 13).

In a similar manner, Jaspers defines the goals of the therapeutic process as the increasing ability of the patient to experience his existence as real. That is, to become more fully aware of his existence and all the potentialities and possibilities that emerge from it. May says that the characteristic of the neurotic is that "his existence has become 'darkened,' blurred, easily threatened and clouded over, and gives no sanction to his acts; the task of therapy is to illuminate the existence" (May, et al., 1958, p. 398).

The existential self should be further defined by the self theorists. It is the real self, the choosing self, and the becoming self. It is the entity that creates the environment and gives meaning to existence. It differs from the phenomenal self in that it is less deterministic and it functions in the "true" reality of existence rather than in a "phenomenal" or perceived reality. To obtain this type of selfhood, the individual must not only free himself from group norms, universal ethics, and mechanistic trends, but also he must become free from a consistent self-definition. When the individual defines himself he is attempting to formulate his essence, which is detrimental to transcendence. In order to achieve existential selfhood, the individual must constantly re-define himself, revise his goals, and revive his possibilities.

Summary and Conclusions

The similarities between self theory and existentialism represent some major trends that are being renewed in psychology. For one thing, the individual is growing in size and importance in relation to other factors, such as drives, urges, conditioned stimuli, etc., in determining behavior. He is viewed as being active and free in making and creating his own world, thus he has the responsibility for doing so. Also, there is a growing conclusion that all sources of values arise within the individual (Maslow, 1961, p. 53). A blind adherence to a set of values, whether external or internal, has the result of self-alienation and, thus, reduces the freedom of choice of the individual.

While self theory may be considered to be a non-deterministic personality theory, it is still built on several causal constructs. Striving toward self-actualization is viewed as an organic-biological tendency; perception is guided by a personal frame of reference; and value judgments are based on either a self structure or, in the case of the better-adjusted individual, on the facts of organic experience. Self theory is therefore existential up to a point, but insists on "explaining" much of the behavior that the existentialists would view as free actions. For the existentialists the first cause of behavior is the individual.

Also, self theory is reductionistic: it brackets off "real" reality and leaves it in metaphysical realms. Yet Rogers' theory is based upon the assumption that there is a real reality and that ultimately the individual has to approach it if he is to function properly and reach his potential. Rogers' theory is caught in the same subject-object dichotomy that the phenomenologists attempt to reduce and the existentialists synthesize. The existentialists neither reduce nor deny external reality, but view it as being contained in existence. Existence is primary, so that neither pure subjectivity nor pure objectivity can be attained.

Rogers' separation of self into "self structure" and "individual" presents another problem. The self structure may come to determine the individual's experiences and behavior, but at the same time the self structure is defined and created by the individual, or organism. The reciprocal and cyclic relationship between these entities implies that they are one and the same—the individual determines the self structure and the self structure determines or restricts the individual's full functioning. An existentialist concept, existential self, may combine self-as-doer and self-as-object in one stroke. The existential self is both what the individual does, and what he is. Or put another way, selfhood is what the individual puts into action.

The use of the construct *existential self* may strengthen and enrich self theory. This holistic term would make divisions of the self, such as self-concept, self structure, individual, and organism unnecessary. Experience or perception would not have to be *caused by* a self-definition, but would be for the *purpose of* attaining selfhood. The concept of the existential self, then, would make self theory even more teleological and holistic and less deterministic. Self theory is unique among personality theories for its advances in these directions. If the teleological, holistic and freedom orientation have been the forte of self theory, then the existential influence should be favorable.

References

Arbuckle, D. S. Existentialism in counseling: the humanist view. *Personnel and Guidance Journal,* 1965, *43,* 558-567.

Braaten, L. J. The main themes of "existentialism" from the viewpoint of a psychotherapist. *Mental Hygiene,* 1961, *45,* 10-17.

Fromm, E. *Escape from freedom.* New York: Holt, Rinehart & Winston, 1941.

Hall, C. S., & Lindzey, G. (Eds.) *Theories of personality.* New York: Wiley, 1957.

Johnson, E. L. Existential trends toward individual psychology. *Journal of Individual Psychology,* 1966, *22,* 33-41.

Kneller, G. F. *Existentialism and education.* New York: Philosophical Library, 1958.

Landsman, T. Discussion of the paper by Patterson, Kilpatrick, Luchins, and Jessor. *Journal of Individual Psychology,* 1961, *17,* 39-42.

Maslow, A. H. In R. May (Ed.), *Existential psychology.* New York: Random House, 1961.

May, R., et al. (Eds.) *Existence: a new dimension in psychiatry and psychology.* New York: Basic Books, 1958.

Pervin, L. A. Existentialism, psychology, and psychotherapy. *American Psychologist,* 1960, *15,* 305-309.

Riesman, D. *The lonely crowd.* New Haven, Conn.: Yale Univ. Press, 1950.

Rogers, C. R. *Client-centered therapy.* Boston: Houghton Mifflin, 1951.

Sartre, J. P. *Existentialism.* New York: Philosophical Library, 1947.

Tillich, P. *The courage to be.* New Haven, Conn.: Yale Univ. Press, 1952.

SECTION IV

Existential Counseling

*Counseling is essentially a process of making-free, a
humanizing of the person who has lost his freedom in
sectors of his existence where he can no longer transcend
his life situation by freely giving meaning to it. He behaves
there more or less as a lower form of being, as a
dehumanized, determined existence. It is the aim of
counseling to assist the person in regaining his freedom in
these areas by creating insight into the meanings he
attributes to these situations, by starting the extinction of
the responses which the counselee—after gaining insight—
no longer likes to retain, and by the conditioning of other
responses corresponding to his new free evaluation of reality.*
                                            —Adrian van Kaam

Existentialism, as a psychological school of thought, has been slow in gaining acceptance among practicing counselors and therapists. In the minds of many it remains a mood, an attitude, a philosophy of life, rather than a systematic therapeutic procedure. It has been overlooked particularly by those professionals specializing in child and adolescent counseling; they feel it is too philosophical, too intellectual, too abstract for an immature clientele. However, this may not remain the case in the future. A theory of personality and a theory of counseling are beginning to emerge from the philosophical predisposition of existential thought, and they can be applied to preadolescents and adolescents. The articles in this section present a thorough exposition of existential counseling theory; therefore only several brief points will be highlighted in this introduction.

An existential theory of personality does not consist of specifically stated assumptions about human behavior. Instead, it relies on generally conceived notions of the nature of man and existence. Human freedom is a central concept; however, responsibility and accountability are inherent in this notion. If people are to be free and live in a democratic community, they must be responsible and accountable for their behavior. Versatility is characteristic of existential counseling techniques. The recommended techniques vary from analytically oriented to behaviorally oriented ones, and the selection of specific techniques depends on the client and his or her life experiences. However, most existential therapists concur on the importance of the counseling relationship; this I-Thou relationship is the basis for all human understanding and growth.

The first reading in this section, by C. Gratton Kemp, is intended as a general introduction to existential counseling, from which the reader can develop specific counseling behaviors and techniques. Kemp presents an excellent sketch of existential counseling and gives a thorough background of the development of existential thought, highlighting the contributions of prominent theorists for the past hundred years. He continues by relating existential philosophy to counseling theory and outlining the basic concepts, assumptions, and techniques of the process. At the close of his discussion, Kemp presents the results of a brief survey of high school students on fear and anxiety, to highlight the appropriateness of the existential approach with adolescent clients. The reader may well wonder what the results of a similar survey of elementary school pupils would reveal. Individual replication of this type of study might elucidate the value of existential counseling for the preadolescent population.

Leif J. Braaten, in the second article, presents the major philosophical assumptions of existential thought. His specific insights into the implications of each assumption are particularly relevant for the practitioner. The third reading, by Gerald Pine, relates existential theory specifically to school counseling. He discusses the role of the counselor, and focuses on effective counseling attitudes and behaviors. This article is more concretely related to the day-to-day functioning of the counselor than the previous two. Existential counseling procedures with adolescent clients are creatively demonstrated in the final article by Marilyn Bates and Clarence Johnson. They isolate six major concepts of existential thought and discuss the implications of each for the counseling process. Client and counselor verbalizations are presented to contrast possible nondirective counselor statements with appropriate existential counselor statements.

C. GRATTON KEMP

Existential Counseling

Existentialism: The Basis for Existential Counseling

Existentialism is an endeavor to understand man as he really is. It takes issue with the assumption of science that to know the essence of man means that we have grasped the reality of man. Existentialism is also critical of the methods of knowing man which are the products of the rational approach since this approach may clarify the essence of man but offers little help in understanding the reality of man.

Reality is not identified with "objective being" but neither is it identified with "subjective being," that is with "consciousness" or feeling. Existentialism is not engaged in contrasting the objective and subjective. Instead it emphasizes the possibility of grasping oneself at a level which makes the subject-object dichotomy irrelevant. Our difficulty in trying to know ourselves is that we think of ourselves in "spatialized" terms approximate to objective things. "The moments in which we grasp ourselves are rare and consequently we are seldom free. Our existence is more in space than in time."[1] Our immediate experience so often has to be screened or put through the sieve of

C. Gratton Kemp, "Existential Counseling," *Counseling Psychologist*, 1970, 2 (3), pp. 2-30. Reprinted by permission.

some objective or subjective necessity. True freedom is experienced in moments when we grasp ourselves as we really are. "When he came to himself" is as infrequent for us as it was for the Prodigal Son.

Kierkegaard and other existentialist thinkers engaged in a desperate refusal to identify Reality with the world of objects. Nietzsche wrote: "When we have reached the inevitable economic administration of the earth, then mankind as a machine can find its meaning in the service of this monstrous mechanism of small and smaller cogs adapted to the whole."[2]

Existentialism is a reaction against the steady encroachment of technology in which existentialist thinkers see man fast becoming like the machines he operates, losing both his claim on human freedom and his ability for self-transcendence. Each thinker in his own way is trying to help man in his search for meaning. Each assists him to reclaim his dignity, to heal the split within him in which the essence of objectivity can be found in the depth of subjectivity. No means of empirical measurement can (as Allport[3] emphasizes) help us to understand the "Johnian in John." It is this kind of understanding with which existentialism is concerned. The expressions of existential thinking in literature, psychology and philosophy analyze and portray man at a level below that of the principles of both materialism and idealism. The one-dimensional man engrossed in the transient objects of his environment is delivering up his true Being for "a mess of pottage."

Why the Existential Attitude Developed in Europe

The existential attitude was a response to the critical conditions of the mid-nineteenth century. It arose through the independent thinking of many minds in a spontaneous answer to the loss of a personal center. It emerged in art, literature and philosophy.

Its beginnings in Europe and especially in Germany go back over a century to the decade of the 1840's when its main contentions were formulated by such thinkers as Schelling, Kierkegaard and Marx. They were sharply critical of the reigning "rationalism" of the Hegelians. They were followed in the next generation by Nietzsche and Dilthey.

The basic critical drive of the Existential philosophy is a part of a more general philosophical movement which counts its representatives not only in Germany but in France, Switzerland, Holland, England and America.

This drive expresses itself in calling men back to "Existence." Especially among the German thinkers there was criticism of the identification of Reality or Being with Reality-as-known, as the object of Reason. They began by distinguishing essence from existence and insisting that Reality or Being in its fullness is not essence, not the object of cognitive experience, but is in fact existence. It is Reality as immediately experienced, with the accent on the person and personal character of man's immediate experience.[4]

Ibsen's *A Doll's House* vividly illustrates what was happening in Europe in the last half of the nineteenth century. It is an attack against the fragmentation and compartmentalization of life in all of its aspects. The play emphasizes the folly of the man who keeps his wife and family in one compartment, his work in another, and his friends in a third. Compartmentalization became the distinguishing characteristic of all areas of life. In all its forms it symbolized an escape from the realities of life, from both existence and nature. Ethics was divorced from business, and religion from daily life.

Even more serious was the compartmentalization within the person himself. Reason, it was thought, told him what to do; his will put it into effect, and if his emotions got in the way, they were suppressed or channeled into compulsive drives and forced rigidly into currently acceptable mores. There was great emphasis on the rational; the "irrational" was consigned to the fairly regular events planned as emotional outlets.

Such compartmentalized individuals conformed well to the demands of a developing industrial society. They were able to manipulate themselves in the same way as they manipulated the machines they operated. Rewards such as the paycheck were the validation of personal worth. Employees' chief and often only significance was reckoned in terms of what they produced. Such individuals are described so well by Erich Fromm in his emphasis on the "marketplace orientation." He writes: "As with any other commodity, it is the market which decides the value of these human qualities, yes, even their very existence. If there is no use for the qualities a person offers, he has none, just as an unsaleable commodity is valueless though it might have its use value."[5]

Men surrendered their self-awareness as a protection against reality and paid the price in anxiety, compulsions for self-negation and despair. But the great analysts of the era, Kierkegaard and Nietzsche, concluded that the sickness of Western man was only partially explained by the specific individual or social problem. Industrialization and technological development nudged him into this condition, but as Nietzsche declared: "This is Europe's true predicament, . . . together with the fear of man we have lost the love of man, confidence in man, indeed, the will to man."[6]

In the fast developing industrial society, increasing importance was placed on the "rational" system of thought. But the interpretation of reason itself changed from "the power of truth and justice embodied in man as man,"[7] to technical reason applied in the making of machines which ushered in a world-wide mechanism and with it a mechanized way of looking at man.[8] This system of thought and life developed by the industrial society and philosophic writings such as those of Hegel was opposed by the philosophers of Existence. Poets, artists, and philosophers in every European country tried to stem the encroachment of the self-estranged form of life which was fast losing contact with the Eigenwelt world of being. Such artists as Van Gogh, Cezanne and Picasso indicate in their works the desperate attempt to express the immediate underlying meaning of the modern human situation, even though this means portraying despair and emptiness. Indeed, Tillich holds that Picasso's painting "Guernica" gives a most gripping and revealing portrayal of the atomistic, fragmentized condition of European society which preceded World War II.

In light of what has happened in the last hundred years, their opposition is more than justified. As Tillich describes it, the implications of this system have become increasingly clear: "A logical or naturalistic mechanism which seemed to destroy individual freedom, personal decision and organic community; an analytic rationalism which saps the vital forces of life and transforms everything, including man himself, into an object of calculation and control; a secularized humanism which cuts man and the world off from the creative Source and the ultimate mystery of existence."[9]

The focus of the transition was the changing attitude toward religion and religious values. All groups faced the problem created by the breakdown of the religious tradition under the impact of the social revolution, bourgeois liberalism and the ideas of the enlightenment. Religion moved to the periphery of life. It lost its relevance for all groups—the educated and the great numbers of industrial workers. It was no longer a present and immediate resource and it offered no unquestioned sense of direction.

There were efforts to try to return religion to its former regency. Hegel attempted to do this by conscious reinterpretation, but he did not succeed. His approach was attacked by a revived theology on the one hand and by philosophical positivism on the other.

It was in this matrix of change that existential philosophers endeavored to find the ultimate meaning of life. For them it could not be found in the "estranged" objective world. It was beyond the reach of reinterpretation, revived theologies and philosophical positivism. They sought it in the inward experience, in reality as immediately experienced in actual living. So they turned to man's immediate experience, toward "subjectivity" as the living experience in which both objectivity and subjectivity are rooted. Such an undertaking had strong mystical overtones but there was no intention of a mystical union with the transcendent absolute. Instead it was an expression of faith toward union with the depths of life whether ventured upon by individuals or groups.

An examination of what was taking place at that period in England reveals a remarkable contrast. England was the only European country in which the existential problem of finding a new meaning for life had no significance. Here positivism and the religious tradition were on friendly terms. This existed partly because social conformism prevented radical questions from gaining the floor of consciousness. During the time of upheaval (1830 to 1930), religion retained its central and unique place in the thinking of the people. This condition suggests that the existential attitude and philosophy arose on the mainland out of the problems created by the breakdown in the religious tradition.

The Slow Acceptance of Existential Thought in America

1. *European philosophy and psychology has made slow progress in America.* It has clearly been eclipsed by the ideas imported from Britain. Allport has compared the influence of the two streams, the philosophy and especially the psychology of the Lockean or British emphasis and the Leibnitzian or European emphasis. In his comparison he writes that the Leibnitzian tradition maintains that the person is not a collection of acts, or simply the locus of acts; the person is

the source of acts.[10] Gestalt theory imported from Europe has become the most influential version of the original meaning in adjusting to Anglo-Saxon empiricism. The idea of intention gave way to the passive concept of expectancy. Planning, foresight and purpose bowed to the cognitive theories of "maps" or "sets."

Even these distorted and weakened versions of the active intellect are challenged by those American positivists who emphasize stimulus response and associationism. Thus positivism, including not only behaviorism and operationism but also associationism, became the right wing of contemporary American psychology. Cognitive theory became the left wing which has remained Lockean. It has little to do with a truly active intellect intrinsic to the personal self which was the insight of Leibnitz and his successors.

Generally speaking there is little enthusiasm for the concept of being or existence when it is differentiated from essence which is the result only of cognition or rational thought. However there are some trends in the direction of making room for the existential point of view. There are those whose central theories parallel Spinoza's doctrine of conatus. The writings of Angyal, Cantril, Lecky, Rogers and Goldstein emphasize self-actualization to varying degrees. Although these authors are not existential thinkers, they do postulate one basic motive in life—the maintaining and actualizing of the organism.

2. *There appears to be at times an almost irrational fear of an encroachment of philosophy into science.* Such a fear or suspicion has several roots. This encroachment is in part a continuance of nineteenth century attitudes when psychological science won its freedom from metaphysics. It is sometimes forgotten that the existential movement resulted from an intense concern to be more rather than less empirical. This movement is in part a reaction to the tendency of seeing the counselee in forms fashioned to the counselor's own preconceptions or to make him over into his own predilection. Counselors have been and still are guilty of the "Procrustean bed" approach. In this respect existentialism is within the household of the scientific tradition.

On the other hand, it is a threat to the purely scientific approach (narrowly conceived) in its acceptance and use of the facts which human beings reveal in art, literature, and philosophy, and in its study of cultural changes which provides insights into the anxiety and conflicts of contemporary man. In the existentialists' search to understand they unite science and humanism.

The aversion to the use of philosophical insights is short-sighted. Counselors need to recognize that every scientific method rests upon philosophical presuppositions. The reality which the counselor sees is determined by his knowledge and use of philosophical undergirding. By examining the philosophical bases of what he is doing and plans to do the counselor must recognize whether or not it agrees with what he believes about human nature and is relevant to real problems.

It is a common but naive and erroneous premise that the counselor is better able to observe facts if he avoids having anything to do with philosophical assumptions. This premise results in his identification with methods of isolating factors and observing them from an allegedly detached base, a method resulting from the split between subject and object made in the seventeenth century in Western culture and developed in its present form in the last hundred years.[11] It is accepted that science should question its own presuppositions. This means that the counselor should analyze his philosophical assumptions, and many counselors find this difficult to do.

3. *Counselors are preoccupied with technique.* They are also action oriented. These two characteristics may explain in part their lack of interest and knowledge of the theories upon which the various methods of counseling are based. One explanation may be found in our pragmatic approach to almost every kind of problem, and our optimistic, activistic concern for helping and changing people. This is demonstrated by our progress in the behavioristic, clinical and applied areas.

Our concern with technique is a worthy one, but what shall be the source of our rationale? It must be apparent that if technique only is emphasized, it will finally become self-defeating. Can we be sure that the environment and our interpersonal relationships will supply the most comprehensive insights for progress?

Why Existential Counseling Has Meaning for Us

Some individuals today are homeless and lost, giving up awareness and sinking into dogmatism and conformism. Others are striving for a heightened self-consciousness by which to become aware of their existence with new convictions. At this time of crisis in history, existentialism and existential counseling become especially relevant.

Counselors are becoming more introspective. They realize that they may be far removed from the reality of those they wish to help. Is the counselee or group member only an object and perceived as the projection of our particular theory of behavioral change? Do we expect him to fit the conceptual system in which we have been trained (this is not to minimize the importance of knowledge and training, but only to suggest that it may be inadequate, biased, and even irrelevant in certain specific situations)?

May Smith, sitting across from us, may not be capable of being understood through the use of any of our conceptual systems. It is difficult for us to accept that she does not have to be logical or consistent, and that she has human freedom. How can we know whether or not we see May Smith as she really is, in the world in which she "lives, moves, and has her being"?

This was the concern of those in Europe who have become known as members of the Daseinanalyze or existential-analytic movement. The movement, as described by its chief spokesman, Binswanger, "arose from dissatisfaction with the prevailing efforts to gain scientific understanding in psychiatry . . . . Psychology and psychotherapy as sciences are admittedly concerned with 'man,' but not at all primarily mentally ill man but with man as such. The new understanding of man, which we owe to Heidegger's analysis of existence, has its basis in the new conception that man is no longer understood in terms of some theory—be it a mechanistic, a biological or a psychological one. . . ."[12] In a time of radical upheaval in the period of transition from Medievalism to Renaissance, Pascal courageously probes the meaning of our existence. He writes: "When I consider the brief span of my life, swallowed up in the eternity before and behind it, the small space that I fill, or even see, engulfed in the infinite immensity of spaces which I know not, and which knows not me, I am afraid, and wonder to see myself here rather than there, now rather than then. . . ."[13]

Pascal could have written this today, to you and me. Many of us also are aware of the contingency of life, its "throwness." Too many of us have wondered why we are here, not there; why it was a friend, a wife or husband and not ourselves. We would like to have a satisfying understanding but find none, and sometimes, to still our disquietude, we take refuge in some superficial explanation of time and space.

It is little comfort that we in the Western world seem to have gained power over and conquered nature. Deep in man's being the result has been not only his estrangement from nature but also his estrangement from himself. Existentialism seeks to overcome the resulting split between subject and object and to grasp reality at a level which is below such cleavages. Oriental thought speaks to our search although it is on a different level and from a very different perspective. In quotations from Laotzu's *The Way of Life,* we read: "Existence is beyond the power of words to define: terms may be used but none of them is absolute." "Existence is infinite, not to be defined and though it seem but a bit of wood in your hand, to carve as you please, it is not to be lightly played with and laid down." "The way to do is to be." "Rather abide at the center of your being, for the more you leave it, the less you learn."[14]

Many conditions in America now parallel those in Europe during the period of the development of existential philosophy. There is a breakdown here of the religious and humanistic traditions. The church is uncertain and pragmatic expediency is in the saddle. For many, the religious tradition is irrelevant to the problems of the times; to others it is an afterthought. Freedom and responsibility are little understood and less respected. Rebellion and force are accepted by many as the means of securing change.

There is a lack of direction which causes deep concern in all levels of society. The trained and educated place much hope in sophisticated systems of analysis and the best insights of the behavioral sciences. There is a hidden assumption that technical reason, successful in other realms, will succeed here too, given a little time and encouragement. In other words, the problems are located in environment and interpersonal relationships. Lofty symbols and productive imagination are reduced to signs, which make creative imagination seem unnecessary. We ask the wrong questions therefore, and seek meaning in the advancements of the technological society. Many assume that man lives by bread alone, and those who wonder seemingly cannot extricate themselves from searching only in the empirical world.

The Counselee's World from the Existential Viewpoint

Each one of us has three simultaneous aspects of world which characterize our existence as being-in-the-world. We live in the natural world, the world of objects around us, generally called the environment and known as Umwelt, meaning "world around." We live at the same time in the world of interpersonal relationships, the world of one's fellow men, and known as Mitwelt, literally the "with-world." Eigenwelt, the third world in which we live, is generally ignored. It is not adequately discussed in modern psychology or depth-psychology. It presupposes self-awareness, self-relatedness, self-transcendence and is possessed only by human beings. It is the potential for grasping what something, such as a snow-topped mountain, a ballet, or a personal relationship means to us. It is the basis on which we see the real world in its true perspective. But whereas we are impelled toward the first two relationships, i.e., to the natural world and to relationships with others, the Eigenwelt aspect of world may remain underdeveloped. We tend to objectify this potential for development known as Eigenwelt, or "own-world." We say "that is a beautiful sunset," but we leave out the "for-me-ness" of the experience. Our dichotomy between subject and object has conditioned us to believe that more is said when we state that it is beautiful—separated from ourselves. In our false attempt to be more scientific, more "truthful," we lose the sense of reality in our experiences.

We live in all three modes of world—Umwelt, Mitwelt and Eigenwelt. They are always interrelated and therefore influence one another. Each of these three worlds has its own host of special meanings.

Umwelt, the first mentioned, is the world common to all organisms. For animals and ourselves, it includes biological drives, needs and instincts. It is the world of natural cycles of sleep and wakefulness, of desire and relief. It is the world of biological determinism. It is appreciated, accepted, and honored by the existentialists. As Kierkegaard wrote, ". . . natural law is as valid as ever." On the other hand, it is to be expected that the existentialists place it in more proper perspective than the essentialists, who emphasize "drives" and "substances" and ignore or place little emphasis on the other modes of world.

Mitwelt, the second mentioned world of interpersonal relationships, does not mean any form of "social determinism" or "collective mind." It refers to a much more complex interaction in which the meaning of others in the group is partly determined by one's own relationship to each of them. Such a relationship carries with it a sense of responsibility, of caring, of commitment and communion. It is a true organic group as opposed to an aggregate group or collection of individuals. The implications of the relationship which exists in

Mitwelt have been developed by Martin Buber in his "I and Thou" philosophy.[15] In the description of Umwelt, the categories of "adjustment" and "adaptation" are accurate, whereas in Mitwelt the term "relationship" describes the interaction. If the counselor induces the counselee to adjust to test results or his analysis of a set of conditions, the counselee loses his personhood and is only an instrumentality, an object. Relationship implies a readiness on the part of both counselor and counselee to change.

The understanding of Eigenwelt is more difficult. For many who are preparing to counsel it is strictly foreign to their way of thinking. Some verbally refute it; others ignore it; still others distort its meaning. It poses a difficult problem for a sizeable proportion of this group. This is unfortunate, but it should not be altogether surprising. Eigenwelt is an unexplored territory of psychotherapeutic theory. What do such terms as "the inner choice" and "a personal center" mean? Or what does it mean to say "the self in relation to itself," or the "self knowing itself"?

This understanding of the self in relation to itself was not dealt with by Freud. Nor have the interpersonal schools dealt with it. Sullivan's approach tends to make the self a mirror of the group around one. This empties the self of vitality and originality and reduces the interpersonal world to one of "social relations." The schools who see relationships within the boundaries of Mitwelt deal inadequately with love as might be expected. Sullivan uses his concept of the meaning of "chum" which leaves it without depth or symbolic meaning. Love cannot be understood if Eigenwelt is omitted. Omit it and love lacks power and the capacity for development. Nietzsche and Kierkegaard insisted that to love one must have become the "true individual."

Kierkegaard insisted that to love presupposes that one "has comprehended the deep secret that also in loving another person one must be sufficient unto himself."[16] Marriage counselors sometimes rephrase this in words such as "the one who makes the best marriage partner is the one who does not need to marry." Such a statement in general proves to be a conundrum to many college students since they are steeped in the Umwelt and Mitwelt modes of being.

Basic Concepts in Existential Counseling

1. *To know the counselee is to relate to him in his totality, to grasp his being.* This is different from knowing *about* him. Valuable

as definitive and comprehensive data may be, we do not learn *of* him, only *about* him. This is not really seeing the other as a person. In fact it may be a means of defending oneself from the anxiety of involvement, of being with him. To encounter the being of the counselee with the readiness to love him is to open oneself tò a profound experience and this involves a creative risk. Sartre wrote: "But what each of us requires in this very effort to comprehend another is that he should never resort to this idea of substance, which is inhuman because it is well this side of the human. If we admit that the person is a totality, we cannot hope to reconstruct him by an addition or by an organization of the diverse tendencies which we have empirically discovered in him."[17]

2. *The sense of being is real.* It is said, generally speaking, in our Western culture the real is only what is measurable. A thing or experience is not real if we cannot reduce it to numbers. It is quite difficult for us to accept our realization that "being" belongs to such realities as love, will and conscience. We cannot be measured or counted or fully explained in terms of relationships. If we segmentize or abstract we lose ourselves, we get nowhere.

It becomes clearly evident to any discussant of being that the psychological need to avoid or suppress the whole idea of "being" permeates our culture. In this matter we are contrastingly different from the Indian and Oriental cultures. Some explain our condition as the result of emphasizing our function (what we do, or what we are, clerk, grocer, teacher), and to the widespread conformist tendencies in our culture. When the counselor has diaries, biographies, inventory results and test results before him, he may conclude he knows everything about the counselee, and he does know everything except the "Johnian in John."

Being is not comprehended in his attributes. Being is the counselee's ability despite his environment and relationships to become aware of the forces acting upon him, of his condition. With such awareness he has freedom to decide in favor of this rather than of that.

Existential therapists Binswanger, Kuhn and others describe man as the being who is *there.* Each man has his particular *there,* his own place in time and space of which he is conscious and for which he is therefore responsible. Binswanger describes him as "The person-who-is-responsible-for-his-existence-choosing."

We fall prey to thinking of "being" as static rather than as a continuous state of becoming. Each of us can best be understood in terms of what we are becoming. We come to grips with ourselves as we project our possibilities in action. The past and present can best be viewed in terms of the future, or what the individual's aims may be.

Man can be and is aware of himself and responsible for himself. But also he is aware of the fact that some time in the future he will not be. Within him dwells being and non-being. His choices determine what will live (have being) and what will die (lose being) within him. Continuously he makes choices "to be and not to be." This dialectical relation is the means of his becoming.

Each time he so chooses he affirms the "I am" of his existence. It is possible to grasp the "I am" experience at anytime. It is most likely to be grasped in times of great change in the life of the individual: success, failure, tragedy, heightened joy.

In the counseling relationship, individual or group, the counselor may help create the conditions in which another feels accepted. This feeling of acceptance and of being able to trust one or more others may be a helpful and necessary condition for the "I am" experience but that is all. This is an experience of Dasein. It is realized in the Eigenwelt, one's own-world, but not in the Mitwelt, the world of social categories. If acceptance is unconditional, it frees the person to experience his own being. The crucial and unpredictable situation is what the individual does with the fact that he is accepted in his own awareness and sense of responsibility for himself. Counselors are prone to assume that love and acceptance are all that are necessary. They may be generally helpful, but are not of themselves sufficient.

It follows then that authentic being is not the result of the introjection of social and ethical norms. Being is not the product of conditioning. If my existence is authentic, it is what I have come to understand and believe is me. The result is likely to bear some resemblance to what others have told me or have not told me; it is not necessarily *because of* or *in spite of* incoming experience but rather what I have done with it. It is from this personal center, "own-world" that I can and should decide upon my future.

3. *Being-in-the-world.* Existential thinkers emphasize that to understand a person is to understand his world. Being together then means being together in the same world. To know the counselee is to know him in the context of his own world. Binswanger, a leading existentialist, emphasizes that too much importance has been placed on the way in which our counselees have deviated from what we call

the norm instead of trying to understand them in their own or private world.

But we don't understand the counselee's world through the results of tests or the accumulation of data concerning him. Neither do we understand him by some sentimental identification. We need to go deeper than the subject-object dichotomy. Difficult as this is, it is of the first importance. It meets the counselee at the point of his greatest need. Counselees like many others suffer because they have lost their world, they have no community. They have lost not only the meaningful relationship with the human world, but are strangers on probation in the natural world itself. Many persons who are to a large degree detached, unrelated and lacking affect, tend toward depersonalization. Frequently they hide their condition by means of intellectualism.

People say the play was well done, or the game was well played instead of saying, "I liked the play," or "I liked the game." Many have written of this condition of personal isolation and alienation, such as Fromm in *Escape From Freedom* with respect to sociopolitical considerations, and Tillich who writes from the spiritual viewpoint. This isolation affects man at all levels of life including his alienation from the natural world itself. It is the result of centuries of the separation of man as subject from the objective world. David Bakan describes this separation of man from his world as "epistemological loneliness." He concludes that it results in part from the inherited skepticism of the British empiricists, Locke, Berkeley and Hume. The alienation arose by thinking of man "as essentially alone rather than as a member and participant of a thinking community."[18]

There was a time when this loneliness was almost non-existent. In the Middle Ages, man in the depth of his being was considered to be related to the real world. The world was experienced as directly real (vide Giotto) and the body as immediate and real (vide St. Francis). Since Descartes there has been a separation; soul and nature have nothing to do with each other. Nature belongs to a different realm and is to be understood mathematically.

In modern times, man's alienation from nature and from himself has deepened. Tillich writes, "The picture of western Europe from Great Britain to Italy as I saw it in the years 1936 and 1937 was the picture of a complete cultural disintegration, especially in the younger generation." He views this disintegration to be characterized by four feelings: fear, uncertainty, loneliness and meaninglessness. At that time, two decades ago, he saw America as living "in a happy backwardness." Today there is hardly a doubt that he would have seen it to be in the midst of a thorough disintegration, similar in degree but otherwise different from what had then already taken place in Europe.

Existentialism is interested in trying to reestablish the possibility of meaning. Existentialists undertake this by showing that man is interrelated with his world. They maintain that the person and his world must be understood as one. Self implies world, and world implies self; one cannot be understood without the other. When we think of a man in his home, in the office, or in a meeting, we frequently think of a spatial relationship, but much more than this is implied.

Ignoring the integral relationship between man and his world leads to oversimplification. Counselors often assume that they can arrive at understanding the counselee's behavior from a study of his environment. We miss the fact that each one of us lives in his own world which in some ways is different from the world of all others, or that persons living in what seems to be an identical environment are really living in different worlds. Binswanger explains that "there is not one space and time only but as many spaces and times as there are subjects."[20]

World and being-in-the-world have a unique meaning for the existentialists. World is that person's unique structure of meaningful relationships and the design in which he participates. It is necessary for the counselor to know the counselee's environment, but the important challenge is to know the *meaning* of this environment to the counselee. The counselee's world consists of past events and the variety of conditioning influences, but their meaning derives from how he relates to them, what he selects from them to build his future. The counselee is continuously using what he selects, molding, forming, and building it into every minute of his relating. Self-awareness and designing is an ongoing process.

This ongoing process is openness to all experiences, it is the "openness of world." The counselee's world—this openness—is not identifiable with culture. Even if man could know all the languages and cultures and experience them, he would know only the historically knowable world; he would not know the infinity of future possibilities. Regardless of his finitude and the limitations of every kind which affect him, the counselee designs his own-world. These future possibilities are the significant aspects of the world of each of us. The counselor ignores or discredits the potentialities of the counselee when he perceives him only in the framework of accepting, adjusting, or fighting. The counselee has many possible ways of behaving but all of these are rooted in this manifold potentiality of being.

4. *"Ego" and "being" are different.* Counselors readily confuse the functioning of the ego with authentic "being." This is understandable because of the current emphasis on ego and the fact that the subject-object dichotomy has become so acceptable in much of counseling therapy.

Since its inception the ego has been considered only a part of the personality and a relatively weak part. Traditionally it was conceived as a passive and derived agent. It is "derived from the id by modifications imposed upon it from the external world" and "is representative of the external world."[21]

The ego is a reflection of the outside world. Its strength or weakness depends upon the approval or disapproval of people and forces outside the person. The sense of being or "being" itself is not the agent of world awareness. It is firmly grounded in one's own experience of existence. It is not the capacity to evaluate events in the world but the capacity to be conscious of oneself as one in the world, as the being who can do these things. In the subject-object dichotomy, ego is the subject, but "being" is prior to this dichotomy. The sense of being is the knowing that I am the one who initiates what is occurring. In my being I am not against the outside world necessarily but my knowing includes my capacity to be so. If I choose I can confront non-being if it seems necessary.

The neglect of recognition and the understanding of "being" has led counselors to settle for adjustment as the goal of counseling. In so doing they assume that the ego is primary, and the socially acceptable satisfaction of ego demands the end result. Such a viewpoint is the handed-down assumption of viewing the individual as the passive recipient of forces acting upon him, and the product of conditioning influences. These influences today are strong and varied but not necessarily all-powerful.

5. *The fact of non-being.* It is common to think of life in terms of being or becoming but to avoid thinking of one's demise in any form. We discuss our "beings," our first days of becoming, but avoid talking about the endings whether they be job, health, friendship,

marriage or life itself. Yet we know that all things come to an end; non-being is not popular but it is real. We know too that "being" in any sphere or activity of our lives is not automatic and should not be taken for granted. Every new experience threatens our being. We can choose escape, or denial, or rationalization and thus deny being within us, and allow non-being to become a reality. We do not consciously create being; it takes place incidentally as we dedicate ourselves to an ideal in the future. We cannot overcome the appearances of non-being by an act of will alone. When we try, we are like the man who cleaned his house of one demon only to find that seven others came in to take up their abode.

Being and non-being are the opposite poles of existence. One cannot and does not have meaning without the other. It is when non-being threatens us that we are most aware of being. The degree of our awareness bears a direct relation to our courage to accept and take into ourselves the evidence of non-being. Non-being becomes actual only in its negation of being. Even in our strong affirmation of being we know that non-being is in the wings ready to come downstage. The vividness of our being is dependent upon our affirmation of it in the face of non-being.

Of course death is the undeniable fact of non-being. But the problem of non-being is ever with us. It is evident in our failure to confront it in the daily pressures to conform. It is in the tendency of each of us to let himself be absorbed in the multitude of superficial collective responses and attitudes. Such absorption robs us of our self-awareness, our potentialities, and the ways in which we are in touch with our uniqueness. Such absorption often serves as a means of escape from the anxiety of non-being (uselessness, emptiness) but at a cost of forfeiting our sense of existence and the development of our potentiality.

But non-being confronted can result in growth, in the experience of being, in aliveness. We confront non-being when we have the courage to accept it or take it into ourselves without suppression, repression, anxiety, hostility or aggression.

It is a mistake to try to preserve our being by running away from situations which could be expected to produce anxiety or from those of potential hostility and aggression. At such times we are left with a weak, unreal sense of being. Nietzsche wrote of the "important people" who escape aggression by repressing it and as a result experience a "drugged tranquility." These situations are not the unusual or infrequent ones which may come to mind, but rather the usual, almost day-to-day kind with which any person has to cope. The person who does succeed in accepting and dealing with the normal forms of these states develops his sense of being, his at-homeness with and in his inner self. The counselor who has not developed his own sense of being may be less helpful in recognizing and helping the counselee whose problem is rooted in this kind of struggle.

6. *The ontological perspective on anxiety.* The majority of counselors consider anxiety to consist of two types: neurotic and normal. Few consider existential anxiety or the anxiety of being. May lists three characteristics which differentiate neurotic anxiety from normal anxiety: (1) Neurotic anxiety is disproportionate to the objective threat whereas normal anxiety is proportionate to the objective threat. (2) Neurotic anxiety involves repression and other forms of intrapsychic conflict whereas normal anxiety does not. (3) Neurotic anxiety is managed by means of various forms of retrenchment of anxiety and awareness, such as inhibitions, the development of symptoms, and the various neurotic defense mechanisms, but normal anxiety can be confronted constructively on the level of conscious awareness or can be relieved if the objective situation is altered.[22]

If anxiety has its roots in the culture, which is the position taken by Freud, Harvey, Kardiner and others, the counselor need only be concerned with its psychological and sociological bases. He may hope to relieve the counselee of his neurotic anxiety when he counsels with him in terms of these understandings.

Counselors are aware that our society is faced with a radical change of structure. Threats felt today by both counselor and counselee are significantly different from any they have ever before experienced. The threats now are those related to "ends" rather than "means," and cannot be removed on the basis of cultural assumptions.[23] The threat today in the Western world is not to subsistence or prestige. Rather the culture is seen as a threat to basic assumptions which have been identified with the existence of the culture. The individual, as a participant in the culture, identifies the threat with his own existence.

Sociological theories of anxiety do not explain some of the anxiety we experience. We suffer from another anxiety: the knowledge that our days are numbered. Our finitude, which impresses itself upon us in many ways, we know as anxiety of a very different kind. Fromm, May, Mowrer, Harvey, Tillich and others recognize this form of anxiety. They have named it Urangst, a name for the existential anxiety of knowing that we are finite, that someday we shall die.

Harvey carefully distinguishes between existential anxiety and neurotic anxiety. Urangst does not connote hostility or provoke inner conflict leading to neurotic defense measures. May emphasizes that existential anxiety should not be identified with fear or termed neurotic.

Tillich has gone further. He believes that existential anxiety is basic to all anxiety. He wrote, "A more exact analysis shows that in the anxiety about any special situation, anxiety about the human situation as such is implied. It is the anxiety of not being able to preserve one's own being which underlies every fear and is the frightening element in it." He distinguishes three types of anxiety, "according to the three directions in which non-being threatens being: (1) Non-being threatens man's ontic self-affirmation (his affirmation of his own being), relatively in terms of fate, absolutely in terms of death; (2) It threatens man's spiritual self-affirmation, relatively in terms of emptiness, absolutely in terms of meaninglessness; (3) It threatens man's moral self-affirmation, relatively in terms of guilt, absolutely in terms of condemnation."[24]

Tillich sees the anxiety of our time as one in which we experience the threat of spiritual non-being. We escape this anxiety by detachment and conformity. We detach ourselves from meaningful relationships with others and with ourselves. We evade any deep search within ourselves concerning the meaning of existence by conformism. We indulge in activity which we hope will assuage the yearning for exhilarating creativity with meaning, frequently with little success.

The counselor in this environment does not escape the threat of anxiety and emptiness either in himself or in the counselee. If he views the anxiety and the behavior which ensues as a result only of environmental conditions, he is at a loss to understand his own uneasiness and the ennui or irresponsibility of the counselees. If our anxiety is basically ontological concern for our own being, then recognition of this fact is the starting place. At present we may be confusing "means" and "ends." In fact, a balanced approach requires the inclusion of the centrality of the existential ground of all anxiety. May writes, "In my judgment, our psychological and psychiatric dealings with anxiety phenomena of all sorts will be greatly helped by shifting the concept to its ontological base."[25]

The ontological approach recognizes that anxiety is a conflict between being and non-being. From this point of view, anxiety occurs precisely at the point where some emerging potentiality or possibility faces the individual. He knows that something must die in order that something is born. The very possibility of the new involves the destroying of present security. Herein lies the anxiety. Although we do not welcome and often evade anxiety, it is prerequisite to the possibility of becoming, of developing the new. It also means that we possess some freedom to change; otherwise there would be no anxiety. To Kierkegaard, anxiety was "the dizziness of freedom"; he explained that "anxiety is the reality of freedom as a potentiality before this freedom has materialized." Unwelcome as it is, anxiety has its constructive aspects.

It is clear that to understand anxiety correctly and fully, those concerned must recognize and accept the fact that each person has a depth dimension. This dimension must be honored and respected, for it is at this level of experience that anxiety should be dealt with.

The counselor is not engaged in trying to free the counselee from anxiety. He recognizes that anxiety is to be valued as an opportunity for growth. Therefore he is interested in helping the counselee to accept anxiety as a constituent of life. He hopes to be successful in helping him to discover and to take issue with his anxiety, accepting what cannot be changed and changing what can and needs to be changed, both within himself and in the external world.

7. Ontological perceptions of guilt. Odier[26] and Tournier[27] describe two forms of guilt: functional or societal guilt, and true or ontological guilt. The first is the guilt one feels when he behaves in a manner generally unacceptable to society. What he does which results in guilt feelings varies with the immediate subculture which has provided the values. A boy in one subculture may feel guilty if he "lifts" small articles in a department store, but a different boy in a different subculture may feel guilty if he does not.

True or ontological guilt has its source in one's "own-world." Each person has potentialities or values, and when he denies them or fails to fulfill them his condition is guilt. Each of us has potentialities given in his "core." One is indebted to actualize these, and failure results in guilt feelings in a thousand forms.

The existentialist does not say in the common manner that one has guilt feelings. It may be that the counselor's reduction of guilt to guilt feelings has contributed to the sense of illusion in counseling. Instead the existentialist's approach to guilt is direct: the counselee is guilty.

This guilt is not necessarily linked to the religious. A person is just as guilty in refusing to accept the corporeal aspects of life as the intellectual or spiritual aspects. For the counselor it means accepting the counselee's life and experience seriously and respectfully.

There are other forms of ontological guilt besides the refusal to accept and develop one's potentialities. Another is our failure to perceive another person as he really is. We are prone to see one another through our own limited and biased views. The result is that we misunderstand, we are unfair and fail to meet the other's needs. This should not be confused with moral slackness, although the guilt may be increased by lack of moral sensitivity. The fact is simply that try as we may, we are unable fully to see the world through another's eyes.

A less frequently discussed but more comprehensive form of ontological guilt is our separation from nature as a whole. This means separation from the source of our being. There is a depth of meaning in the phrase, "from dust we come and to dust we shall return." In some lost sense, nature is our home. Nature, whether beautiful, dramatic or terrifying, has a way of calling us back to ourselves. It disturbs us when we realize that nature has little or no meaning for us.

Ontological guilt differs from other forms of guilt. Its source is not in the culture or in any introjection of authority figures. It is not that one is guilty because he broke the law or because he did not live up to someone's expectations. Rather, it is rooted in his knowledge of himself, his self-awareness, the fact that he can see himself as the one who makes his own choices.

This kind of guilt is different from neurotic guilt. If one does not recognize this guilt, or recognizing it, represses it, it turns into neurotic guilt. If one does accept it, it usually has constructive results on his personality. One who accepts his ontological guilt is likely to become more humble, more sensitive in his interpersonal relationships, and better able to use his potentialities more creatively.

The Meaning of Time

Existential analysts have a distinctive approach to time. Their thesis is that the profound experiences of life, joy, tragedy and anxiety, occur more in the dimension of time than of space. They therefore place time in the center of the psychological understanding of the counselee. In this context, how one relates to the future is of signal importance.

One's capacity to relate to the past, present, and long-term future is the unique characteristic of human existence. The fact that we can look back and see ourselves as we were in the past and project ourselves in self-conscious imagination into the future for weeks, months or years makes intelligent growth and change possible. This is considered to be the distinctive dimension of human personality. Mowrer describes us as "Time-binding—that is, the capacity to bring the past into the present as part of the total causal nexus in which living organisms act and react, together with the capacity to act in the light of the long-term future—is the essence of mind and personality alike."[28]

Existential thinkers culminate their analysis of finitude in the analysis of time. They distinguish "Existential" or immediately experienced time from dialectical timelessness on the one hand, and from the infinite, quantitative, measured time of the objective world on the other. Qualitative time, as opposed to the Aristotelian and common Western idea of quantitative measured time, is characteristic of Personal Experience.

Each existentialist has his own explanation of time as qualitatively and immediately experienced. Kierkegaard writes of the pregnant moment in which eternity touches time and demands a personal decision. Nietzsche uses his doctrine of "external recurrence," which gives to every moment the weight of eternity. Heidegger (the most radical), in his analysis of Kant, indicates that for him time is defined by "self-affection," grasping oneself or one's Personal Existence. In this sense temporality is existentiality.

The meaning the counselor places on time bears a direct relation to his view of being-in-the-world. If time is viewed only in "clock time," it is understood as an analogy from space; that is, it is perceived much like regularly spaced points on a clock or calendar. This approach fits the Umwelt view where the individual is an object, an entity moving among the various conditioning and determining forces of the natural, quantitative world.

But the counselor is interested in the world of interpersonal relations, the world of caring and love. This is the Mitwelt world, in which we realize that time has little to do with the significance of the experience. The degree of affection between two persons is not a measurement of the length of time they have known each other. The remembered moments are those which break through the steady progression of time. Hence the expression, "Time stood still." Strauss quotes the German proverb, "No clock strikes for the happy one."

These two levels of experience require a third level or world for completeness. To varying degrees, we have developed our potential for seeing the meaning of an event for ourselves. This is our own-world, the world of self-relatedness and self-awareness.

The insight into the meaning of an event for ourselves is instantaneous, and the moment of awareness has significance for all time. This insight is not arrived at through critical examination. It arrives, unannounced, in its entirety, complete. Other meanings may attach themselves, but the core of meaning remains as it was when born: whole. When this insight or "break-through" is traumatic, the person may be unable to "have" a future. He may be unable to get beyond the traumatic experience, to think or imagine forward. Repression and related neurotic symptoms are a means of making sure that the usual relation of past and present will not obtain.

Not only is time placed in the psychological center, but the future in contrast to the past or present is the significant mode of time. This is in accord with the view that man is always emerging, always becoming. Kierkegaard wrote, "the self is only that which is to become." The future which is assumed is not the distant future, not an escape in phantasy, but the immediate future. The individual is in a dynamic self-actualizing process only to the degree that he has developed self-awareness. He explores, tests reality and moves into the immediate future.

If the person is always becoming, always emerging, then personality can only be understood as we perceive it on a trajectory toward the future. This does not mean we can neglect the past, but rather that to understand the personality, we must look at the Umwelt world of the contingent, of the natural historical, and of those forces acting upon us. We do not live entirely in this world; neither are we necessarily the victims of pressures from the past.

However, the past is not a collection of unrelated events or a reservoir of memories. The past is the dynamic contingency in which we accept what has occurred. Also, from the past we select what we perceive will give us satisfaction and security in the immediate future and that which will help us to fulfill our potentialities.

It is common knowledge that we select from the past a particular and special event, a critical incident so to speak, and not the thousand and one things we do every day. Alfred Adler considered the form of memory a mirror of the individual's style of life: what the individual seeks to become determines what he remembers of the past. What he seeks to become may be at the level of intentionality and not necessarily part of his conscious awareness. In this manner of thought, the future determines the past in a dynamic sense, and what the counselee is able to recall depends upon his decision or commitment with regard to the future.

We are prone to conclude mistakenly that it is the impoverished past of the counselee which accounts for his indecision. Although the past does have an influence, the counselee's condition is primarily the result of his lack of commitment to the present and future. He does not relate or definitely select from the past because he perceives a future in which nothing matters to him. Unless there is a commitment to work toward changing something in the immediate future, uncovering the past will have no reality.

Counselors slip easily into thinking that given time, matters will work out satisfactorily. It is understandable that counselors may desire to take refuge in some automatic doctrine of historical progress. However, belief in progress is unacceptable to existential thinking. This is true whether it be concerned with historical materialism, technical progress, psychological doctrines of determinism or religious beliefs in predestination or providence. We do not progress in the things that are genuinely human, for example, love. Each generation starts from scratch. Kierkegaard wrote, "Every generation begins primitively, has no different task from that of every previous generation."[29] Of course we make so-called progress in technical areas, and we may even improve conditions conducive to what is genuinely human, but no more.

The usual use of data from the past is in disagreement with the existential point of view. Counselors assume that present behavior bears a significant direct relation to past experience. This use of data is based on the concepts of the Umwelt world and ignores the Eigenwelt or own-world. Existential counselors place primary and first importance on the counselee commitment in the future. The past which enters into the counseling experience is that which is selected by the counselee. The procedure in the use of data is the reverse of the customary method. Usually the counselor decides which data is useful in understanding the counselee. In existential counseling, the counselee decides which has ongoing meaning. He makes the choice not according to the expectancy of the counselor, but rather in terms of what the experience means to him.

Often counselors assume that if the proper conditions for love are developed, the participants will love one another. This is the critical dilemma of T-groups and basic encounter groups. The pressure engendered may only result in pseudo forms of love. The conducive conditions carry no assurance that members will take the creative risk of truly loving.

There is another prevalent assumption among counselors that insight results from an intellectual act. Of course the intellect is necessary and to some degree prepares the conditions for the insight to occur. However, that which Kierkegaard calls the Augenblick, or "the pregnant moment" (generally referred to as the "aha" experience), is more than a cognitive act. For Paul Tillich, it is the moment when "eternity touches time." This is his concept of Kairos, "time fulfilled."

The counselor frequently sees the counselee as static, predictable and somewhat set or "fixed" in his attitudes. Thus he is unlikely to see what is "crying to be born"; the emergent becoming of the counselee escapes him. This is due in part to the counselor's perception of his function. Counselors take over the burden of learning to love for the counselees. Instead they should help the counselees to remove the blocks which keep them from being; the counselors cannot love for them, and in trying to do so run the risk of dulling the counselees' own consciousness.

The Meaning of Self-consciousness

Frequently self-awareness and self-consciousness are mistakenly identified. Self-awareness is present in forms of life other than human, but only human life has self-consciousness or the capacity for self-transcendence. The dog is aware that his owner putting on a coat means he is going outdoors. He is also aware that he is hungry, but he does not have the capacity to know himself as the one who is hungry. This capacity of self-consciousness is unique to man. He knows himself as the one who feels joy or fear; he experiences himself as the subject who has a world. This capacity for self-consciousness is the basis of his capacity to use abstractions and symbols.

Self-consciousness or self-transcendence is the most unacceptable concept to the nonexistentialist. It is the foundation of Existentialism and therefore most crucial to the understanding and acceptance of existential counseling.

Objections stem from several sources. They arise from the suggestion that self-consciousness refers to the unempirical and is unrelated to actual experience. It is rejected by those who retain the traditional way of describing human beings in terms of static substances. Self-consciousness is also rejected by those who view the differences between animal and human behavior only as differences in degree and not differences in kind. Some handle the distressing idea of self-consciousness by means of distortion. For these, it exists only as the capacity to ask the res extensa questions of the horizontal dimension (Tillich), or of the Umwelt and Mitwelt worlds. The general objection is clearly described by Murphy. He asks, "Should the student of personality, at the present stage of research, posit a nonempirical entity, distinct from both organism and its perceptual response to forms and symbols, which is called a 'self'?" His decision is that "a tentative negative answer to this question seems advisable." However, he suggests that another answer may be given when "the present stage of inquiry is more advanced." The dilemma of those who hold to empirical explanations is expressed by Immergluck. He writes: "There is, on the one hand, modern psychology's commitment to the scientific method . . . while on the other hand, there remains the nagging conviction that somehow man must be personally free. How to resolve this antimony?"

The existentialists do not have this dilemma. For them, the capacity of the normal person to transcend the present situation reveals itself in all kinds of behavior. They see this capacity in man's ability to bring the distant past and the long-term future into one's immediate existence. It is demonstrated also in our unique capacity to think and to talk in symbols. It is evident in our attempts to understand ourselves. We think of ourselves as evil, but then we are confronted with the question that if we were truly evil, would we be able to recognize this? At other times we view ourselves as essentially good, but find it difficult to account for evil. We ask if life is worth living and recognize that the ability to ask such a question implies a capacity beyond our rationality.

Communication and communion in human relations presuppose that each of us knows he is the one who is in communion with another. The whole scope of trust and responsibility presuppose that we are able to some degree to understand how others see us.

Nietzsche has described man as "the animal who can make promises." The capacity to make promises is not the result of conditional
"social behavior." It implies a conscious self-relatedness, the ability
for self-transcendence. For Sartre, dishonesty was a uniquely human
form of behavior: "the lie is a behavior of transcendence."

Counselors regularly assume that "introjection," "identification,"
etc. describe the dynamics of social adjustment. This is an oversimplification which is also inadequate. It omits the profound and central
fact that the person is aware at the time that he is the one who is
responding; that is, he is choosing or not choosing to accept and use
a certain model. This supplies the needed explanation of the difference between unexamined social conformity on the one hand and
the creativity and freedom of genuine social response on the other.

For existentialists, the significant world is not Umwelt or Mitwelt
but Eigenwelt. Eigenwelt is the mode of behavior in which a person
sees himself as subject and object. In fact, the term "exist," that is,
"to stand out from," assumes this capacity. Existing is the continual
emerging, a transcending of one's past and present in terms of the
future. This capacity to transcend the situation implies that one is
able to stand apart and look at one's self and the situation, to consider the several alternatives and reach a decision. To ignore or discount this capacity is to settle for a partial view of man and to limit
his possibilities for helping and being helped.

This capacity for transcendence of the immediate situation is not
another attribute or faculty; it is a given in the ontological nature of
man. Some persons develop or make use of this potential much more
than others. Persons vary in their perceived need to make use of this
capacity. Many relate to life and generally make decisions only on
the basis of pragmatic expediency.

Self-transcendence requires imagination in order that alternatives
may be considered and decisions made. Kierkegaard views imagination as of signal importance. He wrote, "What feeling, knowledge or
will a man has depends in the last resort upon what imagination he
has, that is to say, upon how these things are reflected . . . . Imagination is the possibility of all reflection, and the intensity of this
medium is the possibility of the intensity of the self."[32] A modern
philosopher writes, "Our inner life is determined by images, produced by practical imagination."[33] But the person may use a form of
imagination which focuses upon the past and the manifest content.
This leads to a method of interpretation which Jung has called repro-

ductive.[34] Such a method is immediately visible, thoroughly intelligible and may obviate the need for deeper understanding. This is imagination at work in the Umwelt and Mitwelt modes. The imagination of the Eigenwelt mode is productive imagination. Such imagination leads to a method of interpretation that is purposive. This does not ignore either the past or manifest content, but transcends these in a manner that permits them to point to other meanings in which both the past and manifest content participate—i.e., permits symbolic meanings to arise.

The interaction of imagination and sign or symbolic thinking influences change in behavior. When the counselee thinks with the use of signs he makes use of productive imagination. He engages his imagination to visualize what has been the outcome of his thinking. This kind of thinking is unlikely to initiate the new, except perhaps incidentally. The power lawnmower stops. The operator knows that the motor uses gas. His imagination proposes to him that the gas tank is empty. This is reproductive imagination. It is a kind of imagination which finds wide and useful application. However, used by itself it lacks adequacy and comprehensiveness in the counseling relationship.

A counselor complained about the unrealistic attitude of some of his counselees. "Imagine," he said, "John with an I.Q. of 120 and in his circumstances (father in lower income bracket) wanting to become a medical doctor." This may have been a situation in which the counselor was using reproductive imagination and "old sets." To John, being a medical doctor could have been a symbol—a symbol of doing his part to reduce the misery of the world, concerning which he already has some understanding.

Implicit in the capacity of self-transcendence and the use of one's imagination is the basis of human freedom. It is difficult to accept this freedom, and as a result, many do not energize the depth dimension of the Eigenwelt world. "Some counselees do not get beyond the pseudo-freedom of rebellion. Rebellion easily becomes confused with freedom because it is a normal interim move toward freedom. Rebellion acts as a substitute for the more difficult process of struggling through to one's own autonomy, to new beliefs, to the state where one can lay new foundations on which to build."[35]

The counselor who is aware of this potential for human freedom remains alert to the ways in which the counselee proceeds to use his freedom. He may use it to move forward, to have the "courage to be," or he may relinquish his freedom, thus having only the "courage to be as a part." One psychologist writes, "the urge to grow, pursue meaning, seek unity is also a 'given' . . . . Growth toward this end is a law to which most personalities seem to conform. The promise I see for myself is the essence of my freedom. When a critical situation challenges me I call forth this promise—it becomes a major factor in the solution of the problem in hand."[36]

The counselor should be sensitive to the counselee's use of his freedom to decrease his self-awareness, to withdraw from life. A very common and almost unconscious method of the counselee in relinquishing his freedom is the submergence of himself in a group, society or cult. He becomes very adaptable, meeting each situation without effort. He fulfills the expectations of others. The risk is that he relinquishes contact with himself; gradually genuine individuality and spontaneity disappear.

"The counselee may also relinquish his freedom by rejecting the poignant feelings of doubt concerning the meaning of existence. He discontinues the question, 'Why?' The counselor assumes routine duties, working on a 'horizontal' level that makes real confrontation with life unnecessary. Thus we escape from our freedom by asking only the questions that can be answered and by accepting answers imposed upon us authoritatively. Such retrenchment unfortunately provides a false sense of being in command of life, a feeling of belonging. Doubt is rarely present."[37] "Meaning is saved but the self is sacrificed. And since the conquest of doubt was a matter of sacrifice —the sacrifice of freedom of the self—it leaves a mark on the regained certitude; a fanatical self-assertiveness."[38]

Not all counselors recognize and accept this potential of human freedom. Carl Rogers characterizes assumptions that man has potential freedom as simply speculations. His lack of acceptance of this potential of human freedom becomes apparent in his contention that freedom can be researched. He thus removes human freedom from the Eigenwelt to the Mitwelt world. Such counselors may have no basis for hearing and understanding the Eigenwelt concerns of counselees. Such concerns, if and when expressed, are perceived as having their roots in the Mitwelt world of interpersonal relationships. Counselees soon become aware of those counselors for whom the Eigenwelt world is foreign or out-of-bounds and therefore do not express these concerns. In any case, when these concerns are expressed they are apparently carefully disguised, often appearing only as a prefix or suffix in the expression of an idea.

Basic Assumptions in Existential Counseling

Existential counseling is a radically different approach to the counselee and counseling. A review of the foregoing concepts reveals that it differs from other approaches in at least the following significant ways:

1. *Technique follows understanding.* The simple can be understood only in terms of the complex. This principle differs from the usual counselor assumptions. Counselors generally assume that the simple, the Umwelt and Mitwelt modes of relationship can be understood by direct study. Pierre Teilhard de Chardin in his book, *The Phenomenon of Man,* takes the position that when a new function emerges such as self-consciousness in man, the whole gestalt shifts; and the organism can now be understood only in terms of the new function. The potential of self-consciousness introduces a new complexity which significantly affects all the simpler elements and their resultant relationships.

This is the direct opposite of much of the current national emphasis. Customarily it is assumed that if the right technique is used, we can then understand the uniqueness of the counselee. The existential counselor's primary goal is to understand the counselee as a person, a being and as being-in-the-world. This does not mean that he has a low respect for technique, but rather that technique takes its legitimate place in a new perspective. The new perspective is to help the counselee recognize and experience his own experience.

This approach places emphasis on the context in which counseling occurs. The usual context of viewing the counselee as an object, the product of psychic dynamisms or mechanisms does not obtain. The context in existential counseling is one of seeing the counselee as a person who is choosing, committing and orienting himself toward something emerging in the present.

2. *Existential counselors ask different questions.* Ordinarily the counselor begins with the manifestations of the problem and moves toward treatment of the conditions which are presumed to have caused the problem. He asks questions which may help him to relate the manifestation to the condition and to the cause. He is working within the Umwelt and Mitwelt modes. The existential counselor asks, "What will help me understand the counselee's existence at this moment in his history? What will help me understand his being-in-the-world, his ontological viewpoint as a person?" He is working

primarily in the Eigenwelt mode. For example, the college student complains of his inability to speak before a large class of students but feels that he does quite well in small groups. Counselors working only in the Mitwelt world might view this as the counselee's need to overcome his fear and hesitancy. He might even plan steps of how this could be accomplished. He also might set up means whereby his performance with increasing numbers of students could be positively reinforced. The existential counselor working chiefly in the Eigenwelt world would view the fear and reticence of speaking before the large group as a holding back of potentia of the existence of this person. He may or may not deal immediately with the problem, but more important, he would see it not only as a mechanism of inhibition, but as a limitation of the counselee's being-in-the-world.

3. *In existential counseling problems take their meaning from the counselee's own immediate ontological existence.* This concept has three aspects: (1) It is not the counselee's past per se that throws light on the present, but rather his perception of it. (2) His present behavior is indicative of what he has learned or not learned to date. (3) Each significant sample of behavior (normal or deviant) is looked at on an ontological basis.

This approach places traditional theories and concepts on an existential basis. Repression in other approaches is viewed as the counselee's need to present an acceptable picture of himself which leads to the inhibition of thoughts, desires and actions unacceptable to the cultural moral codes and religious beliefs. The existential approach views this within the framework of the counselee freely accepting his potentialities. When he represses, he becomes unaware of his freedom. Aware of it, he can decide what to do with it. The chief concern here is how the counselee relates to his freedom to express his potentialities in the first place, repression being one way of relating it.

Instead of treating resistance in the traditional way, the existential counselor is interested in what makes such a phenomenon possible. Looking at it ontologically, he may conclude that it was this person's way of avoiding the development of an original potential. The counselee avoids the recognition of a potential to be developed by becoming absorbed in the Mitwelt world, in the anonymous mass of humanity.

Emphasis, then, is not placed on understanding the phenomena through recognition of the interplay of forces or drives behind them.

These forces or drives are not denied; nor are they understood on the basis of energy transformation. They are viewed, rather, as the person's potentia of existence.

One advantage of this approach is that there can be direct and immediate entering into the counselee's framework instead of screening or putting through a sieve the counselee's communication in order to determine the source of its initiation. The counselor is open to the counselee as a being and takes seriously any indication from the counselee of the nature of his being-in-the-world. To the degree that the counselor achieves this, he increases his "translucency," becoming a vehicle and medium through which the counselee sees himself.

4. *Existential counseling requires a unique relationship.* The counselee may be an object to be diagnosed or a person to be understood. To the existential counselor, the relationship is one in which he is concerned in understanding and in experiencing the being of the counselee. The existential counselor disagrees with the traditional position that "the less we are involved in a given situation, the more clearly we can observe the truth."

The counselee may be telling the truth although from the objective standpoint what he is saying may be false. The counselor is prepared to abide by the realization that there is a kind of truth which may be false for everyone except for the counselee who expresses it. The counselor directs his reflection to the relationship between the counselee and his belief. If what he says follows logically from his perception of the matter, then it is considered true for the counselee, even if his criteria and referents are objectively false.

The counselor is assumed to be an expert, but if he remains completely one and proceeds as such, the counselee soon feels he is an object to be done something with or to. In this case, a professional distance exists which severely limits the possibility of the counselee being helped. The existential counselor accepts the need for training and skill, but first and last he is a person. For the time being he is working to understand the problems of someone else rather than his own. The existential approach is distinctive in that the training and discipline necessary for understanding another is not left up to chance or intuition but becomes a significant undertaking.

Such an approach means that two persons are directly relating to each other in a real, basic relationship. The counselor is not escaping or hiding behind some diagnosis he is making to himself of what is taking place. The counselor's direct involvement helps to make clear to the counselee that he is relating, doing something to one who is involved with him. It is assumed that new insights emerge for the counselee when what he is really doing and saying grasps him or "gets to him." This is a different kind of happening than if the counselor told the counselee what the counselee finally understands for himself.

This points to an important aspect of the counselor's functioning: the counselor does not impose himself, his ideas or feelings on the counselee. Instead he follows the affect and leads of the counselee. The counselor is alive and aware; he sticks to his function of helping the other person to bring to birth something from within himself. He does not allow his own involvement to become a means for the counselee to escape his own problem.

The counselor who is too conscious of the technique which he uses is limiting his availability to the counselee. He is blocking presence; he is not coming through. He is in this matter much like the actor. The actor uses technique, but it has become so much a part of him that he is not conscious of it. This is a necessity if he is to be able to be creative, that is, to create an authentic role. The counselor completely gives himself over to understanding the counselee.

5. *Existential counseling requires a unique purpose.* Karl Jaspers contends that we are now in the process of losing self-consciousness, and that this may usher in the last age of historical man. William Whyte is concerned that our emphasis on conforming behavior and adjustment is tending towards the destruction of individuality. In his book *Organization Man,* he concludes that therapists may turn out to be our enemies in their counseling for adjustment. He characterizes them as a "mild-looking group of therapists, who . . . would be doing what they did to help you." Rollo May suggests in *Existential Psychology* that we may be engaged in helping the individual adjust and be happy at the price of loss of his being.

Adjustment may be a last-ditch attempt to preserve one's centeredness by accepting non-being. When counselors promote adjustment they frequently are encouraging the counselee to live in a smaller world. Instead of neurosis being viewed as a failure of adjustment, it may be more correctly viewed as an indication that the person had adjusted and that this is his trouble.

Counseling for adjustment comes under criticism in existential counseling. Counseling for adjustment means that the counselee comes to accept a narrowed, distorted world. Without conflict, he makes his world identical with the culture. In this manner he reduces his anxiety and is relieved of his symptoms, since he surrenders the possibilities which caused his anxiety. He has accepted living with only the "courage to be as a part." In this manner, counselors become agents of the culture whose task is to adjust people to it. Counseling becomes an expression of the fragmentation of the culture, not a means of freeing counselees to transcend it. Many schools of counseling are described by the above method. In due time we can expect to reap the results of the resentment and despair of those who have been deluded into using one's self as a machine.

The existential counselor considers himself engaged in an undertaking much more fundamental than releasing the counselee from symptoms and helping him to adjust. He is engaged in helping persons to experience their existence. This is a difficult undertaking, for counselees do not come to be helped to experience their existence; this is about the last thing they want to do. They come instead to find a better, more acceptable way of operating themselves as a mechanism much as they would operate a machine. Many counselees talk of themselves as mechanisms. It is a Western, twentieth century, cultivated escape. Infused with the idea of being scientific and objective, they talk *about* themselves. It is a culturally acceptable way of rationalizing their detachment from themselves and others. Such a procedure has helped them to hide from ontological awareness. Talking *about* rather than *of* themselves saves them from seeing existence as it really is and themselves as they really are.

6. *Commitment is primary.* To the degree that the counselee succeeds in escaping his ontological consciousness he has his being in the Mitwelt world. But the purpose of existential counseling is to have the counselee experience his own-world, the Eigenwelt world. However in order to explore his being-in-the-world, he must be committed to doing so. The usual assumption in counseling has been that after the counselee possesses more knowledge about himself and gets more insight he will make the appropriate decision. The existential position is the reverse; commitment is primary.

There is another significant difference, namely, that the counselee does not see the truth until after he has committed himself. The counselee cannot permit himself to receive knowledge or to allow an insight to come into being until he is ready to decide and has moved to give his decision expression. But this decision is neither a sudden or "conversion" experience. The possibility or readiness to take such action is a necessary condition, but is based upon many small decisions along the way. Decision indicates a decisive attitude toward existence, an attitude of commitment. This is not a pseudocommitment. It is not the counselee doing what is expected. Nor is it because the counselee sees no alternative or is making a commitment which he does not intend to keep. These kinds of commitments are escape mechanisms to allay anxiety. They are in the Umwelt and Mitwelt mode. This is the situation in which the self-conscious person is taking himself seriously. It is in the Eigenwelt mode.

7. *Attitude toward anxiety.* The counselee finds it difficult to relate to what is troubling him. He talks about it at length but the experience or situation doesn't become real to him. Not until some inner suffering or outer threat unsettles him has he the incentive necessary for revealing his illusions of inner change. At this time, silence is important in helping the counselee gain insight.

Since a certain degree of anxiety and uneasiness is necessary in order that the counselee confront himself directly, questions arise as to how this condition can be facilitated. On the one hand, for the counselor to arouse anxiety is considered a questionable procedure (it is interesting to compare this conclusion with the usual practice in the T-group and basic encounter groups). On the other hand, any attempt to quiet the anxiety of the counselee may hinder the counselee's seeking further help.

The existential counselor asks himself what is keeping the counselee from committing himself unconditionally in some area of his existence. The counselor needs to be able to enter into this existential anxiety. He needs to be able to permit the counselee to recognize that there is the possibility that he may forfeit or lose what is possible in the present. In so many ways and from many sources, counselees have the unarticulated assumption that something will save them, that the counselor or someone will see that nothing harmful happens to them, that somebody "will soften the blow."

The concern that we need to engender anxiety in order for learning to take place is a direct outcome of the degree to which we have watered down anxiety. Life provides enough anxiety, real crises, and the existential emphasis is to help the counselee to confront both joy and tragedy directly. The counselee finds it difficult to accept the fact that if he chooses he can indeed destroy himself. The counselor accepts this fact and its importance is not disregarded. The counselor takes existence seriously and hopes to help the counselee to do likewise.

Functioning of the Existential Counselor

The counselor with existential leanings is no less scientific in his outlook and practices, but he does not assume that the scientific encompasses all the insights and understandings he needs. He takes seriously joy, triumph, despair and tragedy as they occur in living and in his own life. He focuses on the meaning of an experience and secondarily on the experience itself. He does not protect himself or others from the impact of situations and circumstances. He has respect for the carefully conceived and well-supported logical conclusion and also for the penetrating immediate grasp of experience of one's own-world. He stands apart from himself and his environment and examines both within the context of the future and his state of becoming-ness. He is acquainted with doubt and fear, but is capable of hearing that without courage, without concern, without commitment life is hollow. He doesn't aim or set out to be an existentialist. He just tries to be an honest man.

Not only does the existential counselor place importance on all three modes of being, but he himself lives in these three modes. Since he has developed the potential of self-transcendence, he is in touch with his own being and non-being-in-the-world. Since he does not ignore or repress his ontological anxiety or his "functional" guilt, he is more able to allow others to experience themselves in depth.

He views himself as a person and accepts the "mystical" in his life and others. His acceptance of the "mystical" signifies a venture of faith toward union with depths of life. He sees himself as a person, in the words of Jaspers, as "completely irreplaceable." He also accepts the fact that he cannot completely know himself. He does not treat himself as an object nor does he treat others as objects. He dissociates what a person does from what he is. A person remains a person regardless of his behavior.

Because he lives in each of the three worlds and has developed his potential for self-consciousness and self-evaluation, happenings in the Umwelt and Mitwelt worlds are viewed from the Eigenwelt perspective. It follows then that he looks at interpersonal relationships (including counseling) from a different viewpoint, and with different concerns and different questions. Insights gleaned from understanding the counselee's Umwelt and Mitwelt worlds are the basic data used by counselors in general. For the existential counselor, these are useful but not basic. The basic data is that obtained from knowing the meaning of this data to the counselee and the potential of the counselee's Eigenwelt world for designing his own-world.

Many counselors are satisfied when the counselee makes adjustments leading to constructive outcomes. The existential counselor considers these worthwhile but less than adequate. He does not counsel for adjustment or for self-actualization. For him, the chief value lies in the degree to which the counselee comes to understand his being-in-the-world and the meaning of personal events in relation to it. This does not mean that the existential counselor is unrealistic, that he does not realize that the counselee has to make adjustments. But the existential counselor believes the counselee's becoming bears a direct relation to his own-world, his world of self-consciousness, to conscience and productive imagination.

When the existential counselor grasps the world he does so in terms of his own being, his own-world. He has developed to some degree his potential for making judgments. Heidegger has called this capacity "the call of conscience," and Gordon Allport has described it as "the arbiter of adult values."[39] The kind of decisions or judgments a counselor makes is a function of the modes which describe his existence. If he lives in the Umwelt and Mitwelt modes, his judgments are based on societal norms. In this situation, conscience is the emotional reaction to the harmony between self-relatedness and relatedness to others. The questions or ideas which the counselor considers necessary are directly related to his own existence. If, in dealing with matters calling for moral decisions, he has not developed the Eigenwelt mode of being, he is unlikely to expect the counselee to look at concerns from this perspective. The counselor who lives in all three modes has a broader perspective for understanding the counselee whose behavior some authority has judged unacceptable or heroic.

Customarily the counselor's orientation focuses on doing something with and for the counselee. He hopes that the counselee's release of ideas and feelings regarding the Umwelt and Mitwelt worlds will make it possible for him to acquire information for making an analysis which will aid his future planning. He hopes that this experience will help the counselee to become more amenable to a consideration of the necessary changes to be made. He may use various methods of positive reinforcement to ensure that the counselee will accept and act upon constructive plans for the future.

The existential counselor is engaged in trying to understand what life means to the counselee. He wants to know the nature of his being-in-the-world. He is interested in information about the counselee not for itself or as a means for making judgments and plans, but rather he hopes to understand what the experiences mean to the counselee. Likewise, he is not only interested in test results and other data because they give indications of the counselee's ability and interests, but chiefly in what they mean to the counselee.

The counselor is interested in how the counselee views significant events and problems in his own life. He is not so much interested in these because they throw light on the counselee's flexibility and critical thinking efforts, but rather because they help the counselor to understand the depth at which the counselee meets life—whether he has existential understanding and concerns, or if he moves only in the Umwelt and Mitwelt modes of being.

He is interested in the counselee's past as a means of being with the counselee, but not as a means of making prognostications regarding what is possible and best for the counselee in the future. Rather, he is more interested in the counselee's grasp of the future, what the counselee decides regarding his future. He feels he can better understand the counselee's own world from knowing what he sees for himself in the future than by studying the counselee's past in order to predict his future. He is also interested in the counselee's past, since what the counselee selects from the past as being meaningful to the future provides the counselor with another source of understanding.

He does not discount the importance and usefulness of technical and diagnostic concerns, but he recognizes that they are on a different level from the understanding that can follow from the phenomenological grasp of what is immediately occurring in the interview.

He avoids confusing these two methods and levels of understanding or of absorbing or of subsuming one under another. He uses constructs and does not assume that he counsels in some atmosphere of diagnostic purity unrelated to all else.

He is just as much aware, however, of the temptation counselors experience in becoming preoccupied with techniques. He knows that such techniques allay anxiety and save one from the turmoil that comes from being with the counselee. He also knows that they can effectively block him off from the full presence in the encounter which is essential to understanding what is taking place. He is convinced that understanding does not follow from a knowledge of dynamics.

He tries to facilitate the counselee's connection with his own world. He places some importance on motivation, but is more concerned in understanding the will and intentionality of the counselee. He views will and decision as central to therapy. He holds that in the exploration of the counselee's life, the counselee is exerting his will as evident in the direction of his choices. They may sometimes seem insignificant, but even then the counselee is using his freedom and willing a future moving toward being or non-being. Such an assumption on the part of the counselor enables him to avoid the subtle pushing of the counselee in one direction or another. The counselor is also interested in the social (and other inter-personal) relationships of the counselee, but more interested in the counselee's perception of his being in relation to them; the significance these relations have for him. He is interested in the traumatic episodes of the counselee's life not only as a means of judging his ego strength, but also in the context of enabling the counselee to see life and situations as they really are, not to hide, distort or camouflage them, but to face them and relate to them.

Rather than strengthen the impression which the counselee may have that the counselor will save him from the impact of the folly of his ways, the existential counselor is interested in having the counselee confront his existence seriously. He hopes that the counselee recognizes that he is free to deny his possibilities and opportunities if he so chooses. Unlike many counseling relationships in which the tendency is to water down or even avoid anxiety, despair and the tragic aspects of life, this counselor is interested in having the counselee see them for what they are.

The result of the practice of dodging or minimizing the realities of life is often a passive withdrawal from much of what needs to be faced if the counselee is to develop his own-world. Some methods of counseling, such as T-group or basic encounter, engender anxiety. If such is necessary, it is because the real anxieties of life have been circumvented. The existential counselor assumes that life itself produces enough of such anxieties, and the only real crises and emphasis is placed on confronting these directly.

Counselors are aware of the importance of motivation in counseling. Techniques have been developed to initiate, maintain and enhance motivation. They depend on motivation for change to take place. The general assumption is that if the counselee sees the wisdom of the alternative he chooses, he will carry it out. The counselor is interested in having the counselee make an intelligent and constructive choice. Despite their best efforts, counselees sometimes do not carry out a choice which they seemingly enthusiastically choose.

When this occurs, counselors may become critical of their methods. They then consider ways in which it might be possible to increase motivation. One of the most comprehensive summaries of the conditions most likely to induce desired behavioral outcomes is that provided by McClelland in his article, "Toward a Theory of Motive Acquisition." He lists in table form the "variables conceived as entering into the motive change process."[40]

A second and very different approach for enhancing motivation is that developed by Self Theory. The assumption is that the person who is not motivated does not need reward or punishment, but rather assistance in understanding, accepting and working through the psychological problems that prevent him from knowing what he desires. As he understands, clarifies and accepts for himself, he becomes motivated from within toward a constructive direction.

These kinds of approaches commend themselves to many counselors who develop a great skill in incorporating either of these principles for increasing motivation in their counseling. Methods which are built on the precepts and understanding of the Umwelt and Mitwelt worlds appear generally satisfactory to counselors who themselves experience life in these modes.

These methods do not encompass the means for fully understanding why the counselee behaves as he does. Reinforcement and unconditional acceptance are useful but do not help to the degree we assume they do in explaining the behavior of counselees. They lack comprehensiveness since from the existential viewpoint they omit insights from the Eigenwelt mode, or the world of self-consciousness.

However, Allport in *Existential Psychology* edited by Rollo May, cautions against the conclusion that all counselee problems have existential roots. He suggests that "sometimes at least" an acquired world outlook may constitute the central motive of a life. Those who have not developed the potential of self-consciousness or who rarely consider meaning in depth may have different counseling needs from those who do. Allport concludes that psychology urgently needs to distinguish between lives in which "the existential layer is, in effect, the whole of the personality, and other lives in which it is a mere mask for the rumblings of the unconscious."

One psychologist is foremost in directing our attention to other considerations: Otto Rank gave the will a central place in his counseling theory. He wrote, "Whence comes the will and why psychologically must we interpret this will, not understood in its origin, now as will to power (Adler) and again as sex drive (Freud) and more than that, why must we interpret it at all, instead of being able to recognize its true psychological nature?"[41]

The will has been a controversial subject through the centuries. Whether the will is free to act or is in bondage to the self has been an issue of long standing. These two positions were the subject of the debate between Erasmus and Luther. Erasmus conceived the freedom of the self over its impulses. This point of view originating in the Renaissance has had great influence even to the present time. Luther, a representative of the Reformation viewpoint, considered the will to be in bondage. That is, he believed the will as part of the self was subject to the internal change in the self in exercising its influences. From the Renaissance point of view, the will located in the Umwelt and Mitwelt modes may be influenced by forms of conditioning. In the Reformation point of view, the will functions in relation to the awareness and decision of the self and is thus located in the Eigenwelt mode.

Rollo May places the will and decision in the center of counseling. Will and decision does not refer only to the life-shaping decisions. These words have a broader and more subtle meaning than we customarily ascribe to them. Decision even in small things involves a leap. There are always some elements not determined in the outside situation, but even when they become known, one is unable to predict his reactions to them. In this sense, decision requires the movement of one's self in a direction not completely predictable or known.

Thus the existential counselor considers the will seriously. This does not mean that he is not interested in motivation or what increases it. He is concerned when reinforcement is used to motivate a counselee to do something which does not concur with what the counselee intends and wills. On the other hand, if the counselee intends and wills something, the existential counselor would see inducement via some method of motivation to be useful but only secondary, and in many situations unnecessary.

The existential counselor is interested in understanding the various forms of conditioning and the development of a permissive climate and unconditional acceptance. But he is more interested in and places more importance upon the intentionality and will.

Rollo May defines intentionality thus: "By intentionality I mean the structure which gives meaning to experience."[42] He considers intentionality to be the heart of consciousness and the key to the problem of wish and will. Intentions are decisive with respect to how we perceive the world. May illustrates this by his reference to a house in the mountains. He makes the point by bringing to our attention that if the visitor is a real estate man, he will look at it in terms of its saleability, the profit potential. If the visitor is an artist, he will notice its pattern of lines, how it fits into the landscape, and its ramshackle condition will heighten the artistic possibilities. In each of the situations, the visitor may be the same man responding to what he sees; it is the same house but his intentions differ.

One side of intentionality originates with the perceiver. The other side is that the object itself influences the perception. May sees it as the bridge between these two. He considers it to be the structure which makes it possible for us to see and understand the outside world. In intentionality the dichotomy between subject and object is partially overcome.

The explanation of why the counselee does not act or why he acts differently from the counselor's expectations lies with the intentionality. Consciously or unconsciously he intended something which was different and which in turn resulted in a different perception and outcome. The counselor who uses reinforcement, or attempts to increase motivation by some other means, may be working at cross-purposes. And when he succeeds with some result in the Umwelt or Mitwelt world, he may only be increasing the counselee's problems.

The degree of willing is seen in the vitality with which an action is carried out. Tillich relates vitality to intentionality in these words: "man's vitality is as great as his intentionality: they are interdependent . . . . Only man has complete vitality because he alone has complete intentionality . . . . If the correlation between vitality and intentionality is rightly understood one can accept the biological interpretation of courage within the limits of its validity."[43] Tillich insists that being in man is never given automatically as in plants and animals. Being in man depends upon his courage, and without courage he loses his being.

Intentionality and willing go hand in hand; one cannot be understood without the other. The counselor who describes the counselee as lacking in motivation is describing appearances, not the basic cause. The cause is a lack of intentionality. Intentionality and vitality show themselves not simply as a biological force, but as a reaching out, a forming and re-forming of the world in various creative activities. Nevertheless, as counselors we are unable to supply intentionality or directly modify it; we can only encourage the conditions within the counselee which make it possible.

Preparation for Existential Counseling

If existential counseling becomes a perspective which is perceived as useful and necessary for counseling, what changes in the preparation of counselors should be considered?

Currently it is assumed that studies in the behavioral sciences with appropriate emphases on theory and practice, followed by an internship and periodic in-service training are adequate. Such preparation is occasionally embellished by a course or two in sociology, anthropology or political science.

Plainly this type of preparation focuses on counseling using insights from those disciplines whose chief concerns are within the Umwelt and Mitwelt modes of being. This type of preparation is necessary, but it provides no formal basis for thinking and experiencing in the Eigenwelt mode. In fact, this preparation grounded in the behavioral sciences may direct the counselor-in-training away from an appreciation of, and interest in, sources of information in other disciplines.

Granting the necessity of this further perspective, what emphasis and what means could be expected to facilitate the existentialist approach for the counselor? It is not expected that all counselors would be interested or able to engage in existential counseling. This is true not so much because of lack of skill or knowledge as from an inability to be at home with looking at life and living it from within the Eigenwelt mode. In fact, the chief problem may be in a scarcity of those who now look at life and themselves from this depth dimension or are interested and ready to commit themselves to becoming able to do so.

Although all of us as humans possess this potential for self-transcendence and freedom, we do not develop it. It remains undeveloped until we choose to look at life from this perspective or until circumstances force us to do so. We are unlikely to embrace our existence until we are willing to accept the fact that there are understandings which are not necessarily or completely the product of rational thought. We deal then with ourselves and others as essences, measurable quantities and qualities.

This potential for self-transcendence cannot be taught or imposed. But the following thoughts and beliefs may indicate a minimal readiness:

1. The recognition that no person can be completely understood by the use of rational thought and its products.

2. An awareness that information about John, however well organized and sophisticated, does not assist us in understanding "the Johnian in John."[44]

3. The recognition and growing acceptance that there is a kind of truth which may be false for everyone except him who expresses it. Although the counselee's criteria and referents seem objectively false, it is considered true if what he says follows logically from his perception of the matter.[45]

4. An inquiring attitude regarding the significance of productive imagination and the function of symbols.

5. The ability to accept ambiguity. "Instead of accepting change as an academic concept, he must be willing and able to recognize and work with change in its serious dimensions and bewildering unpredictability."[46]

It is not possible to plan with any degree of certainty the experiences necessary and helpful in the preparation of a counselor to do existential counseling. It is logical to assume that he will need the background of knowledge currently obtained in his studies of the behavioral sciences. However, the content may be viewed from a different orientation and subjected to questions arising from experiences planned to aid in the development of his existential potential. The following are suggestions as to the direction these needed experiences might take.[47]

Experiences in the Study and Interpretation of History

A foundation for understanding existential counseling could be developed through the study of (1) the roots of existentialism in the Biblical and Greek worlds; and (2) the historical changes in Europe which encouraged and led to the development of existential thought in Germany, France, Holland, Russia and other countries.

The meaning of these historical changes and changes in thought patterns should be sought through a study of the interpretation of history, especially European history during the time when Existentialism was developed, approximately 1830-1930. Such an interpretation should focus on political, philosophical and religious elements.

In order to understand the thought patterns and attitudes of our own people toward Existentialism and existential counseling, the influence of pragmatism and of British empiricism should be studied and interpreted from the three foci mentioned above.

Experiences in Literature and Drama

The study of noble characters in literature encourages the counselor to consider joy, tragedy and ambiguity in depth, to relate to myths and symbols, and to be open to the intuitive searching of the artist concerning the meaning of life. He might wish to read, study and discuss in small groups great prose and poetry in Greek, Shakespearean and modern plays. The discussion might well focus on what the characters experienced, possible reasons for their reactions, and how each counselor's perception of these situations would affect him and his counseling effort. Consider the possibilities for the grasping of existence in a small group discussion of such symbols as Hamlet's "To be or not to be . . . ."

Experiences in Philosophical and Religious Thinking

These could provide the counselor with the opportunity to grasp the significance of what the various existential thinkers, such as Schelling, Kierkegaard, Marx, Nietzsche, Dilthey, Bergson, Heidegger and others are saying. Through this study and that of religious literature chosen both from Eastern and Western thought, he could come to understand the meaning of Being and the centrality of Time in the existential approach.

A second kind of study and understanding would focus on imagination and symbols. Through reading and discussion, the counselor could come to recognize the signal importance of imagination in that (1) it submits the material of sense perception to our understanding and is an important element in the attempt to understand another from his frame of reference; (2) it encompasses the counselee's goals and represents the concrete life of his convictions. The counselee's desired accomplishment is the language of the imagination; and (3) it unifies sensation and reason, and through imagination each counselee views the future goal.[48] Not only should the counselor know the significance of productive imagination, but he should become aware of its use in his own problem solving endeavors.

A third kind of study is that concerned with symbolic thinking. Our horizontal living, marketplace orientation, pragmatic thinking, emphasis on the tangible and other subtle, pressing influences have caused us to evade consideration of the symbolic. Yet without the symbolic, which, as Martin Buber states, is a covenant "between the Absolute and the concrete,"[49] we cannot reach the depth of meaning for which we yearn in our human relationships. It is not that we do not sense this, for we sprinkle the description of counseling with an abundance of symbols, such as freedom, love, sense of responsibility, and personal center. In our attempts to explain them, we treat them as signs, and in so doing we remove them to Umwelt and Mitwelt worlds.

When symbolic meanings are ignored or treated as signs, counseling is forced to become counseling for adjustment. Signs suffice when only adjustment to the world of signs is desired. However, without the probing use of the symbolic, existential meanings are unlikely to be found, and personality changes are unlikely to take place.

To interpret life in terms of signs is to remove the meaning and significance of depth from our experience. Conceivably, then, freedom would mean the license to do what we can get away with; peace, the absence of conflict; and justice, penalty in proportion to the infraction. The true symbol has the following characteristics: (1) it points beyond itself to something else; (2) it participates in that to which it points; (3) it opens up levels of reality which are otherwise closed; (4) it opens up hidden depths of our being; (5) it cannot be produced intentionally; and (6) it dies when it no longer produces a response in the group in which it originally found expression.[50]

In his becoming, the existential counselor will resist his nominalistic tendencies. He will tolerate the ambiguity that accompanies symbolic thinking. He will refuse to try to define the symbol or make it concrete, knowable, and attainable. Not only will he discipline himself in this manner, but he will cultivate symbolic thinking in his own approach to reality. He will build an appreciation of the symbol and its meaning through study and discussion, and will endeavour to realize its significance for interpersonal growth and community self-renewal.

Experiences Through Art

The basic constituent of counseling cannot be taught. The conditions conducive to its development grow out of experiences which are meaningful and understood. They are the experiences of joy, tragedy, doubt and despair which the counselor shares with all men. Art quickens his perception and understanding of others and opens doors to awareness of self. It can do this since it makes accessible to him both the feelings experienced by predecessors and those expressed by contemporaries.

Not all art enhances the possibility of communion of the counselor with his inner self and with others, but only that art which calls forth his productive imagination, causes him to feel, and to become aware. Whatever form the art may take, the degree to which it intensifies these qualities determines its usefulness. No two counselors can be expected to be equally and similarly helped by any art form.

The degree to which the counselor experiences his own-world depends in large measure on the depth to which he is accustomed to examine and experience being-in-the-world. For the counselor who dwells in the Umwelt and Mitwelt worlds, art in any mode is less likely to deepen his sensibilities or attune his understanding to the mystery of life. For the counselor who deeply reflects upon his existence, art in some form can engender understanding of his own-world, a prerequisite for participation with others in the same quest. Counselors can benefit from the confrontation which good art, regardless of subject matter, makes possible. Such an experience deepens the counselor's self-consciousness, preparing him to participate in the counselee's search for meaning, confidence, and hope.

Issues

1. Can we as counselors become able to distinguish a problem of the counselee which is centered in the Umwelt (environment) or Mitwelt (inter-personal relationships) from one which is centered in the Eigenwelt, or the counselee's self-consciousness, his being-in-the-world?

2. Can we as counselors keep the proper perspective between essence which indicates the use of techniques, and existence which indicates direct understanding and communication with the counselee? Can we further avoid confusing them or permitting one to be absorbed in the other?

3. Can we posit self-consciousness as an entity in and of itself and use existential concepts as such, or shall we interpret them in the Mitwelt or Umwelt modes and then try to research them?

4. Can we accept human freedom, that is, the capacity of the individual to decide against any odds between being and non-being, and therefore understand the meaning of Existentialism and existential counseling without distortion?

5. Can we accept the fact that there may be something about man which is not now or ever will be understood completely within the framework of scientific research and thus value and use existential insights without reducing them to the terms of the Mitwelt mode?

Conclusions

Existential counseling adds a perspective and depth which is especially relevant today. A high school counselor interested in the fears of students asked three hundred high school students from five different urban schools to write the name of the first fear they thought of. When the results were examined, forty-five per cent had fears which may have been expressions of existential anxiety. About twelve per cent wrote fear of death, five per cent feared the death of parents, five per cent wrote fear of failure, five per cent fear of the future, eight per cent fear of car accidents, five per cent fear of war, and five per cent fear of loneliness.

This may be indicative of an increase of existential concerns. If such is the case, there is a need for counselors who, because of their own self-consciousness and depth of their life experiencing, appreciate and to some degree understand the existential concerns of others. If such counselors will continually prepare themselves through study, reflection and practice, many more students may be helped.

These counselors will use those techniques and skills which accord in principle with their beliefs about men. Their use of them will be in the manner and to the degree that these are viewed as helping them to help the counselee understand his own-being-in-the-world. They will assume that if the counselee can be helped to discover who he is, whom he desires to be, and what has true meaning for him, then the means and information will be used in proper congruence with the counselee's own becoming.

Existential assumptions are controversial. To some they may seem "foolishness." To others they may be a "stumbling block." But to still others they are a call to have "the courage to be."

Notes

1. Henry Bergson. *Essai sur les donnees immediates de la conscience.* German tr., Jena: 182 (1911).

2. Walter A. Kaufman. *Nietzsche, philosopher, psychologist, antiChrist.* Princeton: Princeton University Press (1950), 140 ff.

3. Gordon W. Allport. *Becoming: basic considerations for a psychology of personality.* New Haven: Yale University Press (1959), 18.

4. Paul Tillich. Existential philosophy. *Journal of the History of Ideas* (1944), Vol. 5: 1, 44-70.

5. Erich Fromm. *Escape from freedom.* New York: Holt, Rinehart and Winston, Inc. (1941), 19.

6. *Ibid.,* Kaufmann. *Nietzsche, philosopher, psychologist, antiChrist.*

7. Paul Tillich. The world situation. *The Christian answer,* ed. by Henry P. Van Dusen. New York: Charles Scribner's Sons (1945), 2.

8. C. Gratton Kemp. *Intangibles in counseling.* Boston: The Houghton Mifflin Company (1967), 66.

9. *Ibid.,* Tillich. Existential philosophy.

10. *Ibid.,* Allport. *Becoming: basic considerations for a psychology of personality,* 7-16.

11. Nietzsche. *Wille zur macht X.*

12. L. Binswanger. Existential analysis and psychotherapy, in *Progress in psychotherapy,* ed. by Fromm-Reichmann and Moreno. New York: Grune and Stratton (1956), 144.

13. Blaise Pascal. *Pensees of Pascal.* New York: Peter Pauper Press (1946), 36.

14. Witter Bynner. *The way of life according to Laotzu, an American version.* New York: John Day Company (1946).

15. Martin Buber. Distance and relation. *Psychiatry,* 1957, Vol. 20, No. 2.

16. Soren Kierkegaard. *Fear and trembling.* Trans. by Walter Lowrie. New York: Doubleday and Company (1954), 55.

17. Jean Paul Sartre. *Being and nothingness, an essay on phenomenological ontology.* Trans. by Hazel Barnes. New York: The Philosophical Library (1956), 52, 58.

18. David Bakan. Clinical psychology and logic, *The American Psychologist,* December (1956), 656.

19. Ernest Cassirer. *An essay on man.* New Haven: Yale University Press (1944), 22.

20. *Ibid.,* Binswanger. Existential analysis and psychotherapy, 196.

21. William Healy, August F. Bronner and Anna Mae Bowers. *The meaning and structure of psychoanalysis as related to personality and behavior.* New York: A. A. Knopf (1930), 38.

22. Rollo May. *The meaning of anxiety.* New York: Ronald Press (1950), 194, 197.

23. *Ibid.,* Kemp. *Intangibles in counseling,* 93.

24. Paul Tillich. *The courage to be.* New Haven: Yale University Press (1952), 41.

25. Rollo May et al. *Existence: a new dimension in psychiatry and psychology.* New York: Basic Books Inc. Publishers (1961), 52.

26. Charles Odier. *Les deux sources, consciente et inconsciente de la vie morale.* Neuchatel: La Baconniere (1943).

27. Paul Tournier. *Guilt and grace.* New York: Harper and Row Publishers, Inc. (1962), 66, 67.

28. O. Hobart Mowrer. Time as a determinant in integrative learning, in *Learning theory and personality.* New York: Ronald Press (1950).

29. Soren Kierkegaard. *Sickness unto death.* Princeton, N.J.: Princeton University Press, 163.

30. Gardner Murphy. *Personality, a biosocial approach.* New York: Harper and Row Publishers, Inc. (1947), 490.

31. Ludwig Immergluck. Determinism—freedom in contemporary psychology, *American Psychologist* (1961), Vol. 19, 270-281.

32. Soren Kierkegaard. Concluding unscientific postscript, in *A Kierkegaard anthology,* ed. by Robert Bretall. Princeton, N.J.: Princeton University Press (1951), 210-211.

33. Richard Kroner. *The religious function of the imagination.* New Haven: Yale University Press (1941), 9.

34. Carl Jung. *Psychological types.* New York: Harcourt, Brace and World, Inc. (1923), 577.

35. Rollo May. *Man's search for himself.* New York: W. W. Norton and Company, Inc. (1953), 154.

36. Gordon W. Allport. *Pattern and growth in personality.* New York: Holt, Rinehart and Winston, Inc. (1961), 563.

37. *Ibid.,* Kemp. *Intangibles in counseling,* 105.

38. *Ibid.,* Tillich. *The courage to be,* 49.

39. Gordon W. Allport. *The individual and his religion.* New York: The Macmillan Company (1950), 87.

40. David C. McClelland. Toward a theory of motive acquisition, *American Psychologist* (1965), Vol. 20, 321-333.

41. Otto Rank. *Will therapy.* New York: W. W. Norton and Company, Inc. (1936), 12.

42. Rollo May. *Love and will.* New York: W. W. Norton and Company, Inc. (1969), 223.

43. *Ibid.*, Tillich. *The courage to be,* 81-82.

44. *Ibid.*, Allport. *Becoming: basic considerations for a psychology of personality,* 18.

45. *Ibid.*, Kierkegaard. *Concluding unscientific postscript.*

46. C. Gratton Kemp. *Foundations of group counseling.* New York: McGraw-Hill Book Company (1970), 229.

47. Kemp. *Foundations of group counseling,* based upon 230-235.

48. C. Gratton Kemp. *Perspectives on the group process.* Boston: Houghton Mifflin Company (1964), 15.

49. Maurice S. Friedman and Martin Buber. *The life of dialogue.* New York: Harper and Brothers (1960), 320.

50. Paul Tillich. *Dynamics of faith.* New York: Harper and Brothers (1958), 42-43.

LEIF J. BRAATEN

The Main Theories of "Existentialism" from the Viewpoint of the Psychotherapist

The philosophical movement loosely designated as "existentialism" has recently been received with renewed interest by serious thinkers in psychology, psychiatry, and theology. Schaffner (12) describes this trend as follows:

... the existentialists performed a valuable service in starting to free contemporary thinkers from the shackles of philosophic, ethical, and religious systems that were keeping scientists and laymen alike from seeing man more clearly and more realistically.

Another sign of such an interest is that the American Psychological Association incorporated a symposium entitled "Existential Psychology and Psychotherapy" into its 1959 annual conference.

The writer has read a great number of published books and articles on this subject. The interested reader is referred to some of the more significant contributions (1, 2, 3, 4, 6, 7, 10, 11, 13). Nowhere, however, was there available a systematic survey of the main themes of "existentialism." The present paper is an attempt to provide such a survey and relate the themes to the clinical experience of a psychotherapist.

Leif J. Braaten, "The Main Themes of 'Existentialism' from the Viewpoint of a Psychotherapist," *Mental Hygiene*, 1961, *45*, pp. 10-17. Reprinted by permission.

Several attempts were made to abstract these main themes. The list which is presented here is the last one, and it is open for further revision. Each theme is stated in terms of a brief, freshly formulated message. Then the theme is paraphrased and related to "existentialist" writing. This section is followed by some selected comments and reactions from the viewpoint of psychotherapy.

The Main Themes of "Existentialism" and Psychotherapy

Man, You are Free; Define Yourself

Nobody has perhaps been a more vigorous advocate for the roads of freedom than Sartre (11). He is constantly puncturing all alibis of unfreedom which man has invented such as heredity, environment, upbringing and the current culture. He claims that you are only what you make of yourself. In other words, man has to invent man. This is man's greatest achievement in life. Just as there are endless vistas ahead in space, there are many unexplored ways of becoming more genuinely "human." Within the psychological profession, Gardner Murphy has recently explored "human potentialities."

The experience of feeling free necessarily involves some anxiety or trembling, but this is a driving force in seeking out the new possibilities. Every new venture of the human spirit implies a certain loneliness in the process of exploring and groping into the unknown.

From the external frame of reference, the scientist (9) believes that under certain conditions, such as the therapist's congruence in the relationship, his empathic understanding, and his unconditional positive regard, the client will display movement along particular dimensions of personality change. On the other hand, it seems that psychotherapy would be inconceivable without some subjective experience of freedom to choose on the part of the client.

The essence of therapy is the client's movement from feeling unfree and controlled by others toward the frightening but rewarding sense of freedom to map out and choose his new personality. When he, for once, has realized that it is possible to break away from old patterns, his appetite for creative newness increases progressively. It is a challenge to the therapist to become especially sensitive to the client's struggle for a more satisfying self-definition. In so doing, the therapist must alert himself to the client's readiness for freedom which varies considerably along the therapeutic process for each client, as well as between clients.

Cultivate Your Own Individuality

Several "existentialists" have been strong individualists. Nietzsche once made this famous statement: "Be a man and do not follow me—but yourself." One is advised to develop whatever is unique and special about oneself. Only in this way can mankind show progress. Every human being is challenged to cultivate what is *special* about himself, whether this involves becoming creative with ideas or objects. We all have to find out what is particularly satisfying for ourselves.

One of the greatest individualists of all times was Kierkegaard. He wanted the following inscription on his gravestone: "That Individual." Among psychologists, Jung (5) is convinced that the client would like to be understood in all his separateness, rather than as the average person. An experienced therapist knows that many clients are quite obsessed with a need to be understood accurately. Nothing but a full understanding will suffice.

The writer has some research evidence to the effect that an increased emphasis upon this private, inner self is positively and significantly correlated with one dimension of "success" in psychotherapy: namely, the mental health rating by the TAT-diagnostician. Heidegger calls this inner self *Eigenwelt*. According to Rollo May, et al. (7), Freud taught us much about the average, dynamic human being; Fromm, Horney, and Sullivan enlightened us on the interpersonal aspects of the person; yet there is still much to learn about how to facilitate man's relations with his own unique self.

Live in Dialogue with Your Fellow Man

The "existentialists" believe that there are some qualities of being which can only be distinctly developed in relation to another person. In other words, you are dependent upon your fellow man for certain exceptional experiences. Buber (2) has devoted a lifetime to spell out the characteristics of a genuine meeting of two human beings, in which each person brings about significant change in the field of the other. The proper focus to discover what is particularly human is, according to him, *between* man and man.

Such a life in dialogue requires an open awareness, and occasionally a human encounter will shake one's foundations as a person. But the recommendation is rather to make a difference in the field of your fellow man than to be ignored, even if the meeting may temporarily be disturbing for both. During a recent convocation address at the University of Chicago, Dr. Joshua Taylor made this recommendation to a new group of academicians. We were urged to take a stand in society, to participate in the community, and to let our knowledge make a real difference in our dealings with other individuals.

The psychotherapist is more challenged than many other professionals to live in dialogue with his fellow man. The very essence of therapy is a person-to-person meeting. Once the therapist has learned to appreciate the anxieties and the rewards of helping the client to develop a truer self, he is missing the experience of such a relationship when he periodically is not active in the performance of therapy. Part of this feeling is that his need to be helpful toward others is frustrated, but, more importantly, the therapist is deprived of enjoying a certain quality of emotional coexistence. He cannot *be* some important mode of himself outside a deep relationship to another human being.

This mutual dependency is even more significant from the client's point of view. The client can only develop certain human qualities, such as trust and understanding, to the extent that the therapist is able to demonstrate these qualities in action. Therefore the ambitious therapist is constantly trying to push the limits of freedom and safety within the relationship. Thus he becomes less and less limited by his own attitudes in his desire to help others.

If you are going to live successfully in dialogue with your fellow man, it is essential that you learn to recognize the true "boundaries" between yourself and the other person. We are not surprised that children often operate as if other persons—the parents, siblings, etc.— form a part of their extended self. But it is shocking to realize how difficult it is even for adults to act as if both they and others are free centers of subjectivity rather than ego-extensions to manipulate.

Through the help of therapy, the client ceases to expect specific reactions to stimuli he emits toward others. Instead, he learns to accept the more modest goal of just making some difference to his fellow men in a broader sense. The client realizes that he can only take responsibility for his part of a relationship. What the other person does with it, he can only decide. Similarly, the therapist should be judged by how well he can provide optimal growth conditions for the client. Ultimately, it is up to the client to decide whether he wants to make use of the therapeutic relationship. One implication of this principle is that the therapist should not always be held responsible if significant personality change does not take place.

Your Own Experiencing Is the Highest Authority

The "existentialists" urge you to live your own life, to become sensitive to important happenings in your own existence, particularly choices at significant crossroads. Your own experiencing is your best guide. This greatly limits what you can learn from others because they have to interpret their experience. Therefore, you cannot trust, fully, even the wisest men; they can only provide you with stimulation. You can receive their impact, but you should never forget that your own uniqueness necessarily will color your interpretations. Binswanger has much to say about the importance of discovering one's *Eigenwelt*. If this development does not take place, a person will never achieve a real sense of his own existence; he will not develop toward an authentic human being.

Within the client-centered group, nobody has been a more vigorous advocate for the "function of experiencing" than Gendlin. His thesis is that therapy is "successful" to the extent that the client is helped to become open and sensitive to his ever ongoing stream of experiencing. If a person is completely aware of his experience, he will tend to make the most intelligent and satisfying choices in life.

Rogers has also emphasized experiencing as the ultimate guide for human existence. He says: "No one else's ideas, and none of my own ideas, are as authoritative as my experience. It is to experience that I must return again and again, to discover a closer approximation to truth as it is in the process of becoming, in me." A declaration of a similar nature, which is even more meaningful to me, runs as follows: "Neither the Christian church nor the priests—neither Freud nor Rogers—neither the revelations of others nor research—can take precedence over my own direct experience."

Such an approach toward life will necessarily involve some conflict with other people. But if a person is fully open to his experience, he will consider all the relevant factors and decide when it is appropriate to yield or take a fight. One such factor will be the other person's right to be guided by *his* experience.

Be Fully Present in the Immediacy of the Moment

"Existentialism" is focused upon the individual's existence from moment to moment. The past is not so important; it is what you are *right now.* Jaspers once exclaimed: "What we are missing of full human presence!" Rollo May has pointed out that in therapy and life in general there are so-called "pregnant moments," occasions when a radical change can take place in a person's existence. Many "existentialists" show an awesome respect for the significance of certain emerging developments. Tillich (13) has coined the word *kairos* for the moment when "eternity touches time," when some critical fulfillment can occur.

The writer found in his doctoral research that the more "successful" the client was, seen by both the therapist and the TAT-diagnostician, the more likely it was that he showed a movement toward greater emphasis upon an immediate, emotional experiencing of the self. In other words, "successful" clients tend to become more truly open to their existence *right there and then* within the therapeutic relationship. Rogers believes that the essence of therapy is that the client is experiencing such deep moments of integration of the self. These moments he considers the real "molecules of therapy."

There are critical points during the treatment process when the therapist's wisdom and skills are particularly called for, when what he *is* as a total person determines whether the client is given a chance for a spurt of growth or quits, when therapy is immensely speeded up or temporarily upset. Sometimes the client may go through such critical moments more quietly. At other times he may experience fully for the first time certain denied aspects of himself dramatically. This intensive experiencing may give the client what the psychoanalysts call "abreaction" which implies that the denied material will never any more have the same threatening character.

There Is No Truth Except in Action

The "existentialist" is disgusted with thinking which is not reflected in action. He feels that a small action is often more significant than a thousand words. Sartre argues that "existentialism" implies that you are willing to accept the full consequences of your viewpoints. There must be congruence between belief and action. There is an emphasis upon commitment: that is, to be an aware participant in society rather than merely an observer. Accordingly we find that several "existentialists" have been very concerned about the predicament of man. They have been uncompromising in their criticism of depersonalization in our mass culture.

The relevance of this message for psychotherapy is that the therapist must not only experience the proper conditions for constructive personality change within himself; he must actively communicate these attitudes to the client so that they make some perceived difference in his field. Frieda Fromm-Reichmann has eloquently stated this rule in psychotherapy: "What the patient needs is an experience, not an explanation!" It is more important what the therapist is able to *be* and *do* than what he just says. One implication of this principle is that the therapist must not try to be somebody he is not. Pretense is detrimental to good therapy. The client often senses, at some level within himself, to what extent the therapist strikes him as an authentic person. A basic requirement for progress in treatment is that the therapist is able to transparently be himself, that there is congruence between his inner awareness and his actions.

You Can Transcend Yourself in Spurts

Although modern "existentialists" acknowledge some historical roots, they believe that it is possible, even characteristic, for the authentic man to throw off the burden of the past and transcend his old self. According to their position, a person's development cannot always be accounted for by a gradual, stepwise evolution. In Sartre's "existential psychoanalysis" the therapist tries to help the client perform significant choices which will make him rise above old, unsatisfying patterns of behavior.

The transcending of oneself is naturally more characteristic late in "successful" therapy than earlier in the treatment. During the beginning of therapy, the client feels very much chained to his past; he moves around, psychologically speaking, only with the greatest efforts. But as treatment progresses, the client becomes quite excited by planning a truer, more satisfying self. He feels dissatisfied by merely repeating old "personal constructs."

The client feels less compelled to appear consistent over time. There is a keen enjoyment in experimenting with oneself. A high value is placed upon surprising oneself as well as others. It even happens that a client feels free to throw overboard a whole old set of rules and assumptions and replace them with something radically new and different.

Live Your Potentialities Creatively

When Nietzsche wrote about *Übermensch,* he had in mind a person who is creatively actualizing himself, an individual who refuses to be bound by his past, somebody who, rather, is a continuous process of becoming. With the expression "will to power" Nietzsche was referring to the individual's power for self-fulfillment, not to his desire to dominate his fellow man. He wanted everybody to push toward his own unique potentials.

This creative approach toward oneself and different subject matters implies a certain distrust of the past as the source of understanding and inspiration for future development. For the creative person, the past holds only a small part of his attention. He is rather preoccupied with the present and the future and assumes that there are infinite areas of human endeavor yet to be explored. He takes it for granted that he can change and develop.

Toward the end of "successful" therapy the client does not feel fixated by his past conditioning, abilities, and interests. He knows that the challenge is to grow beyond himself. Areas where his potentials are best tend to be selected for further improvement. A playful spontaneity is characteristic of his behavior. He is toying with ideas and materials. New combinations are tried out. As therapy progresses, the client is groping for fresh expressions which more accurately reflect significant experiencing. He is becoming fond of his *Eigenwelt* regardless of recognition from others. He is joyfully pushing toward the frontiers of his own talents for living and self-expression.

In Choosing Yourself You Choose Man

Existentialism has often been accused of leading to moral nihilism. Such critics argue that there would be no two sets of values which would be similar in important respects when everybody is challenged to define himself. According to Sartre, this line of reasoning is unjustified because in choosing for yourself you are also choosing for mankind. When you are planning some course of action, you would always have to ask yourself: "What would our society be like if everybody did like me?" In other words, the existentialists strongly emphasize man's responsibility toward his fellow man. One of the heroes of Camus is going through agonies because he was not given a second chance to save a woman whom he saw commit suicide. An implicit assumption in this theme is a belief in the basic unity of man, a feeling that we are all faced with the same task of having to learn to live constructively with ourselves and other people.

In theories of therapy and personality, some lean toward a conception of man as basically evil, destructive, and sinful, while others think they have observed that man is rather good, sociable, and forward-moving. Freud and many of his followers seem to belong to the first group, and so do many theological thinkers on pastoral counseling. Mowrer seems to fall into the second group, emphasizing what he has called the "pleasure of consciousness," that man often finds pleasure in doing what would be constructive for all men. Rogers is certainly closer to Mowrer than Freud; he has observed that human nature is basically self-actualizing and good. As I understand him, this does not mean that Rogers denies man's freedom to choose between good and evil; rather it means that when man becomes more "fully functioning," he tends to make socially constructive choices because this tendency is part of his basic nature.

You Must Learn to Accept Certain Limits in Life

Earlier in this paper much was said about man's capacity to transcend himself creatively. This does not mean that there are no limits to self-actualization. The "existentialists" feel that contemporary man has to be reminded that he shows a little more imagination in the way he defines himself. On the other hand, the "existentialists" are certainly also very concerned about limits in our existence, especially the ultimate limit—death. In European "existentialism" the concern with death is central.

It has often been said that being in the world can only be fully grasped in relation to not being. Since the opportunity to commit suicide exists for every human being, great importance is attached to an active confirmation of living. In other words, you have to be "born again" to become an authentic person. An individual who has worked through his feelings in relation to death often achieves a new quality to his living. He becomes very concerned about making the most of his existence right here and now.

It can be argued that since death is the ultimate limit, death is the prototype of all limits. In psychotherapy very significant events are connected with limits of one kind or other. Rogers early recognized that the setting of limits for himself and the client was an integral part of constructive treatment. From the therapist's point of view there is a certain limit to how much responsibility he is willing to assume, how much time he can offer his client, and how much affection and aggression he can tolerate. It is important for the therapist to be aware of his limits at all times and behave accordingly. He must also strive to push his own limits farther.

From the client's viewpoint it is often one of his most significant achievements that he learns gracefully to accept certain limits of reality both within and outside the therapeutic relationship. Sometimes his whole emphasis, then, changes toward becoming more concerned about what he can do *within* the limits of the therapy hour, his level of intelligence, his present marriage situation, etc.

Summary and Perspectives

In this paper the writer has endeavored to discuss the main themes of "existentialism" from the viewpoint of a psychotherapist. Since no systematic survey of "existentialism" seemed feasible for our topic, an attempt was made to arrive at a fresh list of the most important "existentialist" themes. Each theme was then presented and discussed in relation to selected issues of psychotherapy.

Our tentative list of the main "existentialist" themes includes: (1) Man, you are free, define yourself; (2) Cultivate your own individuality; (3) Live in dialogue with your fellow man; (4) Your own experiencing is the highest authority; (5) Be fully present in the immediacy of the moment; (6) There is no truth except in action; (7) You can transcend yourself in spurts; (8) Live your potentialities creatively; (9) In choosing yourself, you choose man, and (10) You must learn to accept certain limits in life.

It is the conviction of the writer that the "existentialists" have an important message to communicate to modern man in general and the psychotherapist in particular. The stimulation from this movement may also open up new, fresh perspectives for the scientific investigation of psychotherapy and personality change.

References

1. Barrett, W., *Irrational Man: A Study in Existential Philosophy* (New York: Doubleday & Co., Inc., 1958).
2. Buber, Martin, *Between Man and Man*, translation by R. G. Smith (Boston: Beacon Press, Inc., 1955).
3. Collins, J., *The Existentialists: A Critical Study* (Chicago: Henry Regnery Co., 1952).

4. Herberg, Will, ed., *Four Existentialist Theologians: A Reader from the Works of Jacques Maritain, Nicolas Berdyaev, Martin Buber and Paul Tillich* (New York: Doubleday & Co., Inc., 1958).
5. Jung, Carl G., *The Undiscovered Self*, translation by R. F. C. Hull (Boston: Little, Brown & Co., 1957).
6. Kaufmann, W., ed., *Existentialism from Dostoevsky to Sartre* (New York: Meridian Press, 1956).
7. May, R., E. Angel and H. F. Ellenberger, eds., *Existence: A New Dimension in Psychiatry and Psychology* (New York: Basic Books Inc., 1958).
8. Rogers, Carl R., "What It Means to Become a Person," in *The Self: Explorations in Personal Growth*, C. E. Moustakas, ed. (New York: Harper & Bros., 1956), 195-211.
9. Rogers, Carl R., "The Necessary and Sufficient Conditions of Therapeutic Personality Change," *Journal of Consulting Psychology*, 21 (April, 1957), 95-103.
10. Rogers, Carl R., "A Process Conception of Psychotherapy," *American Psychologist*, 13 (April, 1958), 142-49.
11. Sartre, Jean Paul, *Existentialism and Human Emotions* (New York: The Wisdom Library, 1957).
12. Schaffner, B., "Thoughts About Therapy Today," *Mental Hygiene*, 43 (July, 1959), 339-50.
13. Tillich, Paul, *The Courage To Be* (New Haven, Conn.: Yale University Press, 1952).

Acknowledgment

Although the writer is fully responsible for this paper, he wishes to acknowledge the value of his dialogical encounters with Drs. Eugene Gendlin, Carl R. Rogers, John M. Shlien, and Mrs. Hellene Sarett.

GERALD J. PINE

The Existential
School Counselor

Introduction

Today's students are deeply concerned with questions regarding
the meaning of human existence. These questions are expressed in
such terms as Who am I? Where am I going? What is the meaning of
life? What is the meaning of *my* life? What is the purpose of learning?
How relevant is education to life? The search for the answers to these
queries is a significant element in the existential counseling relationship.

Because existentialism emphasizes freedom with accountability
and focuses on man as the creator of his culture and the master of his
destiny, it has become an attractive and dynamic philosophical force
in counseling. Its potential for school counseling is now being fully
explored and translated into the reality of schools.

Common Existential Principles

A great deal of diversity may be found among such existential
writers as Sartre, Heidegger, Kierkegaard, Marcel, Jaspers, and Buber.
As a philosophical movement existentialism embraces a variety of

Gerald J. Pine, "The Existential School Counselor," *Clearing House*, 1969, *43*, pp. 351-354.
Reprinted by permission.

viewpoints. However, running through these various existential viewpoints are several common denominators which can be identified and which have special relevance for those who hope to arrive at a more effective counseling approach through the medium of existentialism.

(1) The basic philosophical principle of existentialism is that *existence precedes essence.* Man chooses his essence; he exists first and then defines himself through the choices he makes plus the actions he takes. Thought without action is meaningless. Man is what he does.

(2) At every moment man is free. He is free of external forces. He is free of himself—of what he has been. An individual's past life is history, it no longer exists *now* in the present. An individual is influenced by external agents or by his past life only when he chooses to be influenced by these forces.

(3) Accompanying man's freedom is the awesome burden of responsibility. Each man is responsible for what he is. In choosing and acting for himself each man chooses and acts for all mankind. Man cannot avoid the weight of his freedom. He cannot give away his freedom and responsibility to the state, to his parents, to his teachers, to his weaknesses, to his past, to environmental conditions.

(4) Every truth and every action implies a human setting and a human subjectivity. There is a world of reality but it cannot be reality apart from the people who are the basic part of it. Reality lies in each man's experience and perception of the event rather than in the isolated event; e.g., two men may hear the same speech, the same words, the same voice. One man's reality may be that the speaker is a political demagogue, for the other man the reality is that the speaker is an awaited political saviour.

(5) Man must rely upon himself and upon his fellow creatures to live out his life-span in an adamant universe. Man's relationship to others must be that of self-realization for all and creature comfort (empathic love).

(6) Man is not an object; he is a subject. Each man is unique and idiosyncratic. To view man scientifically is to view man as an object. Science fails to find the "I" in each man.

Existential Counseling Principles

Flowing from these common and vital existential principles a special helping and facilitative human relationship between student and counselor has evolved. The existential school counselor has translated

existentialism into a counseling approach designed to increase freedom within the pupil, to assist the pupil in discovering meaning for
his existence, and to improve his encounter with others.

*The existential school counselor sees counseling as more an atti-
tude than a technique.* It reflects the self of the counselor and represents a sharing of the counselor's self in a personal and human relationship with a fellow human being.

School counseling is viewed primarily as an encounter which implies a special kind of relationship requiring the counselor to be
totally present to the student, to participate in the student's existence, to be fully with him. The counselor strives to know the student by entering the student's reality, and seeing as the student sees.
He empathizes with the counselee.

The counselee is not reduced to an object to be analyzed according
to theoretical constructs. He is not diagnosed and evaluated by the
counselor because diagnosis and evaluating are conducted in terms of
externally established norms and standards.

The counselor who depends on cumulative records and test data to
work with the student locks himself outside the student's internal
world. Entrance into that world is gained by an emotional commitment in which the counselor risks himself as a person.

Knowing the student as a person becomes more important than
knowing about him. This demands counselor movement away from
the traditional diagnostic approaches which mirror an external objective perspective to an internal, subjective, and personal experience
with the counselee.

*The existential school counselor operates on the immediate view
of human experience.* Counselor behavior is a function of the immediate view of the student. There is no reliance on historical or external determinism.

The immediate view stresses that it is the way the student sees his
situation today, at this instant, which produces his behavior at this
instant. The student behaves at this time on the basis of his ways of
seeing, choosing, and acting at this moment in time. What the counselor is and what he does in his relationships with students is the key
to developing facilitating and enabling relationships among counselees.

This implies that the counselor and the student can effect change
together without the counselor knowing the case history of the student; it suggests that change can evolve in students without neces-

sarily effecting change in parent behavior or in the neighborhood environment.

The existential school counselor knows that no matter what the student has endured elsewhere, a positive facilitating *present* experience is enabling and growth-producing. Providing positive present experiences does not depend on knowing what a person's past experiences have been.

"Student Responsibility and Role"

Directing, guiding, and advising students are not part of the existential approach to counseling. Choices must be made by the counselee. *The student assumes full responsibility for choice and action.*

Whenever the counselor structures the counseling situation toward a counselor choice he infringes upon the freedom and the commitment of the student. The student increases his freedom and his sense of personal responsibility only when he experiences freedom and responsibility.

Counseling provides him with such experiences when it is built upon an authentic belief in the potentiality of the student and his capacity for choosing. The more the counselor acts on that belief the more he discovers the student's potentiality and capacity for choosing and acting in self-actualizing ways. This demands enormous faith and consistency on the part of the counselor.

The counselor conveys his faith in the student through his attitudes which indicate to the student, "You can become more independent and self-sustaining" and "The direction for your life ultimately must come from you." Through his attitudes the counselor communicates the feeling that the student *can be* more than he is rather than the feeling he *must be* more than he is.

The existential heart of counseling is the recognition of the student's right to make his own choices and his own "mistakes." Counseling is an encounter in which the counselee is free to become more free. The student who feels trusted to make his own choices begins to trust in himself more and becomes aware that the meanings of his experiences, the meaning for his existence emerge from within himself.

The ideas of freedom and accountability indicate that *the student must be free to choose whether he wishes to participate in the counseling process.* Counseling should not be imposed nor bureaucratized.

As one student put it, "Counseling is one of the very few things that students feel they have freedom in. I think it is their choice alone whether they would like to use the program. I think we are adult enough to decide for ourselves whether we need or want counseling."

Unfortunately, in all too many school systems, the practice is to require every student to see the school counselor a given number of times during the year. Such practice is perceived by students as a routine mechanical assembly-line process of interviewing. To some counselors allowing the student to decide whether or not he will make use of the counseling service poses a real threat because it puts their counseling program "on the line."

The existential school counselor would not hesitate to allow students the right to choose whether or not they would make use of counseling since he would feel that (1) a counseling relationship that has been initiated by the student is built on a firmer footing than one into which he has been forced; (2) a counseling program will attract voluntary self-referrals in proportion to the quality of the counseling; and (3) required and routine counseling negates what existentialism stands for—it infringes on freedom.

For the existential school counselor the central role in the relationship must be left to the student. Counseling exists primarily for the student and must be used by the student on his terms. The more the counselor focuses on the needs, problems, and feelings of the student, the more he emphasizes the existential character of counseling.

Focusing on the student and his frame of reference enables the student to become more aware of his internal resources and facilitates in the student an understanding of the reality of his being in the school, in the home, in the world. In this kind of atmosphere the student learns that it is *he* who is important; it is *his* experience which counts and not someone else's; it is *his* being that is significant; it is *his* internal advice that is relevant.

"Tuning In"

Non-evaluative listening is a particularly important dimension in existential school counseling. This doesn't refer to a polite or social listening in which the counselor tolerates the student's verbalizations or waits for the student to finish talking and then jumps in to get a point across. Listening, in an existential sense, means tuning into the experiential wavelength of the counselee, being in complete emotional and cognitive contact with him.

While the counselor listens he does not analyze, evaluate, or judge what is being communicated. He immerses himself completely in the counselee's perceptions and experiences so that he is sensitive to all levels of communication—the verbal and the nonverbal—the affective and the cognitive.

It is essential that the existential school counselor know himself. He can only like students as much as he likes himself; he can accept students to the degree that he accepts himself; he can understand students in so far as he can understand himself. When he knows his own values he can become more sensitive to the dangers of imposing those values on others.

By looking at himself as he is and is becoming the counselor becomes more aware of the influencing dimensions of his behavior and how they affect his counseling function. He develops a deeper sensitivity and richer appreciation of the unique potentialities in those counselees who differ from him in behavior and values.

MARILYN BATES
CLARENCE D. JOHNSON

The Existentialist
Counselor at Work

When Beck (1963) integrated philosophical foundations of guidance with psychological models of man, counseling completed its
rites of passage from childhood to maturity. In the childhood of
counseling, the various models of personality served as useful conceptual tools that allowed counselors to function from a scientific base,
but counseling could not come of age until larger ontological questions at least were raised. Asking questions, however, remains an
academic exercise until philosophical and theoretical answers are
translated into operational procedures in the counseling office.

The purpose of this paper is to translate one philosophy—existentialism—into behavior for the counselor at work. This paper attempts
to spell out the nitty-gritty of what the givens of existentialist philosophy might mean to counselors working in public school settings.
Relevant existential postulates are identified and briefly elaborated.
Main emphasis is placed on implications of the concepts for a counselor as he works in his office. The reader is referred to other sources
for more thorough presentation of existentialist philosophy (see References).

Bates, M. & Johnson, C. D. The existentialist counselor at work. *The School Counselor,*
1969, *16*(4), 245-250. Copyright 1969 American Personnel and Guidance Association. Reprinted with permission.

Since a source of confusion among various theoretical counseling positions seems to lie between existentialist and self-theory practices, each existentialist postulate is translated into dialogue that contrasts a representative non-directive response with a representative existentialist response.

Concept: Existence Precedes Essence

Man is flung into the world from an unknown and doomed to struggle toward an unknown—death. His only known is that he is. His existentialist task in life is to define himself through his being in the world. Throughout life man is in process of becoming.

Implications for Counseling

If man's task in life is to define himself through the process of becoming, it follows that the counseling function of midwifing the self-actualizing process ought to be available throughout an individual's life. The existentialist concept of life as a continuous process of definition implies that counseling services ought logically to begin with pre-school play therapy and to end in a geriatric setting. In public schools the existentialist counselor, who is developmentally oriented rather than crisis-centered, would most certainly begin his activities in elementary school and ideally would work with families before children reached school age. Follow-up counseling to the existentialist would be routine rather than exceptional.

Another implication of the concept that living is a process of self-definition lies in the area of record-keeping. To the existentialist, collection of data concerning a counselee is fairly futile until these data enter the awareness of the counselee. "Pure" practice consonant with existentialist theory would suggest that the counselor develop jointly with each client a developmental folder for relevant data (test scores, physical development charts, records of interest patterns, autobiographies written at various grade levels, cumulative transcripts, teacher's anecdotes, etc.) gathered in the process of the counselee's education. The isolation of collected materials beyond immediate reach of the counselee is inconsistent with the school counselor's existentialist concept of defining essence.

The following dialogue illustrates the translation of concepts into operational terms—verbal behavior.

Client: I don't really know who I am or where I'm going, or how I'm going to get there.

Non-directive: You're pretty confused right now about what life is all about.

Existentialist: Before you can make choices about what you want to do, first of all you somehow have to find out the sort of person you are.

Concept: *Man Is Condemned to Freedom*

Existentialist man is free. No matter how he tries to escape this awesome, terrible freedom, he cannot. Man must choose for himself and accept full responsibility for the consequences of those choices. There are no responsibility-free wombs into which existentialist man can retreat. His life sentence is a freedom which carries no possibility of reprieve or commutation.

Implications for Counseling

Since man must choose, his best chance of being human is to make as many choices as possible *in awareness.* If man bungles through his life a puppet on a string, strung out by chance and only activated by deus ex machina choices, his life style will be at best a series of blunders and at worst a meaningless tragedy. Only when man uses his sentence of freedom to make conscious choices is he really alive. The existentialist counselor who conceptualizes man in this fashion will see as one of his counseling functions the clarification of alternatives open to the client. In the counseling relationship counselor and client examine realistic courses of action open to the client and their probable consequences. The client, condemned as he is to freedom, then chooses his actions with awareness, and in his consciously made choices finds that he is human. Clarification of alternatives might involve course selection, college choice, job opportunities, changes of program, dropping out of school, etc. The constant need for decision-making in the school setting, whether changing a program or selecting a job field, offers an opportunity for counselor and client to experience an encounter. Functions which other theoretical orientations may label *routine* and *clerical* can be used by the existentialist counselor to assist clients to make conscious choices with awareness of responsibility for consequences. Every client contact, brief or extensive, is seen by the practicing existentialist as a potential encounter.

Verbal behavior illustrative of applied theory might be:

Client: I'm not sure whether I should drop chemistry or not. I know I need it for college, but I'm not doing well in it.

Non-directive: You know you need chemistry for college, but you are not quite sure whether you can make it or not.

Existentialist: It seems to me that we should explore together whether or not to drop chemistry. I'm willing to help you in any way I can, but it will be your choice and your decision.

Concept: *When Man Chooses, He Chooses for All Men*

Condemned man makes free choices as he must, but existentialist man is aware that every choice he makes carries in it the implication that it is the best choice for *all* men since each man, in his lonely freedom, is the only representative of mankind he will ever know.

Implications for Counseling

The term *responsibility* is not an unctuous, moralistic pronouncement to the existentialist, but an inescapable fact of being in the world. As a counselee constructs his alternatives and clarifies possible consequences of his choices he must be helped to realize that *he* is the only representative of mankind he has. Thus inherent in each choice he makes is the implication that this is best for *every* man. The counselee who chooses to cheat is by his behavior stating that this is best for all of us. He cannot place responsibility for his choices on an unhappy childhood, or a poor teacher. Neither can he excuse himself by saying, "I didn't mean to do it." Rationalizations may be interesting but, in the existentialist's counseling office, irrelevant. The client, with the help of his counselor, becomes aware of the responsibility inherent in his every choice, and comes to understand that he *is* man, whether he likes it or not. He is condemned to choose for himself, but he is also condemned to choose for all mankind.

The contrasting responses of non-directivists and existentialists to one client's verbalizations might be:

Client: I know I should have done my homework, but the teacher just didn't make it interesting, and I was bored, so I didn't get it done.

Non-directive: You know better, but somehow you just couldn't seem to work up enough interest to get at your homework.

Existentialist: You chose not to do your homework last night and would like to shift blame to your teacher. This sounds like a cop-out to me.

Concept: Man Defines Himself Only Through His Actions

Good intentions, to the existentialist, are not paving on the road to hell. They are simply irrelevant. Man is defined exclusively through what he *does,* not what he *says* he is going to do, or what he intended to do. The only final relevancy is action.

Implications for Counseling

As the existentialist counselor works with his client, the client will constantly be confronted with his visible behavior—what he actually did, not just what he felt. Intending to do homework is meaningless and of no concern. Did he do it? Feelings are relevant and worth exploration only in understanding the barriers to action. Counseling will tend to emphasize actions and feelings in the here and now, rather than to dwell on historically remote causes of behavior or to focus mainly on feelings alone. Confrontation, then—with relevant "what's" rather than irrelevant "why's" or futile "wish I had's"—is the major emphasis.

The implications for research on the effectiveness of counseling are apparent in this concept. If the only relevant end product of counseling is what the client *did,* measuring the results of counseling can be done in operational terms, just as research can focus on observable behavior rather than on elusive attitudes.

The concept of man defining himself through his actions also has major implications for vocational counseling, since in Western culture modern man defines himself particularly through his occupational choice. What man does with his productive time is one of his major ways of stating who he is. Thus the existentialist counselor sees occupational choice as a means of self-definition and gives serious attention to vocational exploration. He will use all occupational media—interest tests, career materials, individual counseling, group counseling, group guidance, career days and units—as useful tools in helping each client, boy or girl, seek out his statement of occupational choice.

Non-directivists have traditionally been little interested in occupational exploration except as it involved self-concept, while the existentialist counselor addresses himself to vocational counseling with serious intent:

> *Client:* I'm not sure what I want to be. Sometimes I think nursing, then again, no. I think I would like to be a secretary. I'm just not sure at all.

Non-directive: The whole picture of choosing a job seems pretty dim to you right now.

Existentialist: Right now you seem to have at least two choices in mind. Could we think out loud what's in each job for you?

Concept: The Encounter—The "I-Thou" Relationship Defines Counseling Process and Content

The existentialist concept of encounter emphasizes that, while man essentially is alone, the bridge from "I" to "Thou" is the basis of the counseling relationship. Risk and pain for both counselor and counselee are ever-present, especially in the necessary process of confrontation.

Implications for Counseling

Each encounter between counselor and counselee is a unique event and does not necessarily imply a long-term relationship. The three-minute interview concerning a program change may be an "I-Thou" encounter. Every contact the counselor has with his counselee has potential for encounter, whether the purpose is college choice exploration, personal problems, or corrections of unsatisfactory behavior referrals. The therapy requirement of many interviews over a long period of time is not essential for a public school existentialist counselor to consider himself "really counseling." The realities of time limitations can be met with a minimum of frustrations when each encounter, no matter how brief, is considered important. The quality of the relationship is far more important to the existentialist than is the quantity of time allotted to it.

The "I-Thou" relationship implies a deep commitment by the counselor to his counselee, a commitment that involves concern for *all* his behavior. The encounter must include dealing with mistakes a counselee makes in behavior, even if the mistakes involve discipline. The existentialist counselor is committed to the counselee, and remains "I-Thou" involved, whether the counselee is behaving appropriately or inappropriately. The counselor-administrator team and the counselor-teacher team working *with* a counselee would be routine for the existentialist.

This existentialist posture of dealing with all a counselee's behavior demands that the counselor be very aware of his own limitations and responses. For example, if he is not able to separate his perceptions of a counselee's behavior from perceptions of the counselee as a person of value, the counselor may then be entangled in his own hang-ups. If the counselor is operating from "I-Thou" he must be authentic, and this involves committing himself to the risk and pain of a counseling encounter that may include self-confrontation. Awareness of this risk should be made a part of professional training that includes provisions for self-exploration.

Dialogue between a faculty member and a representative non-directive and existentialist counselor might go something like this:

> *Faculty Member:* That hood, Jim J., has been acting up in my class again. I wish you would do something about his behavior.
> *Non-directive:* It seems to me that this is a problem better handled by the vice-principal.
> *Existentialist:* I'll be glad to talk with Jim. Send him in fourth period: but would you take a little time right now to tell me how he's bugging *you*?

Concept: Two Worlds Exist—The World of Objective Reality and the World of Subjective Reality

A world of objective reality, governed by more or less known scientific laws, exists and is knowable by man. Another world of subjective reality governed by more or less unknown psychological laws exists and is only tentatively knowable by man.

Implications for Counseling

The concept of two different worlds operating from two different sets of laws is particularly useful for the existentialist school counselor. It allows him to use tools indigenous to *trait* and *factor* counseling governed by a set of statistical laws, presumably knowable. It also allows him to explore with the counselee the phenomenological world of the latter, while realizing that the life-space of a counselee is never fully knowable. Objective measuring instruments can be used on an "as if" basis, but are subject to alignment with the interface of the counselee's subjective world and the realities of the objective world. Because of the concept of two worlds, the existentialist counselor is highly sensitive to dangers involved in using normative data to draw ipsative conclusions.

Within the framework of the concept of two worlds the existentialist counselor is responsible for the acculturation process as well as the individualization process. One of the tools he uses to facilitate both processes simultaneously is group counseling. The safe cocoon of individual counseling is a necessary but not always sufficient condition for helping a counselee cope with his two worlds with their often contradictory dimensions, and thus the existentialist counselor often finds himself group counselor.

A final example of verbalizations of a non-directive counselor-at-work and an existentialist counselor-at-work concerns a reconciliation of these two worlds:

Client: I don't see the way clear at all after graduation. There has to be something, but I sure don't know what.

Non-directive: You're feeling pretty much up in the air about everything right now.

Existentialist: You know there is a world out there, some place to go, but at this point you don't see how you fit into all of it. Let's talk about it.

Summary

Fitting the concepts of existentialist philosophy into the work of the counselor has been the purpose of this paper, in which various existentialist postulates have been enumerated. An attempt was made to tease out the implications of the philosophical concepts for the work of the counselor as he operates within the framework of the school setting.

References

Arbuckle, D. S., Landsman, T., Tiedeman, D., & Vaughan, R. P. A symposium on existentialism in counseling. *Personnel and Guidance Journal,* 1965, *43,* 551-573.

Beck, C. E. *Philosophical foundations of guidance.* Englewood Cliffs, N.J.: Prentice-Hall, 1963.

Bugental, J. F. T. *The search for authenticity.* New York: Holt, Rinehart and Winston, 1965.

Dreyfus, E. A. The counselor and existentialism. *Personnel and Guidance Journal,* 1964, *43,* 114-117.

Johnson, E. L. Existentialism, self-theory and the existential self. *Personnel and Guidance Journal,* 1967, *46,* 53-58.

Van Kaam, A. *The art of existentialist counseling.* Wilkes-Barre, Penn.: Dimension Books, 1966.

Wahl, J. *A short history of existentialism.* New York: Philosophical Library, 1949.

SECTION V

Individual/Developmental Counseling

A new professional discipline has emerged: child psychiatry. It is based on an assumption we cannot share, that children who need help are "emotionally sick." Few of them are really sick; most are misguided. Who is best qualified to help them—the teacher, the parent, the counselor, the psychiatrist, the social worker, the minister, or any adult friend or relative? In our experience, any one of them can be effective in influencing the child and helping him to adjust. The disturbed child has wrong ideas about himself and life and uses socially unacceptable means to find his place. Anyone who can win his confidence, who understands him, who can show him alternatives, can redirect the child.

—Rudolf Dreikurs

Individual/developmental psychology, as we know it today, is a direct result of the work of Alfred Adler at the beginning of this century. A colleague of Sigmund Freud's, Adler eventually rejected the tenets of psychoanalytic thought and developed his own system, which he termed *individual psychology*. This system is more widely known today as Adlerian counseling.

The basic theoretical concepts of Adlerian counseling focus on the following:

1. Teleoanalytic goals: behavior is seen as a movement toward

future goals. The counseling process involves an analysis of these future goals.

2. Striving for superiority: all individuals are attempting to become better than they are at present. This striving carries a person from one level of development to the next.

3. Inferiority feelings: these feelings arise from a sense of incompletion or imperfection. They are normal and are the cause of all improvement in a person's life.

4. Social interest: each individual possesses a natural interest in the welfare of society. By working for the common good, a person compensates for his or her individual weakness.

5. Style of life: this concept is the sum total of an individual's attempts to be superior and to overcome his or her basic inferiority feelings. The style of life is unique for each individual.

6. Creative self: human beings create their own personalities. They search creatively for experiences that fulfill their unique styles of life.

7. Consciousness: each individual is capable of planning and guiding his or her behavior with full awareness of its meaning for his or her self-realization.

Rudolph Dreikurs extended the work of Adler specifically to include the family constellation. Most of Dreikurs's work has concerned the development and management of children and adolescents. He titled his approach *family counseling,* since the focus of therapy was the family unit. Dreikurs readily adopted the Adlerian concepts of inferiority feelings, superiority striving, style of life, birth order, and teleoanalytic goal orientation. This last concept he translated into four goals of a child's disturbed behavior.

More recently, Don Dinkmeyer has extended the work of Adler and Dreikurs, incorporating their concepts into the approach that he terms *developmental counseling.* Dinkmeyer begins this section of readings by briefly, yet comprehensively, surveying Adlerian psychology and its application to school counseling. His description of the stages in the counseling process may be especially helpful to practicing counselors. Dreikurs, in the second article, focuses more specifically on the four goals of a child's misbehavior and their remediation by counselors and parents. In the final article, Dinkmeyer applies the philosophy of Alfred Adler to developmental counseling.

DON DINKMEYER

Contributions of Teleoanalytic Theory and Techniques to School Counseling

School counseling demands competency in a variety of psychological areas in the dimensions of educational, vocational, and personal-social problems, and in the area of consulting teachers and parents.

The most noticeable deficiency in some counselor-education experiences is the lack of familiarity with a theory demonstrated to be effective in school counseling. The purpose of this paper is to present the contributions of Adlerian psychology to school counseling.

An Overview of Personality Theory as Related to Counseling

Adlerians perceive man as an indivisible, social, decision-making being whose psychological movement and actions have a purpose. The fundamental assumptions for understanding personality are:

1. *Human personality is best understood in its unity or pattern.* This is the holistic approach, which views man as a unified organism, a unity moving by definite life patterns toward a goal. He is seen as a total unit and regarded as an irreducible whole. From this vantage point, we do not add to our understanding by fragmentary analysis,

but instead are required to see the pattern and relationship between the data.

2. *Behavior is goal-directed and purposive.* A contrast is apparent here. There are theorists who adhere to the view that behavior is caused, and can always be explained in mechanical terms. From this point of view, motivation can be understood in the light of its goal-directed nature; such goals give direction to man's striving which becomes the final cause or final explanation. In contradistinction, Adlerians look forward to determine the cause; they comprehend the goal as the cause.

Furthermore, the goals are recognized and treated as subjective, creative, and unconscious goals, that may be only dimly perceived by the individual. It is recognized that they direct the person's selective responses in two areas: in the cognitive life (revealing his private logic) and in the emotional life wherein emotions may be employed as social tools.

3. *Motivation can be understood as the striving for significance or the movement to enhance self-esteem.* Striving for significance receives its direction from the individual's unique, subjectively conceived goal of success (self-ideal). This search for significance emerges when man experiences the subjective feeling of being less than others and then engages in various attempts to compensate. His inferiority feelings are often due to a faulty self-evaluation. This situation suggests that we seek a master motive, a concept common in organismic psychology. It has sometimes been called self-actualization, self-expansion, or competence (Dreikurs, 1950; Rogers, 1951; Maslow, 1954; Combs & Snygg, 1959; White, 1959).

4. *All behavior has social meaning.* Man is primarily a social being, and his behavior is understood in terms of its social context. The significance of behavior really lies in our interaction and transaction with others. Social striving, from this point of view, is primary, not secondary. Behavior is highly influenced by the consequences of the reactions of other persons. Behavior often makes sense in terms of an ironic social regard, e.g., a child's bothering the teacher and forcing her to deal with him so that he can have a special place among the peers of the class and the school.

5. *Each individual has the creative power to make biased interpretations.* Biased apperception influences our every process. Behavior is not only reactive, it is creative. The individual has the power of choice. His uniqueness ultimately rests in this creative power. Behav-

ior is thus understood not only within the purview of stimulus and response, but also in terms of the intervening variable of the organism or person who makes a creative decision about that stimulus (S-O-R).

6. *The individual is understood in terms of his phenomenological field.* The individual, being always understood in terms of his subjective point of view, impels us to be concerned with the meaning that a given event possesses for him.

7. *Belonging is a basic need.* Man has the desire to belong to someone or something. His social significance derives from belonging. He is not actualized without belonging. Many of man's fears and anxieties arise out of the fear of not belonging or of not being acceptable.

8. *The emphasis is on idiographic, not nomothetic laws.* There is a greater concern with finding laws that apply characteristically to the individual in relation to his style of life (idiographic) than in the development of nomothetic laws that apply generally but include many exceptions.

9. *The psychology of use has priority over the psychology of possession.* We are concerned with determining the conclusions the person has drawn from his experiences. The individual at any moment does that which is most useful or best accomplishes his purposes and strivings at that moment. That which interferes with his goals is not done. This principle is noted in the varying ways in which individuals make use of their heredity or their environment.

10. *The development of social interest is crucial for mental health.* Social interest is based on our capacity to give and take. It is demonstrated by a readiness to demand less than one is able to offer and in the desire to cooperate. Social interest becomes a criterion of mental health. This method of counseling places as much emphasis on cognitive change as it does on affective change.

Counseling Procedures

The foregoing assumptions, fundamental to Adlerian psychology, lead naturally into a set of procedures.

Counseling is seen as a learning process that provides a re-educative bridge for solving the tasks of life. Counseling involves communications for the purpose of modifying concepts, convictions, and attitudes.

The counseling process is divided into four parts: (1) the relationship; (2) the investigation of dynamics and motives; (3) insight; and (4) the reorientation phase.

The Relationship

There is an emphasis upon an alignment of the goals of counselor and counselee. Effective counseling cannot take place unless the counselor and the counselee are working within a framework of similar purpose. This type of relationship transcends rapport.

Since school counseling often involves contact with children who are not self-referred, the aspect of goal alignment becomes crucial to the relationship from the very start. A bridge to such alignment can be found, more often than not, through the development of intermediate goals. The counselor may ask, for example, "Would you like to find out why you feel that way?" Or he may choose to work with the counselee on a current problem which may lead to the major concern.

Indispensable to the relationship is mutual trust and respect. The child is treated with respect even when his ideas are diverse and opposed. It is axiomatic that one of the functions of the counselor is to listen and to understand. A child seldom has situations in which adults show that they really care about what he says. It is this unique understanding that leads to and provides a therapeutic relationship. Empathy in this relationship is the result of being understood. Stated another way, when the child is in contact with an adult who shows he understands how that child feels and can guess his private logic, the highest form of empathy is achieved. It becomes important, through motivation, to win the child, and gain his confidence, revealing enough to convince the child that the counselor does understand, anticipates success, and that the child has found an individual with whom he can align his goals.

The Investigation

The counselor begins by exploring the current situation and the way in which the child approaches social relationships and responsibilities as they appear, first in the home and then at school. The counselor might systematically raise certain questions and investigate them further by listening attentively to what is said and what is not said. It is seen that the investigation begins with "here" and "now" problems, and always with focus on determining "for what purpose?"

The family constellations and the relationship between siblings are important in this system also. The individual's ordinal position in the family can show how he uses his situation to create his style of life, while a systematic study of the relationship between the siblings is made to derive the psychological position of the child in the family.

Early recollections provide another method of understanding individual goals and mistaken assumptions about life. The first incidents in life that a person can recall are consistent with the pattern of life as seen by the individual (Mosak, 1958; Ferguson, 1964). Adlerian clinicians using early recollections can develop a type of diagnosis that might be made by a clinical team. Therefore, early recollections are used as an aid in comprehending individual life style (Hedvig, 1965).

Adler placed emphasis on utilization of hunches and the ability to guess correctly the psychological movement of the individual. Dreikurs developed a technique that he calls the "hidden reason." This technique is effective in understanding what transpires in a person's private logic. It is used when the person does something out of the ordinary that is puzzling. Thereafter, when he is quizzed about it, he does not seem to understand why he did it. The person is really not aware of the reason. The "hidden reason" technique attempts to determine the individual's rationale for his behavior; it involves guessing what he is thinking. The counselor attempts to determine under what circumstances certain behaviors make sense. The counselor asks the individual if he wants to change, and then asks him to cooperate by telling what goes on in his mind. If one can get the exact words that were on his mind at the time, then he immediately will acknowledge it (Dreikurs, 1966).

Techniques such as these are devised to assist the counselor to understand how the client thinks and how he came to hold these convictions. The understanding, in this procedure, often exists in the counselor first and then is transferred to the counselee's awareness so that he ultimately develops self-understanding. These techniques are concerned with understanding the life style and self-image.

Insight

During this phase the counselor should be concerned with making the individual aware of why he chooses to function in the manner he does.

Interpretation, when used within this frame of reference, places emphasis upon the goals and purposes of the symptoms that are seen. It is usually based on a tentative hypothesis, e.g., "Could it be . . . ?"

or "Is it possible ... ?" In this way the individual is actually confronted with his goals. The private logic which he may not see for himself is mirrored for him. During the confrontations the child will often produce a "recognition reflex." This reflex has been described by Dreikurs (1957, p. 47):

This automatic reaction consists of a roguish smile and a peculiar twinkle of the eye, a so-called "recognition reflex." The child need not say one word or he may even say "no" but his facial expression gives him away.

The proper sequence in disclosure involves: (1) asking "Do you know why you are doing this?" "Would you like to know why you are doing this?" (2) If there is a willingness for such discussion, interpretation in a tentative manner is also involved, such as: "Could it be ... ?" or "I have the impression . . . ."

This procedure is referred to as the "mirror technique." The individual is confronted with his goals and his intentions.

Empathy in this form of counseling involves making the individual aware of his private logic and showing interest in helping him change. Little time is spent in description of feelings or straight reflection of feelings. The emphasis is focused on the purpose of the feelings.

It is important to find one point or place where the counselee may want to change. If the counselor cannot find the place, as in the case of a difficult child, then in all probability the counselor cannot change him at all. In some instances the child has been referred to counseling because of a conflict with a teacher or parents; perhaps the child really does not choose to change. However, in a case wherein the child would like to get along better with his peers, this may be the proper point or place to begin the attempts toward change.

Reorientation

In this phase of counseling the counselor and counselee think the situation through together. The counselor's basic responsibility is to help the individual see the alternatives in attitude and behavior. But mere awareness of alternatives is not enough. It is still necessary to develop the courage to try to change. Encouragement restores the individual's faith in himself (Dinkmeyer & Dreikurs, 1963). Encouragement helps one to realize his own strengths and abilities and develops a belief in his dignity and worth. If a person is discouraged, neither insight nor change is possible.

It is in the reorientation aspect of counseling that the counselor strives to help the counselee become aware he is functioning in a way that inevitably will cause problems of his own choosing. Eventually he is confronted with choice, one of the most important therapeutic agents of all. He can then decide the way in which he will choose to function.

There is an investigation of values involved in these premises. It is vital to the counseling relationship that the counselor does not moralize. The "oughts" and "shoulds" are to be discreetly avoided. Most certainly the therapeutic experience can help to provide some success experiences within and external to the counseling process.

In other situations the counselee will be helped by a setting of tasks. If he does not get along well with his peers, for example, perhaps he can learn to deal effectively with just one child. In some instances children have been helped by learning to act as if they were aggressive, as if they were happy, etc.

Adlerian psychology contributes to school counseling theory by establishing certain assumptions about personality and providing unique procedures in the counseling process. The "compleat" counselor will want to become well acquainted with Adlerian theory and practice as he develops his personal theory of counseling.

References

Combs, A. W., & Snygg, D. *Individual behavior.* New York: Harper & Row, 1959.

Dinkmeyer, D., & Dreikurs, R. *Encouraging children to learn: the encouragement process.* Englewood Cliffs, N.J.: Prentice-Hall, 1963.

Dreikurs, R. *Fundamentals of Adlerian psychology.* Chicago: Alfred Adler Institute, 1950.

Dreikurs, R. *Psychology in the classroom.* New York: Harper & Row, 1957.

Dreikurs, R. The holistic approach: two points of a line. In *Education, guidance, psychodynamics.* Chicago: Alfred Adler Institute, 1966. Pp. 21-22.

Ferguson, E. D. The use of early recollections for assessing life style and diagnosing psychopathology. *Journal of Projective Techniques,* 1964, *28,* 403-412.

Hedvig, E. Children's early recollections as basis for diagnosis. *Journal of Individual Psychology,* 1965, *21*(2), 187-188.

Maslow, A. *Motivation and personality.* New York: Harper & Row, 1954.

Mosak, H. Early recollections as a projective technique. *Journal of Projective Techniques,* 1958, *22,* 302-311.

Rogers, C. R. *Client-centered therapy.* Boston: Houghton Mifflin, 1951.

White, R. Motivation reconsidered: the concept of competence. *Psychological Review,* 1959, *66,* 297-333.

RUDOLF DREIKURS

The Four Goals of
the Maladjusted Child

Every action of a child has a purpose which is in line with his effort toward social integration. A well-behaved and well-adjusted child has found his way toward social acceptance by conforming to the rules governing the social group in which he lives. He senses the requirements of the group and acts accordingly. He is active when the situation warrants it and passive if need be; he talks at the proper time and knows how to be quiet. He can be a leader or follower. A perfectly adjusted child—if there ever was one—would hardly reveal any individuality of his own, since he would reflect only the social needs of his environment. Only in the slight deviation from perfect adjustment does he reveal his individual personality through the characteristic approaches which he has found and developed for himself.

Accordingly, individual behavior is already a slight deviation from absolute conformity. We cannot consider such deviations as maladjustments because the needs of any social group are not static. The social group requires improvement, growth and evolution. The individual who imposes his own ideas on the group acts as impetus for development. If his ideas are beneficial for the group and his method

Rudolf Dreikurs, "The Four Goals of the Maladjusted Child," *Nervous Child*, 1947, *6*, pp. 321-328.

constructive, he is still—and only then—well-adjusted, although not completely conforming. Mere conformity can be an obstacle to social development and thereby become an expression of social maladjustment.

Maladjustment may be defined as behavior which disturbs the functioning of the group and its development. The psychological dynamics underlying maladjustment are very complex in adults. It takes time and great effort to unveil the variety of factors at work beyond consciousness and the mask of adulthood. Adults have the same fundamental attitudes which they had as children; but in the process of adolescence they learn, for appearance's sake, to subordinate them to the pattern set by society. The successful accomplishment of covering up one's real intentions and motivations is then called maturity. The child who has not yet reached this stage of "maturity" may openly demonstrate his attitudes. It is possible, therefore, to recognize the goals of child-behavior by mere observation.

All disturbing behavior of the child is directed toward one of four possible goals. They represent his interpretation of his place within his group. He tries either to:

(1) gain attention;
(2) demonstrate his power or superiority;
(3) punish or get even; or he
(4) gives up in complete discouragement.

The same child may display a certain behavior pattern in one group, while under special circumstances he may behave according to another goal. However, it is possible to establish in most cases the predominant classification of his behavioral goals.

The attention-getting mechanism (A.G.M.) is prevalent in most young children. It is the result of the way in which children are brought up in our culture. Young children have few opportunities to establish their position by socially useful contributions. Older siblings and adults do everything that has to be done. The only way a young child can feel accepted and a part of his family group is by means of the older members of the family. *Their* contributions bestow value and social status on him. As a result, the child seeks constant proofs of his acceptance through gifts, demonstrations of affection, or at least through attention. As none of these increases his own feeling of strength, self-reliance and self-confidence, he requires constant new proof lest he feel lost and rejected. He will try to get what he wants in socially acceptable ways as long as possible. However, when he loses confidence in his ability to use socially constructive means effectively, he will try any conceivable method of putting others into his service or of getting attention. Unpleasant effects like humiliation, punishment, or even physical pain, do not matter as long as the main purpose is obtained. Children prefer to be beaten rather than to be ignored. To be ignored and treated with indifference is the worst thing that can happen to a child; then he feels definitely left out, rejected and without any place within the group.

The desire for attention can be satisfied through constructive methods. The child is naturally inclined to be constructive as long as he feels able to succeed; but if his requests become excessive, or if the environment refuses to meet his demands, he may discover that he gets more attention by disturbing. Then the struggle starts. For a while the parents may succumb to the provocation without getting too angry and annoyed. Pleasant and unpleasant episodes are held in balance: the child's desire to occupy them with himself is met and a workable equilibrium is maintained. However, there may come a time when the parents decide to subdue the child, to stop him from being annoying and disturbing. Then the child changes his goal, and the child and the parents become deadlocked in a struggle for power and superiority. The child tries to convince the parents that he can do what he wants and they will not be able to stop him. Or he may demonstrate in a passive way that they can not make him do what they want. If he gets away with it, he has won a victory; if the parents enforce their will, he has lost and the next time perhaps uses stronger methods. This struggle is more fierce than his fight for attention. His maladjustment is more obvious, his actions are more hostile, and the emotions involved more violent.

This struggle between parents and child for power and dominance may reach a point where the parents try every conceivable means to subjugate the culprit. The mutual antagonism and hatred may become so strong that no pleasant experience is left to maintain a feeling of belonging, of friendliness or cooperation. Then the child moves into the third group. He no longer hopes for attention, his ability to gain power seems hopeless, he feels completely ostracized and disliked and finds his only gratification in hurting others and getting even for being hurt by them. That seems for him the only way to play a part. "At least I can make them hate me," is his despairing motto. In groups where he can still gain personal superiority and power, his actions may be less violent and cruel than in those where he has lost all status. Children of this type are the most violent and vicious; they know where it hurts most and they take advantage of the vulnerability of their opponents. Power and force impress them no longer. They are defiant and destructive. As they are sure from the beginning that nobody likes them, they provoke anyone with whom they come in contact to reject them. They regard it as a triumph when they are considered horrible; that is the only triumph they can obtain, the only one they seek.

A passive child will not move in the direction of open warfare. If his antagonism is successfully beaten down, he may be discouraged to such an extent that he cannot hope for any significance whatsoever. He then may become completely passive and give up any participation. This complete passivity may be limited to certain activities and groups if the child's discouragement is only partial; it may lead to complete inertia if the discouragement is total. As the hostility is not displayed openly, he may provoke less antagonism; but this lack of acute disturbance should not make us consider this maladjustment as less grave than the one of the child in the third group. Both have reached extreme forms of antisocial attitudes. (In certain cases we can actually speak of "violent passivity.")

Maladjusted children may be classed as active and passive and they may use constructive or destructive methods. The choice of constructive or destructive methods depends on the child's feeling of being accepted or rejected by people or groups; his antagonism is always expressed in destructive acts. This feeling of belonging or the lack of it is a decisive factor for the switch from constructive to destructive methods. Active or passive behavior, on the other hand, indicates the amount of courage. Passivity is always based on personal discouragement. The combination of the two pairs of factors leads to four types of behavior patterns:

1. Active-constructive,
2. Active-destructive,
3. Passive-constructive,
4. Passive-destructive.

The sequence as presented is based on the actual progression of maladjustment. Many parents and educators are inclined to regard an active-destructive child as much worse than a passive-constructive one. However, this is not necessarily true. If the child's antisocial attitude has not developed too far, as in cases of attention-getting, he can be induced with relative ease to change his destructive methods into constructive ones; but it is extremely difficult to change a passive child into an active one. The passive-constructive child is less unpleasant, but needs more assistance for the development of self-confidence and courage.

A short discussion of the four types of attention-getting mechanism may illustrate the significance of these four patterns. The *active-constructive* A.G.M. resembles a very cooperative and conforming behavior. These children are the sheer delight of parents and teachers. But they actually are not as good as they seem to be. They merely try very hard to make an impression of excellence in order to gain praise and recognition. Their deficiency becomes apparent if they fail to get it, for then they generally start to misbehave. Their social relationships within their groups are often disturbed; they cannot be equals—if they do not excel they feel lost. Their desire to be perfect, to be correct, to be superior is often stimulated by parents who encourage such traits, either because they themselves are over-ambitious and perfectionistic, or because they play up this one child against the other children. Competition with another sibling is a frequent factor in this striving for applause. In order to maintain his superiority over a younger brother or sister, or to catch up with and possibly surpass an older sibling, the child tries to become good, reliable, considerate, cooperative and industrious, seeking and accepting any possible responsibility. The excellence of the model child is only too frequently achieved at the expense of the problem child who becomes discouraged and frustrated in this competition.

It is this group of over-ambitious children who develop *active-destructive* methods when their efforts to attract attention with socially accepted methods fail. They may try the most bizarre means to put themselves forward when they are discouraged in the field of tangible and useful achievement. They may show off, clown, be obtrusive, keep others occupied with constant questions; they may become "enfants terribles" and in many other ways force parents and teachers to pay attention to them. They may resemble the children who seek goals two and three; but they differ from them by the lack of violence and antagonism. Their goal is still attention-getting, and their misbehavior stops when this goal is achieved; while the child who wants to demonstrate his power (goal two), and still more the child who wants to punish (goal three), is not satisfied with mere attention and continues his provocative behavior after this is achieved.

A very significant group consists of the children who use *passive-constructive* methods for attracting attention. Many parents and teachers do not recognize these children as misbehaving. Their pleasantness, charm and submission cause the observer to overlook the discouragement in their passivity and dependence on others. In the masculine culture, passive-constructive behavior patterns are deliberately stimulated in women and almost required from them. For this reason the passive-constructive A.G.M. is found more frequently in girls than in boys and is considered in the latter as effeminate. The passive-constructive child is certainly less unpleasant than the active-destructive one, but requires more efforts for adjustment.

A child who seeks attention with *passive-destructive* methods is generally so much discouraged and feels so much rejected—mostly through the methods which are used with him—that he may very easily reach the fourth group of completely discouraged children (goal four) whom he resembles anyhow. His bashfulness, instability, untidiness, lack of concentration and ability, self-indulgence and frivolity, his fearfulness, his eating difficulties, and his backwardness in taking care of himself and in developing skills, make him the most difficult child in this group.

The distinction between the various groups in which a child belongs can be made by mere observation. It may require some training to evaluate properly the behavior patterns of a child. Such training is essential, as the establishment of a correct psychological diagnosis is a prerequisite for the proper way of dealing with a child. Any one disturbing behavior may serve for several or for all four goals. In each child it may have a different function in his relationship to others; and the specific dynamics of a disturbing behavior must be recognized in order to evaluate its significance. Laziness, for instance, can be a passive-destructive A.G.M., serving to occupy the parents and to make them pay attention and give assistance. But it can also be used by the child as a tool in the struggle for power, by demonstrating his helplessness to a forceful and determined parent or teacher. Regardless of threats and punishments the child will not move or do anything. In certain instances laziness has been used as a specific means to punish an over-ambitious parent. And finally, laziness may indicate complete discouragement; the child just gives up because he has no hope of succeeding.

The function of a certain behavior becomes obvious when correction is attempted. The following example may illustrate this. A child is brought to a new group of children and stays outside, refusing to join the group. The teacher tries to draw him in. If his first hesitation was an attention-getting device, he will probably respond readily to the teacher, because he was only waiting for special attention. If his reluctance to join is based on his desire to demonstrate his power, he will act differently. He may run away as soon as the teacher approaches, inviting the teacher to chase him and putting up some active resistance to being drawn in. On the other hand, if the child is set on revenge because he is sure to be disliked and rejected, he may look defiantly at the approaching teacher and scratch, bite or spit at anybody who tries to get him. The completely discouraged child may accept the teacher's hand and join the group, but will remain passive and stay where he is left.

The trained observer has no difficulty in recognizing the child's goals and in classifying the category in which a particular behavior belongs. The reaction which the child provokes generally indicates what he expects and wants. In case of doubt a very simple technique can be used to determine with absolute accuracy the goal which the child pursues. This technique affords a reliable diagnosis, verifying the impressions based on observations.

The child does not know why he behaves in a certain way. It is futile to ask a child, "Why did you do it?" When he answers, "I do not know," it is generally true. The child follows his impulses without clear realization of his motives. If he tries to give an explanation for his behavior, his explanations are mostly rationalizations and excuses, but not the real reasons. Instead of asking the child why he did something, one must explain it *to him*. Such disclosures, however, should not refer to the *cause* of his behavior, but only to the *purpose* of it. Reasons such as being jealous, having no self-confidence, feeling neglected, dominated or rejected, feeling guilty or sorry for himself, regardless of how correct they may be in explaining the child's behavior, are accepted by him at best with friendly indifference. His reaction is quite different when his purposes and goals are disclosed to him. Such interpretation, when correct, evokes immediately a very definite and characteristic reaction. This reaction is automatic as a reflex; for this reason I call it the "Recognition Reflex." It indicates with certainty the correctness of an interpretation. It consists of a roguish smile and peculiar twinkle of the eye. The child need not say one word, or he might even say "no"; but his facial expression gives him away. Disclosure is not only of diagnostic value; it leads often to an immediate change in the particular behavior, especially in a young child. Psychological interpretations are understood even by very young children, as soon as they comprehend the meaning of the words. If the interpretation is correct, they show the typical reflex and are inclined to change their attitudes when they are made aware of them, as they are not reconcilable with the already established conscience. This does not imply a complete change of the life style, but only a change of methods.

To evoke the reflex the child must be approached in a friendly way without humiliating or belittling him; the disclosure should never impress the child as fault-finding and criticism. It is advisable not to make a definite statement but to start the remarks as a vague conjecture, "I wonder whether you don't want to get attention" . . . "to show your power" . . . "to be a big boss" . . . "to punish your mother?" Or, "Could it be that you want to . . . ?" Such discussions can never do any harm. If the interpretation was wrong, there is no reaction. Then another conjecture can be tried and the child's reaction will indicate which one was correct.

A five-year-old boy repeatedly threatened to hit and bite other children, especially a little girl cousin. Our first impression was that he felt neglected and wanted to hurt them, to get even. Our voiced interpretation encountered a blank face. We went on probing. Maybe he wanted to show how strong he was. Again no reaction. "Could it be that your mother gets very upset about such threats, and you want her to make a fuss over you, to talk to you about it and tell others what you have done?" His face beamed (Recognition Reflex). He was in his glory. The same behavior in another child would have meant something different. For him, it was only a tool to keep mother concerned with him.

A nine-year-old boy had his hair hanging over his right eye. I met him with his mother. In his presence I asked her why she thought he wore his hair over his eye. She did not know; neither did he. My surmise was that he probably wanted his mother to keep reminding him to push his hair back. She could not understand how I knew that she constantly had to remind him. Very simple—if he could not gain her attention in that way, he would not like to have his hair always getting into his eyes. He beamed. That was all that was said. The next day she called me up, quite excited. The boy had asked for money to have his locks cut by the barber.

Two boys, nine and ten years old, annoyed their mother by using bedtime for fighting in their beds. The mother could not stop it and did not know what to do. I had a talk with the boys. I asked them why they went on fighting after going to bed. I did not expect the correct answer to this question, but wanted to hear what they had to say. They both explained that it is so much fun to fight in bed when it does not hurt to be thrown down on the pillows. That was their rationalization. I asked them whether they would mind if I told them the real reason. Of course, they wouldn't mind. Then I ventured, "Maybe you do it just so that mother will come several times to remind you to be quiet." The younger one said indifferently, "Could be." The older one said nothing, but beamed. One should know that the older one was the favorite of the mother and depended upon her, while the younger one felt somewhat excluded and relied upon himself for his position in the world. Generally he was the one who started the fights, but in this particular situation the older brother obviously had instigated the fights for the sake of getting his mother's attention, bringing her back to the bedroom ever so often. Nothing more was said or done about it; but after our short discussion the evening fights stopped and never were resumed. That does not mean that the older boy suddenly became independent of his mother. But this particular method was no longer useful once he recognized his purpose.

The recognition of the child's goal is the basis for his treatment. Children who drive for attention must learn to become independent, by recognizing that *contributing* and not *receiving* is the effective instrument for obtaining social status. Within the four groups of A.G.M., the attempt should be made to help children to become active and to change destructive methods into constructive ones, until the child is able to overcome the need for any special attention. Children who drive for *power* should no longer be exposed to power and pressure against which they have successfully rebelled and still rebel. Acknowledging their value and even their power is essential for making them self-confident so that they no longer need verification of their power. Children who want to *punish* and to get even are usually those who are convinced that nobody likes them or ever will like them. Helping them involves a long process of demonstrating that they are and can be liked. Children who *give up* in discouragement have to be brought back slowly to the realization of their abilities and potentialities.

The recognition of the child's goal is an important prerequisite for any educational effort. However, knowing, and even changing, the goal of a child does not necessarily affect his fundamental concepts of life, his life style (Alfred Adler). Understanding and altering the conclusions which a child drew from his experiences with the world around him, his outer environment, and with his hereditary endowment, his inner environment, requires a more thorough analysis of the child. It implies an exploration of his family situation, the dynamics of his relationship with parents and siblings, the methods by which he was brought up, the economic, religious, racial and national conditions which influenced the atmosphere in which he lived.

For this reason, efforts to reach the deeper levels of the personality structure must be reserved for special child guidance work. Teachers, group workers, physicians, and others who want to influence children will rely mostly on their ability to understand and evaluate the child's goals, which they can determine without involved investigation. The knowledge of a child's goal permits a better approach and, above all, prevents unwitting acceptance of the child's provocation which only increases his maladjustment and misbehavior. Doing what the child expects, confirms his belief that his wrong approaches are effective.

DON DINKMEYER

Developmental Counseling in the Elementary School

With the greatly increased extension of counseling and guidance services to the elementary school level, counseling theorists have become aware of a greater need for a theory of developmental counseling with children. This theory must take account of such basic factors as the nature of the child, the elementary school setting, and the goals, techniques, and process of the counseling. Furthermore, those who would counsel in the elementary school must become aware of the research in the broad area of child development and child psychiatry.

Nature of the Child

The most obvious difference between secondary school and elementary school counseling stems from the nature of the child. The elementary school child is still in the process of becoming—physically, socially, emotionally, and as a total personality. He is in a process of unfolding and there are still certain developmental changes that will come about as the result of this growth process.

Dinkmeyer, D. Developmental counseling in the elementary school. *The Personnel and Guidance Journal,* 1966, *45*(3), 262-266. Copyright 1966 American Personnel and Guidance Association. Reprinted with permission.

Research in child development points to the importance of considering developmental changes. Thus, the counselor would need to be aware of "normal developmental problems" as contrasted with serious adjustment difficulties. He should know that there are wide individual differences in developmental patterns that are due to basic differences in rate of development. These developmental differences create adjustment problems for the child both in the tasks of school and social life.

The counselor, therefore, should have available developmental data that tell him about individual rates of development and enable him to infer something about the child's feelings about himself in the peer group.

Mussen and Jones (1958), in their study of the self-concept in late and early maturing boys, have indicated a variance in the self-concepts and motivation of these two groups.

It is important that each counselor be familiar with the basic needs of the child. The child has specific needs that relate to the guidance process. He needs to mature in self-acceptance, in his understanding of self, and in his comprehension of his assets and liabilities. The child needs to develop a more realistic self-evaluation and the counselor can help in this process. The counselor can also assist the child to develop, to mature in social relationships, to belong, and to identify. The child needs to develop independence, to take on responsibility, to make choices, and to be responsible for these choices. He needs to mature in his ability to plan. The counselor provides an environment in which the child is independent, makes choices, and becomes responsible for his decision. The child also needs to mature in understanding the role of work in life as it first appears in educational achievement and then as it appears in the environment as related to jobs and employment opportunities. The child needs to develop a realistic self-appraisal of his capacities, interests, and attitudes as they relate to the work tasks.

The counselor, at the elementary school level, will recognize that he needs to work with the significant adults in the child's life. This includes the teacher and the parents. With the teacher he will encourage intensive child study that takes into account developmental information and the developmental factors significant in comprehending the way in which the child approaches the developmental tasks of living. He will help the teacher to have available cumulative records that provide information about rate instead of status, dynamics of behavior instead of descriptions of the past. The cumulative record should show the pattern of development both physically and psychologically.

Behavior is purposive, and acquires its meaning in the social setting. Beyond the understanding of need, the counselor must understand the purposes of behavior in specific children. Purposes are the directive forces in the child's life, even though the child may not be aware of these goals and purposes. We need to look at the purposes of misbehavior as they are illustrated in attention-getting, the seeking to be powerful, to get even, or to demonstrate inadequacy (Dreikurs, 1957). As we become cognizant of the individual's purposes, we are able to deal with the child's private logic, and become aware of the basic style of life and concept of self and others. Psychological growth is patterned, and we must focus on the unity of behavior and the style of life, avoiding the collection of fragmentary data and instead looking at the direction of psychological movement.

Recent research tends to indicate that the early elementary years are much more significant than any of us have been truly able to determine prior to now. The research of Bloom (1964) indicates the significance of the first three grades in predicting the total pattern of achievement. Kagan and Moss (1962) at the Fels Research Institute recently released a study indicating that many of the behaviors exhibited by the child during the period from six to ten years of age, and a few during the period from three to six, were moderately good predictors of theoretically related behavior during early adulthood. This study indicated that the child who was achieving well early in school will generally continue to achieve well. There is a need to provide early encouragement for the academic achiever, and to identify those who are not meeting the academic tasks at this stage of life.

The elementary counselor should also be aware of the developmental task concept as first formulated by Havighurst. He needs to recognize that the pertinent tasks of middle childhood involve learning to get along with age-mates, and participating in the give and take of social exchange.

Most human problems are interpersonal problems and these problems increase as the child moves into a peer society. The research of Piaget (1929), which has increasingly attracted the attention of American psychologists, shows that during preadolescence the child begins to develop a concept of self quite distinguishable from the outer world. This is the time when the clarification of feelings, concepts, attitudes, goals, and an understanding of self would be most significant.

The development of conscience, morality, and values begins early in the elementary school. The child is in the process of developing this internal moral control and set of values. The child learns that rules are necessary and thus develops what Piaget calls the morality of cooperation. Piaget believes that middle childhood is a crucial period for the development of this cooperation. The counselor could be available to help the child through this stage as an awareness of values and goals emerges. The child will frequently need help in reconciling his values, his ideal self, and his actual performance. However, the child needs to learn to make plans, and to act in the present and immediate future independent of other parents and other adults. Counseling can provide the opportunity to assist in the making of choices, planning, and deciding.

Caroline Tryon and Jesse Lilienthal (1950) have provided an interesting presentation of the developmental tasks and their importance for the counselor. They indicate that these might be used as guideposts that permit us to assess the rate at which the child is developing in regard to the tasks of life. They suggest that the counselor might be aware of some of the following pertinent tasks:

a. achieving an appropriate dependent-independence pattern;

b. achieving an appropriate giving-receiving pattern of affection, learning to accept self as worthwhile, learning to belong;

c. relating to changing groups, establishing a peer group, and learning to belong and behave according to the shifting peer code.

Counseling in the Elementary School Setting

The counselor cannot counsel without an awareness of the elementary school setting, and the fact that he is part of an educational team. He should be aware of the philosophy, objectives, and practices of the school. He should be familiar with the curriculum and the opportunities within the curriculum for the student's development. He must be cognizant of the teacher's crucial role in classroom guidance. The teacher should be encouraged to provide regular guidance activities, to identify problems, and to provide guidance through the teacher-counselor role.

Developmental counseling, which can be contrasted with adjustment, or crisis counseling, is not always problem-oriented in terms of assuming that the child has some difficult problem. Instead, the goals are the development of self-understanding, awareness of one's potentialities, and methods of utilizing one's capacity. Developmental counseling truly focuses on helping the individual know, understand, and accept himself. This type of counseling, then, becomes personalized learning, not individualized teaching. The child learns not only to understand himself but to become ultimately responsible for his choices and actions.

Unique Factors

The type of counseling we are considering Hummel (1962) has referred to as ego counseling. This implies that it may be a short-term service in which the relationship is basically collaborative and the child works on problems that are of concern to him. The counselor helps the child investigate, analyze, and deliberate to solve more effectively certain developmental problems. Thus, exploration, examination, and resolution are basic techniques. There is mutual survey of the facts, clarification of feelings, consideration of alternatives, development of problem-solving techniques, and arrival at decisions.

The counselor provides a non-evaluative relationship and offers his collaboration. His job is to clarify, to reflect, to restate as precisely as possible the meanings he perceives to be implied in the counselee's statements. However, the counselor, at times, will interpret, confront, question, and thus facilitate the child's capacity to solve his own problems.

The elementary school child is in the process of formulating a style of life and self-concept. There is a considerable body of evidence that indicates that the child with a poor self-concept, compared with those who have more positive self-concepts, will be more anxious, less well-adjusted, less popular, less effective, less honest, and more defensive (McCandless, 1961). One of the tasks of the school counselor is to assist each child to feel accepted as he is. The counselor seeks to help the child discover his potentialities, to acquire a realistic appreciation of his assets and limitations, and to set certain goals. This should enable the child to accept himself rather than seek to conform to standards that are out of harmony with what he is or would hope to be.

Principles in Child Counseling

What, then, are the fundamentals we need to be aware of in child counseling?

1. Counseling is a learning-oriented process carried on in a one-to-one social environment. It must utilize the best that we have available from learning theory.

2. The relationship is crucial in the counseling process. It should be one in which there is mutual trust and mutual respect, enabling the counselee to become more open to communication and more motivated to change. Change is always more possible in a non-evaluative, non-judgmental atmosphere.

3. The counselor helps the client to understand and accept what he is, and to use his newly acquired knowledge about self to realize his potential, to change in attitude, behavior, and, eventually, style of life.

4. The child is frequently not a volunteer. There is a real need for common purpose and a motivation for counseling. It is important that the goals of counseling be mutually aligned between counselor and counselee. It is important to understand the individual's objective viewpoint, to be empathic, to recognize his private logic.

5. We need to listen not only for the words, but what is behind the words. We need to become skilled in guessing the child's psychological direction. Behavior is purposive and has social implications. We need to make the child more aware of his purposes, goals, convictions, and attitudes. As the child becomes aware of his faulty assumptions, he can "catch" himself.

6. There are certain dependency factors that will restrict the child from changing certain things in his environment. His choices may be limited in terms of restrictions placed upon him by adults such as parents and teachers.

7. There is a necessity for working intensively both with parents and teachers if we are to change the child's environment. Contact with the significant adults is directed at changing the adult's behavior and thus the child's perception of self and human relationships. The counselor most of all must become aware of the goals and the unity in the pattern of the counselee's behavior. Maladjustment is characterized by increased inferiority feelings, underdeveloped social interest, and uncooperative methods of striving for significance (Dreikurs,

1950). These dynamics help the counselor to explain and understand the child's behavior.

8. Because the child may not be as verbal as the adult, there is need for sharper sensitivity on the part of the counselor in working with non-verbal cues and non-verbal factors. We need to listen with the child's ears and observe to determine what is behind the total psychological movement. Our observation of a recognition reflex in his facial expressions sometimes enables us to comprehend his goal. Disclosure of the child's goals and purposes when given in appropriate fashion can be a most significant technique.

9. The counselor provides encouragement as a major therapeutic technique. He enables the client to accept himself so that he has the courage to function (Dinkmeyer & Dreikurs, 1963).

10. Some children have a minimal ability to relate their feelings. They may not always be sensitive to reflection, and they need a tentative statement in regard to feelings such as: "Could it be you feel the children are against you?"

11. The individual's perceptions are more important than the objective reality of the situation.

12. People will move in positive directions when they are really free to choose. We need to provide the atmosphere that permits them to make these choices.

13. The feeling of basic trust between counselor and counselee opens the channels of communication. The mutual alignment of goals also assists this development.

14. Counseling is looked upon as a reeducative process directed towards the development of self-understanding, the changing of convictions, and the development of increased social interest. It is not heavily oriented toward vocational guidance; instead it deals with the developmental tasks, problems, and needs of the child. Through self-understanding, self-acceptance, and clarification of feeling the greatest growth can occur.

15. The cognitive and conceptual development of the child is not always as advanced as we might hope and, hence, the counselor must be certain communication is meaningful. Children have limited experiences and, hence, will have a limited ability to comprehend certain concepts.

16. The counselor becomes aware that he needs to empathize so closely that he can guess what it is that the client is thinking, and that he can put this into the client's words. The effective counselor is

one who understands the way in which the individual strives to be significant and helps the individual to accept himself. He sees the developmental problems as interpersonal problems. His communication with the client helps the client to understand new ways of relating to others.

Developmental counseling provides the child with an opportunity to explore his feelings, his attitudes, convictions. The counselor starts with the problems that the child perceives and helps him to solve them. The counselor in this situation provides a relationship that accepts, understands, and does not judge. It provides the counselee with constant clarification of his basic perception of life. This relationship enables the counselee to become increasingly self-directed so that the goal is one of enabling the counselee to deal with both the developmental tasks and the general problems of living. This type of developmental counseling suggests that counselors would not only be problem-oriented, but would be concerned about all students in the school population.

The goal is to take certain grade levels and to offer assistance to each student by providing an opportunity for some four or five contacts devoted to the specific objectives as they have been presented. When we can provide this form of counseling at the elementary school level, we can probably insure a greater productivity academically and hopefully much more effective social relationships between children and also between children and the significant adults in their atmosphere. Thus, we can see that elementary school counseling may need a new theory and a new set of practices. Developmental counseling might provide a direction quite different from that of typical secondary school counseling.

References

Bloom, B. *Stability and change in human characteristics.* New York: John Wiley, 1964.

Dinkmeyer, D., & Dreikurs, R. *Encouraging children to learn: the encouragement process.* Englewood Cliffs, N.J.: Prentice-Hall, 1963.

Dreikurs, R. *Fundamentals of Adlerian psychology.* New York: Greenberg, 1950.

Dreikurs, R. *Psychology in the classroom.* New York: Harper, 1957.

Hummel, R. Ego-counseling in guidance: concept and method. *Harvard Educational Review,* 1962, *32,* 463-482.

Kagan, J., & Moss, H. *Birth to maturity.* New York: John Wiley, 1962.

McCandless, B. R. *Children and adolescents: behavior and development.* New York: Holt, Rinehart and Winston, 1961.

Mussen, P., & Jones, M. The behavior inferred motivation of late and early maturing boys. *Child Development,* 1958, *29,* 61-67.

Piaget, J. *The child's conception of the world.* New York: Harcourt, Brace, 1929.

Tryon, C., & Lilienthal, J. Developmental tasks: the concept and its importance. *Fostering mental health in our schools.* 1950 Yearbook, Association for Supervision and Curriculum Development. Washington, D.C.: The Association, 1950.

SECTION VI

Play Therapy

The younger elementary school child is only beginning to emerge from the stage wherein all objects are toys, all the time is for play, and work is a construct developed through role playing. While he is being indoctrinated successfully into the concept that his work is school work, he remains a creature who, largely through play, develops his social roles and concepts, and works through his frustrations and concerns. In contrast with his older sibling who can and does verbalize frustrations, love, anger, and acceptance, the younger child acts these feelings.

—*Richard C. Nelson*

In counseling, even with children, professionals have a tendency to emphasize verbal interaction at the expense of nonverbal communication. As professionals, we ask our clients to relate to us in the mode that we are most familiar with, namely spoken language. However, language is a fairly sophisticated process, requiring the manipulation of symbols and dependent on prior verbal experience. Children, particularly younger children, have not completely mastered the maze of symbols inherent in verbal communication, and frequently they have insufficient experience in the use of language. We may be asking children to relate in a mode that is at least difficult for them if not foreign to them in some respects. How then can we communicate with children who are verbally immature? One method of choice is through the medium of play therapy. Play is the child's natural mode of communication. It provides him or her with a symbolic way of expressing internal thoughts and feelings. Children learn, rehearse, and reality-test different behaviors through the medium of play. They are continually communicating with their environment in nonverbal, play-oriented ways. Boys and girls play with dolls, cars, soldiers, and animals. They draw, mold clay, shape sand castles, and make mud pies. They play house, play doctor, and play at other occupational roles. They do all these activities in an attempt to explore their world, gain expertise about their environment, and communicate with each other and with adults. Play, then, can be an effective mode for entering into the life-space of the child.

Play therapy can be a highly structured diagnostic tool, or it can remain relatively unstructured. It can be counselor-directed or client-directed. It can be conducted in an expensively equipped clinic or in the corner of a classroom. Sophisticated play things and expensively equipped offices are not necessary for working with children in play therapy. In fact, they may at times be inhibiting factors. Basic raw materials are all that is required in most situations. Recommended materials include paper, pencils, crayons, hand puppets, small dolls, small animals, clay, games, and a mirror. Imaginative counselors can build their own play therapy kits from materials purchased at their local department stores.

This section explores some of the various uses of play therapy, applying the unstructured, nondirective approach. In the first reading, George Murphy outlines a brief history of the development of play therapy. He discusses the setting for therapy, and some of the tools a counselor can use in the process. His comparison of structured and unstructured models is particularly informative. Murphy concludes by presenting general guidelines for the counselor to consider when using play therapy.

Jean Waterland, in the second reading, discusses play therapy from a nondirective point of view, using concepts developed by Virginia Axline that are based on the client-centered philosophy of Carl Rogers. She focuses particularly on counselor behaviors that are important for effective nondirective play therapy. A case study is presented using the nondirective model.

The third reading, by Eugene Alexander, deals with the use of play media in elementary school counseling situations. The author favors the use of unstructured play and offers constructive suggestions for the counselor considering play therapy.

The fourth article by James Widerman and Eileen Widerman is a departure from the traditional concept of play therapy with young children. The authors demonstrate how play methods can be used effectively with older children and adolescents to facilitate the development of a counseling relationship and to stimulate verbal interaction with the client. The case of a resistant, nonverbal, adolescent client is used to illustrate the process.

GEORGE W. MURPHY

Play as a
Counselor's Tool

The intent of this article is to summarize psychological literature in an attempt to determine the value of play as a technique for understanding the child, and as a tool for the elementary and junior high school counselor.

The study of play as a means of understanding the child is a comparatively new approach in the field of psychology. It is a technique whereby the child can express his feelings and emotions with something he is familiar.

Rousseau was the first to advocate that the child be educated through play. He offered the suggestion that the teacher himself enter into the play activity (10). Although Freud used play as a means of therapy, he only touched the surface of its possibilities. Only in the last thirty years have people become interested in play as a technique for better understanding the emotions of a child.

Prior to 1919 little work was done with children, because of the difficulty of utilizing free association as is achieved in adults. Prior to this time no work was done with children under six years of age (9). After 1919, Melanie Klein and Anna Freud began to employ the

Murphy, G. W. Play as a counselor's tool. *The School Counselor*, 1960, *8*(1), 53-58. Copyright 1960 American Personnel and Guidance Association. Reprinted with permission.

technique of play as a means of analyzing children. Melanie Klein feels that the super-ego is highly developed in the child under six years of age, and Anna Freud feels that the child at this age has not developed a complete super-ego (10).

Since the first use of play as a technique in understanding the child, much has been written about the use of toys, the type of toys, and techniques that should be used. The tools employed have broadened to include all types of toys, psychodrama, drawings, finger-paintings, clay, music, and almost everything that is known to the young child.

Before one can fully understand the use of play as a technique, it is important for him to understand the development of play in the child. Play involves all types of activity, beginning in the very young child. He passes through sequential developmental stages including motor activities of grabbing, picking up objects, and placing special meanings to things. As the child progresses in age, so do his play activities. He begins to incorporate what he has learned in the past to carry out present activities. As he matures his realm widens, first it includes friends in the neighborhood, and then those at school. With each new group of friends his scope of play activities increases.

Many types of play rooms have been described in the literature. In the beginning, Melanie Klein used play in the home of the child as a technique. She felt that the child would relate better in an environment with which he was most familiar. After experimentation she found that the child would relate much better outside the home in a setting which was geared for play. By this means the child was removed from the many threats the home offered to his security (9).

The play room should be kept as simple as possible. With the exception of the basic furniture, the only things which should be there are toys. There should be a sink, and the floor should be washable. The toys should be the type that would instill the child to use his imagination as much as possible to reveal his emotional needs.

It should be emphasized that the type of toy used in therapy is not really important. It is far more important that it be something that will motivate the child to structure as well as endow the materials with conceptional and functional content (14). Toys used should be inexpensive, for during acts of aggression it is not uncommon for the child to break the toy. It has been suggested that the child's toys be kept locked, allowing only the same child to use the toys each time. This offers the child a sense of security, feeling they are his own and no one else's (9). Another suggestion is that the child be allowed relative freedom in selecting the toys with which he desires to play.

Studies have been made of the type of toys which are available for the use as tools in therapy with the child. The supply of such toys is practically unlimited, and new ones are coming on the market each day. The following toys are examples of those used to demonstrate motor activity, pattern activity, mechanical activity, and unstructured activity: guns, soldiers, farm animals, baby dolls, telephone, doll family, furniture, trucks, planes, balls, nok-out bench, goose, clay, scissors, paste, pencils, crayons, and paper. The child was then observed to see which toys he picked to best express his needs. It was found that the doll family was chosen most by the child. The conclusion was that he seemed to be able to best express his feelings through this medium (2).

There are two schools of thought with regard to the manner in which play therapy should be carried out. The first is unstructured play. The child is given complete freedom in his choice of toys, and in setting his own stage for play. In this approach, the therapist becomes an observer, watching what the child does. He may enter into the play on the request of the child, taking whatever part the child desires. The second, is the structured plan. The therapist sets the stage for play, gives the child the toys, and asks him to act out what would happen. The main advantage of this plan is that it enables the patient and the therapist to get to the root of the problem more quickly. It also enables the therapist and child to join forces in order to reach a common goal (8).

There are certain facts to be kept in mind in dealing with play as therapy. The person should have a genuine respect for the child as a person. At all times he should display patience and understanding. As in any work with a child, the therapist should first understand and accept himself. The therapist should allow himself sufficient objectivity and intellectual freedom in understanding the things the child is attempting to tell him. Sensitivity, empathy, and a good sense of humor are essential qualities demanded of the personality of the therapist (1).

The child should be helped to understand that he can do anything he likes in the room—that this is his play room. He should also understand that the therapist will not tolerate any physical violence to either himself or the child. Under no circumstances should the adult display any emotion when the child shows aggression and destroys a toy. At the same time, the therapist should not try to force the child to play with a certain toy. He will return to it when he is ready.

In periods of aggression, the child will often destroy the toy with which he is playing. The child will completely ignore the toy for a while, but eventually come back to play with it. Once the child has expressed his aggression and again plays with the toy, he shows the therapist that he has mastered the cause of the aggression and is accepting it in a new light. The child will often discuss how he feels using the doll family to show his emotions (13).

Often in play therapy the child takes the part of the adult and asks the therapist to take the part of the child. Transference takes place between the child and the therapist. Through his role-playing as a child, the therapist can feel with the child in his dealings with the world of adults. Through this medium the child is given an opportunity to learn about himself in relationship to the therapist (1).

The statement made by Lawrence K. Frank in his article *Play in Personality Development* sums up the theory behind this technique: "This approach to personality development emphasizes the process whereby the individual organism becomes a human being, learning to live in a social order and in a symbolic cultural world. Thereby we may observe the child from birth on, growing, developing child play as a means to exploring the world around himself" (4).

One of the basic factors reported in the literature was that the toys used with each child should be within his realm of play. A child should not be exposed to toys that are too old for him because he would not be able to express his true emotions through them. By using toys he is used to playing with, the child will feel freer to play and enter into the world of make-believe. The adult observing him will also obtain a truer picture of what the child is experiencing.

In order to do any work with children it is necessary for the person (psychologist, analyst, or a school counselor) to understand children and have a desire to work with them. The qualities of acceptance and empathy are the most important qualities. It is essential that the person working with the child accept him as he finds him—advancing the child forward from that point toward mutual understanding of the problem. It is also necessary that the adult understand, as well as feel, what the child is experiencing if he is to be enabled to help the child.

In general all the authors were in agreement concerning the type of toys that can be used. The writer found two main differences of thought expressed in the literature. First, there is disagreement regarding the importance of the strength of the super-ego in the young child. Second, authors do not agree on the merits of using the structured techniques or the unstructured. In the case of the first, this writer feels, the therapist will be guided by his own psycho-analytical theories. This should not produce a disagreement. Basically it is a difference in ideals and training. The second difference involves the technique employed, and this will be determined by the amount of training of the therapist, as well as his ability to understand what the child is trying to say through play.

It was a general fact that the doll family was considered the best means of getting the child to express his true feelings about the home situation. When this device is used, it is important to keep the doll family limited to the size of the child's family. Quite often the child will destroy the person within the family that is causing the problem. This may be done by either breaking the doll, completely ignoring it, or stating that he is going to send him away. It is not uncommon for feelings of guilt to follow the removing of the threat to his security. Eventually, the child will again include the doll that had been out of the play. When this happens the therapist knows that the child is showing acceptance of the problem, and is ready through the world of make-believe to attempt to cope with his personality conflicts.

Everyone agrees that it is extremely important for the person in therapy to be non-emotional. He should not show any display of emotion if a toy is destroyed. By keeping control, the therapist helps the child feel that the room is a place where he can do as he pleases. Usually the first time the child destroys an object, he will look at the adult for rejection. When this is not forthcoming, it will give the patient the security of acceptance. This is one of the basic factors in the use of play therapy. It helps the child understand his personality, and its relation to himself as well as the world around him.

Play therapy is a comparatively new and underdeveloped field. Its scope is wide—ranging from toys to art and music. This paper has dealt only with the use of toys employed to help the therapist better understand the child.

The three objectives of the study were to determine: (1) the value of play in understanding the child, (2) the possible use of play by the school counselor, (3) the extent to which it could be applied to the junior high school.

Due to the child's lack of ability to understand himself and the world around him, play therapy is an invaluable tool. It allows a trained person to observe the child in a certain setting. In adults this is done through talking and reasoning, using past experiences. Due to his limited experience, the child is not capable of doing this. Through the use of play, he can accomplish what the adult does by talking.

The use of this technique in our schools can be very helpful to the counselor in his efforts to aid the child to understand himself. However, it is important that the counselor always keep in mind that he is not a trained psychologist, or therapist. It should never be used to analyze a child, for that is not the counselor's job. With training, this technique could become a valuable tool to the school counselor as he endeavors to help the child achieve maturity and self realization.

The use of toys in the junior high school guidance program is not advisable. The main objection is that chronologically the majority of junior high school pupils have little interest in toys. At this age, the child has the power to reason. Play can be used in the junior high school through such techniques as music, draw a person, draw a house—a tree—a person, finger painting, scatter drawing, and psychodrama.

References

1. Axline, Virginia M., *Play Therapy Procedures and Results, Amer. J. Orthopsychiat.*, 1955, 25, 618-627.
2. Beiser, Helen R., *Play Equipment for Diagnosis and Therapy, Amer. J. Orthopsychiat.*, 1955, 25, 761-771.
3. Conn, J. H., *Play Interview Therapy of Castration Fears, Amer. J. Orthopsychiat.*, 1955, 25, 747-755.
4. Frank, L. K., *Play in Personality Development, Amer. J. Orthopsychiat.*, 1955, 25, 576-591.
5. Frank, L. K., Goldenson, R. M., and Hartley, Ruth, *Understanding Children's Play*, Columbia University Press, New York, 1952.
6. Gessell, A., and Ilg, F., *The Child From Five to Ten*, Harper Brothers Publishers, New York, 1946, 359-374.
7. Graham, T. F., *Doll Play Phantasies of Negro and White Primary School Children, J. Clin. Psychol.*, 1955, 11, 11-25.
8. Hambridge, G., *Structured Play Therapy, Amer. J. Orthopsychiat.*, 1955, 25, 601-618.
9. Klein, Melanie, *The Psychoanalytic Play Technique, Amer. J. Orthopsychiat.*, 1955, 25, 223-283.
10. Lebo, D., *The Development of Play as a Form of Therapy, Amer. J. Psychiat.*, 1955, 12, 418-442.

11. Moustakas, C. E., and Schalock, H. D., *An Analysis of Therapist-Child Interaction in Play Therapy, Child Develpm.*, 1955, 26, 143-157.
12. Piaget, Jean, *Play, Dreams, and Imitation in Childhood,* W. W. Norton & Company, New York, 1951, 147-168.
13. Soloman, J. C., *Play Technique and the Integrative Process, Amer. J. Orthopsychiat.*, 1955, 25, 591-601.
14. Woltman, A. G., *Concepts of Play Therapy Techniques, Amer. J. Orthopsychiat.*, 1955, 25, 771-784.

JEAN C. WATERLAND

Actions Instead of Words:
Play Therapy for the
Young Child

Play therapy may be used to modify behavior by allowing the young child to express his thoughts and feelings partly or entirely through acting them out rather than talking them out. The counselor tries to convey to the child that he has the right to feel and act as he does. By creating an acceptant atmosphere, the child can be free without worrying about how his behavior affects the counselor's opinion of him. The counselor acts as a selective mirror, reflecting for the child his emotionalized perceptions and attitudes so that the child can become aware of them and in time change them. The decision to change or not to change his behavior always remains with the child, because the counselor cannot take the initiative in this respect without destroying the atmosphere of total acceptance of the child as he is.

Theoretical Position

Within the framework of *relationship theory,* the counselor's ability to communicate with the child in play therapy is stressed so that

Waterland, J. C. Actions instead of words: play therapy for the young child. *Elementary School Guidance and Counseling,* 1970, *4*(3), 180-187. Copyright 1970 American Personnel and Guidance Association. Reprinted with permission.

the counselor does not direct the child's actions or verbalizations. The counselor helps the child understand his thoughts and feelings through the cautious use of reflective phrases rather than interpretive statements which are usually analytical in nature. Nelson (1966) states that ". . . the objective of counseling should be to create conditions for expression and communication, and to avoid, generally, viewing play from an analytical frame of reference." Muro (1968) recently discussed a child's progress during play therapy where the counselor's behavior was guided by the philosophical tenets of relationship theory derived in part from the earlier work of Axline (1947) and Moustakas (1953).

Axline advocates nondirective play therapy and bases her ideas on Rogers' work. In her opinion, play represents a more natural medium of self-expression for children than does mere verbalization. Axline not only emphasizes play therapy with individual children, but also stresses its use in groups and its application to education. Proponents of relationship theory stress that the counselor develop a warm relationship with the child, establishing good rapport. The counselor must respect the child's ability to solve his own problems and should not direct the child's actions or conversations. The counselor endeavors to accept the child as he is, recognize his feelings, and allow him to express them. The counselor tries not to rush the play therapy process and only sets those limits needed to keep the child's therapy within the realm of reality. A central feature of Axline's philosophy is the belief that warmth, respect, and acceptance must be integral parts of the counselor's personality.

Moustakas' approach to play therapy, based largely on Axline's ideas, emphasizes attitudes. He believes that the feelings of the counselor are of major importance. The counselor should communicate three basic attitudes to the child: (a) faith, expressed as a belief in the child's ability to work out his own problems; (b) acceptance, shown through encouraging the child to express his feelings freely; and (c) respect, conveying to the child that he is regarded as worthwhile and important. The goal of Moustakas' approach is that children achieve feelings of security, worthiness, and adequacy through emotional insight. According to Moustakas, the therapeutic process begins with the child expressing negative attitudes culminating in anger and hostility. Eventually these feelings become mixed with positive feelings, and finally the attitudes become separated and consistent with reality.

The Need for Play

The play therapy approach is vital to the counselor as he works with children who have difficulty communicating with adults (Nelson, 1966). The counselor, however, must know when and how to use play. This does not imply that the counselor needs to use play therapy with all children. Only the counselor's sensitivity to the child and his situation will determine when play materials should be used. If the counselor has confidence in himself and in the child, he does not need to be concerned with how the play materials will be used; the child will start to play when he is ready.

Three Components

Play therapy has three components—the setting, the child, and the counselor.

The Setting: Playroom and Play Materials

In an ideal situation, the setting consists of a playroom and play materials. The room should be large enough to accommodate group play sessions. The room should be soundproof, have a sink with hot and cold running water, and protected windows. If the room is to be used for teaching, it should include a one-way mirror and be wired for audio and visual tape equipment.

The toys should be arranged in an unstructured fashion so that the child feels at liberty to do what he wants (Axline, 1947). Suggested play materials include water, a sandbox, clay, paint, dolls, shovels, telephones, blocks, balloons, nursing bottles, etc. Dolls are important when working with family relations. Toys for working through aggressions include trucks, mallets, and soldiers. Play materials that do not inhibit the child's activities are preferable.

If a playroom and play materials are not available, some ingenuity on the part of the counselor can do much toward turning an ordinary room into a playroom.

The Child: Feelings and Actions

Most children the counselor sees in play therapy have failed to develop individual identities: development of the real self has been inhibited because of inadequate personal relationships. These children probably have been rejected by others, and subsequently have learned to reject themselves; they are struggling to establish themselves in what they perceive as a frightening environment. In their own eyes, adjusting to the environment by either withdrawing or showing aggressive tendencies gives them needed status. The children's real difficulties might be disguised by academic or health problems.

These children have behavior problems they do not know how to solve. Their maladjustments may be caused by misdirected energy, which must be channeled into constructive areas.

The Counselor: Techniques, an Implementation of One's Personality

The role of the counselor is to convey to the child, sincerely and consistently, attitudes such as permissiveness, acceptance, and respect. To transmit these relationship characteristics to the child, the counselor must possess the personal qualities of an effective counselor. Since the child is quick to sense insecurity and insincerity, the counselor cannot just play a role. In addition to these personal qualities, the counselor needs to be adept at using a variety of counseling techniques. Some of the basic counseling techniques as applied to play therapy follow.

Reflection. Reflection is one technique used by the counselor to develop the child's self-understanding. The counselor listens carefully to what the child says and how he says it. In reflecting the child's feelings, he is cautious not to add or subtract from the original meaning. For example, when the child buries the baby doll in the sand and says, "She hates the baby," the counselor reflects, "She hates the baby." The counselor is in error if he reflects, "Mother hates the baby," because the child has not named the person involved. The object of the child's feelings must be stated by the child before being reflected by the counselor (Ginott, 1961).

The counselor must be sensitive to the child's reactions to the reflection. Some children accept reflections from the counselor which may be simply restatements of what the child has said. For example, the child says as she plays with the doll, "She makes me mad." The counselor responds, "She makes you mad." Other children will be saying, "I just said that," or "Aren't you listening to me?" When the child responds this way the counselor needs to begin rephrasing, in his own words, what the child has said. For example, if the child says, "I hate the teacher because he tells me what to do," the counselor could respond, "Being told what to do makes you angry." The counselor, however, should refrain from using indiscriminate reflective phrases because such phrases are meaningless. When the child makes an offensive statement the counselor reflects using his own words (Ginott, 1961). For example, the child expressing feelings about his mother by saying, "She is a dirty rat," could be reflected by the counselor's responding, "Oh, your mother seems to be pretty bad."

Interpretation. Interpretation should be used cautiously to avoid expressing something to the child before he is ready to accept it. The child's nonverbal behavior represents how he thinks and feels. Whenever the counselor tries to translate nonverbal behavior into words he is interpreting—stating what he thinks the child's behavior means (Axline, 1942). Actually, what the counselor thinks and feels the child's behavior means is not important. How the *child* thinks and feels about his own behavior is important to the counselor. "Susie, you're crying because you want your mother," is an example of an interpretation; "because you want your mother" is only an educated guess on the counselor's part. Susie might be crying because no one is telling her what to do or because she does *not* want her mother. The counselor must examine carefully the meaning of a child's verbalizations and actions before making rapid and perhaps erroneous interpretations.

Silence. Correct handling of silences in the playroom is very important. The counselor should not push the child into conversation or play. Silence must be accepted and then gradually interpreted to the child by the counselor. Possible interpretations of silence include, "You are at a loss to know what to do," or "You don't know what to do first." These interpretations leave with the child the responsibility for initiating activity and/or a conversation. The counselor is helping the child to become independent by allowing him to assume the responsibility for making decisions and choices.

The counselor is in error if he says to a silent child, "Why don't you start playing in the sand box," or "Tell me something about your family." In these examples, the counselor has told the child what to do or what to talk about. An unlimited number of sessions may pass before the child becomes active. The child's reaction to the counselor and to the playroom is probably an indication of his past relationship patterns and the sensitive counselor can learn a great deal about the child this way. The child should make the decision to play or not to play, to talk or not to talk. The counselor must not push or hurry him.

Structure. Because structure helps create a framework for the relationship between counselor and child, the counselor must structure the play therapy sessions. Doing so also facilitates the child's keeping the relationship reality-oriented. Structuring is an on-going process and should be used as the need arises. The following are examples of the kinds of structure the counselor provides and how he can verbalize these limits to the child.

The counselor sets the departure time: "We leave the playroom at four o'clock."

The child makes the decisions: "You may play with these toys any way you want."

The child is responsible for his safety: "This is not safe for jumping."

Certain toys are built to take aggression: "Why not beat up the clown?"

The child cannot attack the counselor: "Instead of painting me why don't you use the easel?"

Play material is for use only during the session: "The car must stay in the playroom."

Once a limit is set by the counselor it should be followed consistently to provide a feeling of security for the child. When the limit is broken by the child, the counselor must follow up the infringement by reflecting the child's feelings. For example, "You are angry with me for not letting you do that." The counselor should handle the incident in an accepting manner so as not to make the child feel guilty.

The three components of play therapy—the setting, the child, and the counselor's personal qualities—are illustrated in the following case study.

Julie

Julie appeared to be a well-adjusted six year old. Her academic work was average and her social relationships were satisfactory. Last December, however, the teacher reported that Julie was acting babyish, sucking her thumb, and crying. Upon inquiry the teacher discovered that there was a new baby in the family. The teacher and counselor hypothesized that Julie was having difficulty accepting her new role in the family structure. The school counselor felt that play therapy might help Julie clarify this unfamiliar role. A brief conference was held with Julie's mother to explain the purpose of play therapy.

During the first session, the counselor introduced Julie to the playroom. Although the counselor felt she had established good rapport, Julie remained guarded in her activities. Julie was sometimes very verbal and other times not. She seemed to be struggling with herself in order to stay within socially acceptable limits. She explored the room commenting on the various play things. Her comments included: "We have puzzles like this in our classroom." "Would you like me to do a puzzle for you?" "Can I use the crayons to make a Christmas picture?" Julie was trying to seek permission from the counselor in order to feel free to pursue a chosen activity. The counselor would have been in error if she had responded by saying, "Yes, Julie, why don't you do a puzzle for me," because the counselor would have assumed the responsibility for Julie's activities. Instead, the counselor reflected by saying, "Only if you want to," which gave Julie the responsibility for making the final decision. Soon Julie started to paint a picture and to splash the paint around. The counselor observed Julie's nonverbal behavior and concluded that she enjoyed splashing paint, and accepted Julie's behavior by responding, "You are enjoying this." An erroneous response would have been to ask Julie to stop splashing the paint; this would have imposed an unjustified limit on Julie. Later Julie explored the doll corner and commented offhandedly that their family had a new baby. Julie did not express any particular attitude about the new baby nor did she pursue the topic. The counselor let Julie's comment pass because she felt Julie was not interested in pursuing the statement any further at that time. The counselor structured the end of the session for Julie by saying that just a few minutes were left. Julie touched on her problem only briefly, but it was apparent that she sensed the counselor's attitude of acceptance.

The beginning of the second session was similar. Julie casually reexplored the room and the play materials, and then sat silently by the doll corner. Cautiously she began to assume the part of a mother taking care of her baby. Once in a while she looked quickly at the counselor and then returned her attention to the doll. Julie made no attempt to involve the counselor in her play activity. She quickly stopped playing the role of the mother and assumed the role of a small child drinking from the baby bottle, sucking her thumb, and talking in a babyish manner. After awhile Julie directed her attention to one of the grown-up dolls. She began telling the counselor about the doll. "She's a bad mother," she said. "She just feeds the little baby. She makes the little girl eat by herself." The counselor listened carefully and reflected some of Julie's important comments: "You feel she is bad," and "The little girl needs help when eating." Julie continued with a flood of negative comments about the bad mother until the end of the session.

Shortly after the beginning of the next session, Julie again became involved with the dolls. Julie acted out and expressed very negative feelings toward the mother and baby dolls. The counselor used silence, acceptance, reflection, and interpretation to help Julie express her deeper feelings. Before the end of the hour, Julie very casually began expressing some positive feelings toward the grown-up doll. She mumbled, "Mother likes to hear me read." The counselor responded by making a casually stated tentative interpretation to Julie about her verbal and nonverbal behavior: "You feel that perhaps Mother has time for both you and the new baby." The counselor felt she could make this interpretation because Julie had started to talk about "me" and not the little girl doll. This interpretation was accepted by Julie and helped her explore more positive feelings regarding her mother and the new baby.

The counselor would have been in error if she had started to ask Julie questions about what she was saying and doing. In this session Julie began to minimize the negative attitudes toward her mother (the grown-up doll).

Julie began the next session by pretending the grown-up doll was her mother, the little girl doll represented herself, and another doll was the baby. Julie appeared to be equally attentive to the grown-up doll and baby doll. This time, however, Julie started to make such statements as, "Mommy has to help the baby 'cause she's so little," and "She and I can eat together." Julie began to express the feeling of accepting her role in the new family situation. Because Julie was ordinarily a very stable child and because the counselor had accepted both her negative and positive feelings, Julie could resolve her problem.

This gradual behavioral change in Julie was substantiated by a classroom episode. Julie said, "Oh, Mrs. Jones, the baby cried all night. My mother had to get up and take care of her." Her tone of voice and the sympathy she expressed for her mother displayed an understanding of the family situation. Julie was beginning to understand that the extra care needed by the baby was a necessity. It did not mean that her mother loved the baby more than she did Julie. This episode plus Julie's mother's comment on her improved behavior indicated that Julie was beginning to overcome the momentary but important conflict over the new baby.

References

Axline, V. M. *Play therapy*. Chicago: Houghton Mifflin, 1947.

Ginott, H. G. *Group psychotherapy with children*. New York: McGraw-Hill, 1961.

Moustakas, C. E. *Children in play therapy*. New York: McGraw-Hill, 1953.

Moustakas, C. E. *Psychotherapy with children*. New York: Harpers, 1969.

Muro, J. J. Play media in counseling: A brief report of experience and some opinions. *Elementary School Guidance and Counseling*, 1968, 2, 104-110.

Nelson, R. C. Elementary school counseling with unstructured play media. *Personnel and Guidance Journal*, 1966, 1, 24-27.

EUGENE D. ALEXANDER

School-centered
Play-Therapy Program

There were times when Chucky sat in the corner with his back to other children. Sometimes he would stand up and shake his hands as if they were foreign appendages stuck onto his body. There were occasions when he would desperately hug the teacher's leg and hide his face in her dress. At other times he had a faraway look in his eyes and would not respond at all when spoken to. Often when you talked to him he would answer in irrelevant, unrelated sentences. Yet somehow he was learning to read and much of the time he would sit in his seat trying to take part in classroom activities. There were even occasions when he was seemingly able to share openly in activities with the other children. His teacher had warm feelings for him. She was concerned and worried. She talked with his parents and found that they rationalized his different behavior. The parents also indicated that they did not have time and were not interested in taking him someplace for help. The teacher was desperate. She felt deeply for this child. She knew that he was profiting from his school experience. She wanted to keep him in her class, yet she feared that if he did not get some help very soon it might become more difficult for

Alexander, E. D. School centered play-therapy program. *The Personnel and Guidance Journal,* 1964, *43*(3), 256-261. Copyright 1964 American Personnel and Guidance Association. Reprinted with permission.

him to function in the school situation. What was she to do for Chucky? She guessed that he needed some psychotherapeutic help.

A Rationale for Play Therapy

Psychotherapy is most often practiced in either the hospital or the clinic setting. In the hospital the children are usually very severely emotionally disturbed and are treated as medical cases. In the clinic setting it is almost mandatory that the parents participate actively. There are very few facilities available to the relatively mildly disturbed youngster or to the youngster whose parents are accepting of help for their child but not willing to participate. To fill this gap there have been recent attempts to help the child in the school situation. In the school setting it is not necessary to involve the apathetic parent. It is also possible to help the disturbed child who is manageable in the classroom, without upsetting his immediate academic situation. This relieves the load from the other facilities so that they can concentrate upon children with more intensive difficulties. This paper describes one approach to play therapy in the school setting.

Play therapy in the school has a somewhat different emphasis from the way in which psychotherapy is usually conceived. It is an integral part of the educational program and like the rest of the educational program, is not medically oriented. The general goal of education is to increase the individual's knowledge and understanding of the universe and of himself. Educational play therapy concentrates on the latter aspect of this task.

Most children who come for play therapy are referred because they have problems in their relationships with other people. The teacher finds them hostile, withdrawn or possessed of an atypical perception of their environment. Through the one-to-one relationship in the educational play therapy setting the child is given the freedom to express and to explore himself in an accepting climate. Educational play therapy as here conceived is not a method but an attitude. Through creative listening (an involved alertness to underlying feeling and a sensitivity to the meaning of this feeling in the child's existence) and intense empathy the therapist is able to share the fundamental inner experience of the child. By responding in terms of this inner experience, the therapist helps the child struggle through to a better self-concept.

The therapy relationship has the basic essentials of any genuine human relationship. It differs only in that the therapist is able to give his undivided self completely to the child and is totally alert and sensitive to the child's feelings. The therapist shows complete acceptance, faith, hope and trust in the child. This frees the child to express himself openly and to allow his feelings of fear and distrust to emerge. He is able to examine those aspects of his self that he regards as negative as well as the ones he regards as positive and to see them both as meaningful aspects of existence.

This approach to children has been referred to as Relationship Psychotherapy by Moustakas (1959b). In this approach the child is not regarded as mentally ill. There is no effort to change the child, to manipulate him, to categorize him, to adjust him to the society. The child is seen as an individual in his own right. It is assumed that he has his own goals, his own needs, his own mode of perceiving and these are respected. Therapy creates a free situation in which the individual is given the opportunity to self-actualize. The basic human tendencies that Maslow (1954, 1962) describes are allowed to emerge. The child needs to expend less energy in defending and protecting himself and can devote more effort in exploring and expressing his potential as a being.

There are times when a sensitive, responsive teacher is able to have a therapeutic relationship with a child. This is frequently quite difficult for teachers because of the large number of children in the class and the teacher's lack of awareness and experience with the possibilities of such an experience. The school play therapist can offer his undivided attention for a 50-minute period once a week. There are no other children demanding the therapist's attention, there are no academic requirements limiting the relationship, and the therapist has been highly sensitized to respond to the feeling tone of the child.

Fortunately for Chucky (the child mentioned at the beginning of this paper), his school system was one of the few that employed a child therapist as a regular member of the staff. Chucky's teacher discussed his situation with her principal and the school therapist. They decided that psychotherapy would be a helpful experience for the child.

The psychotherapist set a regular time for him and Chucky to meet. The therapist's mode of operation was unique to the public school environment. He worked in several schools and had no permanent room. He carried toys in a suitcase and spread them out in any reasonably quiet room that might be available. He knew that it was the relationship, not the toys, that was the key to emotional growth.

Therapy Begins

Chucky entered the therapy situation with suspicion and wariness. He did not look directly at the therapist. He went to the corner of the room and began to shake his hands in the air. Then he went to the toys, examined them for a while, and walked to the other side of the room. The therapist said, "You don't feel like playing with the toys today." Chucky looked at the therapist with a surprised expression. He spent most of the rest of the session alternately looking at the therapist and just standing with his inner thoughts. The therapist sensed Chucky's feelings and said, "You're not quite sure what to make of all this. You're surprised that there are not things you have to do." The therapist said very little during the first session. He shared the silence attentively with Chucky. He was alert to Chucky's being. Even though little was said, Chucky and the therapist felt closer to each other by the time the session was over.

The therapist is different from most adults the child has experienced. He listens attentively to what the child has to say and responds with real understanding. He is honest with the child and the acceptance the child experiences is an active one with sincere encounters when limits are reached. The child does not find the therapist demanding of him or threatening, but waiting attentively to share and to explore those things most important to the child.

Chucky began to talk a little bit more each session. A little of his talk hinted about things that raised his anxiety. The walls of the building, storms, big animals, time, all seemed to disturb him. Most of his talk was about irrelevant, unimportant things that had little meaning in his life. Often he would just sit and stare at the clock or at the therapist's watch and call off the time. Soon he was able to sit close to the therapist and to hold onto his watch hand for comfort. This seemed to make him feel more secure and he began to pour out his anxieties. Would the next minute follow this minute or would time stop? Would the walls fall in? How could you be sure that they would stay up? Would a big snake come and eat him? Would the wind blow the building down? The therapist did not try to minimize these fears or to reassure Chucky. He shared Chucky's worries and tried to feel them the way they appeared to Chucky. He made such remarks as, "You want to be sure that the next hour will come," "You are still afraid of the room," "When it is raining outside you want to hide from the storm," "You are afraid of animals you do not know." But primarily the therapist tried to concentrate his whole being on the inner experience Chucky was having. He tried to let this sharing be communicated by the minimal cues that Chucky had learned from his incidental everyday experience.

A play setting is provided because it is in play that the child has been most familiar and comfortable in expressing himself. The toys give the child a means of acting out feelings and experiences which he is incapable of expressing verbally, due not only to their threatening emotional content, but also because of the child's limited experience with the language. The play setting also facilitates the exploration of experiences not accessible to awareness and in fact the greatest growth most often takes place at this level. The child can explore his feelings through the toys until he is ready to explore them more directly in his relationship with the therapist. Toys, in their very existence, usually represent a freeing, playful atmosphere. They are the one means available in everyday life by which the child can escape the restrictions and distortions of the adult world. To find an adult that can enter and share the playful world of toys helps to build up a trusting relationship.

Before Chucky was able to come over to the therapist and to explore his watch, he spent much time examining a toy watch and placing it on a doll's wrist. After he had tested the watch on the doll, he was able to explore the therapist's watch. This examination of the watch initiated a physical closeness to the therapist. This physical closeness in turn initiated a closer relationship that gave Chucky enough security to make a more involved exploration of the toys. At first he spent most of his time arranging the toys in neat order. As he began to feel more free, he started to use the toys more expressively. He shot the guns, moved the cars, played with the toy soldiers and even fed the baby doll. He became less concerned about the neatness of the toys and left them strewn around the room. He even began throwing some of the toys and on several occasions hit the doll. Later on he began to focus on a male puppet. He called it names and would alternately hit it and run from it. Still later he began to call the therapist names and pretended to hit him. On other occasions he came over and sat on the therapist's lap, putting his head on the therapist's shoulder.

The child finds himself in a situation with a very minimum of limit from which he can branch out and discover his true feelings. The limits serve as a superstructure from which he can build rather than a fenced-in enclosure from which he cannot escape. By struggling through the limits the therapist and child come closer to each other and the child gains security in knowing where he stands. The limits emerge from the requirements of the situation and are not arbitrarily imposed in terms of external values. This in itself is a learning experience. The child learns to appreciate realistic structure.

Testing of Limits

During the third session Chucky wanted to leave early. The therapist pointed out that he had to remain the full time limit if he came, but did not have to come at all if he so desired. The next session Chucky not only asked to leave early, but tried to sneak out. The therapist had to stand by the door to prevent this. When he came for the following session, Chucky belligerently stated, "I am not going into that old room." The therapist acceptingly said, "If that is what you wish Chucky, it will be all right. You may go back to your classroom if you want." Chucky looked at the therapist in disbelief.

The therapist actually had to reassure Chucky that he was free to go. Chucky went back to his classroom. Nevertheless this was the last time that he challenged the time limit. He came promptly and never missed another session for reasons other than illness. The therapist sensed that Chucky was so used to being ordered to do things that a real feeling of freedom was necessary before growth could take place. This resolution of limits also had the effect of bringing the therapist and Chucky closer together. They had faced an issue together and had remained friends.

After Chucky was at ease in the therapy situation and had begun to play freely with the toys, other kinds of limits were necessary. Because the toy budget was small, the therapist could not let the children break toys randomly. Chucky began to toss the toys all over the room. Then he began to jump on them. He smashed one of the little plastic cars. The therapist explained, "I can understand the fun you have in smashing that car, but the school doesn't have enough money to buy new toys. I'll have to ask you not to smash any more toys." Chucky began to smash another car and the therapist again set the limit. Chucky refused to listen and continued to break the car. The therapist quietly said, "Chucky, if you try to break one more toy, that toy will have to be put away." Chucky tried and the therapist removed the item. This continued until half of the items were placed in the suitcase. Chucky then stopped playing with any of the toys and glared at the therapist. Angrily he said, "You are a mean man. I hate you. I'm not going to come to this dirty old place anymore." The therapist sympathized, "I certainly can understand your anger, Chucky. It is natural to feel hurt and angry when you want to do something very much and someone stops you." He added, "You are especially angry at me because I let you do so many other things. You are afraid that my stopping you means I don't like you." Chucky got even more angry and stamped his feet. He again began to throw toys around, but being careful not to break any. The therapist continued to accept Chucky's anger. Finally Chucky tried to break another item and the therapist took it away also. This really aggravated Chucky and he struck the therapist. The therapist held Chucky's arms to prevent Chucky from striking him again. Chucky stamped his feet, screamed and cursed the therapist. "I hate you! I hate you! I hate you!" Still holding Chucky, the therapist said, "You are terribly angry with me and you are being honest about your anger. You have to feel the way you feel and I understand." Chucky relaxed a little and the therapist continued, "I have to stop you from breaking toys and hitting me, Chucky. That has nothing to do with whether I like you or don't like you." A little while later the therapist added, "I know saying it might not mean very much, but, Chucky, I like you very much." After a while Chucky quieted down and sat fingering some toys. He left the therapy session without saying a word.

The Relationship Is Explored

Something had taken place in this session that brought Chucky and the therapist still closer together. They had had a real encounter and Chucky discovered that the therapist could accept him even when he was at his angriest. He expressed physical aggression toward the therapist and he was still accepted.

Significant growth does not take place only in the therapeutic situation. The therapeutic situation actually serves as a demonstration experience exposing the child to the possibilities that can emerge from a sincere relationship. It is a guidance experience with the real growth frequently taking place outside of the therapy hour. The therapy experience helps the child to free himself to more open and trusting relationships in everyday life. In therapy he discovers himself to be a worthwhile individual, a person others can like and respect. He begins to have warm relationships with other individuals and each relationship in itself by its very existence is therapeutic. The child has less need to defend or to withdraw. He learns to value the truly human aspects of relationships.

Chucky lost interest in the toys and focused completely upon his relationship with the therapist. He began to approach the therapist physically. He touched all parts of his body, occasionally pinching or twisting, but always stopping when the therapist asked him to. Later he sat on the therapist's lap and hugged him. He began to talk about his family. For several sessions he talked in a hostile manner about his father. He said, "I hate my father." Then one day he told how he had climbed up on his father's lap and how his father had accepted him. His attitude toward his father showed a gradual change and it was obvious from his verbalizations that he was having much more of a mutual sharing relationship with his dad.

Therapy may help the child to become better adjusted to his life situation. On the other hand he may refuse to adjust to those aspects of his life situation which he senses as destructive to his integrity and to his humanity. In this sense a child may emerge in some aspects as more maladjusted after therapy than before. Nevertheless, such maladjustment can be seen as the most wholesome way to respond to an environment that is detrimental to his creative self-actualization.

From Chucky's conversation it appeared that much of his anxiety was related to his father's attempt to control and mold him. Several conversations with Chucky's father confirmed this. Through his interviews with the father the therapist was able to help him become more accepting of Chucky. It was a very difficult experience for both Chucky and his father when Chucky began to assert himself. For the first time they were confronting each other in an open and honest way. Slowly Chucky learned to accept the love that his father had for him and at the same time his father learned to accept Chucky as an individual in his own right who could not be molded into something he was not. Chucky's new confidence in himself helped him to insist upon his rights, and his father's glimpse of understanding helped him to accept what first appeared to him as defiance.

The Therapist and the Teacher

The therapist does not work in isolation from the rest of the school program. He attempts to create a therapeutic attitude throughout the school system. He relates in an accepting, respecting attitude with other school personnel. He realizes that both the teacher and the parent spend a much longer time with the child and as a result often influence a child's behavior more significantly than the therapist. The therapist shares experiences with the teacher. Because of his on-going relationship with the child he can really share with the teacher in a very concrete way rather than in the more abstract way usually occurring if he were to function in a consultative capacity. By this very intimate sharing he can relate closer to the teacher than he could if he saw the child only occasionally. It is through this sharing that the therapist is able to help the teacher explore herself in relation to all her students and to help her develop a more therapeutic attitude toward them.

Chucky's teacher, though warmly concerned about him, was confused and upset about his behavior. Reassurance that Chucky could be lived with, and that she would eventually be able to communicate with him in a more open manner, was not enough. Knowing that the therapist was actively involved in helping the child gave her real security. They were two people deeply involved with Chucky who could mutually share concrete feelings about him. When the teacher talked about Chucky's reluctant attempts to touch her, the therapist knew the deep feelings involved, for he too had lived with them. When the teacher voiced anxieties over Chucky's new ability to be hostile, the therapist shared the development of Chucky's aggressiveness as it was expressed in therapy. As a result, the teacher could see Chucky's hostility was actually a positive expression for him. She could then feel more at ease and accepting of his hostility. This strengthened her interpersonal relationship with him and she was able to make the classroom experience more therapeutic for Chucky. There were also times when the confidence and hope of the teacher helped alleviate the therapist's own shadow of despair. The teacher-therapist relationship as it developed became mutually supportive. Each helped the other with his struggle to help Chucky. In sharing their beings, Chucky, the teacher, and the therapist each became a little more human in his own way. This was reflected in all their other interpersonal relations.

Moustakas (1959a, p. 343) describes this approach to the teachers. "He listened to encourage further exploration on the part of the teacher, but also to understand and learn for himself from the experiences of the teacher; he encouraged the individual teachers to maintain positions they felt were right and valid, but tried to do this without minimizing the value of majority opinion or suggestion; he expressed his point of view from time to time; but encouraged others . . . to maintain their own perceptions and convictions; he directly supported individuals . . . when he felt their integrity and self-respect were being threatened or destroyed; he encouraged teachers to experiment and try out new ideas that came to them . . . and he tried to show his belief in the worth and dignity of each teacher . . . his belief in their potentialities as a creative teacher and his acceptance and empathy in response to each expression."

Thus the play therapy program in the schools must reflect the therapist's accepting attitude toward the teacher's experience as well as the experience of the children. Though the school therapist may work with parents, he focuses upon the teacher-child relationship. The therapeutic relationship between therapist and child can act as a catalyst to a therapeutic relationship between teacher and child. The therapist is able to support the teacher in her struggle to accept and to understand the child while he is helping the child learn to relate more comfortably with people in general. The child is helped to make an emotional reorganization to his school environment as a step toward emotional growth at home and in his everyday life.

References

Maslow, A. H. *Motivation and personality*. New York: Harper, 1954.

Maslow, A. H. *Toward a psychology of being*. Princeton, N.J.: D. Van Nostrand, 1962.

Moustakas, Clark E. A human relations seminar at the Merrill-Palmer School. *Personnel Guid. J.*, 1959, *37*, 342-349. (a)

Moustakas, Clark E. *Psychotherapy with children, the living relationship*. New York: Harper, 1959. (b)

JAMES L. WIDERMAN
EILEEN L. WIDERMAN

Counseling Nonverbal Students

Counseling, as taught by most graduate programs and practiced by the majority of those in the field, is primarily a verbal activity, a transaction and exchange between an identified client and a counselor. The various schools of counseling differ in their stress on verbal interchange, but all to some extent include in their model a client with a problem and an empathic counselor who listens and responds helpfully.

When the counselee, for whatever reason, is nonverbal, the counseling process breaks down. Since counselors' primary tool is talking, they become uncomfortable when confronted by a client who cannot or will not talk. One setting in which this breakdown often occurs is the school.

Most students who voluntarily approach a counselor are nervous, unsure of the counselor's role. Whether or not they ordinarily are verbal, students respond to the counseling situation, which is strange to them, with feelings of discomfort or uncertainty. It is alien to the adolescent's life style to immediately open up and trust an adult. Even under the most conducive of circumstances, the school counselor is too often associated with authority.

Widerman, J. L. & E. L. Counseling nonverbal students. *The Personnel and Guidance Journal,* 1974, *52*(10), 688-693. Copyright 1974 American Personnel and Guidance Association. Reprinted with permission.

Many students do not come willingly for counseling; they are referred by teachers, parents, or administrators. This referral usually implies a problem; the student is a "discipline problem," a "slow learner," a "truant," etc., whether or not the adolescent sees himself or herself in that way.

The difficulties of dealing with an unwilling or uncooperative client are well documented in the literature. The factor that comprises a significant portion of this difficulty is the unwilling client's tendency not to talk or open up. This article offers a framework in which to view a technique for effectively counseling the nonverbal adolescent, providing a case example. While this technique does not have blanket effectiveness, we have found it useful in dealing with a significant portion of school counseling.

The Problem

Typical counseling interviews with nonverbal students are characterized as follows. The students are sent to the counselor. The counselor responds to their presence with comments or questions designed to put them at ease and to elicit from them their view of why they have been referred. Typical questions are "What can I do for you?" and "Who sent you to see me?" and they are frequently preceded by such small talk questions as "How do you like school?" and "What grade are you in?" Students generally field such questions with nods, grunts, shrugs of shoulders, and other such noncommittal expressions. They rarely maintain eye contact with the counselor, instead staring at the floor or out the window. When asked an open-ended question, they give a monosyllabic answer or say "I don't know."

Students' inability or unwillingness to interact verbally often provokes anxiety in counselors—particularly new counselors. They may respond by increasing their own verbal output—either to speak for the student, to give the student a "multiple choice," or to fill what seems like an endless silence. "I know it isn't always easy to talk." "Did you come because you are in trouble?" "You seem nervous." In this kind of situation, neither counselors nor students have their needs met; the counselors feel that they have not helped and the students feel that they are not yet on the way to a solution of their difficulties. No one has the feeling that a relationship has been established. Too often such an interchange discourages students from seeking further help; this can influence not only their present but also their future adjustment, negatively affecting their propensity to seek help from others as adults. Counselors, then, frustrated by such unrewarding interviews—and desiring to maintain their self-images as professionals operating out of a firm knowledge base—too often label nonverbal adolescents as "not amenable to counseling," a label that can hold numerous undesirable implications for others dealing with them.

A Behavioral Hierarchy

In our work with nonverbal students, we have identified a hierarchy of behaviors leading from nonverbal to verbal through which students pass if counseling is successful. The hierarchy is described and operationally expanded in four steps.

Step 1: Students Attend in the Presence of the Counselor

Rather than maintain eye contact with the counselor, students will explore their environment, although this exploration may be initially covert. To avoid relating personally, students may ask such questions as: "Is that a picture of your wife on your desk?" "What time is this period over?" An office stocked with paintings, clay, plants, cards, simple games, a typewriter, felt-tip pens, a drawing pad, a candy dish, magazines, and comics will invite uncomfortable, hesitant, nonverbal students to explore. As they become involved in an exploratory activity, students attend; and this attending becomes an important prerequisite to the attending of protracted conversation. As they become absorbed in activities of high appeal, students become more comfortable.

This transition from an uncomfortable, nonverbal client to a more relaxed one may take more than one session in the counselor's office. The length of the initial sessions can be dictated by the interest and the attention span of the student, some students taking only a part of one session and others taking several complete sessions.

Occasionally an acting-out or a more disturbed adolescent will use this Step 1 activity as an opportunity to test the counselor, the testing usually taking the form of taxing the counselor's permissiveness. The student may pound on the typewriter, handle a toy roughly, try to steal a small item, and so on. The counselor must not reject the student, but the counselor should set limits and in so doing define his or her own role. What is facilitative in this situation is not a direct reaction to this behavior but an attempt to deflect the student's attention by focusing and role definition.

The counselor's main role during Step 1, then, is to invite the student's exploration of the office, to make the student as comfortable as possible, and to encourage the student's return to the office.

Step 2: Students Comment as They Attend

Initially students come to the office and sit in silence. They steal a glance at the distractors, at first perhaps as an aside but gradually more as the central activity. They become more trusting and relaxed as they perform such activities with the counselor present. An important stage has been realized when a student follows a game or activity to completion rather than merely moving from object to object. Often the student will ask the counselor if a particular activity is acceptable and will invite a mutual definition of roles. Regardless, once the student engages in an activity the counselor can encourage comments with such questions as: "What are you drawing?" "What do you think of that puzzle?" Nonverbal students find it easier to talk while they perform than talk while they are not engaged in doing anything.

It is important to keep in mind that the nonverbal student often cannot converse at all without concomitant activity. At this second step, any discussion is encouraged. No discrimination of content is made. Counselors should gauge their own verbal output by carefully and continually assessing the student and the situation. Any conversation should encourage continued activity and should be kept nonthreatening.

Those counselors who lean toward the use of play and/or art as diagnostic tools might wish to integrate them into this step. Care must be taken, however, to allow the student to set the pace and determine the activity. If the student seems to have difficulty in making the transition from private exploration to conversation with the counselor, the counselor might attempt to become involved in the student's exploration. One particularly effective method is to play a game (checkers, dominoes, cards, etc.) and talk to the student as the game is played.

Step 3: Students Are Encouraged to Give More Personal Commentary

Embedded in the students' conversations are statements about themselves. The counselor can respond to these, encouraging students to talk about what they are doing in relation to themselves as persons. Expressions of likes, dislikes, and associations to other events should be noted in an effort to reinforce them. Once the students become used to talking about themselves, they will recall and relate more and more. Wishes and fears may begin to surface during the activity. Students may reveal their feelings about the counselor or the counseling situation. During this stage the counselor, being sensitive to these new elements, can encourage the students to give more of themselves—in both commentary and fantasy. Often at this point students become satisfied to talk without the activity gimmick or to talk after a quick game.

Step 4: Conversation Is Encouraged Without Gross Motor Activity

As students begin conversing for longer stretches, they eventually mention or can be directed to mention their school experiences and problems. They express likes, dislikes, and annoyances. The counselor should respond to—and thus reward—the school-related discussions. Once the student converses comfortably the counselor has reached the presenting problem stage, which completes the transition from a nonverbal to a verbal relationship.

It is apparent that the four-step process is one of making finer and finer speech discriminations. At the start, only gross motor activity is possible (the nonverbal activity). This gross motor activity keeps the client in the office long enough to allow the low rate of fine motor activity (speech) to be increased. Once the rate is sufficiently high and stable, the content of the speech is shaped so as to become personal and then to focus on the problem area. Operant conditioning, then, merges with a client-centered approach and the use of play to facilitate a helping relationship.

A Case History

Three department heads referred Lloyd, an eighth grader, for counseling. He had been suspended numerous times for cutting classes and exhibiting disruptive behavior. He mimicked teachers, ran around the room, danced, and instigated similar acting-out behaviors in others.

The first sessions with Lloyd were conducted in almost total silence. Except to answer questions monosyllabically, Lloyd hung his head, stared at the floor, and took deep, heavy breaths. Because of his obvious discomfort and inability to verbalize, Lloyd was asked by the counselor if anything in the room interested him, and for the first time he raised his head to look around. Careful to avoid eye contact, which might prove too threatening, he surveyed the various "props" in the room. The counselor observed that Lloyd was eyeing felt-tip pens and a pad, so the counselor invited him to draw. Lloyd drew a primitive house with a dog and a person in the yard. At this time the counselor did not discuss the picture. Lloyd was reassured and scheduled for another session.

Lloyd approached this second session by announcing that he had something he wanted to draw. In this second picture he drew a prize fighter in a ring surrounded by spectators. As he drew he said nothing. He seemed to gain satisfaction from what was apparently a working out of his current feelings through the drawing. (The counselor learned later that Lloyd had been in conflict with his science teacher prior to his appointment.)

A third session was marked by Lloyd's discovery of the checkers. As he became more comfortable and trusting, he was able to move beyond drawing to a further exploration of the room. His selection of a game requiring two players was an invitation for interaction. For the next twelve to fifteen visits, student and counselor played checkers. Lloyd kept a careful tally of his win/loss record. (His power struggle—the fighter—was now transferred to the checkerboard.) From grunts, grimaces, and a few infrequent words, he progressed to talking about other things during the games, especially his dislike for the teachers and the effects of his negative interactions with them. The importance of the games and his winning them slowly diminished. Lloyd was now comfortable enough to discuss his difficulties in the context of a verbal, helping relationship with the counselor.

Of course, counseling with Lloyd also involved contact with the administrators, teachers, and family. School testing records indicated that in sixth grade Lloyd had functioned just below the tenth percentile, although up until the fourth grade he had tested at the low average level. Something at that point must have impeded Lloyd's development of verbal skills. The counseling, then, was a series of learning experiences designed to develop the verbal function where it had left off in the fourth grade. When Lloyd's problems were explained to administrators who were concerned with his lack of adjustment, they became more understanding and placed him in a self-contained classroom with remedial reading equipment. Thus, as Lloyd became more comfortable in expressing his anger and frustrations through counseling, he became less of an acting-out student, less of a discipline problem.

Discussion

The methodology presented here for successful counseling with the nonverbal secondary student is certainly broad enough to accommodate a number of different approaches, or counselor styles. For instance, the case history illustrates the use of play primarily as "bait" in the transition from nonverbal to verbal interaction; the fact that feelings were expressed through the play was deemed secondary in importance. Other counselors might want to concentrate on the content of the play or use the play projectively to determine underlying problems and feelings of the student. Counselors of a behavioral bent might use the play as a reward for verbal interchange. It is important, however, not to stop the sequence of steps with the play. The student needs to be brought to the final step of verbalization, as it is verbalization that is recognized and rewarded as a necessary skill by the school and the community at large.

Students vary in their procession through the four steps. Some are quite verbally developed, as can be witnessed by their peer interaction. They become reticent only when confronted by school personnel or by uncomfortable settings—such as counseling. These students move through the outlined steps quite rapidly. Those who are less verbally developed take considerably longer. The counselor needs to be sensitive to the student's progress and needs to tailor reactions accordingly. The length of the sessions can vary according to the amount of time each individual can comfortably tolerate. Experience here is a good guide, as is carefully watching each student. Sessions can vary in length from a few minutes to an entire period and in frequency from one a week to one every other day.

Our experience with this method has been with adolescent students in inner-city junior high school and senior high school settings.

It may also be applicable to children at the elementary level. The characteristics of the given counselee dictate the method more than does age.

Conclusion

Gross motor activities used to bring about increased speech can be a useful device, one that is very suitable for the school counselor. It is especially helpful with students who are verbally underdeveloped, depressed, withdrawn, and anxious. Our experience has indicated that the psychotic, the hard-core characterologically disturbed, and the mature or older student do not respond well to this method. One must then keep in mind that this is only one technique of many that can be employed to facilitate counseling. Counselors must develop their skills generally and then use activity techniques to extend their effectiveness.

SECTION VII

Rational-Emotive
Therapy

*The main goal of the counseling process . . . is to teach
the children the main principles of rational-emotive
psychology—which is based on the assumptions that
people usually become disturbed through acquiring
irrational thoughts, beliefs, and philosophies; and that it
is these philosophies, and not the events that happen to
the individual which truly upset him and which had better
be radically changed if he is to live happily and efficiently.*

—Albert Ellis

Rational-emotive therapy is the result of the therapeutic work of
Albert Ellis. Initially a practicing psychoanalyst, he became dissatisfied with the effectiveness and utility of the classical approach.
What gradually emerged from this dissatisfaction he termed *rational-
emotive therapy* or simply RET. It is a directive model, a cognitive
model, and to some extent a teaching model of therapy. The basic
underlying assumption states that "unreason"—faulty thinking—can
be cured by reason. Rational thought is the key to mental health. It
is the individual's faulty reasoning process that causes disturbance
and maladjustment.

Ellis postulates an A-B-C theory of personality. The "A" factor is
an event that is external to the individual and affects him or her in
some way. The "B" factor is how the individual perceives the event.
In other words, B is what the individual thinks about A. The "C"

factor is behavior of the individual that results from the event (A) and the individual's perception (B). The therapeutic process of RET is primarily focused on the faulty reasoning that frequently takes place at point B and that causes emotional disturbance. The therapist quickly points out the key thought factor and attempts to replace it with a more rational thought. The replacement of irrational thoughts with rational thoughts produces more satisfactory adjustment for the individual and a healthier outlook on life.

The therapist using RET works in a directive manner. It is his or her function to point out faulty thinking and to show the individual how to think and behave more rationally. In this sense, the therapist is a teacher; he or she instructs the client on how to develop a healthier, more adjusted way of behaving. Although the approach was originally developed for adults, it is Ellis's contention that young children can be reasoned with in the same manner as adolescents or adults.

The readings in this section focus on the application of RET to the preadolescent and adolescent population. The opening article, by Ellis, describes in detail the development of rational-emotive therapy and its major theoretical assumptions. In the second reading, Ellis explains how it can be readily adapted to school counseling situations, and he outlines the application process for counselors and teachers. The counselor in this model may function as a therapist or as a consultant to teachers and other professional staff.

The other two articles in this section apply the principles of RET to specific school situations. Edwin Wagner deals with RET from a school psychologist's perspective. His identification of common irrational ideas held by disturbed children may be particularly enlightening for the counselor, and he describes concrete counseling techniques to use with the immature client. Morley Glicken relates RET particularly to the underachieving student.

ALBERT ELLIS

Rational Psychotherapy

The central theme of this paper is that psychotherapists can help their clients to live the most self-fulfilling, creative, and emotionally satisfying lives by teaching these clients to organize and discipline their thinking. Does this mean that *all* human emotion and creativity can or should be controlled by reason and intellect? Not exactly.

The human being may be said to possess four basic processes—perception, movement, thinking, and emotion—all of which are integrally interrelated. Thus, thinking, aside from consisting of bioelectric changes in the brain cells, and in addition to comprising remembering, learning, problem-solving, and similar psychological processes, also is, and to some extent has to be, sensory, motor, and emotional behavior (1, 4). Instead, then, of saying, "Jones thinks about this puzzle," we should more accurately say, "Jones perceives-moves-feels-*thinks* about this puzzle." Because, however, Jones' activity in relation to the puzzle may be *largely* focussed upon solving it, and only *incidentally* on seeing, manipulating, and emoting about it, we may perhaps justifiably emphasize only his thinking.

Emotion, like thinking and the sensori-motor processes, we may define as an exceptionally complex state of human reaction which is

Albert Ellis, "Rational Psychotherapy," *Journal of General Psychology*, 1958, *59*, pp. 35-49. Reprinted by permission.

integrally related to all the other perception and response processes. It is not *one* thing, but a combination and holistic integration of several seemingly diverse, yet actually closely related, phenomena (1).

Normally, emotion arises from direct stimulation of the cells in the hypothalamus and autonomic nervous system (e.g., by electrical or chemical stimulation) or from indirect excitation via sensori-motor, cognitive, and other conative processes. It may theoretically be controlled, therefore, in four major ways. If one is highly excitable and wishes to calm down, one may (a) take electroshock or drug treatments; (b) use soothing baths or relaxation techniques; (c) seek someone one loves and quiet down for his sake; or (d) reason oneself into a state of calmness by showing oneself how silly it is for one to remain excited.

Although biophysical, sensori-motor, and emotive techniques are all legitimate methods of controlling emotional disturbances, they will not be considered in this paper, and only the rational technique will be emphasized. Rational psychotherapy is based on the assumption that thought and emotion are not two entirely different processes, but that they significantly overlap in many respects and that therefore disordered emotions can often (though not always) be ameliorated by changing one's thinking.

A large part of what we call emotion, in other words, is nothing more or less than a certain kind—a biased, prejudiced, or strongly evaluative kind—of thinking. What we usually label as thinking is a relatively calm and dispassionate appraisal (or organized perception) of a given situation, an objective comparison of many of the elements in this situation, and a coming to some conclusion as a result of this comparing or discriminating process (4). Thus, a thinking person may observe a piece of bread, see that one part of it is mouldy, remember that eating this kind of mould previously made him ill, and therefore cut off the mouldy part and eat the non-mouldy section of the bread.

An emoting individual, on the other hand, will tend to observe the same piece of bread, and remember so violently or prejudicedly his previous experience with the mouldy part, that he will quickly throw away the whole piece of bread and therefore go hungry. Because the thinking person is relatively calm, he uses the maximum information available to him—namely, that mouldy bread is bad but non-mouldy bread is good. Because the emotional person is relatively excited, he may use only part of the available information—namely, that mouldy bread is bad.

It is hypothesized, then, that thinking and emoting are closely interrelated and at times differ mainly in that thinking is a more tranquil, less somatically involved (or, at least, perceived), and less activity-directed mode of discrimination than is emotion. It is also hypothesized that among adult humans raised in a social culture thinking and emoting are so closely interrelated that they usually accompany each other, act in a circular cause-and-effect relationship, and in certain (though hardly all) respects are essentially the *same thing*, so that one's thinking *becomes* one's emotion and emoting *becomes* one's thought. It is finally hypothesized that since man is a uniquely sign-, symbol-, and language-creating animal, both thinking and emoting tend to take the form of self-talk or internalized sentences; and that, for all practical purposes, the sentences that human beings keep telling themselves *are* or *become* their thoughts and emotions.

This is not to say that emotion can under *no* circumstances exist without thought. It probably can; but it then tends to exist momentarily, and not to be sustained. An individual, for instance, steps on your toe, and you spontaneously, immediately become angry. Or you hear a piece of music and you instantly begin to feel warm and excited. Or you learn that a close friend has died and you quickly begin to feel sad. Under these circumstances, you may feel emotional without doing any concomitant thinking. Perhaps, however, you do, with split-second rapidity, start thinking "This person who stepped on my toe is a blackguard!" or "This music is wonderful!" or "Oh, how awful it is that my friend died!"

In any event, assuming that you don't, at the very beginning, have any conscious or unconscious thought accompanying your emotion, it appears to be difficult to *sustain* an emotional outburst without bolstering it by repeated ideas. For unless you keep telling yourself something on the order of "This person who stepped on my toe is a blackguard!" or "How could he do a horrible thing like that to me!" the pain of having your toe stepped on will soon die, and your immediate reaction will die with the pain. Of course, you can keep getting your toe stepped on, and the continuing pain may sustain your anger. But assuming that your physical sensation stops, your emotional feeling, in order to last, normally has to be bolstered by some kind of thinking.

We say "normally" because it is theoretically possible for your emotional circuits, once they have been made to reverberate by some physical or psychological stimulus, to keep reverberating under their own power. It is also theoretically possible for drugs or electrical impulses to keep acting directly on your hypothalamus and autonomic nervous system and thereby to keep you emotionally aroused. Usually, however, these steps of continued direct stimulation of the emotion-producing centers do not seem to be important and are limited largely to pathological conditions.

It would appear, then, that positive human emotions, such as feelings of love or elation, are often associated with or result from thoughts, or internalized sentences, stated in some form or variation of the phrase "This is good!" and that negative human emotions, such as feelings of anger or depression, are frequently associated with or result from thoughts or sentences which are stated in some form or variation of the phrase "This is bad!" Without an adult human being's employing, on some conscious or unconscious level, such thoughts and sentences, much of his emoting would simply not exist.

If the hypothesis that sustained human emotion often results from or is directly associated with human thinking and self-verbalization is true, then important corollaries about the origin and perpetuation of states of emotional disturbance, or neurosis, may be drawn. For neurosis would appear to be disordered, over- or under-intensified, uncontrollable emotion; and this would seem to be the result of (and, in a sense, the very same thing as) illogical, unrealistic, irrational, inflexible, and childish thinking.

That neurotic or emotionally disturbed behavior is illogical and irrational would seem to be almost definitional. For if we define it otherwise, and label as neurotic *all* incompetent and ineffectual behavior, we will be including actions of *truly* stupid and incompetent individuals—for example, those who are mentally deficient or brain injured. The concept of neurosis only becomes meaningful, therefore, when we assume that the disturbed individual is *not* deficient or impaired but that he is theoretically capable of behaving in a more mature, more controlled, more flexible manner than he actually behaves. If, however, a neurotic is essentially an individual who acts significantly below his own potential level of behaving, or who defeats his own ends though he is theoretically capable of achieving them, it would appear that he behaves in an illogical, irrational, unrealistic way. Neurosis, in other words, consists of stupid behavior by a non-stupid person.

Assuming that emotionally disturbed individuals act in irrational, illogical ways, the questions which are therapeutically relevant are: (a) How do they originally get to be illogical? (b) How do they keep perpetuating their irrational thinking? (c) How can they be helped to be less illogical, less neurotic?

Unfortunately, most of the good thinking that has been done in regard to therapy during the past 60 years, especially by Sigmund Freud and his chief followers (5, 6, 7), has concerned itself with the first of these questions rather than the second and the third. The assumption has often been made that if psychotherapists discover and effectively communicate to their clients the main reasons why these clients originally became disturbed, they will thereby also discover how their neuroses are being perpetuated and how they can be helped to overcome them. This is a dubious assumption.

Knowing exactly how an individual originally learned to behave illogically by no means necessarily informs us precisely how he *maintains* his illogical behavior, nor what he should do to change it. This is particularly true because people are often, perhaps usually, afflicted with *secondary* as well as *primary* neuroses, and the two may significantly differ. Thus, an individual may originally become disturbed because he discovers that he has strong death wishes against his father and (quite illogically) thinks he should be blamed and punished for having these wishes. Consequently, he may develop some neurotic symptom, such as a phobia against dogs because, let us say, dogs remind him of his father, who is an ardent hunter.

Later on, this individual may grow to love or be indifferent to his father; or his father may die and be no more of a problem to him. His fear of dogs, however, may remain: not because, as some theorists would insist, they still remind him of his old death wishes against his father, but because he now hates himself so violently for *having* the original neurotic symptom—for behaving, to his mind, so stupidly and illogically in relation to dogs—that every time he thinks of dogs his self-hatred and fear of failure so severely upset him that he cannot reason clearly and cannot combat his illogical fear.

In terms of self-verbalization, this neurotic individual is first saying to himself: "I hate my father—and this is awful!" But he ends up by saying: "I have an irrational fear of dogs—and this is awful!" Even though both sets of self-verbalizations are neuroticizing, and his secondary neurosis may be as bad as or worse than his primary one, the two can hardly be said to be the same. Consequently, exploring and explaining to this individual—or helping him gain insight into—the origins of his primary neurosis will not necessarily help him to understand and overcome his perpetuating or secondary neurotic reactions.

If the hypotheses so far stated have some validity, the psychotherapist's main goals should be those of demonstrating to clients that their self-verbalizations have been and still are the prime source of their emotional disturbances. Clients must be shown that their internalized sentences are illogical and unrealistic at certain critical points and that they now have the ability to control their emotions by telling themselves more rational and less self-defeating sentences.

More precisely: the effective therapist should continually keep unmasking his client's past and, especially, his present illogical thinking or self-defeating verbalizations by (a) bringing them to his attention or consciousness; (b) showing the client how they are causing and maintaining his disturbance and unhappiness; (c) demonstrating exactly what the illogical links in his internalized sentences are; and (d) teaching him how to rethink and re-verbalize these (and other similar) sentences in a more logical, self-helping way. Moreover, before the end of the therapeutic relationship, the therapist should not only deal concretely with the client's specific illogical thinking, but should demonstrate to this client what, *in general,* are the main irrational ideas that human beings are prone to follow and what more rational philosophies of living may usually be substituted for them. Otherwise, the client who is released from one specific set of illogical notions may well wind up by falling victim to another set.

It is hypothesized, in other words, that human beings are the kind of animals who, when raised in any society similar to our own, tend to fall victim to several major fallacious ideas; to keep reindoctrinating themselves over and over again with these ideas in an unthinking, autosuggestive manner; and consequently to keep actualizing them in overt behavior. Most of these irrational ideas are, as the freudians have very adequately pointed out, instilled by the individual's parents during his childhood, and are tenaciously clung to because of his attachment to these parents and because the ideas were ingrained, or imprinted, or conditioned before later and more rational modes of thinking were given a chance to gain a foothold. Most of them, however, as the freudians have not always been careful to note, are also instilled by the individual's general culture, and particularly by the media of mass communication in this culture.

What are some of the major illogical ideas or philosophies which, when originally held and later perpetuated by men and women in our civilization, inevitably lead to self-defeat and neurosis? Limitations of space preclude our examining all these major ideas, including their more significant corollaries; therefore, only a few of them will be listed. The illogicality of some of these ideas will also, for the present, have to be taken somewhat on faith, since there again is no space to outline the many reasons *why* they are irrational. Anyway, here, where angels fear to tread, goes the psychological theoretician!

1. The idea that it is a dire necessity for an adult to be loved or approved by everyone for everything he does—instead of his concentrating on his own self-respect, on winning approval for necessary purposes (such as job advancement), and on loving rather than being loved.

2. The idea that certain acts are wrong, or wicked, or villainous, and that people who perform such acts should be severely punished—instead of the idea that certain acts are inappropriate or antisocial, and that people who perform such acts are invariably stupid, ignorant, or emotionally disturbed.

3. The idea that it is terrible, horrible, and catastrophic when things are not the way one would like them to be—instead of the idea that it is too bad when things are not the way one would like them to be, and one should certainly try to change or control conditions so that they become more satisfactory, but that if changing or controlling uncomfortable situations is impossible, one had better become resigned to their existence and stop telling oneself how awful they are.

4. The idea that much human unhappiness is externally caused and is forced on one by outside people and events—instead of the idea that virtually all human unhappiness is caused or sustained by the view one takes of things rather than the things themselves.

5. The idea that if something is or may be dangerous or fearsome one should be terribly concerned about it—instead of the idea that if something is or may be dangerous or fearsome one should frankly face it and try to render it non-dangerous and, when that is impossible, think of other things and stop telling oneself what a terrible situation one is or may be in.

6. The idea that it is easier to avoid than to face life difficulties and self-responsibilities—instead of the idea that the so-called easy way is invariably the much harder way in the long run and that the only way to solve difficult problems is to face them squarely.

7. The idea that one needs something other or stronger or greater than oneself on which to rely—instead of the idea that it is usually far better to stand on one's own feet and gain faith in oneself and one's ability to meet difficult circumstances of living.

8. The idea that one should be thoroughly competent, adequate, intelligent, and achieving in all possible respects—instead of the idea that one should *do* rather than always try to do *well* and that one should accept oneself as a quite imperfect creature, who has general human limitations and specific fallibilities.

9. The idea that because something once strongly affected one's life, it should indefinitely affect it—instead of the idea that one should learn from one's past experiences but not be overly-attached to or prejudiced by them.

10. The idea that it is vitally important to our existence what other people do, and that we should make great efforts to change them in the direction we would like them to be—instead of the idea that other people's deficiencies are largely *their* problems and that putting pressure on them to change is usually least likely to help them do so.

11. The idea that human happiness can be achieved by inertia and inaction—instead of the idea that humans tend to be happiest when they are actively and vitally absorbed in creative pursuits, or when they are devoting themselves to people or projects outside themselves.

12. The idea that one has virtually no control over one's emotions and that one cannot help feeling certain things—instead of the idea that one has enormous control over one's emotions if one chooses to work at controlling them and to practice saying the right kinds of sentences to oneself.

It is the central theme of this paper that it is the foregoing kinds of illogical ideas, and many corollaries which we have no space to delineate, which are the basic causes of most emotional disturbances or neuroses. For once one believes the kind of nonsense included in these notions, one will inevitably tend to become inhibited, hostile, defensive, guilty, anxious, ineffective, inert, uncontrolled, or unhappy. If, on the other hand, one could become thoroughly released from all these fundamental kinds of illogical thinking, it would be exceptionally difficult for one to become too emotionally upset, or at least to sustain one's disturbance for very long.

Does this mean that all the other so-called basic causes of neurosis, such as the Oedipus complex or severe maternal rejection in childhood, are invalid, and that the freudian and other psychodynamic thinkers of the last 60 years have been barking up the wrong tree? Not at all. It only means, if the main hypotheses of this paper are correct, that these psychodynamic thinkers have been emphasizing secondary causes or results of emotional disturbances rather than truly prime causes.

Let us take, for example, an individual who acquires, when he is young, a full-blown Oedipus complex: that is to say, he lusts after his mother, hates his father, is guilty about his sex desires for his mother, and is afraid that his father is going to castrate him. This person, when he is a child, will presumably be disturbed. But, if he is raised so that he acquires none of the basic illogical ideas we have been discussing, it will be virtually impossible for him to *remain* disturbed.

For, as an adult, this individual will not be too concerned if his parents or others do not approve all his actions, since he will be more interested in his *own* self-respect than in *their* approval. He will not believe that his lust for his mother is wicked or villainous, but will accept it as a normal part of being a limited human whose sex desires may easily be indiscriminate. He will realize that the actual danger of his father castrating him is exceptionally slight. He will not feel that because he was once afraid of his Oedipal feelings he should forever remain so. If he still feels it would be improper for him to have sex relations with his mother, instead of castigating himself for even thinking of having such relations he will merely resolve not to carry his desires into practice and will stick determinedly to his resolve. If, by any chance, he weakens and actually has incestuous relations, he will again refuse to castigate himself mercilessly for being weak but will keep showing himself how self-defeating his behavior is and will actively work and practice at changing it.

Under these circumstances, if this individual has a truly logical and rational approach to life in general, and to the problem of Oedipal feelings, in particular, how can he possibly *remain* disturbed about his Oedipal attachment?

Take, by way of further illustration, the case of an individual who, as a child, is continually criticized by his parents, who consequently feels himself loathesome and inadequate, who refuses to take chances at failing at difficult tasks, who avoids such tasks, and who therefore

comes to hate himself more. Such a person will be, of course, seriously neurotic. But how would it be possible for him to *sustain* his
neurosis if he began to think in a truly logical manner about himself
and his behavior?

For, if this individual does use a consistent rational approach to his
own behavior, he will stop caring particularly what others think of
him and will start primarily caring what he thinks of himself. Consequently, he will stop avoiding difficult tasks and, instead of punishing himself for being incompetent when he makes a mistake, will say
to himself something like: "Now this is not the right way to do
things; let me stop and figure out a better way." Or: "There's no
doubt that I made a mistake this time; now let me see how I can
benefit from making it."

This individual, furthermore, will if he is thinking straight, not
blame his defeats on external events, but will realize that he himself
is causing them by his illogical or impractical behavior. He will not
believe that it is easier to avoid facing difficult things, but will realize
that the so-called easy way is always, actually, the harder and more
idiotic one. He will not think that he needs something greater or
stronger than himself to help him, but will independently buckle
down to difficult tasks himself. He will not feel that because he once
defeated himself by avoiding doing things the hard way that he must
always do so.

How, with this kind of logical thinking, could an originally disturbed person possibly maintain and continually revivify his neurosis? He just couldn't. Similarly, the spoiled brat, the worry-wart,
the ego-maniac, the autistic stay-at-home—all of these disturbed individuals would have the devil of a time indefinitely prolonging their
neuroses if they did not continue to believe utter nonsense: namely,
the kinds of basic irrational postulates previously listed.

Neurosis, then, usually seems to originate in and be perpetuated by
some fundamentally unsound, irrational ideas. The individual comes
to believe in some unrealistic, impossible, often perfectionistic goals
—especially the goals that he should always be approved by everyone,
should do everything perfectly well, and should never be frustrated
in any of his desires—and then, in spite of considerable contradictory
evidence, refuses to give up his original illogical beliefs.

Some of the neurotic's philosophies, such as the idea that he
should be loved and approved by everyone, are not entirely inappropriate to his childhood state; but all of them are quite inappropriate

to average adulthood. Most of his irrational ideas are specifically taught him by his parents and his culture; and most of them also seem to be held by the great majority of adults in our society—who theoretically should have been but actually never were weaned from them as they chronologically matured. It must consequently be admitted that the neurotic individual we are considering is often statistically normal; or that ours is a generally neuroticizing culture, in which most people are more or less emotionally disturbed because they are raised to believe, and then to internalize and to keep reinfecting themselves with, arrant nonsense which must inevitably lead them to become ineffective, self-defeating, and unhappy. Nonetheless: it is not absolutely *necessary* that human beings believe the irrational notions which, in point of fact, most of them seem to believe today; and the task of psychotherapy is to get them to disbelieve their illogical ideas, to change their self-sabotaging attitudes.

This, precisely, is the task which the rational psychotherapist sets himself. Like other therapists, he frequently resorts to the usual techniques of therapy which the present author has outlined elsewhere (2, 3), including the techniques of relationship, expressive-emotive, supportive, and insight-interpretive therapy. But he views these techniques, as they are commonly employed, as kinds of preliminary strategies whose main functions are to gain rapport with the client, to let him express himself fully, to show him that he is a worthwhile human being who has the ability to change, and to demonstrate how he originally became disturbed.

The rational therapist, in other words, believes that most of the usual therapeutic techniques wittingly or unwittingly show the client *that* he is illogical and how he *originally* became so. They often fail to show him, however, how he is presently *maintaining* his illogical thinking, and precisely what he must do to change it by building general rational philosophies of living and by applying these to practical problems of everyday life. Where most therapists directly or indirectly show the client that he is behaving illogically, the rational therapist goes beyond this point to make a forthright, unequivocal *attack* on the client's general and specific irrational ideas and to try to *induce* him to adopt more rational ones in their place.

Rational psychotherapy makes a concerted attack on the disturbed individual's irrational positions in two main ways: (a) the therapist serves as a frank counter-propagandist who directly contradicts and denies the self-defeating propaganda and superstitions which the

client has originally learned and which he is now self-propagandis-
tically perpetuating. (b) The therapist encourages, persuades, cajoles,
and at times commands the client to partake of some kind of activity
which itself will act as a forceful counter-propandist agency against
the nonsense he believes. Both these main therapeutic activities are
consciously performed with one main goal in mind: namely, that of
finally getting the client to internalize a rational philosophy of living
just as he originally learned and internalized the illogical propaganda
and superstitions of his parents and his culture.

The rational therapist, then, assumes that the client somehow im-
bibed illogical ideas or irrational modes of thinking and that, without
so doing, he could hardly be as disturbed as he is. It is the therapist's
function not merely to show the client that he has these ideas or
thinking processes but to persuade him to change and substitute for
them more rational ideas and thought processes. If, because the
client is exceptionally disturbed when he first comes to therapy, he
must first be approached in a rather cautious, supportive, permissive,
and warm manner, and must sometimes be allowed to ventilate his
feeling in free association, abreaction, rôle playing, and other expressive techniques, that may be all to the good. But the therapist does
not delude himself that these relationship-building and expressive-
emotive techniques in most instances really get to the core of the
client's illogical thinking and induce him to think in a more rational
manner.

Occasionally, this is true: since the client may come to see,
through relationship and emotive-expressive methods, that he *is* acting illogically, and he may therefore resolve to change and actually
do so. More often than not, however, his illogical thinking will be so
ingrained from constant self-repetitions, and will be so inculcated in
motor pathways (or habit patterns) by the time he comes for therapy, that simply showing him, even by direct interpretation, *that* he
is illogical will not greatly help. He will often say to the therapist:
"All right, now I understand that I have castration fears and that
they are illogical. But I *still* feel afraid of my father."

The therapist, therefore, must keep pounding away, time and
again, at the illogical ideas which underlie the client's fears. He must
show the client that he is afraid, really, not of his father, but of being
blamed, of being disapproved, of being unloved, of being imperfect,
of being a failure. And such fears are thoroughly irrational because
(a) being disapproved is not half so terrible as one *thinks* it is; be-

cause (b) no one can be thoroughly blameless or perfect; because (c) people who worry about being blamed or disapproved essentially are putting themselves at the mercy of the opinion of *others*, over whom they have no real control; because (d) being blamed or disapproved has nothing essentially to do with one's *own* opinion of oneself; etc.

If the therapist, moreover, merely tackles the individual's castration fears, and shows how ridiculous *they* are, what is to prevent this individual's showing up, a year or two later, with some *other* illogical fear—such as the fear that he is sexually impotent? But if the therapist tackles the client's *basic* irrational thinking, which underlies *all* kinds of fear he may have, it is going to be most difficult for this client to turn up with a new neurotic symptom some months or years hence. For once an individual truly surrenders ideas of perfectionism, of the horror of failing at something, of the dire need to be approved by others, of the notion that the world owes him a living, and so on, what else is there for him to be fearful of or disturbed about?

To give some idea of precisely how the rational therapist works, a case summary will now be presented. A client came in one day and said he was depressed but did not know why. A little questioning showed that he had been putting off the inventory-keeping he was required to do as part of his job as an apprentice glass-staining artist. The therapist immediately began showing him that his depression was related to his resenting having to keep inventory and that this resentment was illogical for several reasons:

(a) The client very much wanted to learn the art of glass-staining and could only learn it by having the kind of job he had. His sole logical choice, therefore, was between graciously accepting this job, in spite of the inventory-keeping, or giving up trying to be a glass-stainer. By resenting the clerical work and avoiding it, he was choosing neither of these two logical alternatives, and was only getting himself into difficulty.

(b) By blaming the inventory-keeping, and his boss for making him perform it, the client was being irrational since, assuming that the boss was wrong about making him do this clerical work, the boss would have to be wrong out of some combination of stupidity, ignorance, or emotional disturbance; and it is silly and pointless blaming people for being stupid, ignorant, or disturbed. Besides, maybe the boss was quite right, from his own standpoint, about making the client keep the inventory.

(c) Whether the boss was right or wrong, resenting him for his stand was hardly going to make him change it; and the resentment felt by the client was hardly going to do him, the client, any good or make him feel better. The saner attitude for him to take, then, was that it was too bad that inventory-keeping was part of his job, but that's the way it was, and there was no point in resenting the way things were when they could not, for the moment, be changed.

(d) Assuming that the inventory-keeping was irksome, there was no sense in making it still *more* annoying by the client's continually telling himself how awful it was. Nor was there any point in shirking this clerical work, since he eventually would have to do it anyway and he might as well get this unpleasant task out of the way quickly. Even more important: by shirking a task that he knew that, eventually, he just had to do, he would lose respect for himself, and his loss of self-respect would be far worse than the slight, rather childish satisfaction he might receive from trying to sabotage his boss's desires.

While showing this client how illogical was his thinking and consequent behavior, the therapist specifically made him aware that he must be telling himself sentences like these: "My boss makes me do inventory-keeping. I do not like to do this. . . . There is no reason why I have to do it. . . . He is therefore a blackguard for making me do it. . . . So I'll fool him and avoid doing it. . . . And then I'll be happier." But these sentences were so palpably foolish that the client could not really believe them, and began to finish them off with sentences like: "I'm not really fooling my boss, because he sees what I'm doing. . . . So I'm not solving my problem this way. . . . So I really should stop this nonsense and get the inventory-keeping done. . . . But I'll be damned if I'll do it for him! . . . However, if I don't do it, I'll be fired. . . . But I still don't want to do it for him! . . . I guess I've got to, though. . . . Oh, why must I always be persecuted like this? . . . And why must I keep getting myself into such a mess? . . . I guess I'm just no good. . . . And people are against me. . . . Oh, what's the use?"

Whereupon, employing these illogical kinds of sentences, the client was becoming depressed, avoiding doing the inventory-keeping, and then becoming more resentful and depressed. Instead, the therapist pointed out, he could tell himself quite different sentences, on this order: "Keeping inventory is a bore. . . . But it is presently an essential part of my job. . . . And I also may learn something useful by it. . . . Therefore, I had better go about this task as best I may and thereby get what *I* want out of this job."

The therapist also emphasized that whenever the client found himself intensely angry, guilty, or depressed, there was little doubt that he was then thinking illogically, and that he should immediately question himself as to what was the irrational element in his thinking, and set about replacing it with a more logical element or chain of sentences.

The therapist then used the client's current dilemma—that of avoiding inventory-keeping—as an illustration of his general neurosis, which in his case largely took the form of severe alcoholic tendencies. He was shown that his alcoholic trends, too, were a resultant of his trying to do things the easy way, and of poor thinking preluding his avoidance of self-responsibilities. He was impressed with the fact that, as long as he kept thinking illogically about relatively small things, such as the inventory-keeping, he would also tend to think equally illogically about more important aspects, such as the alcoholism.

Several previous incidents of illogical thinking leading to emotional upheaval in the client's life were then reviewed, and some general principles of irrational thought discussed. Thus, the general principle of blamelessness was raised and the client was shown precisely why it is illogical to blame anyone for anything. The general principle of inevitability was brought up and he was shown that when a frustrating or unpleasant event is inevitable, it is only logical to accept it uncomplainingly instead of dwelling on its unpleasant aspects. The general principle of self-respect was discussed, with the therapist demonstrating that liking oneself is far more important than resentfully trying to harm others.

In this matter, by attempting to show or teach the client some of the general rules of logical living, the therapist tried to go beyond his immediate problem and to help provide him with a generalized mode of thinking or problem solving that would enable him to deal effectively with almost any future similar situation that might arise.

The rational therapist, then, is a frank propagandist who believes wholeheartedly in a most rigorous application of the rules of logic, of straight thinking, and of scientific method to everyday life, and who ruthlessly uncovers every vestige of irrational thinking in the client's experience and energetically urges him into more rational channels.

In so doing, the rational therapist does not ignore or eradicate the client's emotions; on the contrary, he considers them most seriously, and helps change them, when they are disordered and self-defeating, through the same means by which they commonly arise in the first place—that is, by thinking and acting. Through exerting consistent interpretive and philosophic pressure on the client to change his thinking or his self-verbalizations and to change his experiences or his actions, the rational therapist gives a specific impetus to the client's movement toward mental health without which it is not impossible, but quite unlikely, that he will move very far.

Can therapy be effectively done, then, with *all* clients mainly through logical analysis and reconstruction? Alas, no. For one thing, many clients are not bright enough to follow a rigorously rational analysis. For another thing, some individuals are so emotionally aberrated by the time they come for help that they are, at least temporarily, in no position to comprehend and follow logical procedures. Still other clients are too old and inflexible; too young and impressionable; too philosophically prejudiced against logic and reason; too organically or biophysically deficient; or too something else to accept, at least at the start of therapy, rational analysis.

In consequence, the therapist who *only* employs logical reconstruction in his therapeutic armamentarium is not likely to get too far with many of those who seek his help. It is vitally important, therefore, that any therapist who has a basically rational approach to the problem of helping his clients overcome their neuroses also be quite eclectic in his use of supplementary, less direct, and somewhat less rational techniques.

Admitting, then, that rational psychotherapy is not effective with all types of clients, and that it is most helpful when used in conjunction with, or subsequent to, other widely employed therapeutic techniques, I would like to conclude with two challenging hypotheses: (a) that psychotherapy which includes a high dosage of rational analysis and reconstruction, as briefly outlined in this paper, will prove to be more effective with more types of clients than any of the non-rational or semi-rational therapies now being widely employed; and (b) that a considerable amount of—or, at least, proportion of—rational psychotherapy will prove to be virtually the only type of treatment that helps to undermine the basic neuroses (as distinguished from the superficial neurotic symptoms) of many clients, and particularly of many with whom other types of therapy have already been shown to be ineffective.

References

1. Cobb, S. Emotions and Clinical Medicine. New York: Norton, 1950.
2. Ellis, A. New approaches to psychotherapy techniques. *J. Clin. Psychol. Monog. Suppl.*, No. 11. Brandon, Vermont: *J. Clin. Psychol.*, 1955.
3. _____. Psychotherapy techniques for use with psychotics. *Amer. J. Psychother.*, 1955, 9, 452-476.
4. _____. An operational reformulation of some of the basic principles of psychoanalysis. *Psychoanal. Rev.*, 1956, 43, 163-180.
5. Fenichel, O. The Psychoanalytic Theory of Neurosis. New York: Norton, 1945.
6. Freud, S. Basic Writings. New York: Modern Library, 1938.
7. _____. Collected Papers. London: Hogarth Press, 1924-1950.

ALBERT ELLIS

Rational-Emotive Therapy and Its Application to Emotional Education

Rational-Emotive Therapy (RET) is a form of psychotherapy which I originated in the 1950's, after practicing classical psychoanalysis, psychoanalytically-oriented psychotherapy, and various other methods. Although I did as well with these techniques as any of the other practitioners in the field, I began to see with greater clarity that they all were largely ineffective. For no matter how much insight I was able to help my clients achieve, and how emotionally they abreacted and were utterly sure that they now understood themselves deeply and were no longer going to continue their maladaptive behavior, they largely kept making New Years' resolutions to change rather than significantly modifying their actions and actually giving up their phobias, obsessions, compulsions, shirking, psychosomatic reactions, depressions, hostilities, and other complaints. Not that they didn't usually improve to some degree; for they did. But I could see, and they usually could see too, that their improvements were moderate rather than profound, and that they still had a long way to go, after the completion of "successful" therapy, to overcome their basic self-defeating patterns.

Albert Ellis, *Rational-Emotive Therapy and Its Application to Emotional Education*, pamphlet published by the Institute for Rational Living, New York. Reprinted by permission.

I consequently kept trying new techniques and finally realized that unless they included a great deal of activity, both on my part and that of the client, they were not likely to be very effective. For the average client is terribly anxious about doing some act poorly—such as failing in his social, sexual, academic, or vocational affairs—and to quell his anxiety he inhibits himself and stays away from the "dangers" that he has largely created by *defining* these activities as perilous. And no mater how much he tries to convince himself that it is not really too risky or too "awful" to fail, he underlyingly continues to believe that it *is* horrible until he has actually forced himself to do the so-called dangerous act many, many times. Thus, no matter how often he tells himself that seeing black cats is *not* unlucky, he will still tend to superstitiously believe that it is until and unless he forces himself to approach black cats and pats a sufficient number of them on the head.

As I learned this therapeutic truth, I gave up more and more of my psychoanalytic passivity, began to actively disabuse my clients of the irrational beliefs, values, and philosophies that underlay and caused their emotionally disordered behavior, and gave them concrete activity-oriented homework assignments that would help them contradict in practice what I was helping them disbelieve in theory. The better this new therapeutic method worked, the more I thought about *why* it was working and constructed a theory of rational-emotional therapy to back up my procedure.

According to this theory, when an individual becomes emotionally disturbed or suffers from neurotic or psychotic symptoms, which are referred to as point C (emotional Consequences), these are not caused by the Activating events (point A) which occur in his life. These point A events, whether they occur in his infancy or his later years, may cause him all kinds of annoyances, frustrations, and rejections which may *contribute* to his point C Consequences (such as feelings of anxiety, depression, and hostility); but A does not really *cause* C. Instead, the individual has, at point B, a Belief System which more directly and concretely causes his point C dysfunctional Consequences or reactions.

The person's Belief System consists, first, of a set of empirically-based, rational Beliefs (rB's). Thus, when he fails at a job or is rejected by a love partner, at point A, he rationally tells himself, "How unfortunate it is for me to fail! I would much rather succeed or be accepted." If he sticks rigorously to these rational Beliefs, he feels appropriately sorry, regretful, frustrated, and irritated, at point C: but he does *not* feel emotionally upset or destroyed. In order to make himself feel inappropriately or neurotically, he adds the non-empirically-based, irrational Beliefs: "How *awful* it is that I failed! I *must* succeed. I am a *thoroughly worthless person* for failing or for being rejected." *Then* he feels anxious, depressed, or worthless.

In the course of rational-emotive therapy I and my associates show the individual how to vigorously challenge, question, and Dispute (at point D) his irrational Beliefs. Thus, he is shown how to ask himself: "*Why* is it awful that I failed? Who says I *must* succeed? Where is the evidence that I am a worthless person if I fail or get rejected?" And if he persistently and forcefully Disputes his insane ideas, he begins to acquire a new cognitive Effect (at point E): namely, the Beliefs that (1) "It is not awful but only quite inconvenient if I fail." (2) "I don't *have* to succeed; though there are several good reasons why I'd *like* to do so." (3) "I am never a worthless person for failing or being rejected; I am merely a person who has done poorly, for the present, in these particular areas, but who probably can do better later, or can succeed at other things, or can enjoy myself in some ways even if I never succeed at anything very important."

While I am teaching the individual, cognitively and didactically, to see clearly that he *creates* his emotional Consequences by his own values, philosophies, and Beliefs, and that he can understand exactly what these Beliefs are and logically parse them and insist that, to be valid, they'd better be backed by empirical data, I also use powerful evocative-emotive and behaviorist-activity methods of getting him to Dispute his irrational, magic-based attitudes. Thus, on the emotive side, I dramatically confront him, engage in role-playing and behavioral rehearsal exercises, get him to ecounter me and members of his therapy or marathon group, present my own authentic feelings to him, show him that I have unconditional positive regard for him no matter how crummy his behavior may be, and otherwise try to stir him up. Behavioristically, I get him to assume roles that contradict and undermine his irrational Beliefs, give him activity homework assignments that force him to counterattack them in practice, give him practice in assertion training, teach him self reinforcement principles, and otherwise use behavior therapy methods with him. All told, I employ a concerted and comprehensive cognitive-behavior-emotive attack on his self-sabotaging value system, and help change it to a more enjoying, self-actualizing set of values (Ellis, 1962, 1969a, 1971a, 1971b; Ellis and Harper, 1970, 1971).

Although I designed and have kept modifying rational-emotive procedures mainly for the treatment of individuals with emotional disturbances, and although there is now a good deal of experimental and clinical evidence that it works quite well in those areas (Burkhead, 1970; di Loreto, 1971; Maultsby, 1969a, 1969b; Maes and Heimann, 1970; Sharma, 1970; Trexler, 1971), it has also been found that its theory and practice are so simple and direct that they can be used with "normal" populations. Thus, it has been used effectively with organizational executives (Ellis and Blum, 1967; Ellis, 1971b); and it has been found valuable when used with children in regular classroom situations (Daly, 1971; Ellis, 1969c, 1972a, 1972b; Glicken, 1968; Lafferty, Dennerll, and Rettich, 1964; Wolfe, 1970).

How, exactly, can rational-emotive psychology be employed in regular schooling? To answer this question, The Institute for Advanced Study in Rational Psychotherapy has started a private school for normal children, the Living School, which it operates in New York City. The purpose of the school is to teach children the regular elements of academic education; but at the same time to provide them prophylactically with emotional education. And by emotional education we do not merely mean encouraging the children to enjoy themselves, to make freer choices of what they do in school, or to express themselves affectively. These are all worthy goals; but at most they are merely aids to, rather than the essence of, what we conceive of as emotional training.

For in RET we do not merely see the child as a product of his early environment; nor do we believe that he is naturally a fully healthy, self-actualizing, creative creature and that his parents and his society unduly restrict, constrict, and warp him so that he soon becomes alienated from himself and the world, hence moderately or severely disturbed. Instead, we think that his alienation, his ultraconventionalism, and his emotional constriction or over-impulsiveness result from his innate as well as his acquired tendencies to think crookedly, to be grandiosely demanding, and to refuse to accept hassle-filled reality (Ellis, Wolfe, and Moseley, 1966).

Children, in other words, *naturally* acquire several basic irrational ideas which they tend to perpetuate and to sabotage their lives with forever. They religiously, devoutly believe that they "absolutely *need* and utterly *must have* others' approval; that they've *got to* achieve outstandingly and thereby prove how worthwhile they are; that people who act unjustly or inconsiderately to them are bad, wicked, or villainous, and should be severely condemned and punished for their villainy; that it is awful and catastrophic when things are not the way they would like them to be; that obnoxious situations and events *make them* feel anxious, depressed, or angry; that if they endlessly worry about something they can control whether or not it happens; that it is easier for them to avoid than to face certain life difficulties and responsibilities; and that they absolutely *need* a well-ordered, certain, pretty perfect universe. These are the same kinds of crazy ideas which most human adults more or less tend to believe; but children often believe them more rigidly and profoundly.

The main reason for the Living School's existence is to teach its pupils, on innumerable occasions and in many ways, that these typically human irrational ideas do not hold water, will inevitably lead to poor results, can be radically changed, and would better be surrendered and surrendered and surrendered, until the child no longer often holds them. This teaching, moreover, is designed to be done almost exclusively by the regular school teacher, and not by psychologists, counselors, or other special personnel. The teachers are trained—along with the psychotherapists that we train at the Institute for Advanced Study in Rational Psychotherapy—to understand and use rational-emotive methods. Then they employ them with the children. Here are some of the ways in which the rational-emotive philosophy is taught:

1. Regular lessons in rational thinking are given. The children are shown how to distinguish rational ideas—such as "I would like to do well in school because it has certain specific advantages"—from irrational ones—such as "I *must* do well in school because otherwise I am a worthless individual." Discussions of emotional behavior, and how one produces appropriate and inappropriate reactions in oneself, are frequently held.

2. Emotional problems that arise during classroom situations are often dealt with immediately as they arise, and are used for purposes of general emotional education. If Jane is shy about reciting, she may be shown that her shyness really consists of extreme anxiety about what others would think of her if she did not recite perfectly well; and she is shown how to challenge and dispute the notion that she *has* to do well in this or any other respect. If Jane does not soon see what her real problem is and how to handle it, other children in the class are asked what they think she is doing to upset and constrict herself and what she could do instead of this.

3. In situations outside the classroom—as, for example, when the children are in the playground or are on a trip to a museum—destructive and disruptive behavior is called to their attention and alternative, more constructive ways of behaving are considered and suggested.

4. Stories, fables, plays, and other forms of literature are employed to put across rational philosophies of living. Stories, such as the conventional fairy tales, are frequently read and discussed to show the children that the main point of such stories may well be an entirely irrational notion—such as the notion that Cinderella completely *needs* the love of her stepmother and stepsisters, a fairy godmother, and a fairy prince, before she accepts her existence as being potentially enjoyable and worthwhile—and that this notion can be observed, logically parsed, and rejected.

5. Audiovisual aids—such as filmstrips, films, recordings, and video tapings—are employed to help the children understand and utilize some of the rational-emotive principles of living.

6. Group counseling is regularly held, with the teacher (at first under psychotherapeutic supervision and later on her own) talking to six or eight of the children about their personal problems, including their home problems, and showing them (just as regular RET therapists show their group counseling adolescents and adult clients) how to handle these problems.

7. Individual sessions are often held between the teacher and a child who is temporarily upset about something, to get at the basic sources of his upsetness and to show him exactly what he is doing to make himself disturbed and what he can do to undisturb himself.

8. Behavior therapy principles and methods are employed, so that the children are rewarded or reinforced for some of their effective and constructive conduct and penalized for some of their ineffectual behavior. At the same time, however, that the children are penalized if they act disruptively or antisocially, a strong attempt is made to help them distinguish between penalty and punishment—to show them that *they* are never damnable or rotten, even though some of their *deeds* and *performances* are execrable and are not allowable.

9. Instead of trying to create an atmosphere of schools without failure, as Glasser (1969) and certain other affective educators try to do, the teachers in the Living School sometimes deliberately go to the other extreme and pretend that the children have failed at some task or test when they actually have not done badly at it. Their

reactions to this "failure" are then elicited and analyzed, in an attempt to show them that although it is good (for practical purposes) to succeed and unfortunate to fail, they can always unconditionally accept themselves and strive for an enjoyable life *whether or not* they fail at academic or other tasks.

10. Various means of encouraging the children to express themselves openly and authentically and to reveal their real feelings about themselves and others are employed. Through games, plays, role-playing, sports, art, writing, and other means they are stimulated to show what they truly think and feel. But just as rational-emotive group and encounter therapy does not merely *emphasize* authentic self-expression but *also* tries to show the group member that some of his feelings (such as assertion) are appropriate and healthy while other feelings (such as rage) are inappropriate and unhealthy, so do the teachers try to help the children acknowledge and understand the feelings they express, and consider the creation of alternative emotions when they are over- or under-reacting to life's stimuli. Rational-emotive psychology makes concrete use of encounter methods with adults, particularly in the marathon weekends of rational encounter which I and my associates give in many parts of the country every year (Ellis, 1969*b*); and it also uses these methods of affective encountering and release with the children in the Living School. But it always places them within a cognitive-behavioral framework and does not see them as sacrosanct or highly efficient in their own right.

11. As noted above, RET is one of the main psychotherapies that has pioneered in the giving of explicit, activity-oriented homework assignments to adolescent and adult clients. Similarly, the teachers in the Living School use rational-emotive methods of working with the children's problems while they are in the classroom and also of giving them emotionally educating homework. Thus, if Robbie is shy and withdrawn in his relations with his neighborhood peers, he may be assigned the task of trying to make one new friend or acquaintance a week; and if Susan fights incessantly with her sister over which TV program they are going to watch, she may be assigned to try going along with her sister's choices for a few weeks, while convincing herself that it is not awful, horrible, and catastrophic that she is being deprived of the programs she most wants to see.

In many important ways, in sum, rational-emotive methodology is applied to emotional education. And what emerges at the Living

School is a full fledged meaning of this term. For RET is intrinsically didactic, pedagogic, instructional, and *educative*: more concretely and more fully, perhaps, than any other widely used form of psychotherapy. Not every therapeutic orientation is easily adaptable to teaching. Freud's psychoanalysis has largely failed in this respect; while Adler's individual psychology has succeeded much better. I think that we shall eventually show, in our work with normal youngsters, that rational-emotive psychology is as beautifully designed for the educative process as this process is already largely designed for it. For schooling, essentially, is a concerted, long-range attempt to help the child grow up in many ways and assume adult roles and responsibilities which will presumably be creative, productive, and enjoyable. And rational-emotive schooling, as we experimentally practice it at the Living School, is a concerted, long-range attempt to help the child grow up emotionally and to become a reasonably independent-thinking, self-actualizing, minimally disturbed person.

And by person I mean *human* person. For RET is one of the most humanistic psychologies in contemporary use. It has no truck whatever with anything that smacks of the superhuman or the subhuman. It believes that people can fully accept themselves as enormously fallible, incredibly human beings, who have no magical powers, and who reside in an immense but still material and unmystical universe which doesn't really give a special damn about them and most probably never will. It holds that there are no gods nor devils; that people have no immortal souls or immutable essences; that immortality is a silly, grandiose myth; that there is no absolute truth; and that although reasoning and the logico-empirico method of validating reality have their distinct limits (because they, too, originate with and are employed by eminently fallible humans), they are the best means we have of understanding ourselves and the world and would better be fairly rigorously applied in the understanding of life processes.

Rational-emotive education, consequently, teaches children to fully accept themselves as humans, to give up all pretensions of reaching heaven or finding the Holy Grail, to stop denigrating the value of themselves or any other person, to accept their mortality, and to become unabashed long-range hedonists: that is, individuals who heartily strive to have a ball in the here-and-now *and* in their future lives without giving too much heed to what others dogmatically think that they *should, ought,* or *must* do. Is this humanistic way of life, as explicitly taught—and I mean *taught*—in the Living

School going to help us raise saner, happier, and more creative people? I, naturally, think so; but we shall see!

References

Burkhead, D. E. *The reduction of negative affect in human subjects: a laboratory test of rational-emotive psychotherapy.* Doctoral dissertation, Western Michigan University, 1970.

Daly, S. Using reason with deprived pre-school children. *Rational Living*, 1971, 5(2), 12-19.

di Loreto, A. *Comparative psychotherapy.* Chicago: Aldine, 1971.

Ellis, A. *Reason and emotion is psychotherapy.* New York: Lyle Stuart, 1962.

Ellis, A. *How to live with a neurotic.* New York: Crown Publishers and Award Books, 1969*a*.

Ellis, A. A weekend of rational encounter. In Burton, A. (Ed.), *Encounter.* San Francisco: Jossey-Bass, 1969*b*.

Ellis, A. Teaching emotional education in the classroom. *School Health Review*, November 1969*c*, 10-13.

Ellis, A. *Growth through reason.* Palo Alto: Science and Behavior Books, 1971*a*.

Ellis, A. *Rational sensitivity: self-fulfillment for executives.* New York: Citadel Press, 1971*b*.

Ellis, A. *Emotional education.* New York: Julian Press, 1972*a*.

Ellis, A. Emotional education with groups of normal school children. In Ohlsen, M. M. (Ed.), *Counseling children in groups.* New York: Holt, Rinehart and Winston, 1972*b*.

Ellis, A., and Blum, M. L. Rational training: a new method of facilitating management and labor relations. *Psychological Reports*, 1967, 20, 1267-1284.

Ellis, A., and Harper, R. M. *A guide to successful marriage.* (Original title: *Creative Marriage*). New York: Lyle Stuart and Hollywood: Wilshire Books, 1970.

Ellis, A., and Harper, R. M. *A guide to rational living.* Englewood Cliffs, N.J.: Prentice-Hall and Hollywood: Wilshire Books, 1971.

Ellis, A., Wolfe, J. L., and Moseley, S. *How to prevent your child from becoming a neurotic adult.* New York: Crown Publishers, 1966.

Glasser, W. *Schools without failure.* New York: Harper and Row, 1969.

Glicken, M. D. Rational counseling: a new approach to children. *Journal of Elementary Guidance and Counseling*, 1968, 2(4), 261-267.

Lafferty, C., Dennerll, D., and Rettich, P. A. A creative school mental health program. *National Elementary Principal*, 1964, 43(5), 28-35.

Maes, W. R., and Heimann, R. A. *The comparison of three approaches to the reduction of test anxiety.* Washington: Office of Education, 1970.

Maultsby, Jr., M. C. The implications of successful rational-emotive psychotherapy for comprehensive psychosomatic disease. Manuscript, 1969*a*.

Maultsby, Jr., M. C. Psychological and biochemical test change in patients who were paid to engage in psychotherapy. Manuscript, 1969*b*.

Sharma, K. L. *A rational group therapy approach to counseling anxious underachievers.* Thesis, University of Alberta, 1970.

Trexler, L. D. *Rational-emotive therapy, placebo, and no-treatment effects on public-speaking anxiety.* Ph.D. Thesis, Temple University, 1971.

EDWIN E. WAGNER

Rational Counseling
with School Children

Rational Counseling is a newly developed approach to counseling with school aged children which can be easily and effectively applied by the school psychologist and school counselor. It has been developed and adapted in collaboration with a number of school psychologists and is now being successfully utilized within school systems, particularly by Summit County school psychologists. Its efficacy is based not on high sounding and involved theory but on practical, day to day use with children in the primary and secondary grades with a variety of psychological problems. After about two years of experience with Rational Counseling we are able to state, without equivocation that, while it is no panacea, it does work.

Rational Counseling is based on the theory and practice of a psychotherapeutic technique called Rational Therapy which was originated and promulgated by a New York psychologist, Dr. Albert Ellis. Ellis, an erstwhile psychoanalyst, became dissatisfied with the inordinate time demands and uncertain outcomes associated with the use of analytically oriented therapies. Over a period of time he developed Rational Therapy, or as it is sometimes called, Rational-Emotive Therapy, and has used it successfully with countless patients. Ellis has published a great deal of material on his technique

Edwin E. Wagner, "Rational Counseling with School Children," *School Psychologist*, 1965, 9. Reprinted by permission.

and has recently written a definitive textbook entitled *Reason and Emotion in Psychotherapy.*

The fundamental premise upon which Rational Therapy is predicated is that thoughts produce emotions. That is, it is impossible to generate a human emotion without a thought or cerebral signal of some kind which triggers off the feeling. Since, for Ellis, thoughts are largely words or sentences which we tell ourselves (implicit verbalizations), we literally talk ourselves into a disturbed condition. Most people believe that when a situation occurs (let us call the situation "A") they automatically respond with various emotions and attitudes (let us call the response "C"). Actually, there is an intervening process, "B," which follows "A" and causes "C." This process usually consists of simple declarative sentences of "self-talk" which an individual makes to himself and which consequently produces emotions and behavior at point "C." Most of us pay little attention to the "B" part because it happens so quickly and so often that we have become habituated to it. We believe, erroneously, that "A" causes "C" when, in fact "A" causes "B" and "B" causes "C."

Perhaps a brief example will make this clear. Let us suppose that, as you are walking down the street, another person very rudely and forcefully bumps into you. Very likely you would react with anger and would attribute your ire to the fact that you were so roughly and impolitely accosted. That is you believe that "A" caused "C." Actually, what really happened (so Ellis tells us), was that after being jostled you very quickly said something to yourself like, "That big oaf shouldn't have bumped into me—he's uncouth, uncivilized, and downright despicable." Maybe these wouldn't be your exact words but you would have to say something fairly similar to this, perhaps even a resort to a vulgar epithet, in order to make yourself angry.

In order to further develop this contention, let's take the example one step further. Suppose you did become angry and suppose you were all set to give this discourteous ruffian a "piece of your mind" when suddenly, glancing at his face, you realized that he was blind, that he accidentally bumped into you. Perhaps you then would react with a feeling of remorse or embarrassment by saying something quite different to yourself like "What a clod I am, how could I be heartless enough to get angry at a poor, helpless blind man?" The important point is that in either case, whether you became angry or contrite, you did so because of the internalized sentences at "B." Similarly, individuals who entertain irrational and highly charged emotional attitudes toward themselves, their parents, their teachers or the world in general are saying something irrational to themselves at point "B." Rational Therapy and its derivative, Rational Counseling, make the client aware of these "B" statements so that they can be brought to light, analyzed, attacked, and expunged. Thus, with this type of therapy or counseling, the individual's problems are attacked directly and swiftly by dealing with the proximal cause of his disturbances, his internalized sentences. Ellis has listed a large number of typically "neurotic" statements which are common to our culture. For the sake of brevity, these statements can usually be reduced to three categories.

1. Catastrophic sentences, e.g., "Isn't it terrible that I flunked my history exam!" (Actually, it is unfortunate but not terrible.)

2. Shoulds, oughts, and musts, e.g., "My teacher should treat me more fairly." (Why should she? It would be nice if all teachers were fair, accepting, and adjusted, but why must they be?)

3. Blame—either self-blame (guilt) or other blame (hostility), e.g., "My teacher is a dirty rat because she is unfair to me." (Your teacher may be ignorant or disturbed but she is not inherently a blamable person simply because she is unjust or prejudiced.)

During Rational Counseling the client is explicitly asked to pay attention to his sentences. Then, when he recognizes that he does interpret relatively neutral stimuli through exaggerated and emotionally toned internal modifiers, he is helped by the counselor to attack these statements and to replace them with more rational and sensible beliefs. Lately, the client is urged to immediately put his insights into practice by altering his behavior in accordance with his new set of implicit sentences.

With certain modifications this Rational approach can be directly transferred to the school setting. In fact, Rational Counseling embodies a number of distinct advantages which, in our opinion, makes it superior to any other technique yet devised for use by the school psychologist or school counselor.

Here are some of the advantages of Rational Counseling:

1. Rational Counseling is easy to learn and easy to apply. Our experience has shown that the average school psychologist, having familiarized himself with the literature and listening to representative tapes, can do a respectable job with this technique after a few trial runs.

2. School problems are often pressing and require swift intervention and solution. Questions of transfer, promotion, suspension, etc. are sometimes imperative and the counselor is not permitted the luxury of the months of therapeutic contacts usually required with analytic or client-centered techniques. Rational Counseling permits immediate intervention and a direct attack on the presenting problems.

3. Rational Counseling teaches the child to live in his environment. The non-blaming attitude which is the essence of this technique helps the child to accept teachers, parents, and peers and to make the best of an imperfect world.

4. The basic principles of Rational Counseling are easy to understand and apply and can be adapted to children of most ages and IQ's. It gives the child something concrete to work with and provides immediate environmental reinforcement. The child is not burdened with complicated theories and "dynamics" which he often cannot understand but is given a direct explanation of why he is maladjusted and is shown, in simple terms, how to become adjusted.

5. Children, having lived in this neurotic culture for a shorter period of time than their parents, are usually less indoctrinated than adults and make good subjects for Rational Counseling.

6. Rational Counseling, being shorter than most other techniques, permits greater and more effective use of the counselor's limited time and does not necessarily require the cooperation of recalcitrant or hostile parents. Furthermore, should the counselor fail to help the student it is unlikely that he will hurt him. Rational Counseling makes no dangerous incursions into the unconscious, it militates against irrational anti-social behavior, and it discourages rumination, wool-gathering and preoccupation with historical antecedents or "dynamics."

While Rational Counseling was based on Ellis' Rational Therapy, experience indicated that certain modifications were required. For one thing we soon found that typical "neurotic" verbalizations of children differed somewhat from those of adults. To be optimally effective in dealing with children it is necessary to recognize and even anticipate what a child is saying to himself. While the list is by no means exhaustive, here are some common verbalizations and beliefs found in psychologically disturbed children:

1. It is terrible if parents deny love, play favorites, fight among themselves or behave in other irrational ways. (Instead of realizing

that parents are human and while it is too bad if one's parents are disturbed, it is by no means a catastrophe.)

2. Teachers (principals, counselors) should be perfect, e.g., fair, interesting, knowledgeable, understanding. (Teachers are human too and quite often disturbed. It is more rational to accept than to condemn an inefficient teacher.)

3. Self-worth depends on achievement vis a vis a particular peer group, e.g., one must be good at athletics, popular with boys, good looking or tops scholastically. (Real enjoyment comes from doing your best and becoming actively involved in life. Achievement is nice but it has nothing intrinsically to do with self-worth.)

4. Sexual misapprehensions, e.g., it is wrong to masturbate, it is bad to pet, a male teenager must be a sophisticated Don Juan or a sexual acrobat in order to be a "Man." (Sexual thoughts or acts are never wicked in themselves although, to be sure, certain types of sexual behavior are inefficient because they get you in trouble. Sex in this culture is a learned, complicated set of behaviors and it is natural enough for a young person not to be highly knowledgeable and competent.)

5. It is horrible that grownups do not understand or cater to young people. (Why is it horrible? It is not necessary to always obtain sympathy or to always get the car in order to be happy. Frustration is part of living and growing up.)

In addition to being able to quickly spot the kind of verbalization which lies behind the child's disturbance, experience has shown that it also is advantageous to employ some special techniques or gambits such as:

1. Employing the language level or patois of the child. Don't talk down to him but avoid sophisticated or "grownup" language.

2. Using humor liberally, e.g., it is perfectly sound to laugh good naturedly about an obviously disturbed teacher so the child can learn not to take her seriously.

3. Emphasizing the self-defeating aspects of maladjustive behavior and de-emphasizing the moral, social, or disciplinary aspects.

4. Making liberal use of concrete examples.

5. Treating the child as an equal.

6. Using obvious internalized sentences as an ice-breaker, e.g., "Most boys your age tell themselves it's wrong to masturbate. Do you feel this way?"

7. Admitting that other people are often inefficient and disturbed instead of rigidly insisting that significant adults are always right.

8. Emphasizing the need for homework and practice. It is useful to compare the development of rational thinking to a series of homework assignments which take time and effort but pay off in the long run.

Summarizing, Rational Counseling consists of first accepting the client as a fallible but not blamable human being. The counselor then explores the internalized nonsense which the youngster is telling himself, keeping as close to the actual verbiage and individual frame of reference as possible. Next, the self-defeating and irrational nature of these sentences are pointed out and the child is urged to replace them with more logical and realistic thoughts. Lastly, the necessity for practice and follow up is stressed with a final objecctive of eliciting change in behavior. Rational Counseling is thus explanatory, educative and didactic—very much like teaching.

It is not possible, due to limitations of space, to delve into the intricacies and finer points of Rational Counseling. It is our hope, however, that this paper may have whetted the therapeutic appetite for further study in this area and may stimulate the reader to explore this approach in his own counseling. We think Rational Counseling is ideally suited to the problems and limitations of school counseling. Why not give it a try?

MORLEY D. GLICKEN

Rational Counseling:
A Dynamic Approach
to Children

As a by-product of psychoanalytic thought, few treatment groups
have quite the mystique of the latency-aged child. One has only to
read any number of famous studies by Freud, Ericson, Anna Freud
and other psychoanalytic thinkers to be somewhat awed by their
often brilliant "detective" work. The unfortunate result of this complex, difficult approach has been a great deal of illogical, unsup-
ported thinking concerning the latency-aged child with emotional
difficulties and an effective treatment for the resolution of his problems.

Psychoanalytic theory suggests that children are often unable to
discuss their problems because they tend to repress important material. It further assumes that one can often uncover relevant motives,
events, and traumas by providing an atmosphere in which the child
can relate freely. We call this atmosphere or approach "Play Therapy." It is assumed that, either in play or in his random dialogue
with the therapist, the child will often unconsciously bring to the
surface important material. As the child forms a close, healthy relationship with the therapist, he begins to develop insight into his

Glicken, M. D. Rational counseling: a dynamic approach to children. *Elementary School
Guidance and Counseling*, 1968, 2(4), 261-267. Copyright 1968 American Personnel and
Guidance Association. Reprinted with permission.

feelings. This insight, when properly developed, frees the child of his difficulties and allows changes in behavior to develop gradually.

While few therapists in the school setting rely completely on the analytic approach, many remnants of it remain which tend to decrease the effectiveness of the therapist in his treatment of children.

To begin with, it is, in the author's opinion, fallacious to assume that most children cannot readily and quickly discuss their problems in regard to either school or home. Most children in the author's elementary school social work caseload can and do discuss their difficulties without being coaxed by saccharine words or play therapy.

Too often we overtly or covertly convey to the child the same ego-deflating attitudes of the parent when we assume that, because of his age, the child is incapable of involving himself in a treatment-oriented verbal dialogue. By assuming that we need play objects or other gimmicks with most children, we effectively undermine the child's ability to discuss problems and resolve conflicts and we may often avoid facing important issues by turning the therapy session into a fun-and-games time for clay throwing and paint splashing.

This avoidance of issues seems grounded in our illogical premise that disturbed children are too brittle to face their problems actively. This is just not true. Many disturbed children have undergone years of the most violent psychologically damaging conditioning one can imagine and still function beyond our expectations.

Another psychoanalytic remnant too often inculcated in our treatment of children is the notion that once a child understands his feelings more accurately change will take place. Understanding feelings seldom precipitates change since disturbed feelings are end products of pathological decision making and are in themselves only symptoms. What occurs too often is that the therapist is a "nice" person and the child consciously improves to please the therapist or to gain the therapist's love. Such improvement sometimes is long term, but more often than not it disappears when treatment ends. When treatment fails we often wooden-leggedly assert that the child has only intellectual understanding and lacks the emotional understanding necessary for change, or that the child lacks motivation and doesn't really want to change because he fears losing the attention of his mother, with whom he is still involved.

What should be obvious to most child therapists is that we are woefully inefficient, ineffectual, and inaccurate in our treatment of children. We have neither a very good theory nor a very useful treatment approach in psychoanalytically oriented therapy, counseling or casework—all of which mean the same. We, particularly those of us who work within the reality confines of a school setting, should be thinking more in terms of an effective, short term, truly depth-oriented approach.

If the author's experiences are at all transferable to other school counselors, it is suggested that Rational-Emotive Psychotherapy might be just such an approach. The rational approach holds that disturbed emotions, the outward sign of malfunctioning, develop because the child acquires irrational thoughts, beliefs, attitudes, or philosophies about himself and his environment (Ellis, 1962). When a child bases a decision upon an illogical idea the outcome is often a self-defeating emotion or act. It is held that if the counselor can, by aggressively challenging him, help the child see the illogic of his thinking then the child can often significantly improve his functioning. This means that the therapist must be able to isolate the illogical idea, prove to the child why it might be illogical and what harm it does to him, and then help the child accept a saner view of himself and his world by actively encouraging and supporting the child in his attempt to live more logically.

It might sound at this point as if the rational therapist is a walking logician without feelings or emotions. Not so. He challenges only disturbed ideas, not all ideas. People will always emote and feel no matter how logical or bright. But the healthier the internal logic and self-spoken sentences, the healthier their outward manifestations. This assumes, of course, that people think before they act even if the thought is spontaneous or illogical. If we see a dog at the door we might react a number of ways, usually not violently. However, if the dog is foaming at the mouth, our reaction often indicates fear or panic. We then consciously make choices based upon past experiences before we act.

Probably most helpful to the rational therapist is a good working understanding of common irrational ideas. Most of the children seen by the author use one or more of the following irrational ideas in making self-defeating decisions (Ellis, 1962).

1. It is a dire necessity to be loved or approved by virtually every significant person in our environment.

2. One must be thoroughly competent, adequate, and achieving in all possible respects if one is to consider oneself worthwhile.

3. It is catastrophic when things are not the way one would very much like them to be.

4. It is easier to avoid than to face life difficulties and self-responsibilities.

5. One's past history is an all important determiner of one's present behavior; because something once affected strongly one's life, it will indefinitely have a similar effect.

Along with isolation of illogical ideas must come the counselor's belief, conveyed directly to the child, that the child is capable of resolving his problems with minimal intervention from the therapist. The therapist functions essentially as an educator by teaching the child a new way of looking at himself and his world. In no way does he, as is so common in many forms of therapy, subtly encourage the child to improve by offering the child his love. The child is encouraged to improve for his *own* benefit, *not* the benefit of parents or therapist. Too many children who function well in the school setting mainly to win the approval of their parents face extreme frustration when the parent's interest wanes. The rational approach attempts to help the child learn that achieving to win the acceptance or love of others is often self-defeating. Not everyone can possibly like or accept us. If one attempts to win the approval of virtually everyone, the few who refuse to accept us, particularly if they are parents or other significant persons in our environment, tend to negate the other 98 percent who like us. More important than demanding total acceptance of others is the child's ability to relate more positively toward difficult objects in his life, be they disagreeable parents or a rejecting teacher. The concept of forming healthy working relationships rather than unhealthy "love" relationships should be stressed by the therapist.

Once the child has a fairly good understanding of the rational approach and has been able to isolate his irrational thoughts, the therapist begins assigning homework in the form of practical experiences geared to help the child overcome his school or home difficulty.

A most common type of difficulty in the worker's caseload is the underachiever. Very often the underachiever is a relatively bright child so brainwashed into perfectionist thinking by his demanding parents that school becomes a nightmare of continual defeat. The underachiever often is convinced that unless he can do virtually everything well, he is really a terribly worthless person. If he fails to achieve competence in a subject quickly, he gives up. Effort, he irrationally maintains, might indicate that he really isn't a very competent person. After all, he might really try to master a subject and only get a B or C, and that, he equally illogically declares, would be catastrophic, indicative of the fact that he really *is* the worthless, inadequate person he believes himself to be. Consequently, the defeatist attitude or belligerent facade is often an excellent coverup for his own fears (Glicken, 1967). Not trying but still passing at least gives him the excuse that had he *tried* harder, he would have done better. He easily lapses into lethargy, continues avoiding the issue, and is, to all practical outward appearances, poorly motivated. On the contrary, the underachiever in almost all instances is a terribly ambitious, power hungry, perfectionistic child.

Once the therapist isolates the underlying illogical ideas of the underachiever, he begins to encourage attempts at new behavior by assigning homework. The child might be encouraged to complete his classroom paper no matter how poor a job he does just to prove that part of a job is better than none at all and that improved competence in anything requires practice. The child might also be assigned the task of trying to point out to the parent that the more he (the child) attempts to do all things well, the more difficult it might become, because of his increased internal stress, to do *anything* well. The child attempts to show the parent that he can't become the perfect student overnight and possibly that he never will. He might, however, by continued practice significantly improve with time. The therapist at no time lectures the child on the need to get good grades. Instead, he helps the child see that if he wants good grades for the right reasons (his own feeling of accomplishment, *not* just to please his parents), practice and effort rather than Jehovian thinking are the most realistic means to achieve his goal.

Of course, no child lives in the therapist's perfect world and he sometimes makes mistakes in his attempts to change. The therapist non-judgmentally helps the child break through these blocks. In most cases children do follow through on assignments, and over the past two years the author has noted significant improvement in about 90 percent of all cases referred using such measurements as pre- and post-therapy personality testing, improvement in grades, teacher reports, and evaluation of parents. (The author's caseload is unscreened and consists of a good number of underachievers, acterouters, pre-delinquents, neurotics, and even some borderline psychotics.)

To serve the children in the author's caseload more effectively, teachers are seen in group consultation sessions and an attempt is made to help them gain insight not only into the child's problems, but also into ways in which the teacher can cope more effectively with the troubled child in the classroom (Glicken, 1968). This often means that teachers must begin questioning their own ideas and attitudes toward teaching, particularly as it relates to the troubled child. The group acts as a stimulating force to educate, to motivate, and often to change the way teachers teach. Many school mental health workers facing the awesome number of troubled children in the school as compared to static treatment resources, are beginning to see the importance of preparing teachers to cope with children, not necessarily as therapists, but as knowledgeable, helpful adults who are in contact with the child a good part of his day. No thinking therapist should ever underestimate the treatment impact of a good teacher on a child.

Parents too are seen by the worker and an attempt is made to help them cope with their troubled child more rationally. The author has been impressed with the similarities between the Rational and Adlerian approaches and has been active in developing, for the referral of parents in his school district, a family education facility which uses the Adlerian concept of counseling families before groups of other parents. Such a facility helps parents resolve their child management difficulties by questioning their internal logic as it relates to the child and his behavior and role in the home.

It should be clear to the reader that the rational approach is not effective for all therapists. Its effectiveness is highly dependent upon the therapist's ability to aggressively intervene in the therapeutic dialogue by challenging the child's illogical thinking and then by encouraging new thinking so that improved behavior may result. What must also be stressed is the therapist's acceptance of the *person,* though not necessarily his *behavior.* If properly done it is possible to be therapeutically critical of the child's behavior and thinking and yet convey to him your acceptance of his worthiness as a person.

The rational approach also challenges the premise that one's past behavior is the all-important determiner of one's present and future behavior. It stresses instead changing "here and now" thinking. As such, it has been found to be a highly effective treatment approach for use in the school setting with all varieties of pathology.

References

Ellis, A. *Reason and emotion in psychotherapy.* N.Y.: Lyle Stuart, 1962.

Glicken, M. Counseling children: two methods. *Rational Living,* 1967, *1, 2,* p. 36.

Glicken, M. The training of teachers: a mental health issue. *Illinois School Journal,* 1968, *47*(1), 259-261.

SECTION VIII

Reality Therapy

*Through accepting responsibility for one's own behavior,
and acting maturely to constructively change their
behavior, individuals find they are no longer lonely,
symptoms begin to resolve and they are more likely to gain
maturity, respect, love and that most important success
identity.*

—*William Glasser*

Originally developed for adolescent and adult clienteles, reality therapy has recently been successfully applied to young children and to elementary school situations. This therapy approach has developed from the psychiatric practice of William Glasser. Working primarily with delinquent adolescents and disturbed adults, he found his method to be more effective in a shorter period of time than the classical model of psychotherapy. The factor of a typically short duration of therapy time appears to have heightened its appeal for counselors working with children and adolescents. The relatively uncomplicated theory of behavior and the direct therapy process are undoubtedly additional positive factors.

The primary propositions of reality therapy are:

1. A focus on present, conscious behavior.
2. An examination of the value system by the client.
3. A concern with the process of need satisfaction in the client.

4. An insistance on responsible behavior from the client.

5. No toleration of excuses for unacceptable client behavior.

6. Encouragement of active, directive counselor involvement.

7. Deemphasis of case histories and diagnostic test data.

8. Acknowledgment of the client's freedom to choose responsible or irresponsible behavior.

Thus, the emphasis in counseling is for the client to shed the shackles of past misbehavior and focus on establishing a future success orientation.

In the first reading, William Glasser demonstrates the principles of reality therapy and its application to therapeutic practice, using case examples. Richard Hawes, in the second reading, applies reality therapy specifically to the elementary school. He uses behavioral incidents in the school setting to clarify the counseling process. In conclusion, Hawes offers several guidelines for anyone wishing to apply reality therapy in school settings.

WILLIAM GLASSER

Reality Therapy: A New Approach to Psychotherapy with Emphasis on the Treatment of Young Offenders

During the past three years I have been under a variety of psychotherapists and in this time I have experienced a number of different attitudes toward myself and toward those who surround me.

My first psychologist was Dr. C—and she was a rather large shoulder to cry on and I learned after a while that if there was something that I wanted and that my parents would normally have denied to me then I could use her as an intercedent and it was almost sure that this request would be granted. She convinced me, or rather helped me to convince myself, that I was emotionally disturbed and therefore I was not to be held responsible for my actions.

This excerpt summarizing her psychiatric experiences was written by Linda, an extremely delinquent girl, shortly before she left Ventura School, where the most delinquent girls in Southern California are confined and treated. She continues,

After I had been in the Juvenile Hall the first time I began to receive the therapy of an institutional nature, and in this way I tended to get my way, when I felt that it was a subject that was worth getting "upset" over. Since it was on my record that I was an emotionally disturbed child there were various exceptions made for me on this premise. I was not to be upset as I became violent and even masochistic at times. This eliminated the possibilities of the confinement unit and I would have been left alone there and would have been required to think,

Paper read at the Governor's Conference on Youth, Chicago, May 9, 1963. Printed by permission of the author.

and this was supposed to be bad for me. It was at this point in my life that I learned the advantages of being emotionally disturbed and I played them to the fullest advantage. I was "upset" a lot, and I managed to time these little episodes so that I was able to either get in or get out of most of the difficulties that I would encounter.

I then entered a school full of girls like myself who had been either in minor or major difficulties. They ranged from assault cases and prostitution to runaway and sex delinquency. But we were all "upset" quite often and found this to be a clear reason for anything that we did. After all we were the emotionally disturbed and high-strung delinquents and this made any and all we did excusable. We had both private and group therapy. These were sessions in which each girl relieved all the frustrations and disturbances. We were allowed the excessive use of profanity, even when directed toward members of the staff. We were not required to give any of the respect their positions demanded. It was through these various therapy sessions that the girls managed to manipulate the staff into their way of thinking and would mold the rules to comply with what they wanted.

Shortly before my release from that institution I struck a staff member and instigated a riot which got me sent to California Youth Authority and found that these people had an extremely different attitude toward the girls. So you were emotionally disturbed, so big deal! There wasn't anything that anyone but you could do about it, so why worry? I was there under the therapy of Dr. Glasser and Mr. Toobert. I found that Dr. Glasser was less interested in what you had done and your past than he was in your immediate and far future. He was a very personable man, and he gave you the feeling that he was interested in you, but not what you had done and never implied that there was any reason to ask why, as there was no fact necessary but that you did it, and that was the reason for your present incarceration. However, there was not any excuse for what you had done, and you were to hold no one responsible for your actions but you. This is good, for it makes you accept the responsibility for your actions rather than giving the fault to everyone who helped compose your environment.

Now I am leaving Ventura [the Youth Authority] in a matter of days. . . . I have learned that I cannot alter the past, but that I control my future and the responsibility lies solely with me as to my future.

In her own words, this is the story of an intelligent, much tatooed sixteen-year-old girl who, since the age of thirteen, had been deeply involved in prostitution—both heterosexual and homosexual—narcotics, suicide attempts, fighting, and general incorrigibility. Not until she was sent to the Ventura School for Girls, where she was treated with "reality therapy" did she begin to develop some genuine respect for herself and others.

Reality therapy, as Linda attempts to explain, is a method of psychiatric treatment in which the psychiatrist develops a strong, active relationship with the patient, the patient is held responsible for his or her present behavior, only conscious behavior is important, and the unconscious is completely disregarded. Excuses for irresponsible acts—that they appear to be the result of a bad environment, emotional disturbance, or unconscious conflicts coming to the surface—are never accepted. The therapy is concerned with what the patient is capable of doing well, not what he or she has done that has led to the present predicament. At our school no one cared about Linda's past, no one excused her behavior because she was emotionally disturbed, no one was frightened of her threats or temper. Expecting high standards, we respected her and treated her as an intelligent young lady, and she soon began to behave like one. Besides the school program, she had both individual and group therapy, because she was considered such a hopeless case when she arrived. Now on parole, she has a good chance of success. She is a completely different girl from the hostile, uncooperative delinquent who entered the school seven months previously.

Reality therapy, however, is far more than a specialized method that can be used only with institutionalized delinquent adolescents. It is equally applicable to all persons with problems. For example: Ralph, a thirty-one-year-old electronics engineer, has been severely depressed at intervals over the last twelve years. Despite treatment with both psychotherapy and shock, he was deeply depressed when he was given my name. We worked for eighteen months using reality therapy. During this time he came once a week for hour-long sessions except for periods up to four months when his job took him out of town. His marriage fell apart, he had to live alone, his work suffered, but we continued therapy. He considered himself hopelessly depressed and talked of suicide. Gradually, however, he began to take a little responsibility for himself as a man, both in his personal life and in his work. We discussed his depression as his way of escaping responsibility for acting in a more aggressive, masculine way. As we continued, we faced and overcame his inability to cope with the present. Now, many months later, long beyond his previous intervals between depressions, he is feeling fine. He is engaged to be remarried and is successful at work far beyond his expectations.

Sue had been in a private mental hospital for eight months when her mother read an article about reality therapy in the *Christian Science Monitor*. She had led an unsuccessful life and now, at age forty, was withdrawn and eccentric. Her history included psychiatric treatment, intensive individual and group therapy, and about twenty electric shock treatments. Treated with reality therapy for four months, she is slowly becoming a responsible citizen. Her cringing pattern is broken. She lives comfortably in a small apartment, reading and renewing old friendships. Having reviewed her typing and shorthand, she has returned to work as a secretary. Although she will need some more therapy, she has already become a more responsible and worthwhile person.

Reality therapy is very successful with people who like to intellectualize. They find traditional therapy a haven of excuses in their intellectual efforts to avoid facing the reality of their immediate situation. For example, Bob came to therapy as an eighteen-year-old bewildered college sophomore. Never having known his father, he was raised by a young seductive mother, who treated him more like a boyfriend than like a son. She presented him with two immature stepfathers, each of whom left him with a young stepbrother. Failing in college, anxious, and depressed, he had traditional psychiatric treatment from the outpatient clinic of the university department of psychiatry, but with no success. Discussing his family, his miserable childhood, and his feelings about his mother seemed only to make matters worse. Although a poor boy, he was instructed in reality therapy to get a job to pay for part of his treatment. We discussed his school and his future, not the past. It was a long, hard process. He sought deep explanations and psychological reasons for his failures. Excellent at rationalizing, he wanted to avoid the present, because it seemed too difficult. He was trying to hide in school and refused to face the reality of selecting a career. Last year, after three years of once-a-week therapy, he entered medical school and now is president of his sophomore class. He is a responsible young man, who works hard. The new relationship that he has created with his mother has greatly helped her and her latest marriage.

These few cases, representative of the wide range of patients whom we have treated with reality therapy, are cited to illustrate that there is another way to approach psychiatric problems besides the traditional way of looking for unconscious conflicts and discovering and understanding hidden motivations. In reality therapy the unconscious is ignored, the patient's history is of little significance, and his particular problem is of little importance. The more serious and disturbed the patient's behavior, the better this therapy works. It has been developed as a joint effort of Dr. G. L. Harrington, who works half-time in the West Los Angeles Veterans Administration Neuropsychiatric Hospital, and the writer, a part-time consultant for the

California Youth Authority Ventura School for delinquent girls. These institutions are considered to house some of the most difficult of all psychiatric cases. In addition to our institutional associations, we both have private practices.

Dr. Harrington successfully applies reality therapy to chronic, hospitalized, schizophrenic veterans, and I use it with good results in treating the most seriously disturbed delinquent adolescent girls in California. Not only do we employ the treatment ourselves, we also teach the basic principles to all who work with our patients. Much of our success is due to the ease with which these principles are learned by aides, counselors, technicians, and nurses. The continuous treatment that then occurs is vital to disturbed patients. Reality therapy is equally effective in our private practices. The results are not as dramatic, because the patients do not need to change as much as the confined patients do. We do find, however, that they respond rapidly, more rapidly than similar patients did with other therapies.

This article is a brief preliminary report. The considerable psychiatric theory underlying this therapy was the subject of most of my last book[1] and will play a central part in a book I am now writing on reality therapy. Here I will outline the process briefly and attempt to show a need to reconsider some of our most accepted and traditional psychiatric concepts. In six years of weekly conferences devoted to trying to analyze what we do that helps people become more responsible, Dr. Harrington and I have been forced increasingly to conclude that much of what is presently accepted as correct in psychiatry seems to obstruct the process of therapy. After working regularly together since 1956, we decided that I would make some of these ideas public to a group attending the meeting of the National Institute of Crime and Delinquency in Seattle in July 1962. Since that talk, which dealt with the application of reality therapy to delinquents, I have been asked by many correctional personnel in the United States and Canada for further information. We have both had encouraging letters from psychiatrists, psychologists, and social workers who are dissatisfied with traditional psychiatry and who have arrived at tentative conclusions very similar to ours. Many of them have expressed discouragement at the reception they received when attempting to present their ideas to traditional groups.

Reality therapy, as the name implies, deals with reality, and holds that what is most important is facing this reality responsibly. The future must be considered, but the patient's past, except as it is directly related to his or her present behavior, is of little importance. Discussing the patient's history is in fact antitherapeutic, because it serves to minimize the importance of present behavior. We also completely disregard any unconscious processes; we are not interested in looking for supposedly unconscious reasons for the person's difficulties. We are interested only in his present conscious behavior and whether he and we think he is acting in a responsible way and pointing toward a responsible future. As a part of our deep concern with present behavior, we help the patient to *acknowledge a set of values* as early in the therapy as possible. We then discuss his behavior in terms of whether he thinks he is doing right or wrong according to these values. There is usually little difficulty in arriving at the values; the difficulty lies in helping the patient to live responsibly in accordance with them.

Much of the therapy time therefore centers on whether the patient is doing right or wrong according to his values. Psychotic patients who have completely denied reality present difficult problems, but the psychiatrist, with his special skill, must insist on responsible behavior. If he has developed a strong relationship with the patient, the latter will soon begin to live in the real world. The acceptance of values and further responsible behavior then follow. The responsibility is never shifted from the patient because he is mentally ill.

We believe that all people, very early in life, begin to learn a basic sense of right and wrong from which their values are derived, and in most cultures these basic values are remarkably similar. Few indeed, are societies where murder, lying, cheating, stealing, cowardice, incest, promiscuity, or illegitimacy are accepted as right. Tolerated to some degree in every society, they are never considered correct behavior.

It seems logical to us, then, that right and wrong must be derived from essential human needs. Following this argument a step farther, we postulate that there are two needs basic to all humans. There is first our need for closeness with ourselves, to feel that we are unique and worthwhile to ourselves. Second there is our need for closeness to others, to give and receive love and friendship with others, to feel others are worthwhile to us and us to them. When a person is responsible enough to live in a way that fulfills these two needs, he or she will do right much more than wrong. Derived from these universal needs, values may differ according to culture, teaching, and experience, but they do not differ very much. Responsibility, which is the goal of reality therapy, means the ability *to live* according to the values derived from human needs, with neither too much responsibility (apparently), which the compulsive person feels, nor too little, which the delinquent or psychotic feels. A responsible person strikes a balance in his attempt to live according to his values. In doing so he may or may not be happy, but, given reasonable opportunities, he has the capacity for deep satisfaction rather than the brief "kicks" sought by irresponsible people who cannot fulfill their needs.

We are not concerned with isolated feelings. If the patient is sad, depressed, angry, empty, fearful, or anxious, he must relate these feelings to what he is doing now and determine whether his behavior is responsible. No one can help a patient *feel* better; he can only be helped to *do* better, which means to live a more responsible life. Never claiming that therapy can make anyone happy, we do not even concern ourselves with happiness, only with responsibility.

Our theory holds that the diagnosis of mental illness is artificial and meaningless, because what we are really seeing is some manifestation of irresponsibility. All mental symptoms and disturbed behavior are the result of a person's inability to live a responsible life according to his or her values. Even in extreme cases this holds true. For example, a veteran who was hospitalized for eighteen years in the West Los Angeles Veterans Administration Hospital had undergone electric shock treatments, insulin shock treatments, extensive psychotherapy, and finally a prefrontal lobotomy. He continually pressured the doctors to let him out of the hospital, but they refused, because his behavior was erratic, his thoughts were delusional, and he was obviously psychotic. No one thought to treat him as irresponsible until six months ago, when Dr. Harrington took over the ward. He immediately took away the patient's ground privileges, locked him up, and told him it was up to him to take some responsibility before they could talk about discharge. He did not accept the veteran as an irrational schizophrenic, only as irresponsible, and all the ward attendants were trained to do the same. In the past six months, during which the patient developed an intense relationship with Dr. Harrington, there has been a dramatic change in his behavior. He has returned to reality and now brings weekly to Dr. Harrington a list of his responsibilities and how he will fulfill them. The same energy he expended to be psychotic he now uses to face reality, fulfill his needs, and begin to live responsibly according to his values. After all these years, he is being considered for discharge as a responsible person. No one thinks of him as a psychotic patient any longer. The psychiatrist's task, therefore, is to avoid the stagnating concept of mental illness and to treat patients as irresponsible, but with the potential of becoming more responsible.

What about the unconscious, insight into the unconscious, and childhood history? What about the biochemical changes that may go on in the brain? We agree that the unconscious is filled with conflict, that every scrap of a person's long history has led to where he or she is now, and that biochemical changes in the brain may accompany severe mental disturbances. We contend, however, that these concepts have nothing to do with therapy, because they are not the cause of the trouble. They are like the fever and pain that accompany a strep throat. No one would deny their existence; they even call attention to the problem; but it is the streptococcus that must be treated. We certainly do not deny that a person's history has led to his or her present behavior. It is the present behavior, nevertheless, that we must treat; in fact, it is all we can treat. *No one can treat past history.* Our experience has shown that a person's conscious acceptance of responsibility must be broadened, and that what is unconscious is of little importance because it merely accompanies the overt symptoms.

When a seemingly responsible man complains of a stomach pain and we diagnose an ulcer, we soon discover that he has many unconscious conflicts raging inside him. The conflicts arise from his lifelong desire to be dependent, to be taken care of. When he comes to understand this through traditional therapy, nothing happens, because it is not the cause of his ulcer. His ulcer is there because he is unable to take enough responsibility for his life now. Responsible as he may appear, he still wants to be taken care of right now. Learning about his lifelong dependency, all of which is repressed into his unconscious mind, is merely learning about another segment of his problem. The unconscious conflicts are only the mental equivalent, the companion to his ulcer; they do not cause it. It would be just as logical to say that the ulcer causes the conflicts, and in protracted cases I am sure that it does make its contribution to additional conflicts. To treat him, however, we need to help him take responsibility now, to face the present reality, not to delude ourselves or him into believing that his ulcer will heal when he understands what is going on in his unconscious. Our job is to help him lead a more responsible life, to do something about his present irresponsibility, or, in the case of the seemingly responsible ulcer patient, to discuss how he may be assuming more than he is capable of handling adequately. We do not tell him he cannot handle his responsibilities; rather we help him evaluate how much he is capable of doing and strengthen him to carry a realistic workload more efficiently.

Actually it is quite appropriate for everyone to have many unconscious conflicts. No one resolves all problems completely, but in strong, effective people the conflicts caused by responsible living reside comfortably in the unconscious, their natural resting place. A responsible person who maintains an unhappy marriage because he thinks divorce will harm his children will have many conflicts safely lodged in his unconscious, but he will be able to live effectively. Contrary to popular opinion and even to much psychiatric opinion, we think that an irresponsible person has fewer conflicts in his unconscious for two reasons: (1) he acts out his conflicts in his disturbed behavior; and (2) he has many conscious aberrant thoughts. Both reduce the conflicts in his unconscious mind.

Such a person is far less capable of deep feelings, because he has a relatively shallow unconscious. This lack causes a wide variety of unpleasant emotions, such as severe anxiety, anger, and emptiness, all of which interfere with his ability to behave responsibly. The less responsible he is, the worse he feels, which then increases his desire to take irresponsible shortcuts, like divorce, in order to feel better. In doing so, however, he only compounds his problem, especially if his children suffer and complain. Investigating his unconscious becomes a superficial dead end. The job is to build up his conscious responsibility and thereby make him capable of deeper feelings. The deeper the unconscious, the more a person can feel and think profoundly, which in turn augments his ability to behave responsibly.

In contrast to the shallow emotions of an irresponsible person, these deep feelings, the psychological reward for behaving responsibly, increase the tendency to be responsible. Responsible people are much more able to have profound emotions, to form lasting and worthwhile friendships, to fall deeply in love, and to produce great works of art. They are genuinely intellectual in contrast to the irresponsible person who intellectualizes. They do not seek psychiatric help, they are able to face the reality around them, and they can live responsibly according to their values. Socrates may have had many unconscious conflicts, but his choice to die for his values was a conscious responsible choice, and no one has ever seriously questioned his mental competence or the depth of his feelings.

Reality therapy, therefore, is a way in which an irresponsible man can be helped to face his values and learn to live responsibly, hopefully, and happily. Happiness is fortuitous, it is evanescent, and no one can obtain it directly. We do know, however, that responsible people are happier for longer periods than irresponsible people. Deep, rich, inner happiness is possible only for responsible people. This is why Australian aborigines, who are among the most responsible people on earth, are often happier than modern men and women whose "civilization" has in many cases served to obscure their values and lead to irresponsible action.

How then is reality therapy put into practice? First of all, the therapist must become deeply involved with the patient. Meeting the patient on as high a level as the patient can attain, the therapist must never be aloof, sacrosanct, or superior. The psychiatrist must be responsible enough to bare his or her own values, feelings, and elements of behavior in the conversation that makes up the therapy. The therapist must show the patient by example that acting responsibly has rewards. A therapist who is not a strong, responsible person can help no one.

The technique of reality therapy is more difficult to learn than the theory. It takes practice and discipline not to fall into the trap of looking for reasons for deviant behavior—reasons that all patients grasp at to avoid responsibility. Patients treated by reality therapy never sing the familiar refrain, "I'm this way because of my mother." We feel that, regardless of what the patient's mother was like, the patient still is responsible for the way he is, and only he can change. Perhaps, if he changes his behavior, his mother may change hers; but whether she does or not, he must.

An essential technique, therefore, of reality therapy is never to ask "why," only "what," to avoid any implication that the patient is not responsible for his behavior. We think the classical question "why?" has led psychiatry down a blind alley because it helps the patient evade reality. Its use condones present irresponsibility and promotes further deviant behavior by making the unconscious a psychological scapegoat for irresponsible behavior.

Let us now consider the four cases presented at the beginning of the article in the light of reality therapy. To help the delinquent girl, the therapist must discuss with her what she did that broke the law, not why she did it, and help her see how she acted irresponsibly and how this has hurt her. He must be the one who expects the most from her, never excuses her behavior, and feels free to initiate discipline when she is irresponsible. He must treat her as an adult, respect her opinions, and praise her when she acts responsibly. Not just a good guy who accepts her as a poor, disturbed child, he is a strong, responsible person who expects high standards, who excuses nothing, who points out that she is basically responsible for everything she does and that she needs to help others as much as to be helped herself. Her whole future life is discussed along with her present feelings. For the first time she is involved in a relationship where she can respect herself for doing right rather than hate herself for doing wrong. With delinquents, when the therapist is tough enough to enforce the rules, when he initiates discipline if a girl breaks the rules but points out to her that the discipline must be imposed, she will readily accept it. When I tell a delinquent girl that she has to be locked up because she has broken rules and laws, I ask her whether it would be right for me to do anything else. Will I help her by excusing or condoning her behavior, or by giving her another chance when she has already had ten? Will she learn anything or even respect me if I do? The answer is always "no," as in the quotation that began the article. Excusing, condoning, or explaining behavior just substitutes psychiatric kicks for the kicks the delinquent girl got previously from her incorrigible behavior.

With the depressed patient the therapy was similar. No discipline was necessary or even possible; his depression constituted suffering enough to motivate him to work in the therapy situation. Thinking that if he were a sweet, passive man the whole world would love him, he was afraid to take a more aggressive male role. When I became involved with all of his present life, rather than offering him explanations or sympathy, he soon saw himself as an angry person, depressed because he was not even responsible enough to express his anger. He learned in our relationship that a man can express himself, that to take an aggressive role is to be responsible, not hostile. He did not learn this by asking "why," poking back into his subconscious, or telling me his history. We both knew that his past had led to his depressions; if it had not he would not have been in my office. Pointing out what he was doing in all areas of his life, I helped him start a new and better life now. When he did so, he stopped asking "why," he began to assume responsibility, and his depression lifted. It was the taking of some responsibility, not talking about it, that made the big difference.

Sue appeared to be a much more difficult case than she really is.

Blaming her recent life partly on her mother, she found psychiatrists who agreed with her; her condition, however, did not improve. Now she finds that when she acts more responsibly her mother is "different," and her mother told me that Sue is so "changed." Actually, the opportunity to take some responsibility, which evolved through our relationship, has made the big difference. The nurses in the mental hospital showed that they did not understand the problem, by saying that Sue would never improve because of her mother. Mothers may have their opinions, but so do children. Forty-year-old children and their parents have many disagreements. Probing into what was wrong with this relationship would take many years. Ignoring it, encouraging Sue to be more responsible, and trusting her enough to live alone is a much faster way to solve the problem. We wish to know what she is doing to her mother and to herself; through our relationship she is beginning to find out by her own efforts.

The young college student with the disturbed family background is typical of the patient who is in therapy for years, learns everything about himself, and does nothing constructive. Although he was most curious about the why—the unconscious causes of his condition—I refused to fall into the trap. He could dream as much as he wanted, but because his dreams were just further evidence of his irresponsibility, I would have little to do with them. I wanted to become deeply involved with him only as a college man with a future, not as the irresponsible person he was. What was he doing now? Could he do better? Could he be more responsible? Could he treat his mother and stepfather better? When his real father hung himself shortly after writing the young man the first letter in years, what was his responsibility? Did his world have to end then, or did he have a job to do in order to prove he could be a better man? Always his problems were related to his present behavior, his conscious decisions, and he made progress. He will be a fine compassionate doctor, because he has learned to accept responsibility.

This, then, is what we believe. We know that therapy that advocates the uncovering of unconscious conflicts seems to work in many cases, especially with people who are not too disturbed and who are already moderately responsible. With mental hospital patients and those with severe behavior disorders, we have never seen it work. When traditional therapy does work, however, we believe it is because of the therapist's involvement and the kind of person he or she is, not the theory. We think that therapy needs to be directed to conscious responsibility, that unconscious conflicts necessarily accompany disturbed behavior, but they do not cause it.

Reality therapy takes less time than traditional therapy. We see patients at most twice a week, usually only once. Half-hour sessions are often adequate, especially toward the end of therapy. It does away with the need for diagnostic testing and interviewing, which probably waste 25 percent of psychiatric time in publicly supported clinics. What we do can be understood, learned, and used by all who counsel disturbed people in all sorts of nonpsychiatric situations, such as clergymen doing pastoral counseling, college guidance counselors, industrial relations counselors, and, perhaps most important of all, teachers working with disturbed children in their classes.

I have taught these principles to school teachers studying in the Department of Education at San Fernando Valley State College, and I now teach them to teachers and school nurses in the Department of Health at UCLA Extension. Applying what they have learned to problem children in their classrooms, they have reported great success. In fact, more than twenty teachers in my classes last year told me they no longer had to ask the guidance office for help in handling serious problems in class. When they eliminated the word "why" from their vocabulary, when they worked with the child's present behavior, when they held children responsible for what they did and allowed themselves to get close to the children emotionally, they found that most children responded by dramatically changing their behavior. We would work out each case in class; then they would apply the approach we decided upon. The results were amazing to them and gratifying to me.

Dr. Harrington and I have waited six years before publishing our concepts; we will continue to work together to improve psychotherapy. Our hope is to stimulate critical thinking, because it is necessary that psychiatry develop better and more efficient methods of treating increasing numbers of people who come to us for help.

Note

1. *Mental Health or Mental Illness?* (New York: Harper & Bros., 1961).

RICHARD M. HAWES

Reality Therapy: An Approach to Encourage Individual and Social Responsibility in the Elementary School

The technological and cultural forces of today seem to have a separating and depersonalizing effect. This situation causes people to experience the gnawing feelings of loneliness perhaps more frequently and more intensely than in the recent past. As authority, tradition, and conformity lose their potence to solve the problems of the day and to protect us from loneliness and uncertainty, self-esteem (to care for oneself—individual responsibility) and the capacity to love (to care for others—social responsibility) become more necessary for human survival.

In an attempt to *be* loved, many people learn ways to "make" people love them. These desperate power plays are sometimes successful in gaining respect, but respect is only a substitute for love, and the pains of loneliness remain. An alternative method is to learn ways to become more self-responsible (worthwhile) and socially responsible (the capacity to love).

This paper is based on the premise that these conditions (self-worth and the ability to love) are learned, that they are essential learnings for survival, and that the educational system needs to look

Hawes, R. M. Reality therapy: an approach to encourage individual and social responsibility in the elementary school. *Elementary School Guidance and Counseling*, 1969, 4(2), 120-127. Copyright 1969 American Personnel and Guidance Association. Reprinted with permission.

at them as major educational aims. The following is a description of an attempt in that direction.

Teaching Self-worth and Ability to Love

At 10:19 a.m. in the third grade class of the Eastern Elementary School, Mrs. McHenry has the following discussion with Jimmy, an eight-year-old boy who has a difficult time completing assignments even though the school records show him to have above average intelligence. Jimmy, slouched in his chair, is blowing on the edge of his science book when, with the rest of the class, he should be copying five arithmetic problems for his homework assignment. Usually, Mrs. McHenry tells him to get busy, but this time she begins by asking a question. In this approach, it's more valuable to ask questions than to make statements or give directions.

Mrs. McHenry: Jimmy, what are you doing?
Jimmy: (Startled, says nothing and shows that he's not sure what to say or do.)
Mrs. McHenry: Show me—tell me what you are doing. It's important to me.
Jimmy: I—I—I was blowing on the edge of the book like this. (He then demonstrates.)
Mrs. McHenry: (Smiling.) That's right, you were.
Jimmy: (Smiles slightly.)

Their smiles suggest that Mrs. McHenry and Jimmy are experiencing a positive relationship and feeling good about it. A classroom situation that usually ends in a strained or distressful relationship has ended in a positive one. Mrs. McHenry has helped to make a potential minus into a plus and the therapeutic value is significant—for both parties. Another similar technique to help create a positive tone is making a "yes" out of a "no."

Example: A child is raising his hand to ask permission to sharpen a pencil. The teacher feels this activity would disturb the class. In place of saying, "No, you can't," she says, "Yes, you may when the bell rings."

A single incident of this nature is of little value, but when many people (children and adults) try to make a "yes" out of a "no," the effect on the school's atmosphere is great.

Mrs. McHenry: (Continues by asking.) Does that help you complete the arithmetic problem?
Jimmy: (Shrugging his shoulders.) No.

Mrs. McHenry without commenting, moves across the room to help another child who has her hand raised, leaving Jimmy with the choice of continuing the behavior discussed, doing something else, or copying the arithmetic problems.

In another classroom, Mrs. Jones' second grade class is lining up in the back of the room for recess. Tom and Sam get into one of their playful shoving matches, which usually results in a rather serious scuffle. This one is no exception, and one of the girls in the class is slightly injured by an unintentional kick in the shin.

Mrs. Jones: What happened?

The children begin to talk all at once, creating a lot of confusion and noise.

Mrs. Jones: I think we had better bring this up for discussion at our regular class meeting later this morning.

Later, after the class has returned from recess and about 20 minutes before lunch, the class moves into a circle for discussion.

Mrs. Jones: Let's review in as much detail as possible what happened between Tom and Sam earlier this morning.

Tom and Sam reenact or "role play" the situation for the class.

Mrs. Jones: What do you think? How do you feel it worked out?

The children begin to comment, express their opinions, discuss various ideas on how it worked out, judge how valuable it was, estimate the effects the incident had on the class, and suggest how a similar situation could be prevented.

Tom: I guess it wasn't so hot, but we were just fooling around.

Mrs. Jones: We've talked this over pretty well now and we've come up with several ideas on how to solve it. Tom and Sam, what's your plan? (The discussion is always directed toward solving the problem. It is not directed toward finding fault or deciding on punishment.)

Sam: I guess we'll do our own idea of lining up at the ends of the line.

Mrs. Jones: When?

Tom: (After exchanging glances with Sam.) At lunchtime.

It's best to spend as little time as possible on classroom behavior problems. Too much concern can backfire and reinforce what you are trying to eliminate. Time is better used on open-end discussion sessions.

The open-end sessions, the most frequently used and perhaps the most valuable of class meetings, are designed to supplement the academic program by stimulating the children to think and respond. The sessions provide the children with a situation that gives each pupil the opportunity for intellectual success without the possibility of failure. The child makes no mistakes by his answers. Thinking rather than memory is accentuated. These regularly scheduled classroom discussions are the backbone of the program's attempt to encourage individual and socially responsible behavior.

The topic for open-end discussion may be introduced by any class member or the teacher. The topic for one day is introduced by a teacher as she asks the children the following series of questions. Enthusiastic discussion usually follows each question, such as What is play? What is work? Is play or work more important? Would you rather work or play? Is school work or play? Do you learn anything when you play?

Later in the afternoon, several teachers are enjoying coffee in the teachers' lounge. Bill, a sixth grade student who is well known for disruptive behavior, poor academic attitude, and a low achievement record is being discussed.

As in the class meetings, the teachers accentuate practical, reasonable, and realistic solutions rather than reasons (excuses) for his behavior, fault finding, where he can get help, or methods of punishment. They ask, "What can *I* do to make him feel worthwhile?" "Who has an idea that will help him to be more successful while he is in school?" "Of all the people available, who can work out something with Bill whereby he can begin to be more successful?" "Is school relevant to him?" "What can we do to make his time in school more important to him?" Before long, a specific plan is worked out which possibly will help him to be more successful in school and lead him to more self-satisfying behavioral patterns.

The plan: Mr. Ackley, third grade teacher who gets along well with Bill, will ask him to help as a teacher's aide during part of the school day. Bill will be given the responsibility of helping younger children to learn. A responsibility of this nature frequently has a very positive effect on the behavior of the pupil who is giving the help. It is far more effective than when one is lectured or punished.

Applying Reality Therapy

These are a few glimpses of how reality therapy may be applied in an elementary school. Reality therapy has been developed by William Glasser, a Los Angeles psychiatrist who has had considerable experience in private practice, correctional institutions, and as a consultant to various groups, schools, and organizations throughout this country and in Canada. Recently he has shown increasing interest in the schools and their relationship to mental health and human development.

Dr. Glasser's work in the schools over the last few years is reflected in a book entitled, *Schools Without Failure* (1969). His earlier books are *Mental Health or Mental Illness* (1960) and *Reality Therapy* (1965).

Reality therapy is based on the idea that everyone needs to have an identity. For some, this may be described as a "successful" identity because the person is able to become involved with life in a manner that allows him to fulfill two basic needs: Feeling worthwhile toward himself and others; and to love and be loved. When one is unsuccessful in fulfilling any part of these needs he suffers. One suffers not only if he is unable to be loved, but also if he is unable to give love—it's a two-way street.

Dr. Glasser (1966), in a speech to primary reading specialists in the Los Angeles School District, has commented:

These are two-way needs: to love and be loved implies someone to love and someone who loves me. If we don't have this we suffer. For some children the form of this suffering is not learning to read and they won't learn to read until they get the idea that someone is able to care for them and they *can* learn [p. 1].

Because these suffering children are in the process of developing failure identities by their very experiences, they are unable to make the kind of relationships with *responsible* people that are necessary for them to fulfill their needs. It then becomes the first responsibility of the teacher to make contact with them in a way that is open, transparent, honest, and congruent. One needs to meet them as a human being who cares. Without this type of encounter, their chances of shifting from a failure identity (characterized by delinquency or withdrawal) to a successful identity (characterized by self-esteem and love) will be slim indeed. People need people. As Glasser (1966) puts it:

Children suffer by not learning or they get tired of suffering and cause others to suffer. . . . The teacher's first job is to make contact with these children . . . as a person who cares . . . a person interested in them . . . not as a teacher but as a person. . . . Everyone is doing the best he can at the time. If he could do better he would. You can't convince them they can do better until they relate to you and begin to meet their needs [p. 1].

By making this authentic and personal contact, involvement is increased while loneliness is decreased. This personal involvement is reflected by the child's increased motivation to learn.

As the discussion so far implies, the first essential step in the application of reality therapy is to get personally involved. With little children particularly, it is important to use personal pronouns as Mrs. McHenry did with Jimmy, when she said, "It's important to me" (that you show and tell me what you are doing). It is important for the child to know that you are interested in him as a person, not only as a pupil in the class, a name on the attendance book, a 1.5 reading level, or a 107 IQ score. Casual, interested, and authentic conversation where you get to know one another as people is extremely important. It is important for *him* to know that you enjoy playing tennis, watching "Bewitched," have two boys and one girl, and a husband who sells carpets at Sears. It is important for you to know personal things about him. Spontaneous, casual give-and-take, one human being to another, creates a quality of involvement that causes one to hurt if the child is unable to read.

Our daily newspapers remind us with foreboding that one of our most serious problems today is lack of involvement or social responsibility. Arthur H. Brayfield (1968) suggests that we need to develop an environment ". . . that will foster the sense of personal worth and self-esteem required to sustain the human spirit, give meaning to our lives, and provide the energizing force to forge our personal destinies and to insure the emergence and survival of a humane society."

A second guideline of this approach is to accentuate the present time. Do not get involved in reinforcing the set that Jimmy is always doing something like blowing on the pages of his book when he is supposed to be doing arithmetic, that Tom and Sam have a past history of scuffles, that Bill has always been a behavior problem, or that Johnny was unable to read in the past. Being successful at not succeeding is a certain kind of success, and so we have some very successful failures. Do not reinforce past failure but rather expect Johnny to be successful at reading in the present, expect Jimmy to complete the arithmetic lesson successfully today, expect Tom, Sam, and the class to come up with a solution to their scuffling, expect Bill to be successful in helping a third grader to learn.

A third consideration is to deal with behavior. The purpose is not to search for *why* he is behaving the way he does or *how* he feels about it. The valuable point is to help the child become aware of *what* he is doing that is contributing to his failure. In the case of

Jimmy, Mrs. McHenry was able to help him become consciously aware of his behavior, not by demanding that he stop and get busy (an approach designed to take responsibility for him, rather than his taking responsibility for himself), but by encouraging him in a non-punitive manner to describe, as best he could, his actual behavior. The process of describing helps to bring the behavior to the most optimum conscious level.

These first three points, establishing personal involvement and accentuating present behavior, put the situation clearly in the open and set the stage for a fourth point, which is one of the most important, relevant, and meaningful learning opportunities anyone can experience: The opportunity for one to reflect upon and make a value judgment about his own behavior. The value of this experience of responsible self-evaluation and direction cannot be overemphasized. It is extremely important when working personally with individuals, small groups, or large classroom groups, to work toward their making value judgments. This is usually best accomplished by asking questions, not making statements. "Is it worthwhile to blow on the book or complete the arithmetic lesson?" "Is it worthwhile to learn to read?" "Is it worthwhile to help another student?" "Is it worthwhile to kick someone in the shin?" "Is it worthwhile to graduate from high school?"

On this point, Glasser (1966) states, "You can't tell them it is important to learn to read. They must make their own value judgments" (p. 3). When the child decides it is worthwhile to change his behavior, the teacher must work with him in an effort to come up with a specific plan and then encourage him to make a commitment to the plan. Making a plan and getting a commitment are steps five and six. The plan should be such that its fulfillment is guaranteed. Nothing succeeds like success. Once again, questions are important, rather than statements or directions: "What can you do about it?" "What is your plan?" "Will you commit yourself to the plan?" "Will you do it?" "When?"

Jimmy could choose to do the arithmetic lesson, Tom and Sam decide to line up at the extreme ends of the line, and Mr. Ackley is going to ask Bill to help in the third grade.

The seventh and eighth steps are to eliminate punishment and not to reinforce excuses. Punishment and excuses are of no value when working with children who already hurt.

As Glasser (1966) remarks:

Discipline is hard because we not only deal with excuses, we ask for them. Discipline is poorly understood—it has nothing to do with hurting or harming children. It is teaching someone that the way he is going is not helping him and getting him to make better choices. It takes a long time for a child to fulfill his commitments. He will check you out. He will try to see if you will take excuses. If you accept excuses, it proves you don't really care and the old failure pattern recurs. If you accept excuses you are saying, "You are worthless." If the assignment is not done say, "When will you do it?" "Can you do it?" "Can you do it in school today?" "After school?" Not "Why didn't you do it?" If you don't ever accept excuses you are saying, "You are a worthwhile person and I'm waiting for you to complete your commitment" [p. 4] .

It should be noted that the cumulative effect of many people becoming personally involved, dealing with present behavior, changing why to what, making plus out of minus or yes out of no, emphasizing thinking and value judgments through techniques such as regularly scheduled classroom meetings, accentuating and expecting successful experiences, eliminating excuses, and not resorting to fear or punishment, creates a distinct environment. This atmosphere itself becomes an added force toward responsible behavior, successful identity, mental health, overall human development, and the capacity to love.

References

Brayfield, A. H. Human .resources development. *American Psychologist*, 1968, 23, 479-482.

Glasser, W. How can we help young children face reality and become responsible human beings? Excerpts from a speech made by Dr. Glasser at the ESEA Workshop for Primary Reading Specialists, Los Angeles, Calif., August, 1966.

Glasser, W. *Mental health or mental illness?* New York: Harper, 1960.

Glasser, W. *Reality therapy.* New York: Harper, 1965.

Glasser, W. *Schools without failure.* New York: Harper, 1969.

SECTION IX

Recommended Additional Reading

This final section is a bibliography on the theory and practice of counseling, offering additional sources for the serious reader who wishes to expand his or her understanding of and expertise with one or more different models. The bibliography is therefore organized by theoretical model, and each theory covered in the preceding eight sections is represented by several texts. In addition, it includes a final group of references on analytic therapy. Because of this model's wide-ranging appeal and its pervasive effect on many other theoretical schools, books dealing with it were included in the bibliography. However, as previously noted in the Introduction, analytic therapy was not included as a separate readings section because of its limited use with counseling populations.

In order to facilitate the reader's selection, most of the sources are annotated. One note of caution: this list is not intended to be exhaustive or divinely inspired. It is merely the editor's selection of references for additional in-depth exploration in the field of counseling.

Behavioral Counseling

Bandura, A. *Principles of Behavior Modification.* New York: Holt, Rinehart and Winston, 1969.

Investigates the underlying principles of behavior modification procedures. The development and control of a behavioral program are adequately covered. The main strength of this text is its comprehensive coverage of behavioral techniques, including social modeling, desensitization, inhibition, positive and aversive control, extinction, and counterconditioning. Both beginning counselors and experienced therapists can benefit from Bandura's comprehensive treatment of the topic.

Buckley, N., and H. M. Walker. *Modifying Classroom Behavior.* Champaign, Ill.: Research Press, 1970.
A small manual that deals concretely with behavioral procedures. Organized as a programmed learning text. The questions presented realistically reinforce the material that the reader has just completed. Because of its diminutive size and readable format, it can easily be perused in several hours. An excellent resource to use in conjunction with a more comprehensive text like Bandura's.

Ferinden, W. E. *Classroom Management Through the Application of Behavior Modification Techniques.* Linden, N.J.: Remediation Associates, 1970.
A small, inexpensive, reference manual for counselors, therapists, and other professionals working in school settings. Surveys a wide range of modification techniques that professionals could use directly with clients, or in consultation with teachers and parents. Ferinden discusses approaches to classroom management, as well as methods of dealing with problem children and problem situations in groups and individually.

Krumboltz, J. D., and H. B. Krumboltz. *Changing Children's Behavior.* Englewood Cliffs, N.J.: Prentice-Hall, 1972.
A good supplement to Krumboltz's previous work in behavioral counseling. Relates specific reinforcement techniques to normal and abnormal behavior situations. School-oriented at both elementary and secondary levels.

Krumboltz, J. D., and C. E. Thoresen. *Behavioral Counseling: Cases and Techniques.* New York: Holt, Rinehart and Winston, 1969.
Presents a collection of techniques for behaviorally oriented counselors. Emphasis is on the "how" of practicing behavioral counseling. Very readable, with a focus on technique rather than theory. An impressive array of techniques for treating a multitude of child and adolescent problems. A very close approximation of "everything you always wanted to know about behavioral counseling," without being too prescriptive or cookbookish.

Ullman, L. P., and L. Krasner. *Case Studies in Behavior Modification.* New York: Holt, Rinehart and Winston, 1965.

An excellent presentation of specific case examples. A wide variety of dysfunctional behaviors are treated, using behaviorally oriented counseling procedures.

Client-Centered Counseling

Hart, J. T., and T. M. Tomlinson. *New Directions in Client-Centered Therapy*. Boston: Houghton Mifflin Co., 1970.

A collection of readings gathered with the professional counselor in mind. Comprehensively presents the Rogerian model in both theory and practice. The main theme is a survey of new developments in this approach. Part one, "An Introduction to Client-Centered Therapy," and part four, "New Directions in Therapy," are the most appealing for practitioners.

Rogers, C. R. *Counseling and Psychotherapy*. Boston: Houghton Mifflin Co., 1942.

The initial work by Carl Rogers that inspired the development of client-centered counseling and therapy. It details Rogers's concepts of counseling goals, stages in the counseling process, and common therapeutic problems encountered by the client-centered counselor. This text is the basis for all subsequent research and practice in the Rogerian model.

Rogers, C. R. *Client-Centered Therapy*. Boston: Houghton Mifflin Co., 1951.

A further exposition of Rogerian concepts as they relate to the counseling process. It expands the initial work of Rogers detailed in his first book and reflects the considerable amount of research and practice that ensued after that book was widely distributed. Play therapy and group therapy from the client-centered perspective are covered, as well as Rogers's influential individual counseling model.

Rogers, C. R. *On Becoming a Person*. Boston: Houghton Mifflin Co., 1961.

This is the final book in what might be considered the Rogerian trilogy, which, taken together, present all the central concepts of client-centered therapy. This one is a collection of speeches presented by Rogers, focusing on the basic counseling relationship and its importance in the progress of therapy.

Further Reading

Rogers, C. R. *Freedom to Learn*. Columbus, Ohio: Charles E. Merrill Publishing Co., 1969.

Eclectic Counseling

Thorne, F. C. *Personality.* Brandon, Vt.: Clinical Psychology Publishing Co., 1961.
Describes the phenomenal personality system developed by Thorne. Emphasis is on personality development of the "normal" person in society.

Thorne, F. C. *Tutorial Counseling.* Brandon, Vt.: Clinical Psychology Publishing Co., 1965.
Written for the professional therapist but without depending on clinical terms and procedures. Describes the eclectic approach of Thorne with a focus on positive mental health for the general population.

Existential Counseling

Frankl, V. *Man's Search for Meaning.* Boston: Beacon Press, 1963.
A basic presentation of *logotherapy*, which is Frankl's interpretation of existential therapy. The central concept is each individual's search for meaning in life. Frankl movingly describes his concentration camp experiences during World War II, which led to his development of this approach. He briefly outlines the concepts and therapeutic methods that he advocates. A short, readable book.

Moustakas, C. E. *Existential Child Therapy.* New York: Basic Books, 1966.
A collection of articles, each dealing with the problem situation of a child client. All the contributors are existential therapists, and they provide a unique and enlightening glimpse into their concept of the helping relationship and the therapeutic change process. A very readable book for either the established professional or the beginning counselor-in-training.

Further Reading

Beck, C. E. *Philosophical Foundations of Guidance.* Englewood Cliffs, N.J.: Prentice-Hall, 1963.

May, R. *Existential Psychology.* New York: Random House, 1961.

Individual/Developmental Counseling

Ansbacher, H. L., and R. R. Ansbacher. *The Individual Psychology of Alfred Adler.* New York: Harper Torchbooks, 1964.
A scholarly and systematic presentation of Adler's psychology. Comprehensively treats the philosophy, the theory, and the technique of individual

psychology. A must reading for any counselor or therapist seriously considering Adlerian or Dreikursian counseling methods.

Dinkmeyer, D., and R. Dreikurs. *Encouraging Children to Learn.* Englewood Cliffs, N.J.: Prentice-Hall, 1963.
A manual for teachers, parents, and counselors assisting children in overcoming their emotional difficulties. The focus is on the educational system, and the authors attempt to integrate psychological principles with educational practices. Encouragement is the major process emphasized.

Dreikurs, R., and V. Soltz. *Children: The Challenge.* New York: Hawthorn Books, 1964.
A thorough presentation of the family counseling model of Rudolf Dreikurs, grounded in the theoretical aspects of Adlerian psychology. Discusses all major aspects of family counseling and provides a good introduction for counselors, teachers, and parents.

Mairet, R. *Problems of Neurosis.* New York: Harper Torchbooks, 1964.
A thorough presentation of Adlerian concepts and techniques. Thirty-seven case histories reveal how personality disturbances develop and are treated, through the eyes of an Adlerian therapist. Good source for the beginning as well as the established counselor.

Play Therapy

Axline, V. M. *Play Therapy.* Boston: Houghton Mifflin Co., 1947.
This text is primarily school oriented but will be beneficial to any professional contemplating or currently conducting play therapy work with children. It is a comprehensive exposition of the nondirective play therapy model that Axline developed from Rogerian psychology. It can be used as a basic primer by the neophyte or as a source of stimulation and reference for the established practitioner.

Axline, V. M. *Dibs: In Search of Self.* Boston: Houghton Mifflin Co., 1964.
A case history of the psychological development of a small boy. With the expert guidance of a professional therapist, he moves from a severely disturbed condition to one of security, happiness, and effectiveness. In the process of telling the story, Axline presents the major techniques of nondirective play therapy. An interesting and professionally enlightening book. Recommended for all practicing child counselors, as well as interested parents and teachers.

Moustakas, C. E. *Children in Play Therapy.* New York: McGraw-Hill Book Co., 1953.
> Play therapy comprehensively covered in a well-written and well-organized text. Deals with a plethora of presenting problems, from normal to disturbed. There is liberal use of case studies and dialogue transcripts to illustrate the author's work with children. A must book for the serious play therapist.

Further Reading

Millar, S. *The Psychology of Play.* Baltimore: Penguin Books, 1968.

Rational-Emotive Therapy

Ellis, A. *Reason and Emotion in Psychotherapy.* New York: Lyle Stuart, 1962.
> The original treatise on rational-emotive therapy. All the fundamental RET concepts and procedures are here. Should be on every counselor's basic reading list.

Ellis, A. *A Guide to Rational Living.* Englewood Cliffs, N.J.: Prentice-Hall, 1971.
> Written for the nonprofessional who is interested in developing new strategies for coping with problem situations. Presents Ellis's RET model in a nontechnical, pragmatic manner. Interesting supplemental reading for the professional, and can also be used as bibliotherapy by the serious rational-emotive counselor.

Ellis, A., J. L. Wolfe, and S. Moseley. *How to Prevent Your Child from Becoming a Neurotic Adult.* New York: Crown Publishers, 1966.
> Oriented toward the nonprofessional. Applies RET principles to common and not-so-common problems of children. The authors emphasize rational ways for parents to treat their children and how parents can teach their children to adopt a rational philosophy of life. Stimulating reading for the professional as well as a good source book.

Further Reading

Ellis, A. *Growth through Reason.* Palo Alto, Calif.: Science and Behavior Books, 1971.

Hauck, Paul. *Rational Management of Children.* 2d ed., rev. Roslyn Heights, N.Y.: Libra Publishers, 1972.

Reality Therapy

Glasser, W. *Reality Therapy*. New York: Harper and Row, 1965.
The original publication by Glasser, which presents the postulates of reality therapy. All his later work is based on this material. Serious students of counseling and therapy should add this book to their reading lists.

Glasser, W. *Schools without Failure*. New York: Harper and Row, 1969.
Glasser's application of the principles of reality therapy to the classroom setting. He suggests that teachers adopt reality concepts in their total conduct in the classroom. In effect, the teacher creates a counseling or therapeutic learning environment. The focus is on positive feedback and instilling a success orientation in the children. Written for both elementary and secondary school situations. A good consultative tool for counselors to use with school personnel.

Glasser, W. *The Identity Society*. New York: Harper and Row, 1972.
Represents an extension of the author's earlier publications. The major portion of the text is devoted to Glasser's views of educational and societal problems and their solutions. Included are loneliness, failure, drug use, sexual behavior, crime, and welfare. Chapter six, "Reality Therapy," is devoted to a discussion of Glasser's counseling model and succinctly describes the major principles, with examples of their application. It provides interesting and informative reading for professional and nonprofessional.

Analytic Therapy

Erikson, E. H. *Childhood and Society*. New York: W. W. Norton and Co., 1963.
A basic presentation of the author's version of analytic psychology, with emphasis on the importance of ego development in the life process. Part three, probably the most valuable, treats Erikson's concept of the eight stages of development in man. He then relates the stages to ego psychology. This text is primarily an exposition of theory, rather than an explanation of techniques.

Freud, A. *Introduction To Psychoanalysis*. New York: International Universities Press, 1974.
An excellent introduction to child analysis. Organized into three sections, each composed of a collection of papers written by Anna Freud from 1922 to 1935. Part I deals with the preparation of the analyst, analytic methods, and general concepts of child analysis. Part II focuses on psychoanalytic

methods for teachers and parents. Part III presents more specific childhood treatment procedures.

Hammer, M., and A. Kaplan. *The Practice of Psychotherapy with Children.* Homewood, Ill.: Dorsey Press, 1967.
A collection of papers that present the psychoanalytic model of treating children and adolescents. In the first paper, the authors develop the theoretical basis for analytical treatment. The remainder of the papers focus on particular presenting problems, ranging from anxiety neurosis to severe psychotic disorders. Those dealing with neurotic problems and learning difficulties are the most valuable for counselors. The practical, specific nature of each paper is the major strength of this text.

Munroe, R. L. *Schools of Psychoanalytic Thought.* New York: Dryden Press, 1955.
A relatively comprehensive survey of psychoanalytic thought presented from the viewpoint of a practicing psychologist. A good starting point for initial exploration of the complex school of analytic psychology.

Upham, F. *Ego Analysis in the Helping Professions.* New York: Family Service Association of America, 1973.
The author relates the theory and practice of ego psychology to child and adolescent counseling relationships. The reader should have some familiarity with the basic concepts of analytic therapy or ego psychology in order to appreciate fully the richness of the material. Given a basic understanding of personality theory and dynamics, this book can be a valuable addition to a therapist's library.

Further Reading

Barten, H. H., and S. S. Barten. *Children and Their Parents in Brief Therapy.* New York: Behavioral Publications, 1973.

Freud, A. *The Psychoanalytic Treatment of Children.* New York: International Universities Press, 1965.

Klein, M. *The Psychoanalysis of Children.* New York: Grove Press, 1960.

Smirnoff, V. *The Scope of Child Analysis.* New York: International Universities Press, 1971.